D0043428

Problem of the Century

LIBRARIES

DISCARD

Problem of the Century

Racial Stratification in the United States

Elijah Anderson and Douglas S. Massey
Editors

Russell Sage Foundation • New York

The Russell Sage Foundation

The Russell Sage Foundation, one of the oldest of America's general purpose foundations, was established in 1907 by Mrs. Margaret Olivia Sage for "the improvement of social and living conditions in the United States." The Foundation seeks to fulfill this mandate by fostering the development and dissemination of knowledge about the country's political, social, and economic problems. While the Foundation endeavors to assure the accuracy and objectivity of each book it publishes, the conclusions and interpretations in Russell Sage Foundation publications are those of the authors and not of the Foundation, its Trustees, or its staff. Publication by Russell Sage, therefore, does not imply Foundation endorsement.

BOARD OF TRUSTEES
Ira Katznelson, Chair

Alan S. Blinder	Jennifer L. Hochschild	Eugene Smolensky
Christine K. Cassel	Timothy A. Hultquist	Marta Tienda
Thomas D. Cook	Melvin Konner	Eric Wanner
Robert E. Denham	Ellen Condliffe Lagemann	
Phoebe C. Ellsworth	Cora B. Marrett	

Library of Congress Cataloging-in-Publication Data

Problem of the century : racial stratification in the United States / Elijah Anderson and Douglas S. Massey, editors.
    p. cm.
   Includes bibliographical references and index.
   ISBN 0-87154-054-1 (cloth)   ISBN 0-87154-055-X (paper)
   1. United States—Race relations. 2. United States—Ethnic relations. 3. Race discrimination—United States—History—20th century. 4. Social stratification—United States—History—20th century. 5. United States—Social conditions—1980– 6. African Americans—Social conditions—1975– I. Anderson, Elijah.
II. Massey, Douglas S.

E184.A1 P74 2001
305.8'00973—dc21   2001019330

Copyright © 2001 by Russell Sage Foundation. All rights reserved. First papercover edition 2004. Printed in the United States of America. No part of this publication may be reproduced, stored in a retrieval system, or transmitted in any form or by any means, electronic, mechanical, photocopying, recording, or otherwise, without the prior written permission of the publisher.

Reproduction by the United States Government in whole or in part is permitted for any purpose.

The paper used in this publication meets the minimum requirements of American National Standard for Information Sciences—Permanence of Paper for Printed Library Materials. ANSI Z39.48-1992.

Text design by Suzanne Nichols

RUSSELL SAGE FOUNDATION
112 East 64th Street, New York, New York 10021
10 9 8 7 6 5 4 3 2 1

—— Contents ——

—— Contributors ——

Douglas S. Massey is professor of sociology and public policy at Princeton University.

Elijah Anderson is Charles and William Day Professor of the Social Sciences at the University of Pennsylvania.

Linda H. Aiken is the Claire M. Fagin Professor of Nursing, professor of sociology, and director of the Center for Health Outcomes and Policy Research at the University of Pennsylvania.

Ivar Berg is professor of sociology at the University of Pennsylvania.

Mary Blair-Loy is assistant professor of sociology at Washington State University.

Camille Zubrinsky Charles is assistant professor of sociology at the University of Pennsylvania and research associate at the University's Population Studies Center.

Randall Collins is professor of sociology at the University of Pennsylvania.

Kathryn Edin is associate professor in the department of sociology and faculty fellow at the Institute for Policy Research at Northwestern University.

Irma T. Elo is assistant professor of sociology and a research associate at the Population Studies Center, University of Pennsylvania.

Frank F. Furstenberg Jr. is the Zellerbach Family Professor of Sociology at the University of Pennsylvania.

Jerry A. Jacobs is Merriam Term Professor of Sociology at the University of Pennsylvania.

Grace Kao is assistant professor of sociology and Asian American studies at the University of Pennsylvania.

Robin Leidner is associate professor of sociology at the University of Pennsylvania.

Janice F. Madden is professor of sociology, regional science, and real estate at the University of Pennsylvania and director of graduate studies at the University's Fels Center of Government.

Ewa Morawska is professor of sociology and history at the University of Pennsylvania.

Timothy J. Nelson is research assistant professor at the Institute for Policy Research and lecturer in sociology at Northwestern University.

Samuel H. Preston is Frederick J. Warren Professor of Sociology and dean of the School of Arts and Sciences at the University of Pennsylvania.

Douglas M. Sloane is an associate professor of sociology at Catholic University of America and an adjunct associate professor at the University of Pennsylvania.

Tukufu Zuberi is professor of sociology at the University of Pennsylvania.

—— Part I ——

Theoretical and Conceptual Issues

—— Chapter 1 ——

The Sociology of Race in the United States

Elijah Anderson and Douglas S. Massey

AMERICAN SOCIOLOGY IS generally thought to have been founded at the University of Chicago early in this century and to have come of age during the 1920s, when visionaries like Robert Park, Ernest Burgess, and Louis Wirth invented modern social scientific research. Grounded in European social theory, Chicago sociologists sought to apply concepts derived from a close reading of Weber, Marx, Durkheim, and others to describe the social organization of industrial urbanism. In contrast to their European counterparts, however, American sociologists sought to test and extend theoretical ideas through a relentless process of empirical investigation that embraced any and all means of data collection. Using the city of Chicago as their laboratory, they combined quantitative and qualitative data, conducted both ecological and individual-level analyses, paired ethnographies with sample surveys and statistics, and married documentary sources to census data, all in an effort to build a comprehensive picture of contemporary urban society (see Bulmer 1984).

The trouble with the standard account of American sociology's birth is that it happened not at the University of Chicago in the 1920s, but at the University of Pennsylvania in the 1890s; rather than being led by a group of classically influenced white men, it was directed by W. E. B. Du Bois, a German-trained African American with a Ph.D. from Harvard. His 1899 study, *The Philadelphia Negro,* anticipated in every way the program of theory and re-

3

search that later became known as the Chicago School. Although not generally recognized as such, it represented the first true example of American social scientific research, preceding the work of Park and Burgess by at least two decades. Were it not for the short-sighted racism of Penn's faculty and administration, which refused to acknowledge the presence—let alone the accomplishments—of a black man or to offer him a faculty appointment, the maturation of the discipline might have been advanced by two decades and be known to posterity as the Pennsylvania School of Sociology. Instead, Du Bois went on to a distinguished career as a public intellectual, activist, and journalist, and the University of Chicago, not the University of Pennsylvania, came to dominate the field.

Fundamental among the subjects studied by the early Chicago sociologists was the issue of race. Robert Park theorized his relations cycle, Ernest Burgess documented patterns of black segregation and neighborhood succession, and E. Franklin Frazier undertook detailed studies of the ecology and social life of the ghetto. It was not until 1945, however, with the publication of St. Clair Drake's and Horace Cayton's *Black Metropolis*, that the University of Chicago produced a study of the black community matching the depth, rigor, and sophistication achieved nearly fifty years earlier by Du Bois in *The Philadelphia Negro*.

An important legacy of the Chicago School's influence was that the sociology of race was thoroughly grounded in human ecology, at least through the 1960s. Indeed, according to Robert Park's widely cited dictum, social relations *were* spatial relations. Thus in building theories and conducting research, American sociologists concerned themselves fundamentally with understanding how ecological factors shaped and constrained interpersonal behavior and social structure. No analysis of racial stratification was complete without describing the ecological configurations of class, race, and ethnicity or outlining how their intersection influenced the life chances and social worlds experienced by individuals.

One of the most important structural settings considered by sociologists was the neighborhood. From the early writings of Park and Burgess through the later work of Frazier, Janowitz, Blau, Duncan, and Lieberson, neighborhoods were seen as fundamental to the broader system of American stratification. Sometime around 1970, however, sociological interest in the connection between spatial location and social position began to wane. As the status attainment model came to dominate American sociology, the study of stratification became progressively despatialized. Socioeconomic outcomes were conceptualized as individual-level processes constrained only by family circumstances.

The predominance of the status attainment model stemmed from both technological and theoretical imperatives. Technologically, computers grew more powerful and allowed the development of sophisticated methods for collecting, manipulating, and analyzing large amounts of information, yielding a proliferation of social surveys. The resulting data sets included detailed information on individuals, families, and households, but little, if anything, on the places where they lived.

Concomitant with computerization, sociology came under increasing pressure from economics, with economists seeking to project their rational theoretical calculus into domains hitherto dominated by sociologists. Whereas some responded by rejecting rationality and quantification outright, others sought to bolster themselves and their discipline by out-quantifying the economists. Thus researchers of status attainment employed sophisticated survey data in complicated new analyses that traced the influence of family background on individual attainment, both within and between generations. Although spatial concerns did not disappear entirely from the literature, they were pushed aside by a new generation of studies using structural equations, path analyses, and log-linear methods, enabling sociologists to compete with economists for scientific respectability.

During the 1970s, the status attainment paradigm seemed to sweep aside everything in its path and soon came to dominate the major sociology journals. Despite early insights and conceptual advances, however, the paradigm eventually reached a point of diminishing returns. Technical sophistication was no substitute for original thinking about the changing nature of social structure and its effects on individual lives. By the mid-1980s, sociologists were employing ever more complicated models to push around a fixed amount of variance in ever smaller ways. Increases in complexity brought diminishing marginal returns in terms of sociological insight, and the explanatory power of status attainment models remained stubbornly stuck.

The key event that broke the conceptual and empirical logjam, and brought ecology forcefully back into the study of racial stratification, was provided by another Chicago sociologist, William Julius Wilson. His 1987 book, *The Truly Disadvantaged*, argued that urban poverty was transmitted and perpetuated not simply through individual- and family-level mechanisms but also through a series of structural transformations playing out ecologically within cities and across neighborhoods. The spatial intensification of joblessness and the accompanying concentration of poverty isolated poor African American men from employment and created an unfavorable marriage market for black women that undermined family stability.

He argued that whatever disadvantages African Americans might experience by virtue of growing up and living in poor families, they incurred *additional* penalties for growing up and living in poor neighborhoods. Thus ecological context mattered in fundamental ways that went well beyond individual characteristics or family circumstances. Wilson was the first American sociologist to realize that the world had changed and that poverty had become much more *geographically concentrated* since 1970. He coined the term *concentration effects* to describe the additional disadvantage—above and beyond individual and family problems—that poor people incurred by virtue of growing up and living in areas of concentrated poverty.

Thus space came to matter a great deal to sociologists once again, and there was a sudden rush to specify, model, and estimate "neighborhood effects" on various outcomes related to poverty and race. At about the same time, sociology as a whole began to move away from the strident, self-defeating debates of the 1970s, which had pitted extreme epistemological positions against one another as if they were mutually exclusive and logically incongruent—quantitative versus qualitative, theoretical versus empirical, survey versus ethnography, individual versus aggregate. Instead, a growing number of sociologists recognized the compensating strengths and weaknesses of diverse methodologies, different levels of analysis, and complementary theories and sought to *integrate* them in the course of their ongoing investigations. During the 1980s, a new generation of multimethod, multilevel, multisite studies came to the fore.

Through a series of fortuitous circumstances, many of these

currents converged at the University of Pennsylvania in the 1990s. Exactly one century after Du Bois published his landmark work on black Philadelphia, Penn's sociology faculty housed a diverse array of scholars working on various aspects of race and using a variety of theoretical and methodological approaches. The prevailing zeitgeist moved them beyond arguments about which methodological approach was "better" or which theoretical concepts were more "sociological." Instead, they worked to develop new ways to combine methods and theories so as to produce sociological knowledge with greater validity than would be possible using any single method or theory alone.

Over the past decade, these sociologists have been in the forefront of developing multimethod approaches that blend, often within a single study, ethnographies and surveys, statistics and content analyses, and census data with historical records to analyze systematically both textual and numerical data; and those faculty members who do not combine quantitative and qualitative styles in their own studies nonetheless remain open and sympathetic to the full range of research methodologies represented in the discipline.

Given the unusually diverse array of sociologists working on one issue in one department at the same time, we resolved to organize a conference that would allow Penn sociologists to share their insights on the issue of race within a formal integrative structure and to make the resulting synthesis of knowledge available to a wider public. The chapters included in this volume are the product of that conference. Across them, one sees a dedication to the scientific principles first exemplified in the work of Du Bois and later institutionalized at the University of Chicago: a marriage of mutual respect between quantitative and qualitative methods, a lively interplay between theory and research, an emphasis on the ecological foundations of intergroup relations, a healthy respect for empirical data as the best way to discern between competing theoretical visions, and a focus on the structures and mechanisms of stratification.

Inspired by Du Bois's widely quoted dictum that "the problem of the twentieth century is the problem of the color line," each of the substantive chapters of this book examines a different aspect of race in late-twentieth-century America. In a way that we hope might please Du Bois and posthumously redress the great injustice done to him by the university a century ago, each of the chapters is written by a member of Penn's standing faculty, which now includes three African Americans. The contributions are organized so as to take up, in turn, a logical progression of issues with respect to race—theoretical, demographic, ecological, and, finally, the socioeconomic issues of work and school.

Randall Collins leads off the volume and the theory section by situating the social construction of ethnic identity in macro-historical perspective, reminding us that conceptualizations of race are ultimately rooted in broader state structures and geopolitical relations. In a similar spirit, Ewa Morawska argues that black-immigrant relations in contemporary U.S. cities are governed not simply by a group's objective deprivation and its subjective sentiments about itself and other groups but also by historically grounded judgments that vary from setting to setting. A full understanding of intergroup relations therefore requires an understanding of how general social processes are filtered through local contexts and structures to determine specific outcomes.

Robin Leidner's contribution focuses on the problems and issues that surface when a movement organized on the basis of one characteristic—gender—seeks to integrate and mobilize women who are simultaneously heterogeneous with respect to other traits, such as race and class. Even in radical sectors of the feminist movement, the dilemmas of class and particularly racial integration can prove quite difficult. Ivar Berg concludes our conceptual analysis by situating the emotional issue of affirmative action historically, pointing out that affirmative action is hardly the first instance of group-based rights built into U.S. law. Indeed, he argues that a great many of today's "winners" are the descendants of persons who benefited from group-based rights granted in the past. Minorities have the burden of having to *earn* group rights that have long been accorded to majority members, including the ubiquitous status of persona ficta.

Penn houses one of the nation's leading population research centers, and its faculty contains three past presidents of the Population Association of America. It is appropriate that this volume explores the social demography of race in some detail. Tukufu Zuberi links our theoretical understanding of racial identity to concrete issues of data and measurement, exploring how the creation of racial data itself can play a role in racial stratification and the perpetuation of difference. He traces the implications for both theory and measurement of the growing diversification of the U.S. population through massive immigration.

Any study of racial stratification requires data, of course, and demographers are nothing if not careful (some might say obsessed) about the quality of the information they use. For a variety of reasons having to do with the unique position of African Americans in the United States, historical data on race suffer from a variety of systematic defects that make it difficult to reconstruct accurately the demographic history of the African American population. Irma Elo and Samuel Preston use the classic methods of demography to correct these data problems and for the first time present an accurate summary of the demographic history of the African American population. Before trying to explain something as complex and charged as race, it is best to get the facts straight.

One of the fundamental demographic processes is nuptiality, and Frank Furstenberg's chapter explores the retreat from marriage that has unfolded in America's inner cities. He argues that the precarious employment situation lies at the core of the phenomenon. Economic uncertainties make marriage a less desirable, predictable, and permanent social form, and children learn not to expect male-female relations to endure. These apprehensions are reinforced during adolescence as both men and women experience fleeting and often unsatisfactory relationships. A culture of gender distrust emerges as men and women increasingly live in separate spheres. The cultural climate of the urban poor creates extravagant fantasies and expectations, bitter disappointments and discontents, and a reliance on maternal kin. Each of these conditions, in turn, renders the conjugal unit less dependable and sturdy as a social form.

Central to the demography of race is the high degree of mortality experienced by African Americans. Linda Aiken and Douglas Sloane document one of the myriad micro-mechanisms accounting for the persistent black-white gap in death rates. Using AIDS care as a model to explore how access to health care varies by race, they show that African Americans constitute a higher percentage of AIDS patients in public than private hospitals and a considerably smaller percentage of patients in magnet and exemplary private hospitals. The fact that black patients have a lower probability of entering dedicated AIDS units is of concern since research has clearly established that these units have beneficial health outcomes.

The third section considers the unique ecological situation of African Americans, who remain the most segregated group in the United States. Camille Charles shows that black segregation is far higher than that experienced even by the most recent arrivals in the multiethnic metropolis of Los Angeles—Asians. And even though Hispanic segregation is higher, it never reaches the heights experienced by blacks, and mostly it can be explained by socioeconomic status and nativity. The same cannot be said for African Americans, however, who remain hypersegregated within the metropolitan area irrespective of socioeconomic status and despite their clear preferences for integration.

Janice Madden examines variation in the degree of residential segregation of African Americans across metropolitan areas. She finds that places with more African Americans are more highly segregated and have poverty more concentrated in their central cities and that current discrimination, not lower productivity, is primarily responsible for racial differentials in income, poverty, and earnings. Finally, Douglas Massey considers the consequences of racial segregation by linking it to ecological conditions that promote the code of violence described elsewhere by Anderson (1999). He shows how residential and economic structures interact to produce neighborhoods of concentrated poverty, which, in turn, yield harsh and violent social conditions to which ghetto residents must adapt by deploying coded displays of ritualized violence.

The fourth and final section considers specific processes of racial stratification, focusing on employment and education. In the United States, blacks and whites are segregated not only by neighborhood but also by occupation. Jerry Jacobs and Mary Blair-Loy show, however, that occupational segregation by race is nowhere near as high or as consistent as occupational segregation by gender. As a result, whereas the percentage of women in an occupation operates to lower significantly the wages of male and female incumbents, the percentage of blacks in an occupation has no such effect. Wage discrimination against African Americans occurs primarily because blacks are paid less for the same work than equally qualified whites, whereas wage discrimination against women also incorporates a systematic devaluation of work considered to be "female." In the United States of the late twentieth century, few occupations remained socially labeled as "black."

Kathryn Edin and Timothy Nelson continue the analysis of race and employment by studying the work done by low-income fathers in Philadelphia. They find that work for unskilled inner-city fathers has not disappeared, but gone underground, in the sense that they are engaged in a lot of work that is not likely to be captured by official employment statistics. In this underground or informal economy, however, they find persistent racial differences between blacks and whites, reflecting intergroup differences in the mechanisms of job acquisition and recruitment. In contrast to low-income whites, African American men almost never mention communal and family ties as a source for jobs, leading to decidedly inferior outcomes. At the other end of the socioeconomic spectrum, Elijah Anderson examines the situation of black executives working in white corporate environments. Using ethnographic data, he documents the difficulties and issues involved when a stigmatized group comes to penetrate an elite institutional environment formerly forbidden to them.

The volume concludes with a nod toward the future, for the roots of tomorrow's economic uncertainties lie partially in today's educational problems. Grace Kao shows how peer influences differ between racial and ethnic groups to produce divergent educational achievements. She finds that pressures of loyalty to one's own group, the desire to find others similar to oneself, and the prevalence of racially segregated activities and classes work together to reinforce race-ethnicity as a primary filter in selecting friends, yielding very different sorts of peer groups. Friends of Asian youth are more oriented to school and less oriented to social activities than their white counterparts. Their friends also are less likely to have dropped out of high school and are more likely to plan to go to college than friends of white youth. Although the friends of blacks are oriented more toward school and less toward social activities than the friends of whites, they also are more concerned with working, more likely to have dropped out of school, and less likely to aspire to a four-year university. Thus black students have greater exposure to others who have already experienced school failure, suggesting that modeling is far more important than normative influences on student academic performance.

Ultimately, this volume brings sociology at Penn full circle. A century after *The Philadelphia Negro*, it offers a comprehensive look at "the problem of the century" by a multiracial group of sociologists working together in one department using diverse methodologies, theories, and levels of analysis. Rather than privileging one approach over another, we, like Du Bois, seek to combine data, methods, and concepts to construct a more comprehensive vision of race in the twentieth century. In doing so, we seek to develop a new sociology of race that uses diverse methods and theories to describe racial stratification as a multilevel process in which individual behavior is shaped by social structures that are firmly rooted in space. If this sounds like the old Chicago School of Sociology, it is not. It is the Penn School of Sociology that should have been founded by W. E. B. Du Bois decades before Robert Park or Ernest Burgess joined the Chicago faculty.

REFERENCES

Anderson, Elijah. 1999. *The Code of the Street: Decency, Violence, and the Moral Life of the Inner City*. New York: Norton.

Bulmer, Martin. 1984. *The Chicago School of Sociology: Institutionalization, Diversity, and the Rise of Sociological Research*. Chicago: University of Chicago Press.

Drake, St. Clair, and Horace R. Cayton. 1945. *Black Metropolis: A Study of Life in a Northern City*. New York: Harcourt, Brace.

Du Bois, W. E. B. 1999 [1899]. *The Philadelphia Negro: A Social Study. With a New Introduction by Elijah Anderson*. Philadelphia: University of Pennsylvania Press.

Wilson, William Julius. 1987. *The Truly Disadvantaged: The Inner City, the Underclass, and Public Policy*. Chicago: University of Chicago Press.

—— Chapter 2 ——

Ethnic Change in Macro-Historical Perspective

Randall Collins

ANALYTICAL UNDERSTANDING OF ethnicity is one of the weak spots in the social sciences. A great deal has been written about it, but much of what is said has an ephemeral quality. In the past century, there have been waves of enthusiasm for and against various kinds of ethnic and nationalist movements. These have been heated topics, caught up in contemporary political moods. In the late twentieth century, the prestige of ethnic autonomy has been high, and discourse in the social sciences has been replete with morally charged concepts such as multiculturalism, the right to one's culture, and cultural genocide. This is a very different mood from that of the early twentieth century and before, when liberals' ideals were often an inclusive nationalism, overcoming petty regionalisms and local animosities in the name of one people cooperating toward a shared goal. The king in Shakespeare's *Henry V* rallying Cornishmen, Welshmen, Irishmen, and Scotsmen into battle as Englishmen applies the same archetype as American films of World War II, which conventionally feature a platoon containing a WASP (white Anglo-Saxon protestant) farm boy, an Italian, a Swede, and a Jew, who learn to put aside their differences in the common cause. Historically there have been still other variants besides ethnic preservationism and the ethnic melting pot; there have been cosmopolitan periods such as the eighteenth-century Enlightenment, when a widespread ideal was a superior culture rising above and cutting across the local and particular.

Analysis has suffered from being unidimensional. We have assumed too easily that everything flows in the same direction, that the world as a whole is on an evolutionary path or has reached a postmodern condition, that there are ages of nationalism or ages of political correctness. Consider the polar visions of the twenty-first (or twenty-second) century that are implied in these different models. Will it be a future in which every ethnic group will be free and independent, even possessing its own state? Or will it be the continuation of a long-term trend from a heterogeneity of small local groups amalgamating into larger national blocs and thence into a single world culture and comprising, by intermarriage, a single world race? These are the optimistic ideals. Their negative counterparts are, on the one hand, a world of multiethnic hostility, a coming century of pogroms, genocide, and terrorism legitimated by the aspirations of still-oppressed ethnicities and, on the other hand, a century of bland uniformity, with world hegemony of the English language and of American mass popular culture. Putting the argument in these terms should make us suspect that the future belongs exclusively to none of the above; history has always been more of a mixed bag than such one-sided models depict.

The analytical basis must be dug more deeply. No single process affects the entire world or even entire regions of it en bloc. We need to model the range of variants in ethnic arrangements and state the conditions that move a region in one direction or the other. A region can move toward greater ethnic pluralism, or toward greater ethnic uniformity, toward what I have labeled, somewhat tendentiously, "Balkanization" or "Americanization." The strength of the state is at the heart of these variations: as a baseline, how the military state mobilizes its population and penetrates it with civilian tentacles and, on this baseline, how it determines the geopolitical fortunes of states. In this chapter, I present a state-centered theory of ethnicity to go along with the state-centered theories of revolution so frequently propounded.

It is a matter of putting things in their context. Researchers have been acutely concerned with ethnicity and its semantic neighbors—race, nationalism, and citizenship—and they have come up with numerous causal conditions and processes. These causal conditions are indeterminate when we try to generalize them; what works for ethnic assimilation in the United States in the 1950s does not work for the Soviet Union in the 1980s because the geopolitical context is different. Any comprehensive theory of ethnicity must be a multicausal theory. But in a jumble of causes, some are more fateful than others. I argue here, as elsewhere (for elaboration, see Collins 1999), that the geopolitical relations among states are the switch that shifts the causal tracks to quite different directions within each state.

WHAT DETERMINES HOW MANY ETHNIC GROUPS EXIST?

For all the research that has been done on ethnicity in the United States, this is not a good place to begin analytical theorizing. Our concentration has been heavily on processes of discrimination; in a more optimistic or self-satisfied era, it has been on processes of assimilation. All these beg the question, why are there ethnic groups in the first place? We have been concerned mainly with why ethnic groups persist or when they disappear; we have not dealt systematically enough with the question of what creates ethnic groups. In part, this is because of ideological assumptions underlying our research; if one is an assimilationist, one tends to think of the dominant ethnic group not as ethnic at all, but simply as the mainstream culture of that society. If one is a radical critic, one can recognize and denounce this, so that Anglo conformity or WASP dominance becomes recognized as the privileged status of one ethnic group among others. Either way, insight is lost by taking for granted the cultural categories of what is, after all, a very particular historical condition. Assimilation is a reduction in the number of ethnic groups, at the extreme, to one ethnicity per state. The tendency to think of the hegemonic ethnic group as the target of assimilation reveals a general process: some ethnic groups have legitimacy, just as political rule can have legitimacy. The number of ethnic groups varies along a continuum, and the legitimacy of a dominant ethnicity varies as well. The question for an analytically comprehensive theory of ethnicity is, what moves a region in one direction or the other?

Take the question from the point of view of an ethnic liberationist. The rhetoric of one's position naturally assumes that one's ethnic group exists. It has a history, and it has roots, an identity reaching back into the past. The political task is to mobilize this identity still more, so that its members will fight for its preservation and autonomy, and ethnic others will be made to recognize the justice of one's claims. The mobilization stance of ethnic conflict is primordialist. This too is data for the detached viewpoint of an analytical theory. It also means that the activist-eye view is not sufficient grounds for a theory or, indeed, for very adequate historical accounts. The primordialist makes history a blinkered search into the past, a clear channel marked by whatever can be construed as one's historical roots. But Italians in the United States at the turn of the twentieth century were in the process of acquiring an Italian identity, while their homeland identities had been as Sicilians, Calabrians, Neapolitans, Genoans, and so on; those regional ethnicities themselves were the product of assimilation among previously fragmented villages or clans. The same is true of "Chicanos," the result of assimilation among Indios, mestizos, Spaniards, and others; the category-in-formation "Hispanics" is further along the continuum still. Ethnic groups not only reproduce or disappear; they also are created. The process of political mobilizing narrows down alternatives as to where the boundaries are drawn for collective action; it is the conflict that creates the framework that becomes projected backward into a primordial past.

An ethnic group is not merely, or even primarily, a community sharing a common culture and identity; it is such identities as constituted by dividing lines, by contrast with others. The key questions are, how many ethnic groups are socially perceived to exist at a given time and place? And, analytically more important, what determines whether the number of ethnic groups, and therefore also the number of intraethnic divisions, increases or decreases? The easy answer to be avoided comes from treating the first question in a matter-of-fact way; by common discourse we know what ethnic groups there are in the United States, or in Bosnia, and we can then go on to examine what seem to be the more important questions of conflict, domination, or harmonization. These kinds of answers, based on research in the short run of the present, are inconsistent from case to case. We need the long-run, macro-historical viewpoint in order to give the short-run processes their trajectories.

Social Construction of Ethnicity in the Long Run

An ethnicity is best described as a meta-community, a framework for a community of communities. Not everyone in an ethnic group knows each other, and not everyone is linked in a dense network; many ethnicities, such as German or Chinese, can number in the millions or more. Ethnicities are often described as cultural units, characterized by distinctive cuisines, clothing styles, ways of life. These are socially constructed by two related processes: (1) the social action, originally without self-consciousness, that went into building these local peculiarities and (2) the cultural labeling of group boundaries when these items became recognized as markers by group outsiders and then, reflexively, by insiders of the group themselves. I focus here on two markers that are analytically more revealing and that bring out the social process that constructs both naive proto-ethnicity and mobilized ethno-nationalism. These are somatotypes and languages.

Social Construction of Somatotypes

People who belong to an ethnic group tend to look alike, or, at least, physical archetypes are found frequently enough so that it is socially recognized what a "typical" ethnic member is supposed to look like. Scandinavians are expected, with above-average frequency, to be blonde, blue-eyed, and fair-skinned, Italians to be black-haired and olive-skinned, and so on. Physical anthropologists have added a modicum of precision, charting relative prevalence of facial bone structures and skeletal dimensions, of dental patterns and blood types. Mentioning such things can be rather bad form today, insofar as it invokes old, discredited theories that imputed distinct historic destinies to "broad-headed" and "narrow-headed stock" or looked for criminal propensities or hereditary pauperism among southern or eastern European ancestries. Very likely there are no important correlations between physical appearance and intelligence, behavior, or culture. I bring in ethnic somatotypes nevertheless in order to make two analytical points.

First, there is no deep and analytically important distinction between "race" and "ethnicity." Conventionally, races are regarded as physically distinctive (for example, by skin color), while ethnic groups are merely culturally distinctive. But ethnic groups also have somatotypical differences (hair, skin color, facial structures, and the like), and these differences are one of the chief markers that people commonly seize on in situations where consciousness of ethnic divisions is high. A sociological distinction between ethnicity and race is analytically pernicious, because it obscures the social processes determining the extent to which divisions are made in the continuum of somatotypical gradations. Race is a folk concept, a popular mythology that elevates particular kinds of ethnic distinctions into an absolute break. As sociologists, our analytical problem is to show what causes placements along the continuum; the racialization of ethnicity is just one extreme of that process. The geopolitical theory of ethnicity proposed here is, by definition, also a theory of race.

Second, the degree of somatic distinctiveness is socially constructed. Here it is social interaction that controls biology. Somatic differences, like everything else, range along a continuum. What determines the degree of similarity or difference in ethnic somatotypes is how separate the breeding pools have been. Peoples who live in areas of the globe remote from one another are likely to have evolved somatotypes that are very different. These geographically separate breeding pools have created the somatotypes of Scandinavians, Celts, Mediterraneans, Sub-Saharan Africans, Chinese, Ainu, and all the other somatic variants of the human race. Conversely, where breeding pools are geographically and socially closer, the somatotypes become more similar; at complete social and territorial propinquity, they merge.

Somatotypes are an index of past global history; they are geopolitical markers, inscribed on the bodies of human beings. Somatic differences among people who currently live near one another depict past patterns of conquest and migration, including the forced migration of slavery. Where somatic differences are very marked (for example, differences between very light- and dark-skinned persons), the causal process must have been migration from remote areas of the world, where the breeding pools had been separate for a long period of time. If the somatotypes continue to remain distinct once the groups are in geographical propinquity, it is because social processes continue to keep the breeding pools separate. Ethno-somatic distinctiveness is socially constructed, first in the form of proto-ethnic somatotypes (black Africans and Celts looked physically different in 500 C.E. because they had never been near each other); later in the form of ethno-national somatotypes upheld by social barriers to interfertilization (for example, in 1970, when they are in contact in Britain or America).

It is not the color of the skin (or other physical features) per se that determines the social relationship. In nineteenth- and twentieth-century Sweden, extremely blonde, blue-eyed, fair-skinned Finns tended to be looked down on, regarded as slatternly and characteristic of the servant class; here, the extremely fair somatotype of the Finns acts as a marker of a geopolitical history in which Finland had been a conquest possession of the Swedish state from the sixteenth through eighteenth centuries, and Finns had been peasant workers and servants for Swedish landlords. In the ancient Mediterranean, Greeks and later Arabs acquired light-skinned slaves from eastern Europe, Russia, and the Asian steppe as well as black slaves from Africa; here both extremely dark and extremely light skins were taken as marks of social inferiority. Geopolitical separation or contact creates proto-ethnic somatotypes; geopolitical dominance gives specific meanings to these markers as signs of social superiority or inferiority.

Skin-color racism is a product, not a cause. Black Africans were not singled out for slavery by Europeans because they were black. The sugar and cotton planters of the Caribbean and the American South initially attempted to work their crops with native American Indians and with white European indentured servants (who were, in effect, slaves for a limited number of years), but they were unsuccessful in reproducing these sources of labor. Planters turned to African slaves because a supply of slaves became available from this region (Williams 1966). Slavery created racism more than racism created slavery. Africa was vulnerable to slave trading, in turn, because indigenous slavery already existed in Africa, so that slaves were readily supplied to coastal ports.

Moreover, the tribal societies of Africa were horticultural and thus much weaker in geopolitical resources than the agrarian states of the Arabs and later the proto-capitalist states of the Europeans, who organized the long-distance slave trade.

A comprehensive macro-historical sociology of the long run would specify, by comparisons and by drawing on the appropriate archaeology and paleontology, how many generations of group separation produce what degrees of somatic distinctiveness. The time process is asymmetrical; differences that could have taken thousands of years to produce can become obliterated within a few generations if extensive interbreeding takes place. Once groups have moved from proto-ethnicity in mutually oblivious separation into the situation of mobilization within an ethno-nationalist arena, the somatic differences will continue only if they are continually reconstructed.

This social reconstruction can happen in two ways. One is that the carryover from older geopolitical differences into contemporary stratification keeps the breeding pools socially separate. Another is that interbreeding does occur, but the offspring are socially defined as belonging to one group rather than the other or to a third, mixed group. If the groups are white Europeans and black Africans, the possible outcomes could be that all offspring are socially classified as black, or as white, or as a third category, such as "Creole"; a fourth alternative is that the black-white distinction could simply disappear, over a period of generations, to be replaced by some other ethno-nationalist category (such as "American").

The issue is not strictly a matter of what range of skin colors would exist in such a society, but of what distinctions are singled out or not singled out. Somatic distinctions once taken as significant markers of group identities have disappeared; for instance, the distinction between Romans of the ancient empire and Visigothic barbarians who overran the peninsula in the fifth century eventually was forgotten as a social marker, even though the mixture of somatic traits found in modern Italy can be traced to this history.

In the world's future, there surely will be further variations in ethnic divisions. The number of ethnic groups is changed by changes in the pattern of breeding pools; in this way, long-standing ethnic groups can disappear, and new ethnic categories are created. The transition period of amalgamating ethnic somato-types may involve heightened ethnic consciousness. In Bosnia, some of the worst atrocities during the ethnic war of the 1990s took place in regions with a high degree of ethnic intermarriage. This is only possible where, first of all, not everybody is intermar-ried, so that there is a pool of "purists" who can put pressure on those who are intermarrying, and, second, the number of genera-tions of interbreeding is not very deep, so that an intermarried family can be socially identified as exactly that.

The contrast becomes clear if one considers ethnic intermar-riage in the United States among groups that migrated in the nine-teenth century. Many families, for instance, are interbred from An-glo, German, and Scandinavian ethnics; although family members at the turn of the twenty-first century might be aware of their fam-ily trees, there are little or no live ethnic identifications with any of their antecedents (Waters 1990). Ethnic cleansing would be vir-tually impossible under these conditions. Three generations of in-termarriage probably obliterate prior ethnic lines of distinction, provided that the proportion of the population as a whole that intermarries is large enough so that there is no longer an ongoing baseline of ethnic communities against which the small minority of persons who intermarry can be defined merely as yet an addi-tional, mixed category. Such reduction in the number of recog-nized ethnic divisions is a move along the continuum in one di-rection. A move in the opposite direction—increasing the number of somatotypes within a region—depends on new sources of mi-gration or new barriers to interbreeding.

Social Construction of Ethno-Linguistic Groups

Turn now to the other macro-historical dimension of ethnic forma-tion. The most readily available, commonsense meaning of ethnic groups is linguistic. Germans are those who speak German or who migrated from a German-speaking area; Poles are those who speak Polish or whose families once did. Ethnicity as language group is a meta-community taken for granted even more deeply than Anderson's "imagined communities" (1983) of those who read the same newspapers or follow the same broadcasts; confronting those who can or cannot speak one's language is as sharp a marker in everyday social life as one can experience.

Ethnicity is a process of socially constructing distinctiveness on what appear to be primordial grounds: both language lines and somatic inheritance appear to be outside the control of the individual, deriving from a communal past far enough back that it seems immemorial. In fact, socially constructed memory is short and deliberately biased. It is our business to ask the macro-historical question about the contours in time that produce various kinds of group distinctions. Having attempted this for somatotypes, let us ask, what determines how many ethno-linguistic groups exist? What does it take to create a language (or what is socially recognized as a distinct language, since borders within the continuum of language variation are not clear-cut)? It is useful to focus on this side of the problem, because we have more evidence for the history of languages than we do for the history of somatic types and breeding pools or for a history of socially recognized distinctions in customs.

In historical linguistics, a popular model is the pool of language speakers, analogous to the biological breeding pool. Language pools that are socially distinct undergo "linguistic drift"; accumulated random changes bring about drift of languages from one another, as Icelandic drifted away from other branches of Scandinavian. Conversely, language groups that come into contact at a stable border produce hybrid languages, "Creoles," interbreeding a new dialect or language. This biological analogy is what I wish to challenge, or at least supplement. The key determinants of language change—those making the most dramatic effects on ethno-linguistic divisions—typically have been geopolitical.

Although states and ethno-linguistic connections move to different rhythms, there is an affinity between them: strong states give an impulsion toward linguistic uniformity, and highly mobilized linguistic ethnicities give an impulsion toward an autonomous state. This striving toward congruence between state and language is one factor among several; hence the congruence is approached only on certain occasions, although analytically fateful ones. The existence of regional dialects within a language does not gainsay the basic situation; rather it adds complexities within it. Ethno-linguistic identities are layered. The very concept of a dialect, as distinct from a separate language, indicates that some language variation is accepted as normal within a larger overriding identity.

From a macro-historical viewpoint, the sharp distinction between dialect and language is artificial; it is a gradation, and Dutch may be regarded as a dialect of Plattdeutsch (that is, so-called "Low German," the German of the northern coasts; see Sperber and Fleischhauer 1963, 79). But the analytical disparity between the continuums found in historical reality, and the sharp-edged categories by which social actors draw ethno-linguistic boundaries, is very much the point of my argument. Ethnicity is constructed. It is a real-life ideal type, constructed not merely by scholars but by people in ordinary life, and this process of constructing ethnic identities is done with varying degrees of inclusiveness or separation. A geopolitical theory of variations along that continuum will give us the outline of a theory of language change.

Proto-Ethnicity and Ethno-Nationalism

Envision an analytical space: at one extreme is the ideal type of a completely isolated community, both for speaking and for childbearing; here the two kinds of ethnicity coincide. But this is only proto-ethnicity, since completely isolated communities have no sense of difference. Self-conscious ethnic identity, strongest at the level of ethno-nationalism, comes from entering the arena of states in geopolitical relationship with one another. Ethnicity is an intrinsically messy topic, because the historical processes that produce it are intrinsically messy. Our analytical problems in coming to grips with it stem from the fact that ethnicity is always a distorted concept, imposing a pure category on social reality that is not pure at all.

Ethnicity is a construction from combinations of markers—somatotypes, languages, family names—that serve as reminders of ancestral differences that may no longer exist, as well as other differences in culture and life style. These may coincide in distinctive, closely integrated local communities. The paradox of ethnicity is that the more locally anchored such patterns are in actual practice, the less likely they are to be important for social action. It is the larger, looser meta-communities that group strangers into categories for political action, as well as for acts of discrimination and hostility or of sympathy and support.

At the level of these larger constructions of ethnic meta-communities, the generalized notion of ethnicity becomes a social reality in itself, shaping macro-divisions in society. It is distinctiveness, however marked, that is operative, not any particular kind of distinction. If one marker is strong enough, other markers are superfluous. For black Americans, the principal socially recognized marker is skin color; language and names are irrelevant. For Jews, it is genealogy imperfectly conveyed by names, plus religiously anchored culture. For Irish Americans, somatic and linguistic markers are too vague or too far in the past to be operative; there remain names, of fading significance, together with special-purpose organizations designed expressly to keep alive ethnic heritage; such deliberately contrived organizations have an artificial quality and are a sign that the stronger social bases of this ethnic division are largely gone.

What would constitute a general theory of the social construction of ethnicity? The degree of construction is a variable on a continuum. Primordial proto-ethnicity is one end of the continuum, in which a group is completely isolated, completely homogeneous as a breeding pool, a language community, and in any other respect we might care to imagine. This picture is imaginary, because real communities probably always have had some awareness of the neighbors from whom they differed; at the end point where groups are never in contact, there is no sense of difference and hence no ethnic mobilization. The ideal type at the other extreme, complete assimilation, is a utopia that coincides with primordial proto-ethnicity, a heavenly goal at the end of history that is the same as the Garden of Eden at the beginning. Complete assimilation is mythical because it assumes that there is no interaction with the region outside the unit in which assimilation finally occurs; it is a state without foreign relations. Ethnicity is meaningful only by contrast; there can never be one ethnic group, but always two or more. Assimilation, in practice, means moving toward smaller numbers of ethnic groups, but never reaching the end point.

Mobilization ranges from proto-ethnicity, or minimal sense of distinction from other groups, through increasing degrees of group consciousness and action vis-à-vis other groups. The boundaries of what is mobilized are variable; the size and extent of the group are constructed simultaneously with its mobilization into political action. Increasing participation in a political arena defines each group membership vis-à-vis other groups that are becoming defined at the same moment.

The most intense degree of ethnic mobilization may be called ethno-nationalism. This is ethnicity oriented to using the state as its instrument. Ethnicity is not identical to nationalism, since some ethnic groups mobilize against the state, or against dominance by the favored, nationally legitimate ethnic group. Antinational, state-resisting ethnic mobilization too is conditioned by the state, both in its internal penetrative capacity and its external geopolitical position vis-à-vis other states. Ethnicity grows up with the state. Full-scale ethnic mobilization carries in its wake aspirations to state autonomy. In practice this depends on the geopolitical strength of the state, and the goal of autonomy may be recognized as politically unrealistic. In these cases ethnic groups may settle for local or de facto regions of autonomy, freedom from being interfered with by the state in matters of language, education, and other means of perpetuating the ethnic distinction. Even less-mobilized ethnic groups, the archetypal sedentary farms in remote mountain valleys, are in my terminology toward the proto-ethnic end of the continuum and have little effect on the ethnic process of the society at large, until they enter the arena of struggling for their position in the queue of national recognition.

A theory of nationalism is a subtype of the theory of ethnicity. The same processes affect both. Nationalism is toward one end of the continuum; ethnicity, as conventionally defined, is at the middle. By the same token, discussions of citizenship belong to the theoretical problem of the ethno-national continuum, whether one is concerned with constructing a highly uniform participatory citizenship ethos (in effect, strong ethno-nationalist citizenship) or a multicultural or tolerant citizenship, backing off from the ethno-nationalist end point and attempting to institutionalize a coalition of ethnic identities as sharing in legitimacy. A theory of nationalism provides a clue to a theory of ethnicity.

POWER-PRESTIGE AND ETHNIC LEGITIMACY

Max Weber (1968 [1922], 901–40), in discussing the phenomenon of nationalism, noted that the boundaries of a state do not originally or necessarily coincide with linguistic, religious, or ethnic divisions. What makes a difference for national identity, he argued, is what is constructed through the political experience of people with their state. Nationalism is not primordial; it waxes and wanes. The most important of these collective experiences, in Weber's view, is all-out military mobilization. French nationalism was forged above all in the levée en masse of the Napoleonic wars. German nationalism, overcoming the regionalism of the Kleinstaaterei, was molded in the war of liberation against Napoleonic conquest (which not incidentally destroyed many of the minor states and left Prussia, the leader of the liberation war, as the center of national identity).

Weber's argument resonates with a neo-Durkheimian mechanism of emotional identification around symbols forged in the heat of collective participation. As Weber puts it, military participation bonds not only soldiers into a "community of fate" but, to the extent that warfare is fateful for conquest, migration, or extermination, bonds their families and other noncombatants as well. The more widespread the popular participation in the military, the more thoroughly national sentiments are spread. Hence the strongest forms of national feeling come either in the mass armies of tribal coalitions and migrations or in modern states deeply penetrating their populations. The weakest national feeling occurs in states organized as thin layers of aristocrats monopolizing arms above a mass of disarmed commoners.

In either of the highly mobilized forms of military action, Weber suggests, national feeling can be constructed quite rapidly. In the Volkerwanderung of early German history or the recruitment of Viking bands, and (perhaps by extrapolation) in other tribal migrations as well, coalitions may be formed on an ad hoc basis, drawing fighting men from many solidarities, who acquire a new identity, especially if their migration is long distance and their conquest is successful. The same volatility of national sentiments, I would argue, characterizes the shifting national loyalties around modern states.

Weber's argument is about nationalism, but it can be extended to ethnicity in general. Put another way, nationalism is the form that ethnicity takes when the gradient of movement is toward expanding ethnic boundaries so that they coincide with the state. The classic statements of "assimilation" come from the period of expanding nationalism and implicitly assume that the target boundary is that of the state. Weber's argument takes us onto the terrain of geopolitics. Ultimately the core of the state is its capacity to wield military power to control a territory. Neither the boundaries of states nor their power vis-à-vis each other is static; geopolitics gives the principles that determine the increases and decreases in external state power.

Let me add a corollary: the power-prestige of the state in the external arena affects the legitimacy of its rulers in the internal arena. There are, of course, other domestic sources of legitimacy, but in the dynamics of long-term change, the most important factor affecting legitimacy is external power-prestige (for elaboration, see Collins 1986, 145–66). The strongest evidence of this connection is revolution: revolution depends almost always on delegitimation of rulers and on splits within the elite, and these in turn have reached the necessary extreme proportions typically as the result of geopolitical defeat or accumulated effects of geopolitical strain. Conversely, the prestige of state rulers rises with military success; even in the absence of war, the ability of a strong state to dominate other states in diplomacy reinforces the legitimacy of its rulers. In short, external geopolitics affect internal legitimacy.

This argument can be extended from the legitimacy of rulers to the legitimacy of dominant ethnic groups. Schematically, when a state is geopolitically strong, the prestige of its dominant ethnic group is also high. Conversely, a geopolitically weak state lowers its dominant ethnic prestige. Combined with the process of state organization and penetration into its own population, these principles enable us to predict the main variations in the structure and long-term dynamics of ethnicity.

State formation and inward penetration construct the highly mobilized forms of ethnicity. Under these conditions the proto-ethnicity of isolated local communities moves toward the end of the continuum at which there is stronger consciousness and availability for concerted action. The formation of any state at all is the first step toward ethnic mobilization, insofar as there is a call to participate collectively as a fighting unit. The degree to which ethnic mobilization moves up this continuum varies with the extent of state penetration.

At one end, there is minimal state penetration: the "layer-state" of imperial conquest extracting tribute from indigenous proto-ethnic or religious communities. Even here, ethnic unity and awareness may be moved up a notch by the imposition from above of collective responsibility for taxation and internal order. Although Greeks, Kurds, or Armenians under the Ottoman empire might seem like primordial identities, it is likely that the empire's administrative practices in the millet system of collective responsibility and religious self-government formed these identities into larger units than had previously existed or kept them from fragmenting or drifting into different lines of division (Mardin 1997).

Further up the continuum is the structure of feudal aristocracy in agrarian coercive societies. The volatility of feudal alliance and warfare and the long-distance ties of dynastic marriage politics militate against strong ethno-national identification around the state unit. These antinationalist influences are countered in some degree by the vertical demands of lords on vassals and of the aristocracy generally on their servants, retainers, and peasants, which create some degree of identification with regional ethnicities. Although peasants and servants had little direct political participation under medieval French feudalism, the consolidation of a network of feudal loyalties around the king, branching out from the Ile de France, was a magnetic pole in the space of ethnic identification.

A highly mobilized, long-lasting military alliance can create ethnic solidarity among its participants even if the state structure is minimal. The ancient Greek city-states mobilized local identities as fighting units that transcended the familism of the clans; their larger war coalitions, such as those organized against the Persians, expanded the scope of ethnic identification. The war coalitions of the Germanic tribes in the geopolitical vacuum of the falling Roman empire—ad hoc assemblies of men willing to migrate long distances, cutting family connections and taking alien wives along the way—very likely forged new ethnic identities. One piece of evidence is that distinctive new features of the German languages emerged during the period of these war migrations (Borkenau 1981).

These examples warn us that there is no straight evolutionary development from proto-ethnicity to modern ethno-nationalism. Periods of strong ethnic identification around a polity can occur in the absence of anything resembling bureaucratic penetration of society, provided that widespread military participation keeps people busy at war for long periods of time. Once peace comes, or substantial portions of the populace are demobilized into a stratification of aristocracy and peasantry, the large-scale ethno-national identification may disintegrate or move back toward lower levels of mobilization.

Finally, there is the modern process of state penetration. The bureaucratic expansion of the state, especially from the nineteenth century onward, developed public education, economic regulation, and welfare, along with physical infrastructure of transportation and communications. Individuals became public citizens, inscribed in records of eligibility for military conscription, taxation, compulsory schooling, health and pension coverage, passports, and work permits. National cultures were created among those integrated into the state, reaching down even to the bedroom. Watkins (1991) shows that after 1870 patterns such as marital fertility, illegitimacy, and the propensity to marry became increasingly similar among local regions within European states. Where previously the biggest diversity had been within states, now sexual behaviors diverged at the state borders. State penetration established ties to the center that cut across local households, neighborhoods, and workplaces. An unanticipated consequence was to make people available for mobilization in social movements and political action on an unprecedented scale. The result of state penetration was to unleash a series of movements and to shape identities that had previously been latent or nonexistent: class conflict, ethnic consciousness, nationalism, and eventually feminism and a host of special-issue movements (Mann 1993; Tilly 1995).

A strong move in the direction of sharply drawing ethno-linguistic boundaries to the outside, while homogenizing within, is the creation of a standard national language. At the turn of the nineteenth century, some 40 percent of French subjects spoke a regional language or dialect other than French as spoken in the Paris region. This diversity fell off sharply by 1920, as the result of deliberate government policies, the spread of schooling, and the integration through national transport, communications, and commercial networks (Weber 1976; Watkins 1991, 162–63). This is a typical process of state-centered construction of an ideal type ethno-national identity, a movement along the continuum from larger to smaller number of ethno-linguistic groups. It is simultaneously a refocusing of salient boundaries, a strengthening of the boundaries between a group defined as "French" and all non-French, a form of ethno-national mobilization. The degree of ethno-linguistic uniformity, and the strength of an ethno-national identity, comes from the power of a state to penetrate its population and draw it into a single national arena.

Even at its most extreme, state penetration does not automatically succeed in forming a single ethno-national identity within the bounds of each modern state. It may instead provide an arena in which ethnic groups are mobilized to struggle with each other over which cultural identity will become the legitimate core of the nation, or for institutionalized set-asides, (pieces of the national pie), for local autonomy, or even for rebellion and separation from the existing state. Nor does the state necessarily remain territorially stable; even states that have high degrees of internal penetration may become amalgamated or divided by geopolitical processes. Alongside the process of state penetration, we must also consider three geopolitical patterns.

Geopolitical ascendancy of the state in the external arena elevates the power-prestige of the dominant ethnic group within. The greater the geopolitical power-prestige, the more successfully the state penetrates its own population when the institutions of national political participation and cultural communication are introduced. A geopolitically ascendant state is better able to assimilate regional and other proto-ethnicities into a national language, educational standard, and other aspects of uniform public culture. Our prime examples of the creation of national culture, such as nineteenth-century Britain, come from cases in which not only a national economic market and institutions of transportation and communication are being formed but also the geopolitical power-prestige of the state is high. Lacking this power-prestige, national-level institutions become an arena for ethnic conflict more than for ethnic unification.

Geopolitical weakness of the state reduces the prestige of the dominant ethnicity identified with it. If geopolitical strains are severe, the breakup of the state brings in its wake the destruction of ethno-national identity. The breakup of the Roman empire created the separate ethno-linguistic blocks of southern and western Europe, just as the breakup of the Carolingian empire paved the way for distinctions among French, German, and Italian identities. The revival of militant ethno-national identities out of the component pieces of the U.S.S.R. or of Yugoslavia in the 1990s fits the general pattern. Ethnic strife on the local level is not to be explained as a continuation of age-old ethnic hatreds. Ethnic consciousness is volatile, because geopolitics is prone to abrupt transitions. It is volatile both upward and downward on the scale of particularistic mobilization. A geopolitically strong state demobilizes fragmentary ethnic identifications within it, and the reversal of geopolitical fortunes is responsible for the upsurge of fragmentizers.

If the unification of states produces language uniformity, the breakup of states produces language differentiation. The romance languages date from the fragmentation of the Roman empire. Aside from Italian of the home territories, Spanish, French, Romanian, and a number of others are languages of regions that had been colonized by Latin speakers (some of them ethno-somatically Italian, others not). Conquest by German tribal coalitions brought sharp changes into what are recognizable versions of the present national languages.

Changes occurred not only in phonology, but most strikingly in syntax. The grammar of the Romance languages displaced the densely packed inflections and complex word formations that gave Latin its peculiar pungency and freedom from word order. These traits were replaced with less inflection and more analytical and word-separating forms (Kroeber 1963, 50–51; Sapir 1921, 144–46).

Vocabulary, in contrast, retained many elements of Latin words. It is a challenge for macro-historical sociology of language to explain why syntax, the deep structural framework of language, is amenable to abrupt changes, while drift works mainly on continuous gradations in phonology and vocabulary (Aitchison 1991). It appears that drift is more conservative and continuous, whereas language change by abrupt geopolitical crisis also produces radical linguistic discontinuities.

Language speakers act in a way that differentiates themselves as sharply as possible from those who are perceived as their enemies. The process is found not only in tribal societies and archaic periods. Labov and Harris (1986) produce evidence that in the most alienated parts of the black ghetto in large American cities, black English has been migrating away from standard English. That this divergence has taken place in syntax, not merely pronunciation and vocabulary, suggests the depth of the social conflict. Residential segregation and poverty, compounded by self-enhancing feedback loops, create an ever more deeply ingrained cultural distinctiveness on racial lines (Massey and Denton 1993), what I would call the extreme end of the ethnic distinctiveness continuum. Labov (1971), as well as Aitchison (1991), interprets these instances as displaying a general mechanism of language change. Similarly, after the breaking away of the American colonies from Britain, the informal style of American English and rejection of formal British speaking traditions occurred quite abruptly at the turn of the nineteenth century (Cmiel 1990). This mechanism, operating between Gothic conquerors and once-domineering Romans, may have produced the sharp change in syntax between Latin and the Romance languages.

"Balkanization" is a handy label for movement on the continuum away from ethno-nationalism around an existing state and toward ethnic separatism. The abruptness and militancy of movement along this continuum coincide with the degree of geopolitical strain. A full-scale geopolitical shock, the breakup of an empire, opens the door to full-scale ethnic splits, even creating multiple new ethnicities where a single one had existed before. Lesser degrees of geopolitical weakness encourage corresponding degrees of ethnic consciousness and rebellions.

The Ottoman and to a degree the Austrian empires were the "sick men of Europe" for over a century, and everyone knew it. Hence these were the regions in which local proto-ethnicities became dissidents. In zones that were weakly under control by the empire, ethnic nationalists sought their own state. Other regions, still firmly under military control, experienced the mobilization of movements for political autonomies or, failing these, for ethno-nationalist control of cultural institutions such as official language and education. The latter processes meshed with the growth of institutions of state penetration at this time, but in this case not only did the penetration not strengthen the central state, it weakened it by providing an arena for mobilizing dissident ethnicities.

Geopolitical balance of power fosters cosmopolitanism. On occasion the geopolitical situation is stable over a long period of time, with power split among a number of states of approximately equal power. Alliances and diplomacy become oriented toward preventing any one state from drastically outclassing the others in military strength. Under these circumstances, the power-prestige of states is stabilized, but also denatured. Wars tend to be fought under rules of "gentlemanly" or "chivalrous" combat; large conquests of territory are not expected, and casualties are usually limited. Here ethno-nationalism is devalued.

Several processes contribute to this result. War is regarded as a game of the elite, with relatively little participation from the mass of the population and relatively little effect on their lives. Changes in rulership are not drastic, and the military state acts like a thin layer on society rather than penetrating it. The emotional mobilization of mass participation or of bloody conquest is missing, cutting out this route toward ethno-national identification.

In addition, the practice of shifting alliances to maintain balance of power keeps ethnic identities vague and superficial, in keeping with the principle that ethnicities are constructed by division and contrast with those whom they exclude. If one's military enemies and allies change every few years, there is a much weaker sense of one's place in the ethnic order of the world than in situations where long-term geopolitical rivalries frame the ethno-national cosmos.

Transethnic cosmopolitanism is a permanent analytical possibility, and cosmopolitan periods are possible in the future. Suppose we enter (or are already in) a period in which no state is capable of much geopolitical aggrandizement. Instead loosely knit alliances and international networks are the focus of elite action.

By hypothesis, the very idea of ethno-nationalism becomes repugnant, at least among the elite. Such elites bend over backward to avoid extolling the superiority of their own culture. Late twentieth-century "multiculturalism" and "political correctness" may be a contemporary version of transethnic cosmopolitanism, mixed with peculiar circumstances of geopolitical weakening and ethnic mobilization at the level of nonelites.

THE AMERICAN QUESTION:
ASSIMILATION OR ETHNIC STASIS?

American research on ethnicity has concentrated on the question of assimilation, at one time favorably, more recently negatively. What was once considered the inevitable and general direction of change is now widely considered as fundamentally static. Ethnic reproduction along with class reproduction have become the favored (and at least in the case of the former, the morally presumptive) position. What we have done is truncate conceptually the continuum of ethnic change. A theory of assimilation is an explanation of how ethnic boundaries widen; antiassimilation theories are content to show how ethnic boundaries are stuck. What is left out is consideration of the larger context, which determines whether there is movement in either direction along the continuum of numbers of ethnic divisions.

In this section I overview this assimilation and antiassimilation material cursorily, with an eye to showing how it fits into larger geopolitical dynamics. My main theme is that these meso-dynamics of ethnic reproduction and conflict are short run and of variable strength; they are reinforced by particular geopolitical configurations, overridden by others.

In classic assimilation theories, the baseline was preexisting ethnic groups, taken as if primordial, which had not yet started the process of assimilation because of geographical regionalization. This was the situation in pre-state and agrarian-coercive (feudal/extractive) societies. The evolutionary model posited the stages of contact, transitory conflict, accommodation, and assimilation. Change was driven by development of a market economy, division of labor, and urbanization that break down regionally based distinctions and set in motion a process of assimilation to some larger-size group.

There is a good deal of evidence that this process occurs quite often (for the recent period, see Waldinger 1996; for the turn of the twentieth century, see Lieberson 1980). However, as the experience of agrarian conquest states shows, it is possible for market structures to develop while leaving narrower ethnic boundaries in place or at least producing no more than small-scale movements along the continuum of assimilation into larger groups. The Parsees in India, the "king's Jews" in medieval Europe, and the Hanseatic Germans in the Baltic are only a few examples out of many of ethnic enclaves situated precisely in the centers of trade and administration.

Even a complex division of labor and exchange in industrial societies can reinforce ethnic distinctiveness. Rural or pre-migration regional bases of ethnic division can become reproduced by business location and residential segregation. Ethnic groups can find enclaves as specialties within the division of labor, a tendency of which the Indian caste system is only the most extreme example.

At one time sociological theorists assumed that such ethnic division of labor was characteristic only of pre-industrial and pre-bureaucratic societies, but there is ample evidence from contemporary societies to show that it can continue to exist in every form of economy yet known. The split labor market of high- and low-wage sectors and the protection of particular markets by unionization, by ethnically based credit associations, by monopolization through privileged ethnic groups, or by "racial" discrimination, are some of the structures through which this operates (Bonacich 1972; Hechter 1974; Portes 1994; Light and Karageorgis 1994; Olzak 1992).

The aim should be not merely to draw up a scorecard of how much ethnic segregation happens to be structured into the division of labor in each particular case, but to explain why such patterns vary. Any existing historical situation is the result of a balance between opposing tendencies of differing strengths. The division of labor and structures of administrative centralization can have effects in opposite directions on the continuum of ethnic boundaries. In one direction, any kind of contact and co-participation among distinct ethnic groups has the potential for producing assimilation across their boundary. As long as people come together, there is always the prospect of forming a common culture, a new language or patois, making friendships and intermarriages, and forming a united front in conflict against more remote parties. Whether this potential for assimilation is realized or whether, on the contrary, contact merely heightens sense of boundaries depends on whether tendencies to assimilate across the boundary are stronger than tendencies to quarrel. These tendencies are determined by how much prestige there is for participating in a common culture legitimated by the state.

The same is true with the effects of stratification. We are most familiar with the processes by which stratification reinforces ethnic segregation. Differences in class cultures add onto (and sometimes also create) differences in ethnic cultures, and vice versa. Sociologists have described many such self-reinforcing loops: in the contemporary United States, the material conditions of the suburbs vis-à-vis the inner city flow through familial, educational, and attitudinal patterns that reinforce the distinctiveness between black "street" culture and middle-class white culture, with the circle closed by occupational stratification and the perpetuation of material inequality. Bourdieu's habitus theorizes self-reproducing arrangements generally. The pathos of such self-perpetuating models has become American sociologists' stock-in-trade.

Nevertheless, from an analytical vantage point stratification does not necessarily result in static ethnic boundaries. Stratification can also set up tendencies toward cultural assimilation. Stratification gives prestige to the culture of the dominant class. Such culture has often spread to middle and subordinate classes, by the processes of imitation, trickle down, and imposition by culture-producing institutions. If class stratification is correlated with ethnic stratification, such processes bring about assimilation of ethnic cultures. In addition, stratification fosters motivation for upward mobility; insofar as subordinated ethnic groups move up in the class structure or move laterally into the centralized organizations of the economy and state, there is a tendency toward ethnic assimilation by structural amalgamation of group boundaries.

A large literature examines the structural conditions for occupational mobility, of which the strongest condition is expansion in the size of nonagricultural, white-collar, and professional occupations (Bendix and Lipset 1959; Blau and Duncan 1967). These conditions for occupational mobility cut across societies, whether geopolitical power-prestige is high or low. My point here is not that geopolitical trajectory determines the amount of upward occupational mobility, but rather that geopolitics determines ethnic identification even when different classes are encompassed within the same ethnic group. An ethno-national identity, in which everyone is regarded as belonging to the same ethnic group, necessarily includes class distinctions within it.

Conversely, we may expect that the tendency to assimilate is weakest where contiguous ethnic groups are equal in class position and prestige. The issue is the strength of the tendency of stratification to reinforce ethnic boundaries relative to the strength of the opposite tendency to motivate assimilation. This again depends on the geopolitically given power-prestige of the state and hence of the ethnic culture of its rulers.

An additional loop between economic interests and ethnic antagonism has received much attention. The mobilization of ethnic antagonism has often been attributed to underlying economic conflicts. Insofar as ethnic groups form enclaves in the division of labor and the lineup of classes, any change in the economic standing of these groups mobilizes class conflict, which surfaces most easily in the form of ethnic antagonism. For example, anti-Semitism, rare in Christian Europe before the eleventh century, arose in violent attacks on Jews, initially in the Rhineland during the twelfth century and subsequently in eastern Europe. This has been attributed to the spread of a mercantile economy, of which Jews were the spearheads, often in alliance with centralized rulers, making anti-Semitism a convenient rallying point for traditionalist classes—the peasantry and nobility (Murray 1978, 69). Similar structural patterns are found in the solidarity of Georgian Jews and other ethnic groups of the Caucasus that sustained their own informal economies within Soviet communism (Portes 1994).

Ethnic antagonisms based on enclaves within the division of labor are not mobilized uniformly throughout world history. There are many instances in which they are not mobilized at all. Tendencies to ethnic conflict are just one of several causal forces, which can be overridden by stronger conditions. The most central of such conditions, along with the degree of state penetration, is the geopolitically based power-prestige of the state's rulers.

"Americanization" Versus "Balkanization"

Short-run processes within the division of labor, ethno-class strati- fication, and cultural mobilization have indeterminate effects: they can either promote ethnic distinctiveness and conflict or foster motivations toward assimilation—above all culturally, but also as- sociationally and somatotypically. Which of these happens de- pends on contextual conditions, above all the geopolitical trajec- tory of the state. There are two polar types. The "Americanization" model is the case in which the state has an expanding geopoliti- cal position. Accordingly, the prestige of the dominant ethnic group is high, and the prevailing motivation is toward assimila- tion.

In the "Balkanization" model, in contrast, the geopolitical tra- jectory is downhill; the state is crumbling, the prestige of the dom- inant ethnic group is low, and ethnic separatism rather than assim- ilation is the direction of mobilization. In the "Balkanization" model, the dominant ethnic group is not merely lacking in attrac- tion; it becomes a *negative* reference point, so that anti-Austrian and anti-Turkish sentiments are major mobilizing points for politi- cal and social action. In the same way, Russian ethnic identity at the time when the Russian-controlled Soviet empire came apart became a negative reference point for non-Russians.

The United States was a geopolitically expanding power be- ginning in the early 1800s, reaching a standing of major world power by the time of World War I. The United States from 1800 to 1960, a prime example of the assimilation ("Americanization") dy- namic of expanding ethnic boundaries, expanded into the terri- tory of North America against minimal local opposition. By the late 1800s, the advantage of the United States in terms of size and economic resources was formidable on the world scale, and in the twentieth century the United States was in the position to pick up the pieces of the costly showdown wars among the major Euro- pean powers. After 1960 a mild geopolitical decline took place, due to a costly arms race versus the U.S.S.R., the marchland state on the other side of the old European battle zone. Further strains resulted from logistical overextension against populous enemies in Korea and Vietnam. This historical trajectory explains the high ethnic prestige of Anglo American culture as a target for assimilation for a century and a half, with some falling off in this prestige after 1960.

I have perhaps loaded the dice with the "Americanization" model. The United States has been not only a rising geopolitical power but also a territory of great economic resources, and perhaps it was this land of wealth rather than its power-prestige that attracted large numbers of immigrants. I am tempted to modify the theoretical principles to add not only geopolitical prestige but also economic opportunities, which likewise increase the legitimacy and prestige of ruling elites and ethnic groups.

Conversely, not only geopolitical weakness but also economic decline reduce ruling ethnic prestige. Nevertheless, there are grounds for giving geopolitics primacy in affecting ethnic prestige. The prestige of Anglo assimilation in the United States was high from the early 1800s until the 1950s. If it has been challenged since that time, the correlation is not with economic decline but with geopolitical setbacks: above all the Vietnam War (1963 to 1975), but more generally the Korean stalemate (1950 to 1953), the Iranian-Islamic challenge (becoming acute with the Iranian revolution in 1979), and the emergence of a polycentric world. This underscores the point that geopolitical prestige is a matter of trajectory rather than of absolute standing. "What have you done lately?" is more important than the absolute level of geopolitical resources of a state and its elite.

Geopolitical Prestige and Struggle over the Means of Cultural Production

This discussion of meso-level conditions that affect ethnic boundaries has omitted the cultural media, such as education and language. These have important middle-range effects on both ethnic assimilation and ethnic struggle. As with all such meso-level conditions, the question is, which effect happens when? Thus in one (assimilation-oriented) model, mass education produces a common culture, the mass media spread a common language, and expanding access to these media eventually eliminates ethnic enclaves, except for a few residual traditionalists. In the other (assimilation-resistance or ethnic fragmentation) model, the opposite occurs—the spread of literacy, newspapers, television, and the like becomes the bases for mobilization of cultural separatists; "modernization" does not promote universalism but provides the instruments for reinforcing particularisms.

In this vein, education operates in a "damned if you do, damned if you don't" fashion. If, on the one hand, the state attempts to impose cultural uniformity through the educational system, the result is resentment by aggrieved ethnic groups. Here we have Lithuanian, Urkrainian, or Armenian nationalists keeping their culture alive under Russian educational imposition, ready to burst out when the opportunity arrives. If, on the other hand, the state allows cultural pluralization (as Soviet reformers did increasingly in the 1980s; see Waller 1992), it hands the weapons of group mobilization to its opponents.

The key as to which scenario takes place is not the structure of the education system (or the mass media), but the geopolitical conditions that set the overarching gradient of ethnic prestige. A culturally unified educational system and an imposed linguistic monopoly on the means of dissemination will fail if the prestige of the dominant ethnic group is low; at least this will be the case over the time period (apparently several generations under modern conditions) during which state weakness eventually leads to a crumbling of central controls.

We should not dwell too strongly on the image of a strong, vibrant current of cultural separatism, meeting in basements and waiting for the time when it can come into the open air. Rebellious ethnic nationalisms are to a large extent constructed, and fairly sudden shifts in the political wind can bring about enthusiasm for an ethnic culture of separatism that was carried for a long time by only a few die-hards. The "Balkanization" process can be long and slow, with state control visibly crumbling for decades or centuries; in this case (the Balkans in the nineteenth and early twentieth centuries) overt cultural resistance and mobilization are continuous. Or "Balkanization" can emerge rather rapidly, as in the weakening of central control in the U.S.S.R. from the mid-1980s onward. In this case, whatever twists occur in the rulers' cultural line, all feed the same direction of resistance.

In contrast, the "Americanization" model of cultural hegemony can operate without much more than market processes. Although Anglos made some efforts to impose their culture on migrants in the U.S. public schools of the late nineteenth and early twentieth centuries, the prestige of Anglo culture seems to have been the dominant factor in bringing about linguistic and educational assimilation. There was never any national control over education, and a good deal of local initiative existed. Variant forms of education were tried: a huge Catholic school system staffed mainly by non-Anglos, a huge multiplicity of religious colleges, and a number of foreign language schools, of which only the Hebrew academies have had much staying power. As Jencks and Riesman (1968) demonstrate, the variant forms of education soon lost their distinctiveness, as all emulated the high-prestige model: the sequence leading up to the traditional Anglo-protestant college.

Not that multiethnic competition within the United States had no effect on the educational marketplace, but its effects were to heighten competition over a common currency of educational credentials, resulting in the most massive expansion of schooling at all levels of any society in world history (Collins 1979). The result was inflation of a common educational currency, not fragmentation into separate ethnic enclaves. In the same way, separate ethnic-language newspapers and other cultural media have not flourished in the United States in competition with the Anglo American mass culture. No state restrictions were significant in bringing about this result; the prestige of the Anglo culture merely outcompeted that of the ethnic separatists.

The Future of U.S. Ethnicity

As the geopolitical hypothesis predicts, U.S. global power-prestige produced American ethno-nationalism. What the geopolitical theory does not directly explain is the source of white resistance to black assimilation. Here we could invoke a number of well-studied processes by which ethnic stratification reproduces itself. I have nothing new to add here, except the geopolitical context in which this resistance to assimilation went from legitimate to ille-

gitimate. American integration became a strong theme for all ethnic groups with the world wars, especially the catapulting of the
United States into the front rank of world power-prestige at mid-
century. This also led to geopolitical strains of overextension,
above all the embarrassing defeats of the Vietnam War.

The black movement in the United States involved elements
both of liberalizing ethno-nationalism and of separatism. Ethno-
nationalism came from the strong upward trajectory of American
power-prestige, which brought the black integration movement
institutional support from the mass media and the discourse of
public officials, as well as fervent moral support by the cosmopolitan upper classes of the white population. Black nationalism and
separatism, in its various degrees and forms, were fed by the
mood of delegitimation of the dominant ethnic group, due to a
string of geopolitical setbacks. The U.S. defeat in the Vietnam War
was the equivalent of the breakup of the European colonial empires as a result of the strains of World War II; in both cases, the
ethno-nationalism of once-invincible states was battered. Declining states face moral onslaughts on the legitimacy of their rule,
and these are echoed by their own elites in their loss of self-confi-
dence, a mixture of humiliation and guilt. It is this atmosphere
that has encouraged a rebellious nationalism of unassimilated and
oppressed populations.

In the United States, rebellious ethno-nationalisms have not
gone very far, because the geopolitical strength of the state is still
relatively high. With the collapse of the U.S.S.R. in the 1990s, the
geopolitical position of the United States has climbed again by
default. For all the rhetoric carried over from the upheaval period
of the 1960s and 1970s, black, Hispanic, or Asian ethnic militan-
cies take the form of struggles over the content of schooling in
urban neighborhoods and relatively minor issues of deference to
cultural symbols, not claims for transferring even fragments of territorial power to autonomous ethnic control. To the extent that the
power-prestige of the state remains strong, we can expect that the
prestige of ethno-nationalism will remain paramount as long as
the geopolitical situation remains the same. The long-run trend, in
that case, is toward assimilation.

By this time, the target standard is no longer simply the cultural dominance of white Anglo culture and somatotypes. The

pressures for assimilation of European ethnicities, reaching their peak in the New Deal and the mobilization of World War II, by mid-twentieth century had already produced a hybrid culture (which might well be called American Creole). The hybrid nature of that culture doubtless will continue to change, with the incorporation of Asian and Hispanic elements. In many respects, black American culture has already made its mark on American national culture and vice versa. The differences that remain are largely matters of class culture plus one distinctive marker: skin color. On this point, the geopolitical hypothesis suggests an optimistic future for assimilationists, a pessimistic one for separatists.

The key to the racialization of the continuum of ethnic distinctions is the cultural definition of the offspring of mixed breeding as belonging exclusively to the nonlegitimate category. That cultural definition appears to be dissolving at the turn of the twenty-first century. In the 1990s there was growing recognition of a category of mixed race. The effect of such a change in categorical boundaries would be far-reaching. In the absence of further differentiation of institutional segregation in terms of ranked degrees of racial purity such as have existed in Brazil and elsewhere, the breaking up of the rigid distinction between black and white has potential for the entire category scheme to lose its centrality as a marker.

We may be seeing the beginning of a racially de-dichotomized America, even though assimilation of all groups of the population may not occur for a long time. A distinctive black racial identity may well continue, anchored on a sizable black lower class segregated by mutually reinforcing feedbacks of class and racial hostility legitimated by criminalization. The existence of a culturally distinct and hypersegregated black underclass makes black skin a reference point for everyone, keeping the category alive even as applied to blacks of higher social classes.

Counterbalancing this tendency toward racial dichotomy is the potential of an amorphous mixed-race category to de-racialize the overarching American ethno-national identity. This mixed-race category is not emerging through interbreeding between blacks and whites, as in the scenario of classic expectations and fears. It has come about instead from the blurring of identities among some Asians, Hispanics, Amerindians, and others into a transracial category into which white Euro Americans and African Americans have also been blending, at different edges. Blacks and whites may not blend together in the foreseeable future, but it is conceivable that both eventually will blend into a larger, culturally dominant category.

If high geopolitical power-prestige elevates the prestige of a unitary ethno-national identity, and full mobilization of all its people into the armed forces puts emotional energy into this identification, we might expect that the United States as world hegemon will dissolve the cultural definition of race in the coming generations (see Moskos and Butler 1996 for evidence that the strongest institutional sector of black-white solidarity and integration is found within the U.S. army in the post–Vietnam War era). The geopolitical prominence of the United States attracts worldwide immigration, propelling the tendency toward a transracial identity amalgamating a wide variety of world ethnic origins. Within this context, class-based anchoring of a black-white distinction may well continue, but increasingly as a sidelight to the shifting center of American ethno-national identity. The blended Asian-Euro-Hispanic American would be the category into which all else dissolves. All this depends on how long the geopolitical ascendancy of the United States will last.

REFERENCES

Aitchison, Jean. 1991. *Language Change: Progress or Decay?* Cambridge: Cambridge University Press.

Anderson, Benedict. 1983. *Imagined Communities: Reflections on the Origins and Spread of Nationalism.* London: Verso.

Bendix, Reinhard, and S. M. Lipset. 1959. *Social Mobility in Industrial Society.* Berkeley: University of California Press.

Blau, Peter M., and Otis Dudley Duncan. 1967. *The American Occupational Structure.* New York: Wiley.

Bonacich, Edna. 1972. "A Theory of Ethnic Antagonism: The Split Labor Market." *American Sociological Review* 37: 547–59.

Borkenau, Franz. 1981. "The Rise of the I-Form of Speech." In *End and Beginning: On the Generations of Cultures and the Origins of the West,* edited by Franz Borkenau. New York: Columbia University Press.

Cmiel, Kenneth. 1990. *Democratic Eloquence.* Berkeley: University of California Press.

Collins, Randall. 1979. *The Credential Society: An Historical Sociology of Education and Stratification.* New York: Academic Press.

———. 1986. *Weberian Sociological Theory.* Cambridge: Cambridge University Press.

———. 1999. *Macro-History: Essays in the Sociology of the Long Run.* Stanford, Calif.: Stanford University Press

Hechter, Michael. 1974. "The Political Economy of Ethnic Change." *American Journal of Sociology* 79: 1151–78.

Jencks, Christopher, and David Riesman. 1968. *The Academic Revolution.* New York: Doubleday.

Kroeber, A. L. 1963. *Anthropology: Culture Patterns and Processes.* New York: Harcourt.

Labov, William. 1971. *Sociolinguistic Patterns.* Philadelphia: University of Pennsylvania Press.

Labov, William, and Wendell A. Harris. 1986. "De Facto Segregation of Black and White Vernaculars." In *Current Issues in Linguistic Theory.* Vol. 53. *Diversity and Diachrony,* edited by David Sankoff. Amsterdam, the Netherlands: Benjamins.

Lieberson, Stanley. 1980. *A Piece of the Pie: Blacks and White Immigrants since 1880.* Berkeley: University of California Press.

Light, Ivan, and Stavros Karageorgis. 1994. "The Ethnic Economy." In *Handbook of Economic Sociology,* edited by Neil J. Smelser and Richard Swedberg. Princeton, N.J.: Princeton University Press.

Mann, Michael. 1993. *The Sources of Social Power.* Vol 2, *The Rise of Classes and Nation-States.* Cambridge: Cambridge University Press.

Mardin, Serif. 1997. "The Ottoman Empire." In *After Empire: Multiethnic Societies and Nation-Building,* edited by Karen Barkey and Mark Von Hagen. Boulder, Colo.: Westview Press.

Massey, Douglas S., and Nancy A. Denton. 1993. *American Apartheid: Segregation and the Making of the Underclass.* Cambridge, Mass.: Harvard University Press.

Moskos, Charles C., and John Sibley Butler. 1996. *All That We Can Be: Black Leadership and Racial Integration the Army Way.* New York: Basic Books.

Murray, Alexander. 1978. *Reason and Society in the Middle Ages.* Oxford: Clarendon Press.

Olzak, Susan. 1992. *The Dynamics of Ethnic Competition and Conflict.* Stanford, Calif.: Stanford University Press.

Portes, Alejandro. 1994. "The Informal Economy and Its Paradoxes." In

Handbook of Economic Sociology, edited by Neil J. Smelser and Richard Swedberg. Princeton, N.J.: Princeton University Press.

Sapir, Edward. 1921. *Language: An Introduction to the Study of Speech.* New York: Harcourt.

Sperber, Hans, and Wolfgang Fleischhauer. 1963. *Geschichte der Deutschen Sprache.* Berlin: de Gruyter.

Tilly, Charles. 1995. *Popular Contention in Great Britain.* Cambridge, Mass.: Harvard University Press.

Waldinger, Roger. 1996. *Still the Promised City? African-Americans and New Immigrants in Postindustrial New York.* Cambridge, Mass.: Harvard University Press.

Waller, David V. 1992. "Ethnic Mobilization and Geopolitics in the Soviet Union." *Journal of Military and Political Sociology* 20: 37–62.

Waters, Mary C. 1990. *Ethnic Options: Choosing Identities in America.* Berkeley: University of California Press.

Watkins, Susan Cotts. 1991. *From Provinces into Nations: Demographic Integration in Western Europe, 1870–1960.* Princeton, N.J.: Princeton University Press.

Weber, Eugene. 1976. *Peasants into Frenchmen: The Modernization of Rural France, 1870–1914.* Stanford, Calif.: Stanford University Press.

Weber, Max. 1968 [1922]. *Economy and Society.* New York: Bedminster Press.

Williams, Eric. 1966. *Capitalism and Slavery.* New York: Putnam.

—— Chapter 3 ——

Immigrant-Black Dissensions in American Cities: An Argument for Multiple Explanations

Ewa Morawska

CONFLICTS BETWEEN NATIVES and immigrants over neighborhoods, jobs, political influence, and cultural values are integral to the history of American cities, intensifying during periods of heightened immigration. In the nineteenth and early twentieth centuries, these conflicts counterposed a variety of different groups: old (Northwest) against new (Southeast) European immigrants, native whites against southern African Americans in northern industrial cities, and native whites against Asian immigrants in the West (see Bayor 1993 for an overview of these historical encounters; see also Higham 1975). Renewed mass immigration today has brought new diversity to American cities and also revived intergroup tensions and hostilities. These conflicts often involve native African American residents who are disproportionately and disadvantageously concentrated in urban centers (although native white urbanites are by no means free of resentments, especially as most contemporary immigrants are of color; see Johnson, Farrell, and Guinn 1997; Rose 1993; Simon 1993; Jones-Correa 1998).

Heightened intergroup and, in particular, interracial tensions in American cities during the 1980s and 1990s are generally explained using two kinds of theoretical models. The first locates

47

sources of intergroup conflict in the objective conditions of the groups involved. These circumstances are viewed either as absolute or relative economic, residential, or political deprivation of group members (see Harris and Wilkins 1988; Massey and Denton 1993; Kluegel and Smith 1986) or as a direct result of intergroup competition for economic, residential, and political resources that have been made scarcer by increased numbers of competing groups and individuals or by dwindling resources (see Blalock 1967; Olzak 1992; Olzak and Shanahan 1996; Waldinger 1995, 1996a, 1996b, 1997). Another variation is the middleman theory, which locates the source of dissension in the external, structural position of the minority group that finds itself between two major populations or classes, serving as a convenient scapegoat for both (Bonacich 1973; Zenner 1991; Min 1996a; Ong et al. 1994; Light and Bonacich 1989).

The other type of explanatory model points to the subjective or representational sources of intergroup conflict. Two varieties exist: (1) theories that derive intergroup resentments and conflicts from collective beliefs about the existence of systematic ascriptive or discriminatory barriers to achievement (as opposed to individualistic, open-society orientations) and (2) propositions explaining intergroup hostilities in terms of ethnic or racial ideologies (often referred to as ethnic or racial nationalism) that advocate exclusive control over physical and symbolic spaces inhabited by the group, thus enabling popular mobilization. (For the former explanations, see Huber and Form 1973; Feldman 1988; Bobo 1991; Cheng and Espiritu 1989; for the latter, see Browning, Marshall, and Tabb 1984; Light, Har-Chui, and Kan 1994; Ong, Park, and Tong 1994; Lee 1993; Min 1996a; Kim 1996).

A theoretical framework that incorporates all of these explanations has recently been proposed by Bobo and Hutchings (1996). An extension of Blumer's group position model (1958), it views intergroup tension and hostility as generated not simply by economic and political deprivation, competition, or disempowerment or simply by the internalization of sentiments and orientations toward one's own and other groups, but by the *interaction* of these circumstances with the "historically and collectively developed judgments about the positions in the social order that in-group members should rightfully occupy relative to members of an out-group(s)" (Bobo and Hutchings 1996, 955). In establishing a sense of group position, their model identifies both the external conditions and subjective beliefs and representations. External conditions include changing ethnic or racial composition in neighborhoods and workplaces as well as low or diminishing socioeconomic status or political influence vis-à-vis other groups. Subjective beliefs and representations include the sense of group entitlement to certain resources and statuses, combined with feelings of collective disenfranchisement and grievance regarding the advantages of other groups, negative attitudes toward out-groups seen as competitors for and encroachers on claimed resources, and beliefs about the openness or closeness of the opportunity stratification system.

Although the objects of explanation—intergroup hostility, competition, or both—shift throughout the discussion, the group position model thus far is the most promising attempt to reconcile theoretically different perspectives on contentious intergroup relations. In this chapter, I take Bobo and Hutchings's effort one step further and make the explanation of intergroup conflict at once more complex and more flexible. Specifically, I argue that, propelled by different sets of circumstances, different sets of explanations—or, more precisely, differently composed and "weighted" constellations of contributing elements of the group position model—account for frictions and hostilities between different groups in different cities, ranging from low- to high-intensity vocal (or pictorial) public expressions of resentment to physical confrontations.

To substantiate this claim, I compare three American cities with large populations of new immigrants and African Americans: New York, Los Angeles, and Miami. Intergroup contentions in these cities have been far more intense than in other urban centers, and a sufficient number of studies exist of these adversarial relations during the 1980s and 1990s. In addition to examining sixty-odd studies, I contacted thirteen of their authors, asking for information and comments on specific issues and checking my interpretations with them.

INTERGROUP HOSTILITY
IN COMPARATIVE PERSPECTIVE

Among the purposes of comparative research identified by Ragin (1987, 1994), *exploring diversity*—in this case, the contributing factors and mechanisms of the reported outcomes rather than (as

is more common in this kind of research) the outcomes themselves—has been the immediate goal of this exercise, and the advancement of theory a more distant purpose. Comparing only
three out of the hundreds of American metropolitan areas in
which immigrant–native black relations are tenuous cannot establish the general regularities that might exist across diverse patterns
of intergroup tensions and conflicts, but it suggests one possible
strategy toward answering these questions, through the extension
of such comparative analyses.

Ragin (1987, 1994) distinguishes among different strategies of
comparative analysis (see also Isaac and Griffin 1989; Abbott
1992). The historical-sociological approach applied here is informed by the belief that circumstances of social life constitute
embedded processes rather than isolated events, and, therefore,
temporal sequences of situations matter for the outcomes. Explaining *how* things happen thus explains *why* they happen
(Abrams 1982; see also Aminzade 1992). To establish the how and
why of social situations and processes, a case-oriented comparative historical-sociological analysis reconstructs the specific configurations of circumstances that have contributed to the reported
outcome—here, intergroup tensions or open hostility—in particular localities.

Using studies of immigrant–native black relations in New
York, Los Angeles, and Miami and drawing on general studies of
intergroup conflicts in postwar urban America, I have compiled a
list of twenty-two factors that contribute either individually or in
clusters to intergroup tensions and hostilities. In table 3.1, I divide
them into national-level conditions (present in all cases, but exert-
ing a stronger or weaker and more or less direct influence) and
local-level conditions. Within each city, having identified the
groups most often reported to have had contentious relations with
each other during the 1980s and 1990s, I reconstruct the configu-
ration of factors responsible for these tensions and then propose
the best-fitting theoretical explanation.

NEW YORK

Late twentieth-century New York City is a textbook exemplar of
the "New America": its population is nearly 30 percent foreign-

TABLE 3.1 **Factors Contributing to Immigrant-Black Conflicts in U.S. Cities During the 1980s and 1990s**

Level and Reference Number	Factor
National-level factors	
1	Effects of the postindustrialization of the American economy and, especially, the emergence of an urban underclass and the informalization of labor markets
2	Dwindling of the American public sector and its welfare state
3	Shared sense of alienation from the larger society experienced by:
(3a)	Native racial minorities in view of the challenges to affirmative action policies and in the situation of factors 1 and 2
(3b)	New immigrants in view of factor 6 combined with intensified anti-immigrant sentiments and nativism on the part of the dominant American society
4	National (mainstream and immigrant or racial group) media-propagated negative images of and reports on immigrant and racial groups fostering inimical stereotyping
5	Contagious incidents of intergroup conflicts occurring in and reported from other cities
6	U.S. immigration policies and the impact of American foreign policy interests and priorities
Local-level factors	
7	Size and proportions of immigrant or racial groups over time
8	Dynamics of city's economy (sectoral loss and increment in jobs, labor market segmentation, enduring unemployment and underclass, size and areas of the informal economy, existence of ethnic occupational niches)
9	Occupational location over time of immigrants and native blacks, including ethnic occupational niches
10	Overt and covert competition for jobs and wages among immigrants and native blacks
11	Residential concentration, segregation, and interaction of immigrants and native blacks over time; and
(11a)	Intergroup competition for space, housing, and local social services

(Table continues on p. 52.)

TABLE 3.1 *Continued*

Level and Reference Number	Factor
12	Liberal versus conservative local civic-political climate and incorporation or exclusion of outsiders and newcomers
13	Immigrants' and native blacks' participation in local politics and share of public offices
14	Competition for public offices among immigrant and native black groups
15	Institutionalized racism or constraints on achievement of nonwhite, particularly dark-skinned, groups (native more than foreign-born)
16	Group sense of dislocation resulting from (a) one or some (weaker) or (b) all (strong) factors 7, 8, 10, 11, and 15
17	Shared beliefs or ideology of immigrant and native black groups regarding:
(17a)	In-group superiority vis-à-vis other(s)
(17b)	Rewards and statuses due to the group versus the reality, especially vis-à-vis the position of other group(s)
(17c)	Openness versus closeness of the American social structure
18	In-group negative perceptions and stereotypes of other immigrants or racial groups
19	Local ethnic or racial group media representations of other groups and their attitudes to and relations with the in-group
20	History of local intergroup hostility
21	Absence of outstanding, (re)conciliation-oriented city and immigrant or black leaders and organizations
22	Absence of tradition or instances of intergroup collaboration

Source: Author's compilation.

born, made up mostly of Hispanic, West Indian, and Asian immigrants. Its postindustrial services-fueled economy has generated a highly skilled global elite, hundreds of thousands of small firms, a large informal sector, and an underclass disproportionately composed of black (African American and Puerto Rican) residents trapped in dilapidated inner-city neighborhoods by economic re-structuring, a shrinking welfare system, and persistent racism.

New York's ethnic and racial composition, the sectoral distribution of its workers, and other socioeconomic indicators for the period 1970 to 1990 are summarized in table 3.2. Only in the 1970s, after implementation of the Equal Opportunity Employment Act (1972), did New York's pluralist, but distinctly ethnic-conscious and competitive civic-political system, begin to incorporate the city's racial minorities, in particular African Americans. Circulating between the city and their home island, and not well organized politically, Puerto Ricans thus far have remained largely outside the system. As a result of the massive entry of African Americans into white-collar public sector employment (36 percent of the total, rising from 25 percent in 1990), a new black middle class has emerged that is residentially and economically isolated from the blacks who are trapped in poor inner-city neighborhoods (see Glazer and Moynihan 1970; Shefter 1988; Mollenkopf 1993; Joyce 1997; Sanjek 1998; Katz forthcoming; see also Torres and Bonilla 1993; and Cordero-Guzmán 1994, 1999).

The immigrant-native tensions and hostilities in New York that attracted the most media and scholarly attention during the 1980s and 1990s involved, in order of intensity of the conflict, native blacks and Korean merchants, followed by native blacks and Hispanic immigrants. Relations between native- and foreign-born (primarily Caribbean) blacks were more ambivalent and contradictory, shifting between resentment and collaboration, depending on the issue at hand.

African Americans Versus Koreans

In 1990 more than 50 percent of adult Korean immigrants in New York City were self-employed, and another 30 percent worked for Korean-owned businesses specializing primarily in produce, apparel, wholesale and retail Asian imports, nail salons, and dry cleaning. Razin and Light (1998) cite a much lower figure, 23 percent, for Korean self-employment in New York in 1990, but their figure was derived from the U.S. census, whereas the percentage quoted here was developed by Min (1996a, 1998) from his survey

TABLE 3.2 **Selected Indicators of Social, Economic, and Ethnic Composition in the New York Metropolitan Statistical Area, 1970 and 1990**

Metropolitan Area and Indicators	1970	1990
Population (number)	7,895,000	7,323,000
Foreign-born (percentage)	18	28
Racial or ethnic composition (percentage)		
Non-Hispanic whites	63	43
Native blacks	19	23
Hispanics	16	22
Asians	2	10
Non-Hispanic Caribbeans	1	2
Sectoral employment (percentage)		
Manufacturing	21	11
Services	24	39
Public sector	18	17
Household poverty rate (percentage)		
Non-Hispanic whites	12	14
Native blacks	21	25
Puerto Ricans	27[a]	39
Dominicans		31
Non-Hispanic Caribbeans	—	17
Unemployment rate (percentage)		
Non-Hispanic whites	4	6
Native blacks	11	14
Young black males	23	44
Puerto Ricans	14	16
Dominicans	—	17
Non-Hispanic Caribbeans	—	9
Residential segregation (D)		
Black-white	0.810	0.822
Black Hispanic	0.547	—
Black-Asian	0.704	—
Hispanic-Asian	0.512	—
Intergroup residential contact (P*)		
Black-white	0.051	0.062
Black Hispanic	0.193	0.210
Black-Asian	0.013	0.026
Hispanic-Asian	0.022	0.065

TABLE 3.2 *Continued*

Metropolitan Area and Indicators	1970	1990
Public sector employment participation		
(percentage)		
Native blacks	24[b]	35
Hispanics	5[b]	11
Asians	—	3

Source: Data compiled from Massey and Denton 1993; Massey 2000; Logan and Alba 1999; Grassmuck and Pessar 1996; Torres and Bonilla 1993; Waldinger 1996b; Mollenkopf 1993; and Cordero-Guzmán 1994.
— Not available.
[a]Includes Dominicans.
[b]Figures are for 1995.

of New York's Korean community. Most Korean businesses are small, labor-intensive enterprises operating on limited capital and frequently dependent on—and exploited by—white landlords and wholesalers.

Poor English-language skills, high education (more than one-third of recent Korean immigrants in New York are college educated), and lack of access to professional licenses, along with widespread disadvantage and discrimination in the general labor market, are the reasons that Korean merchants commonly give for entering small business. Although in 1990 fewer than 10 percent of Koreans resided in neighborhoods heavily populated by African Americans, 30 percent of all Korean stores were located in these areas, principally lower-class black neighborhoods in Harlem, Flatbush, and Bedford-Stuyvesant or middle-class black neighborhoods such as Jamaica in Queens. Most prevalent in black neighborhoods are Korean grocery and liquor stores and fashion and apparel stores, which their owners typically purchased during the 1970s to early 1980s from Jewish and Italian owners who were seeking to retire or move to the suburbs (see Min 1996a, 1996b, 1998; Waldinger 1995; Kim 1996; Park 1997; Yoon 1997; Alba et al. 1995).

The presence of Korean businesses in black neighborhoods, which residents perceive to be an invasion of territory and an exploitation of African American interests, constitutes the core of the conflict between these two groups. Local residents resent Korean store owners' rudeness and "lack of respect" for and "unwarranted surveillance" of their customers. More than that, blacks complain that Koreans do "not return into the black community what they take from it" (by employing local residents and contributing to local community causes) and, in particular, that they "become rich by exploiting black people (like Jews before them)" and reduce "the opportunity of blacks to open their own businesses." Only 4 percent of African Americans in New York were self-employed throughout the 1980s and 1990s.

Studies indicate, however, that Koreans tend to move into stores vacated by white-ethnic or other black merchants and do not obstruct African American entrepreneurship (Boyd 1990; Waldinger 1996a; Light and Rosenstein 1995; Sanjek 1998; Razin and Light 1998). The considerable literature on why African Americans have such low rates of self-employment in postwar American cities offers several explanations, none of which has much to do with Koreans (for a review, see Waldinger 1996b, ch. 8). For example, the massive movement of blacks into public sector employment "diverted" their interest from small entrepreneurship, the existence of ethnic entrepreneurial niches forecloses the entry of outsiders, and the individualistic, rather than collectivistic, orientation of blacks makes the survival of small business very difficult.

For their part, Korean merchants in poor black neighborhoods resent what they perceive as black customers' arrogance and "misbehavior," such as an inclination for shoplifting. They consider black employees to be "lazy" and "unreliable." Similar negative images are presented in local and national black and Korean media (see Min 1996a, 1996b; Yoon 1997; Park 1997; Thornton and Taylor 1988).

African Americans' discontent erupted in five major boycotts of Korean stores in New York during the 1980s and early 1990s, in poor as well as middle-class black neighborhoods. In each case, the picketing of stores, actively supported by local black nationalist leaders, was accompanied by racial threats and verbal attacks against Koreans. The first such incident occurred in Jamaica, Queens, in 1981 and started over a dispute between a Korean grocery employee and an African American customer accused of shoplifting. It was followed by the 1984 to 1985 Harlem boycott, with black leaders calling Korean shop owners "vampires" who "sucked our money in[to] their blood." The 1988 boycott in the Bedford-Stuyvesant section of Brooklyn followed the first two scenarios. The longest and most aggravating episode (to the Korean merchants at least) was the 1990 to 1991 boycott in Flatbush, which was initiated by a dispute between a Korean store owner and a black (Haitian) customer over the amount paid for merchandise.

Korean stores were repeatedly burned during the 1990s. In the spring of 1992, in particular, as New York's African Americans demonstrated in support of the Los Angeles riots, windows of several Korean shops were broken in Manhattan, and almost all Korean stores closed for a few days after witnessing the rampage through Korean stores in Los Angeles (Min 1996a, 1996b, 1998; Waldinger 1995; Park 1997; Sanjek 1998: 147; Jones-Correa 1998; Van Deburg 1997).

Although each confrontation eventually was appeased through settlements negotiated by local bilateral committees (in which Koreans generally agreed to support more actively the black neighborhoods in which they did business), these agreements did not remove the root cause of African American discontent toward Korean merchants: their very presence in these neighborhoods. As a result, the settlements did not prevent subsequent eruptions of hostilities. The absence of a permanent black-Korean institutional alliance invested with watchdog and public educational functions and the lack of active conciliatory involvement of city leaders exacerbated tensions between the two groups (Sanjek 1998; Min 1996a; Yoon 1997). Although the Dinkins administration established Korean, Caribbean and African American, and Hispanic ethnic affairs offices to coordinate the workings of what the mayor called a "gorgeous mosaic," Korean-black conflicts were not given sustained attention except during confrontations, and Mayor Dinkins himself remained aloof from the prolonged 1990 to 1991 black-Korean conflict in Brooklyn.

To summarize, a constellation of core and reinforcing factors was responsible for the persistence of African American hostility toward Korean merchants in New York during the 1980s and 1990s (see table 3.3 for a list of contributing factors). First, African Americans resent the presence and commercial activities of "others" in their neighborhood—in this case, Koreans. Second, black-nationalist ideologies of self-determination enhance and

TABLE 3.3 Core and Supporting Factors Contributing to Intergroup Animosity in Three Metropolitan Areas

Conflict and Metropolitan Area	Core Factors	Supporting Factors
New York		
Native blacks → Koreans	17b in context of 8, 9, 15	19, 20, 21, 22, 4, 5
Koreans → native blacks	18 in context of 17a, 9	19, 20, 21, 22, 4, 5
Native blacks → Hispanics	10, 14 in context of 8, 9, 15	21, 22
Hispanics → native blacks	10, 14 in context of 9, 13	18, 21, 22
Native blacks → foreign blacks	17b (offense to race status)	10, 11a, 18, 19
Foreign blacks → native blacks	17a, 17b, 17c	14, 18, 19
Los Angeles		
Native blacks → Koreans	16b, 17b in context of 8, 9, 15	19, 21, 22, 4, 5
Koreans → native blacks	18 in context of 17a, 9	16 (status loss), 19, 21, 22
Native blacks → Latinos	10, 11a, 14, 16b in context of 9, 11, 15	19, 22
Latino → native blacks	10, 11a, 14, 17b in context of 13	18, 19, 22
Miami		
Native blacks → Cubans	16b, 17b in context of 7, 8, 15	3, 8, 9, 12/6, 13, 18, 19, 20, 22
Cubans → native blacks	17a, 17b, 17c	18
Native blacks → foreign blacks	18, 10 in context of 17b (undeserved rewards)	8, 9, 11, 12, 18, 22
Foreign blacks → native blacks	17a, 17b	11, 18, 22

Source: Author's compilation.
Note: See table 3.1 for explanations of factors.

mobilize this resentment, asserting that "blacks must own the businesses in their communities so that they can recapture the multiplier effect of black consumer spending for the further economic development of the African American communities" (Light, Har-Chui, and Kan 1994, 7). Both of these elements are sustained by, third, a generalized sense of racial alienation from the larger (national) society.

Among the circumstances responsible for the Korean immigrants' resentment of blacks, of greatest consequence have been: racial prejudices, supported by their belief in their own group's cultural and moral superiority and their belief in the openness of the American system, both of which are sustained by the ethnic and national media (home-country and American); and the economic and psychological insecurity of small middleman entrepreneurs who are recent arrivals in a new country.

These hostility-generating factors are reinforced on both sides by negative group stereotypes sustained by local and national media, a history of conflict, the absence of permanent institutional channels for negotiating intergroup conflicts, the lack of sustained conciliatory involvement of city leaders, and, finally, the indirect effect of black-Korean confrontations in other cities.

The best-fitting theoretical explanation of the black-Korean conflict in New York is a variant of the group position model, whereby the most important element explaining the persistence of antiblack resentment among Koreans is a sense of their encroachment (on family business prospects rather than community rights) by a group that they perceive to be inferior.

An ideologically legitimized belief in a "group proprietary claim to certain areas of privilege and advantage" (in this case, control of economic activities in black neighborhoods), combined with the perception that an out-group "harbors designs on the prerogatives" of the in-group, plays the most important role in generating and sustaining African Americans' animosity toward Korean merchants (Blumer 1958, 4). This interpretation encompasses the black nationalism explanation proposed by Min (1996b) and Light, Har-Chui, and Kan (1994). It finds strong support in the absence of similarly intense animosity toward Koreans by other socioeconomically disadvantaged groups (such as Hispanics) who live in neighborhoods where Koreans also have established themselves as merchants. Recent, largely undocumented Hispanic immigrants do not share the African American sense of structural barriers to achievement, racial alienation, or an ideology of exclusive entitlement (see Min 1996a; Yoon 1997). The only notable incidence of violence—a 1992 Hispanic riot in Washington Heights in which Korean stores were damaged—was instigated by the shooting of a Dominican man by a black police officer (see Sanjek 1998).

Hispanics Versus African Americans

Tensions between Hispanics and African Americans involve more issues and are fueled by different mechanisms than black-Korean animosity. Except for the poorest inner-city sections shared by African Americans and Puerto Ricans, most New York Hispanics, including shopkeepers, do not live and work in the same neighborhoods as blacks (Community Service Society 1984; Massey and Denton 1987; Alba et al. 1995; Rosenbaum 1996; Massey 2000). The main issues of intergroup contention do not concern the control of territory (neighborhoods) or the economic activities carried out within them. Rather, they concern competition for private and public sector jobs and for political influence. Expressions of intergroup tensions likewise differ. Hispanic-black conflicts generally involve public complaints, protests, and civic actions rather than physical confrontation (except for occasional altercations between youth gangs).

Hispanic-black relations are more complex than black-Korean relations in one additional respect. African by heritage and Hispanic by ethnicity, Puerto Ricans and a large proportion of Dominicans (the second largest Hispanic group in the city) occupy a unique position in these encounters. In the competition for low-skill jobs in the private sector, they share a racial disadvantage with African Americans (although they enjoy an escape not available to native blacks), yet in conflicts over public and political rewards they frequently side, however ineffectively, with other Hispanics.

The occupational position of the most rapidly growing Latino group, Dominicans, is similar to that of Central and South Americans in contrast to that of non-Hispanic blacks and Puerto Ricans. As of 1990, nearly 60 percent of New York's Dominicans were employed in ethnic occupational niches, mainly in apparel manufacturing, the hotel and restaurant industry, domestic and custodial services, and construction. Throughout the first two postwar decades, native blacks and Puerto Ricans held low-skill jobs in New York's garment shops and back-of-the-house positions in hotels and restaurants. A massive shift of African Americans into public sector employment between 1970 and 1990 opened up these occupational slots, which were subsequently filled by new immigrants. (On ethnic occupational niches in New York, see Waldinger 1996b, 1996c; Logan and Alba 1999; Rosenfeld and Tienda 1999; and Pessar 1995; on Hispanic immigrant–black competition for low-skilled jobs, see Hamermesh and Bean 1998; Bailey 1987; and Borjas and Freeman 1992.)

Other than Puerto Ricans, Dominican immigrants were among the first Latinos to arrive in New York. In the 1960s Puerto Ricans helped to train them and served as translators and mediators between Dominicans and native employers. Once established, Dominican immigrants pulled in others, creating tightly networked ethnic occupational niches in the formal sector, such as unionized garment manufacturing, hotels, and restaurants, as well as in the informal sector in unlicensed garment subcontracting, neighborhood ethnic eateries, commercial and residential construction and renovation, and child and geriatric care in private homes.

Many inner-city poor African Americans and Puerto Ricans, particularly men, have difficulty competing for low- and, especially, higher-level blue-collar jobs in the formal and informal sectors of the economy. Since the 1980s these jobs have been appropriated by new immigrants. As ethnic occupational niches constrained the employment opportunities for outsiders, employers deliberately discriminated against blacks, further diminishing the ability of African Americans and Puerto Ricans to compete for low-skill jobs in New York (see Waldinger 1996a, 1996b; Stafford 1991; Torres 1995; also Kasinitz and Rosenberg 1998; Kirschenman and Neckerman 1991).

African Americans are in a weaker position than white Hispanics to compete for low-skill jobs in the private sector; the opposite is true in the public sector. Although not entirely secure, and certainly in a weaker position than native whites, African Americans have a competitive edge in the public and political arena. Puerto Ricans do not share this advantage, largely because of their ethnicity rather than their racial heritage.

Providing employment for 35 percent of the city's African Americans in 1990, New York's public sector has served as the ethnic niche for this group. In contrast, Central Americans held only 11 percent of government jobs, and Puerto Ricans held just 4 percent (compared with their 24 percent combined share of the city's population). As expected, Latinos repeatedly lodge official and unofficial protests, charging successive administrations with "neglecting Latinos' and Hispanic concerns," not giving "the [Puerto Rican] community its fair share," and "caving in to the blacks" (see Model 1993; Waldinger 1995, 1996b; Joyce 1997; Reimers and Chernick 1991; Stafford 1991; Torres and Bonilla 1993; also Mollenkopf 1993; Mladenka 1989). Three principal factors have kept these protests ineffective and limited the political influence of Hispanics in New York City. These are the low rate of naturalization among Hispanic immigrants (only 28 percent of Dominican immigrants are U.S. citizens, compared with between 11 and 15 percent of other Hispanic immigrant groups in 1990); the strong orientation toward their region of origin (including Puerto Rico); and the internal fragmentation of Hispanics along ethnic, cultural, racial, and ideological lines (see Reimers and Chernick 1991; Sanjek 1998; Guarnizo 1997; Pessar 1997; Mollenkopf 1993; Joyce 1997; Rumbaut 1997; and Grassmuck and Pessar 1991).

Progressive cuts in the number of municipal jobs since the 1980s have exacerbated the competition between groups. This increased competition, combined with fragmentation of the Hispanic population and the ethnic-divisive politics of the Koch and Giuliani administrations, has made it difficult for African Americans and Hispanics to resolve their conflicts. Even committed pluralists such as Mayor Dinkins have been unable to blur the sharp boundaries in New York's multiethnic mosaic.

Factors quite different from those at the source of black-Korean hostilities are at the root of tensions between African Americans and Hispanics in New York. The first factor is economic and involves job competition in the context of an emerging inner-city underclass created by national and local economic restructuring and reduced public assistance, along with the persistence of racial discrimination in employment and housing. The second factor is political and involves intergroup competition for political influence and public sector employment, which has intensified in the context of dwindling federal and municipal resources. Reinforcing these circumstances—or hindering the reconciliation of intergroup conflicts—have been the divisive ethnic politics of the city and the absence of institutions for channeling intergroup contacts and negotiations (see Jones-Correa 1998 for a different assessment of New York's institutional capacity to mitigate intergroup tensions).

The best-fitting theoretical explanation of tensions between blacks and Hispanics is the group position model, with its emphasis on the self-interest of low-skill African Americans and Puerto Ricans in the competition for private sector jobs threatened by changes in the ethnic composition of the workplace, racial discrimination, and economic restructuring, and the competition between white and black Hispanics for public sector jobs that are distributed unequally by race and ethnicity.

African Americans Versus Non-Hispanic Caribbeans

The West Indian–African American relationship in New York is ambivalent. For West Indians, this ambivalence is informed, on the one hand, by ethnicity or the desire to retain their cultural differences and distinctive ethnic identities and, on the other hand, by race or the painful realization that skin color, more than anything else, defines their identity and opportunities in the United States. For African Americans, ambivalence toward West Indians is basically reactive, ensuing from the equivocal attitudes of West Indians toward their own (and African American) blackness.

The two groups have remained faithful to the long-standing, tension-ridden relationship dating back to the beginning of the twentieth century (see Kasinitz 1992 for an overview of the history of African American and West Indian relations in New York). Constrained by the positive, solidarist "pull" of the relationship, its inimical side remains by and large at the level of verbal expressions of discontent. Acrimonious and hurtful, these expressions perpetuate mutual resentments, but they rarely turn into organized public protests or physical confrontations (except for youthful "gang wars").

West Indian immigrants downplay their racial identity for several reasons. The ideology and cultural practices of their home countries allow them "to sidestep race as an issue in their every-

day lives" (Vickerman 1999, 37) and to reinforce instead the belief
that individual merit ultimately accounts for lifetime achievement.
This orientation is sustained by the intentions of the majority of
immigrants to return home and by their intense, ongoing contact
with their homelands during their (even years-long) sojourns in
the United States. Very important, too, is the West Indians' (not
unfounded) belief that assuming a black identity, which they accurately perceive as inferior in the United States, entails a loss of
social status and downward mobility (see Kasinitz 1992; Charles
1992; Foner 1987; Waters 1994, 1999; Stafford 1987; Zephir 1996;
Bryce-Laporte 1987).

In New York the preference for an immigrant/ethnic identity,
supported by concerns about loss of status, is more common
among (although not unique to) middle-class West Indians than
among lower-class ones. This middle class, which includes professionals, managers, the self-employed, and white-collar service
workers, is larger among English-speaking (49 percent) than
among French-speaking (36 percent) West Indians. Conversely, in
1990 the poverty rate was 11 percent among English-speaking
West Indians and 19 percent among Haitians.

The West Indian middle class lives predominantly in the
Queens neighborhoods of Cambria Heights, Springfield Gardens,
and parts of Elmhurst and Flushing. Although some African Americans also live in these areas, social contacts between the two
groups are rare (Crowder 1999; Foner 1987; Kasinitz 1992; Waters
1994; Kalmijn 1996; Model 1995). Supported by mutual stereotypes implying in-group superiority (African Americans are seen
as undisciplined spendthrifts and unambitious "system blamers"
reluctant to take responsibility for their own lives; West Indians
are seen as uppity, arrogant, and "crafty" over-achievers), thus far
cultural distancing is the main expression of negative feelings (see
Foner 1987; Stafford 1987; Vickerman 1999; Zephir 1996; Kasinitz
1992).

However, frictions are emerging over the competition for
white-collar public sector jobs between native and foreign-born
blacks (primarily English-speaking West Indians). At issue also is
the distribution of local political offices, which unfairly privilege
African Americans, in the opinion of West Indian groups, especially the English speakers (most Haitians tend to concentrate on

their home-country politics). This view dates back to the 1960s, when a new generation of civil rights leaders began to replace the older cohort, in which English-speaking West Indians occupied a prominent place (see Kasinitz 1992). The tension is aggravated by the recent appearance and the divisive effects of West Indian politicians campaigning under the banner of ethnic politics (see Kasinitz 1992; Vickerman 1999).

The option of racial solidarity is employed mostly in poorer and, especially, the poorest inner-city neighborhoods, especially those shared by West Indians and African Americans, such as Bedford-Stuyvesant and Crown Heights in Brooklyn (Crowder 1999; Foner 1987; Rosenbaum 1996; Kasinitz 1992; Zephir 1996). In these isolated ghetto neighborhoods, a common, race-derived fate is difficult to escape, especially for English-speaking West Indians. (Their "immediate otherness" makes foreign-language speakers targets for considerable abuse by young African Americans in schools and neighborhoods, reinforcing the distance between Haitians and native blacks; see Stafford 1987.)

Despite the apparent commonality of experience and, therefore, of interests, racial solidarity of low(er)-class West Indians and African Americans tends to be situational rather than consistent. In addition to ethnic "othering," the following circumstances create tensions and operate against it. Like Hispanic immigrants, West Indians have created ethnic occupational niches in both formal and informal sectors of the New York economy (in garment manufacturing, services to dwellings, truck and taxi driving, construction, and low-skill hospital and household care). As with Hispanics, African American men do not compete well in higher-skill manual occupations. They do not have appropriate networks and are faced with discrimination from employers who prefer "hardworking island boys" to native black workers. In contrast, African Americans by and large do not seek the lowly manual jobs taken by West Indian women (see Kasinitz 1992; Vickerman 1999; Model 1993; Waldinger 1995, 1996b; Foner 1987; Newman 1998; Waters 1999; Grassmuck and Grosfoguel 1997; and Kasinitz and Vickerman 1995.). African Americans likewise have more difficulty finding lodging than foreign-born blacks (Foner 1987; Rosenbaum 1996; Crowder 1999). These experiences prompt many African Americans to perceive West Indians as "taking [things] away from them" and to resent them as rivals. West Indians reciprocate by labeling lower-class native blacks as "lazy," "burglars," "drug addicts," and the like.

Although they do not resolve intergroup tensions, collaborative undertakings joining native- and foreign-born blacks temporarily overcome them. Most cooperative actions have been instigated by abuses of blacks or racial conflicts with the dominant society, notably the harassment of blacks by white police officers and the victimization of blacks by white mobs. There also have been instances of proactive rather than reactive cooperation for common political causes, supported by West Indian immigrant leaders who view the strategy of organizing neighborhoods, schools, and churches around racial identity as a more effective way to obtain resources than ethnic politics (see Min 1996a; Vickerman 1999; Kasinitz 1992; Zephir 1996; Foner 1987; Charles 1992).

The main factors that cultivate anti–African American sentiments among West Indian immigrants also constitute major explanatory elements in the group position model. They include the immigrants' beliefs, conditioned by their home-country experience and the length of time spent in the United States; in individualistic (nonascriptive) achievement and an open society; and in their cultural superiority vis-à-vis native American blacks; reinforced by the fear of social degradation through association with African Americans. Sustained by these sentiments and, in turn, upholding them are the negative stereotypes that West Indians hold about native blacks and competition with native blacks for jobs and offices in the public sector.

A different set of position-defining elements has played the most important role in generating and sustaining negative feelings among African Americans toward West Indians. A core factor (not considered in Bobo and Hutchings's model, which was not designed to explain intraminority relations) is African American resentment of the West Indians' attempts to escape their racial membership. An additional, emergent circumstance generating animosity toward West Indians is the competition for housing and jobs. This better treatment of the latter in housing markets is taken as proof that an escape from racial membership is at least partially possible for Caribbean islanders, further intensifying the African American resentment of the newcomers.

LOS ANGELES

Like New York, Los Angeles is a global and multiethnic city with declining white European and growing Hispanic and Asian populations. It differs from New York in important ways. As an open-shop city offering cheap labor, Los Angeles expanded its industrial sector during the 1970s and 1980s, becoming the country's leading industrial metropolitan area. During these two decades, the number of manufacturing jobs in New York fell dramatically (Soja et al. 1989; Bozorgmehr, Sabagh, and Light 1996; Scott 1996; Waldinger and Bozorgmehr 1996).

This dynamic economic growth did not prevent the emergence in Los Angeles of an inner-city underclass typical of American postindustrial cities. This underclass is composed primarily of African Americans, as elsewhere in the country, and, specific to the region, of undocumented Mexicans and recently arrived, economically depressed Filipino, Vietnamese, and Central American immigrants.

Changes in the city's ethnic and occupational composition, residential segregation, and other socioeconomic indicators are summarized in table 3.4 for 1970 and 1990. The immigrant population of Los Angeles has grown rapidly, making it the largest immigrant city in the country. From a mere 10 percent in 1960 (compared with 20 percent in New York), the share of foreign-born persons in Los Angeles more than tripled by 1990 (growing only one-third in New York).

Los Angeles's immigrant population is primarily Latino and Asian, with Mexicans being by far the largest group. Between 1970 and 1990, the Latino population alone quadrupled to nearly 40 percent of the city's population and is expected to reach 60 percent by 2015. At 13 percent of the total in 1995 (a fourfold increase since the 1960s), Asians now outnumber African Americans. This rapid ethnodemographic change—and its implications for city culture, politics, and social institutions—has sparked anti-immigrant sentiments among both whites and blacks. Proposition 187, passed in 1994, is just one indicator of intensified nativism (see Clark 1996; Sabagh and Bozorgmehr 1996; Ortiz 1996; Grant, Oliver, and James 1996; Soja et al. 1989).

TABLE 3.4 Selected Indicators of Social, Economic, and Ethnic Composition in the Los Angeles Metropolitan Statistical Area, 1970 and 1990

Metropolitan Area and Indicators	1970	1990
Population (number)	7,036,430	8,863,164
Foreign-born (percentage)	20	34
Racial or ethnic composition (percentage)		
Non-Hispanic whites	71	41
Native blacks	11	10
Latinos	15	38
Mexicans		80
Asians	4	12
Sectoral employment (percentage)		
Manufacturing	26	21
Services	37	45
Public sector	12	10
Household poverty rate (percentage)		
Non-Hispanic whites	9	7
Native blacks	22	18
Latinos	20	25
Unemployment rate (percentage)		
Non-Hispanic whites	5	6
Native blacks	10	13
Young black males	21	37
Latinos	8	9
Residential segregation (D)		
White-black	0.910	0.731
Black-Latino	0.438	—
Black-Asian	0.789	—
Latino-Asian	0.438	—
Intergroup residential contact (P*)		
White-black	0.023	0.440
Black-Latino	0.110	0.326
Black-Asian	0.037	0.064
Latino-Asian	0.046	0.092
Public sector employment participation (percentage)		
Native blacks	22	22
Latino	9	20
Asians	4	7

Source: Data compiled from Massey and Denton 1993; Massey 2000; Logan and Alba 1999; Rosenfeld and Tienda 1999; Waldinger and Bozorgmehr 1996; Sonenshein 1993; and Morales and Ong 1993.
— Not available.

As in New York, since the 1970s African Americans have been incorporated into the city's civic-political system, and their increased share of white-collar public sector employment has been crucial to the formation of a new black middle class (see Sonenshein 1993 for a detailed history of this process). Whereas the pool of public jobs in Los Angeles is less than one-fourth the size of the pool in New York, during the 1990s Latino and Asian residents significantly increased their demands for public employment. Less open to immigrants than New York's civic-political structures, the system in Los Angeles is being forced into a competitive ethnic politics constrained by limited resources. As a result, the demographically stagnant African American population is having to compete with Latinos and Asians, groups that are large and growing rapidly (Sonenshein 1993; Henry 1994; Brackman and Erie 1995). The frictions and hostilities between blacks and Koreans and between blacks and Latinos were most intense during the 1980s and 1990s.

African Americans Versus Koreans

The basic mechanisms generating black-Korean hostility in Los Angeles and New York are remarkably similar. Koreans in Los Angeles are highly concentrated (45 percent) in self-employment and in an ethnic occupational niche (more than 75 percent). Moreover, Korean businesses are disproportionately located in poor minority neighborhoods (60 percent of the total, about equally distributed between black and Latino sections of South Central Los Angeles), although the owners reside elsewhere and their stores are mostly dependent on white suppliers. Korean businesses also have taken over limited-capital family enterprises such as liquor stores, corner groceries, and fashion and apparel lines vacated by white-ethnic (primarily Jewish) merchants who either retired or moved away (see Min 1996a, 1996b; Light 1998; Umemoto 1994; Sonenshein 1996; Chang and Leong 1994; Light and Rosenstein 1995).

African Americans in Los Angeles voice complaints about Korean merchants in their neighborhoods that are similar to those recorded in New York: discourteous service, underemployment of blacks, and failure of Koreans to make capital or social investments in the black communities from which "they get rich." As in New York, Koreans see blacks as lazy welfare recipients who are drug addicts and general no-goods, stereotypes that are bred in their home country through American movies and television shows (see Light 1998; Chang 1994; Light, Har-Chui, and Kan 1994; also Light, Bernard, and Kim 1999 on the predominantly Latino employees of Korean firms).

Despite these resentments and occasional harassment of Korean stores in black neighborhoods, black-Korean relations were on the whole better in Los Angeles than in New York during the 1980s, owing to effective local institutional politics, such as the peacemaking initiatives of Mayor Tom Bradley and the conciliatory activities of the Black-Korean Alliance, and the relative weakness of the city's black nationalist movement. Tensions mounted in the fall of 1991 when a Korean grocery owner received a lenient, five-year probation for shooting to death an African American girl while struggling over an unpaid bottle of orange juice, and anti-Korean hostility erupted into mass violence in the spring of 1992 after a jury pronounced white police officers innocent in the beating of black motorist Rodney King. In the course of the burning and looting, one Korean was killed, forty-six were injured, and more than two thousand Korean stores worth more than $350 million were destroyed, primarily in black portions of South Central Los Angeles, but also in Koreatown, located four miles away. In the end, Koreans suffered nearly half of the damages caused by the riots (see Umemoto 1994; Min 1996a, 1996b; Brackman and Erie 1995; Ong, Park, and Tong 1994; Sonenshein 1996; Jones-Correa 1998).

The scope and intensity of this violence, unmatched by any of New York's anti-Korean boycotts, suggests that city-specific circumstances combined with resentment-generating mechanisms common to both cities turned the Los Angeles conflict into a more serious confrontation.

The multifaceted alienation of African Americans in Los Angeles—specifically their heightened sense of displacement by a rapidly growing immigrant population, combined with outrage against the stream of abuse by white police—spread and inflamed the violence against the most visible middleman group. Many observers believe that the city's white establishment, not just the police department, was behind the confrontation. In the opinion of Korean leaders and other, more neutral observers, the local media overly emphasized the Korean-black conflict, contributing to its escalation, in order to turn public attention away from white responsibility for the violence (see Bobo and Hutchings 1996; Min 1996a; also Yoon 1997; Fainstein and Fainstein 1994).

In addition to these core factors, other circumstances contributed to the conflict on both sides. At the national level, ethnic media and anti-Korean hostilities in other cities (specifically, the prolonged 1991 Flatbush boycott in New York) exacerbated the animosity. Locally, the weakening of Mayor Bradley's leadership and the dissipation of his politics of coalition and conciliation, together with the dissolution of Los Angeles's Black-Korean Alliance at the outbreak of the riots, also played a role (see table 3.3 for the list of contributing factors).

The group position explanation of African American hostility toward Koreans in Los Angeles is, therefore, a modified version of that proposed for New York. Rather than being mobilized by intragroup ideologies of self-control and group economic autonomy, the anti-Korean violence in Los Angeles was primarily the result of the African Americans' perception of encroachment and exploitation by forces operating in the larger local society, and secondarily the result of scapegoating the most readily visible "other" group.

This group position explanation is supported by the lack of involvement of Los Angeles Latinos in the 1992 anti-Korean violence. They "only looted" (without destroying) Korean stores in their neighborhoods, although Korean merchants were as numerous there as in African American sections of the city. As indicated by proclamations of Latino leaders that Bradley was "the [first and] last black Los Angeles mayor," Latinos do not feel as displaced or as demoralized by the betrayal of white society as do African Americans.

Korean resentment of blacks in Los Angeles, as in New York, involves racial prejudice fed by the economic and psychological insecurity of middleman small shopkeepers, a shared belief in the superiority of their group (enhanced, perhaps, by a stronger sense of status loss and class distancing by immigrants, two-thirds of whom report a college education, compared with just one-third in

New York), and a vision of America as the land of opportunity for hard-working individuals and families. Because of the scale of the violence and physical damage to the Korean community in Los Angeles, the group position model emphasizes Korean awareness and physical experience of encroachment by savage or morally inferior others (African Americans).

African Americans Versus Latinos

The basic mechanism generating black-Latino tensions in Los Angeles and New York is quite similar: increased competition for private sector and public sector jobs as well as political influence. As with black-Korean relations, however, setting black-Latino competition within the context of massive ethnic change, the specific operation of the city's economy and its political system, and the various perceptions of self and of others calls for a somewhat different cluster of explanatory elements in the group position model.

As in New York, the massive entry of cheap Latino, mainly Mexican, labor into the Los Angeles economy between 1970 and 1990 largely displaced black workers from several economic sectors, such as manufacturing, construction, services, low-skill restaurant and hotel jobs (for men), and textile production and domestic household service (for women). In other fields, such as metal industries, furniture and fixtures, transportation, and higher-level manual jobs in hotel and restaurant services, the growing presence of immigrants and, in particular, the expansion of immigrant occupational niches based on in-group network recruitment are making it increasingly difficult for African Americans to compete successfully for jobs.

In 1990 the proportion of Mexican immigrants in niche occupations (defined as those in which they are significantly over-represented relative to their percentage of the total population) was 72 percent in Los Angeles, representing an increase of 14 percent since 1970; the proportion of niche-employed Central Americans stood at 54 percent. In contrast, African Americans' only occupational niche was, as in New York, public sector employment (see Ong and Valenzuela 1996; Scott 1996; Waldinger 1996d; Grant, Oliver, and James 1996; López, Popkin, and Telles

1996; Ortiz 1996; Logan, Alba, and McNulty 1994a; Valenzuela 1997; Fernández-Kelly and García 1989; and Logan and Alba 1999).

In addition to the sheer mass of "cheap and willing" immigrants and a high-level ethnic "nichefication" that effectively excludes outsiders, a "savage-capitalist" open-shop labor market has combined with the preferences of native white and Asian employers for Latino ("docile") over black ("finicky" and "too ambitious") workers for jobs outside of ethnic occupational niches. Job competition is much tougher in Los Angeles than in strongly unionized New York, making the situation of low-skill African Americans more vulnerable and them more resentful (see Waldinger 1996d, 1997; Johnson, Farrell, and Guinn 1997; Bozorgmehr, Sabagh, and Light 1996; Soja et al. 1989; Min 1996a; Bonacich 1993; Light, Bernard, and Kim 1999).

African Americans feel overwhelmed by outside intruders, and this feeling has deepened since the 1980s as a result of the progressive incursion of poor Latino (and other) immigrants into neighborhoods that were once almost exclusively black. This development has no counterpart in New York. Whereas in 1970, Latinos made up just 10 percent of the population in South Central Los Angeles, by 1990 they constituted about half. Although a majority of South Central Latino residents are concentrated in the rapidly expanding, ethnically homogeneous "mega-barrio," in several neighborhoods they intermingle with African Americans, competing for the same housing.

As in private sector employment, even in predominantly black neighborhoods, African Americans encounter systematic discrimination from real estate and mortgage companies that give preferential treatment to Latinos, who are perceived as more reliable customers. African Americans resent this bias, as well as the problems resulting from the rapidly increasing number of Spanish-speaking children in neighborhood schools and the overcrowding of neighborhood hospitals and other social services (see Massey and Denton 1987; Massey 2000; Johnson, Farrell, and Guinn 1997; Logan, Alba, and McNulty 1994; Grant, Oliver, and James 1996; Clark 1996; López, Popkin, and Telles 1996; Zubrinsky and Bobo 1996; Navarro 1994; Ong and Lawrence 1992).

Holding a sizable one-fifth of city jobs and employing nearly

60 percent of all black residents, the African American niche in the public sector of Los Angeles is, nevertheless, smaller and less secure than that in New York because the black population itself is smaller and declining as a share of the city's population. Demands by Latinos for what they view as their fair share have increased as a result of the growing presence of native-born, better-educated adult children of immigrants and an ethnically homogeneous, largely Mexican, Latino population (compared with the fragmented Hispanic population of New York), along with the dissolution of the biracial (black-white) coalition in 1992. Unlike in New York, these factors have made demands for Latino public employment more effective at all levels of the political system (Waldinger 1996d; Grant, Oliver, and James 1996; Logan, Alba, and McNulty 1994; Navarro 1994; Underwood 1997; Rieff 1992; Sonenshein 1993).

As in the private sector and in the neighborhoods themselves, the competition between African Americans and Latinos for public jobs and political influence generates mutual resentment and negative stereotyping. Latinos see blacks as "having been in power too long" and not wanting to recognize "the fact that they are no longer the majority." African Americans point out that blacks "struggled for years to win power" in the civic service, while immigrants (Latinos) "just arrived" and cannot expect to have everything right away (Johnson, Farrell, and Guinn 1997).

Unlike in New York, however, Latinos in Los Angeles have the upper hand in this conflict over public resources. "Tom Bradley was not only L.A.'s first black mayor," as one observer of the Los Angeles political scene said half in jest, "he was also probably its last [black mayor]. Power has shifted for good here, even though most people don't realize it yet" (Rieff 1992, 149). Not at all secure either politically or economically, blacks see themselves as increasingly outnumbered, and they tend, more than Latinos, to perceive their position in Los Angeles in zero-sum terms: a gain for "them" means a loss for "us" (see Johnson, Oliver, and Bobo 1994).

The core factors contributing to African American resentment of Latinos in Los Angeles thus include the competition of African Americans with Latinos on several fronts (economic, residential, and political) in the context of a progressive dislocation of blacks in all these areas and racial discrimination against them in workplaces and housing, resulting in African American perceptions of encounters with Latinos as a zero-sum game. Latino resentment of blacks, in turn, is generated primarily by competition with them, accompanied by a strong sense of entitlement, for social services in shared neighborhoods and for jobs and influence in the civic-political system. Additional factors sustaining these resentments are the publication by the local media of each group's (often exaggerated) complaints and accusations and the absence of institutionalized cooperation between the leadership and organizations of blacks and Latinos at both city and neighborhood levels.

In addition to self-interest in the competition for economic and political resources within the context of racial discrimination—the most important element in the group position model—the Los Angeles case requires extra local components, namely, self-interest in the competition for residential (housing and social services) resources (with multiplier effects on intergroup conflict) and the collective perception that the out-group (Latinos) intrudes on and harbors further designs on the hard-won prerogatives of the in-group (African Americans). In explaining Latino antipathy toward blacks in Los Angeles, the element of competition, enhanced by a strong sense of overdue entitlement, plays a more pronounced role than in New York.

MIAMI

The principal feature that differentiates Miami (here defined as Metropolitan Dade County) from other postindustrial cities with large populations of recent immigrants is the unusually powerful economic and political position of one group in particular, the Cubans. Fleeing Fidel Castro's communist regime in the early 1960s, large numbers of Cuban exiles settled in the Miami region, and more followed in subsequent decades. By 1990 Cubans made up approximately 750,000, or nearly one-third, of the area's residents and about two-thirds of the entire Latino population, which by the early 1990s had become the area's largest ethnic group (53 percent). At the same time, the proportion of non-Hispanic whites decreased from 80 percent in 1960 to less than 30 percent in 1990, while the proportion of blacks increased from 15 to 20 percent, with foreign-born blacks (mainly Haitians) accounting for most of this growth (see Grenier, Stepick, and LaBorwit 1994; Grenier and Castro 1998; Bowie and Stepick 1998; Pérez-Stable and Uriarte 1997; Stepick 1994; Harris 1994). Miami's changes in ethnic or racial, sectoral, and other sociodemographic distributions from 1970 to 1990 are summarized in table 3.5.

Sheer numbers alone did not make Cuban immigrants a powerful group in Miami (Mexicans constitute an even larger share of the population in Los Angeles, without being empowered). Rather this was due to the emergence of an independent Cuban economic enclave, composed of a middle class of exiles with substantial capital resources and business connections to South America and a large pool of working-class immigrants with diverse manual skills (Portes 1987). The Cuban enclave economy has appropriated significant parts of the tripartite sectoral division that emerged in the process: in banking, international trade, insurance, and real estate services in the primary sector and in apparel manufacturing, construction, and hotel and restaurant services in the secondary and informal sectors (see Stepick 1994; Stepick and Grenier 1994a, 1994b; Grenier, Stepick, and LaBorwit 1994; Portes and Stepick 1993; Bowie and Stepick 1998; Henry 1994; Sassen 1994; Fernández-Kelly and García 1989; Logan, Alba, and McNulty 1994b).

The appropriation by one immigrant group and the resulting exclusion of nonmembers from large segments of all three sectors of the Miami economy, combined with the domination of other sectors by non-Hispanic whites (primarily Anglos and Jews), have made the Miami labor market in general and individual workplaces in particular highly segregated both horizontally (based on ethnic membership) and vertically (based on racial ascription). The segregation of the Miami labor market along ethnic and racial lines has been sustained by the weakness or, in many industries, the complete absence of labor unions, to which both the creation of ethnic occupational niches and the creation of an informal economy have contributed significantly (see Stepick 1989, 1994; Pérez-Stable and Uriarte 1997; Portes and Stepick 1993; Grenier and Castro 1998; Grenier and Pérez 1996).

TABLE 3.5 **Selected Indicators of Social, Economic, and Ethnic Composition in the Miami Metropolitan Statistical Area, 1970 and 1990**

Metropolitan Area and Indicators	1970	1990
Population (number)	1,268,000	1,937,000
Foreign-born (percentage)	—	45
Racial or ethnic composition (percentage)		
Non-Hispanic whites	62	28
Native blacks	13	14
Latinos	23	53
Cubans	91	59
Foreign-born blacks	2	6
Haitian	80	65
Sectoral employment (percentage)		
Manufacturing	15	10
Services	35	48
Public sector	14	13
Household poverty rate (percentage)		
Non-Hispanic whites	—	8
Native blacks	—	27
Cubans	—	17
Haitians	—	34
Unemployment rate (percentage)		
Non-Hispanic whites	—	—
Native blacks	—	—
Young black males	—	—
Cubans	—	—
Non-Hispanic Caribbeans	—	—
Residential segregation (D)		
White-black	0.851	0.718
Black-Hispanic	0.873	—
Intergroup residential contact (P*)		
White-black	0.042	0.105
Black-Hispanic	0.073	0.213
Public sector concentration (percentage)		
Hispanic	—	34
Black	—	25

Source: Data compiled from Massey and Denton 1993; Massey 2000; Logan, Alba, and McNulty 1994b; Portes and Stepick 1993; Perez-Stable and Uriarte 1997; Bowie and Stepick 1998; and Stepick 1994.
— Not available.

The high level of residential segregation in Miami and the dispersion of population throughout the area have reinforced social fragmentation. While Miami's poorest blacks have concentrated in the inner-city sections of Liberty City and Overtown (with native- and foreign-born blacks in adjacent, but separate, neighborhoods), the remaining two-thirds of the black population are dispersed throughout Dade County, mostly in unincorporated areas (Becker and Dluhy 1998; Portes and Stepick 1993; Stepick 1994; Wilson 1997; Massey and Denton 1987, 1993; Massey 2000; Henry 1994).

Cuban dominance in the higher echelons of the civic-political system and its decidedly conservative bent, combined with the residential dispersion of blacks, especially those in the middle class, have kept African Americans from building a fair political representation for themselves. As a result, although their participation in public sector employment exceeds their share in the total population, African Americans are disproportionately concentrated in lower-level positions (Bowie and Stepick 1998; Grenier and Castro 1998; García-Zamor 1998; Henry 1994; Portes and Stepick 1993). The major intergroup conflict in the Miami area has been between blacks and Cubans. Much less intense have been the tensions between native- and foreign-born, mainly Haitian, blacks.

African Americans Versus Cubans

The widespread perception among Miami's African Americans of being overwhelmed by Latinos—specifically Cubans—is not, as in Los Angeles, due to the competition for resources with rapidly growing numbers of immigrants. Cuban refugees arrived in the 1960s, just when the civil rights movement was removing Miami's formal institutions of racial segregation and creating opportunities for blacks. City development embarked on a different track. As African American progress stalled, and Cubans advanced rapidly to economic and political power in the city, the Cuban Refugee Program and other federal initiatives were created to support the émigrés, largely as a result of the priorities and preferences of U.S. foreign policy in the cold war.

By the 1980s the powerful Cuban economic and political enclave was firmly established. Since that time, Cubans (and, in the background, whites) have erected pervasive barriers to competition and advancement by ethnic outsiders, fanning African American resentment and the belief that a historical injustice has been done to African Americans and that, specifically, Cuban immigrants have risen at the expense of blacks (see Mohl 1990; Portes and Stepick 1993; García-Zamor 1998, Grenier and Castro 1998; Bowie and Stepick 1998; Harris 1994).

In the private sector labor market, ethnic recruitment networks and racial discrimination have kept low-skill African American men confined largely to menial jobs such as stevedores, concrete finisher helpers, back-of-the-house hotel and restaurant workers, and the like. African American women likewise have encountered exclusion and racial discrimination, especially in Miami's large apparel-manufacturing industry, although they have been more successful than men in entering lower-level, white-collar occupations. In neither of these sectors have blacks been able to establish group occupational niches.

The strong presence of whites (both non-Hispanic and Cuban) throughout the Miami political system, the unusually high fragmentation of the African American community, and the residential dispersion of African Americans have also prevented the formation of a black occupational niche in the local public sector like that in New York or, to a lesser extent, in Los Angeles. Lacking both the command of Spanish that has facilitated the acquisition of private and public jobs for non-Cuban Latinos and the effective political representation of their minority interests in the resolutely conservative Miami area, African Americans employed in the public sector have encountered more barriers to upward mobility than African Americans in New York or Los Angeles (Stepick and Grenier 1994a, 1994b; Grenier, Stepick, and LaBorwit 1994; García-Zamor 1998; Grenier and Castro 1998).

The accumulated anger of blacks at the enduring white and, in particular, Cuban exile community's economic and political hegemony, repeated police abuses, and other disparaging incidents led to violence in the spring of 1980. Provoked by an accident in which a Cuban man's car struck a black girl, the discontent was aggravated by the differential treatment accorded by Immigration and Naturalization Service (INS) officials to Cuban (being welcoming and helpful) and Haitian (isolating them in camps and threatening deportation) refugees arriving in Miami. Sporadic riots followed throughout the 1980s.

In response to these protests, local political establishments appointed some African Americans to municipal and county offices, and special development programs were created to rejuvenate the black community. Their success was limited, however, partly because black participation was limited and mainly because the rapid economic advance of Cubans overshadowed whatever progress these measures had brought about. When the city refused to honor Nelson Mandela during his visit to Miami in the summer of 1990 (because Cuban politicians were afraid that welcoming a supporter of Fidel Castro would alienate their ethnic electorate), black residents mounted a mass protest and a prolonged boycott of Miami tourism that cost the city millions of dollars (Mohl 1990; Portes and Stepick 1993; Henry 1994; Harris 1994; Herman 1995; Grenier and Castro 1998; Jones-Correa 1998).

Despite this enduring animosity, some attempts at black-Cuban cooperation were made in the 1990s, including, for example, the creation of a black-Cuban coalition against the at-large voting system, which limited both black and Latino participation in county commissions, support by the local National Association for the Advancement of Colored People (NAACP) for the Latino-led opposition to the county's English-only ordinance, and occasional fund-raising balls for black or Cuban causes. These were fragile coalitions rather than a continuous dialogue, leaving intact the roots of African American discontent. The plight of Miami blacks occupies a marginal place on the public agenda of Cubans, which focused on improving their own economic situation and on the political struggle with the Castro regime. In addition, Cuban leaders have persistently denied any intentional racism and refused to commit themselves to fighting its consequences (see Grenier and Castro 1998; also Portes and Stepick 1993).

Produced by area-specific circumstances, the main factors responsible for black animosity toward Cubans in Miami are different than those either in New York or in Los Angeles: the enduring exclusion of lower- and middle-class blacks from the opportunities for upward economic and political mobility by a powerful immigrant community, whose success has been perceived by African Americans as unmerited and detrimental to their own advancement. Reinforcing these factors are blacks' racial alienation from the larger society represented by Miami's (non-Hispanic) whites, a conservative local political system supported by U.S. foreign policy interests during the cold war era, a long history of black-Cuban animosity, widespread anti-Cuban prejudice among local blacks sustained or enhanced by ethnic media, and weak intergroup collaboration.

The best-fitting explanation for the hostility of blacks toward Cubans in Miami is, then, a group position model emphasizing what Portes and Stepick (1993) have called a double subordination of the group (or racial alienation; see Bobo and Hutchings 1996) combined with a profound sense of disenfranchisement and grievance vis-à-vis a group whose dominant position is perceived as unmerited, along with the presence of structural barriers to the in-group's progress.

The Cubans, neither engaged in the competition for resources nor overwhelmed or blocked in any sense by African Americans (except during the riots) have little vested interest in, or explicit opinions about, the predicament of the area's black population. A recent survey of the Cuban press in Miami reveals some subtexts suggesting underlying motives for the persistent failure of Cubans to incorporate blacks into the area's economy and politics (Grenier and Castro 1998). They involve Cuban perceptions of America as the land of opportunity for all who are willing to work and, based on an insidious comparison of Cuban success with the lowly position of blacks, the image that blacks are too ready to blame the system and others, but not themselves, for failure. To the extent that these in- and out-group perceptions are indeed prevalent among Miami's Cubans, their antipathy toward blacks is explained by Blumer's (dominant) group position model (Blumer 1958). According to this model, the source of prejudice against subordinate group(s) is in the sense of superiority of the in-group and the cultural or moral inferiority of the out-group, accompanied by belief in a merit-based proprietary claim to the status and rewards accumulated by the in-group.

Haitians Versus African Americans

As in the case of native versus foreign-born blacks in New York, relations between African Americans and Haitians (the largest group of foreign-born blacks in Miami) are ambivalent. Reflecting the local situation, however, this ambivalence has a different structure in Miami than in New York. Specifically, several circumstances present in Miami, but absent in New York, give greater weight to distance over cooperation in the relationship between immigrant and native blacks.

One important factor has enhanced native and foreign-born black solidarity, namely, a clearly defined enemy for both groups—the Cuban establishment. In comparison, the major enemies of African Americans in New York—the larger society or generalized whites and Korean merchants—have never engaged West Indian immigrants to a significant degree. The mechanisms of this animosity are not identical for the two groups. Native blacks sustain long-lasting anger about the wholesale marginalization of their group by Cuban exiles after the 1960s, while Haitians resent Cuban leaders' openly partisan politics regarding the admission of Cuban versus Haitian boat people between 1977 and 1981. The resulting outrage unites both groups, not only in sentiment but also in action.

The two groups joined forces in street protests during the 1980s, and political actions were taken, such as the intervention of the African American leadership (the NAACP in 1980) on behalf of admitting the Haitian refugees or (the same organization in 1992) siding with the Latino protest against the English-only school ordinance because of its adverse impact on the Creole-speaking Haitian community in Miami (see Portes and Stepick 1993; Grenier and Castro 1998). Pan-African solidarity, although not without tensions, also has been reported among young inner-city native and foreign-born blacks, with foreign-born blacks tending to assimilate downward into the underclass (as opposed to the conventional model of upward mobility; see Portes 1995).

Racial solidarity among Miami's native and foreign-born blacks against what they see as the Cuban oppressors is countervailed, however, by several superimposed circumstances that generate intergroup distance and resentment. Unlike New York Haitians, who melt invisibly into a large mix of immigrants, those arriving in Miami as refugees are singled out and scare-stereotyped by agencies such as the Dade County Health Department and local media as "AIDS carriers," "tuberculotics," and, generally, disease-carrying

immigrants. African Americans accept these anti-Haitian prejudices and the distance they breed (see Stepick 1996; Foner 1998).
The creation of a Little Haiti bustling with immigrant business and
entertainment in the center of Miami has improved the general
reception of Haitians, although this small but vibrant prosperity
contrasts sharply with the bleakness of the native inner-city blacks
and, especially, with Haitians' ambitions to make it into the second Little Havana. This situation breeds resentment among African
Americans, as does the competition between the two groups.
Competition is stronger in Miami than in New York because
blacks face more constrained opportunities in Miami, and neither
group has developed an occupational niche for itself among low-
skill jobs in the secondary sector (see Portes and Stepick 1985,
1993; Stepick 1989, 1996).

Additional circumstances create distance as well. African
Americans and Haitian immigrants live in different neighborhoods
(unlike in New York, where mixed native and foreign-born black
neighborhoods are common, if not pervasive). The pronounced
cultural differences between the two groups (in Miami the majority of foreign-born blacks are Creole-speaking, whereas in New
York, they are English-speaking) have sustained mutual "othering," so that each group thinks of itself as different from and better
than the other. Finally, there is no common political platform in
local politics. Characteristically, political interventions by African
American leaders on behalf of Haitian immigrants have been
made by the NAACP and not by local black politicians (see Portes
and Stepick 1993; Stepick 1996; Grenier and Pérez 1996). In comparison, the New York Democratic party and its African American
caucuses have provided a platform for the political integration of
foreign-born blacks.

The major factors generating anti-Haitian sentiments among
native blacks and at the same time the most important explanatory
elements in the group position model are their failure to accept
Haitians, whom they perceive as "negative aliens," their resentment of economic competition with the newcomers, and their in-
vidious perceptions of the undeserved success (in Little Haiti) of
recent immigrants. The group position model explains the distancing in Miami of Haitians from African Americans as being the result of circumstances similar to those identified in New York:

namely, ethnic "othering" based on a sense of cultural superiority, combined with a fear of loss of status from association with a severely marginalized group, reinforced by the resentment (not quite consistent with the superior distancing) of negative stereotyping and rejection by African Americans.

CONCLUSIONS

This chapter has explored different configurations of circumstances that generate intergroup conflict in American cities, each of which call for different explanations. They can be effectively accommodated within Blumer's group position model as reformulated by Bobo and Hutchings (1996), which incorporates into one encompassing framework both the objective and subjective hostility-generating factors that conventional theories of intergroup relations present as competing explanations.

As this three-city comparison has demonstrated, the contexts and mechanisms of intergroup conflicts are even more complex than accounted for by Bobo and Hutchings, and flexible explanations are required. Some basic hostility-generating factors seem to be present in all cases investigated here. For native blacks, these include shared perceptions of "numerical," residential, economic, or political encroachment by immigrants and competition with them in one or more arenas, combined with the belief that out-groups have made their gains undeservedly and at the cost of the in-group's progress. For immigrants, it includes racial prejudice and distancing vis-à-vis blacks, who are perceived as the lowest-status group in the host society, combined with a competition for resources or a shared belief in entitlement owing to a basic faith in individual and collective merit in the land of opportunity.

However, the particular focuses, intensities, durations, forms of expression, and resolutions of the corresponding conflicts are determined by the interactions of these factors with a wide array of city-specific circumstances and the particular national-level impacts they engage. These include the size and, especially, the pace of immigration; the scope of ethnic niches in the city's economy; the operation of the local political system; U.S. immigration policies and foreign policy interests; the role of national and local media in representing intergroup conflicts; the history of intergroup conflict and the example of similar conflicts in other cities; and the (re)conciliatory involvement of local ethnic or race organizations and political leaders. Comprehensive theoretical explanations of intergroup conflicts in American cities must incorporate these local variations, as I have attempted to do here for the three cases under consideration.

As noted in the introduction, a comparison of just three cities among the hundreds of American metropolitan centers in which immigrant–native black relations have been contentious cannot establish whether more general regularities exist across this variety of context-contingent displays. But it does suggest one possible strategy to answer this question: namely, comparative analyses of the configurations of factors contributing to intergroup tensions. Including a larger number of cases in the analysis would make the narrative-interpretive method of examination applied here increasingly unwieldy and ineffective. But historical sociologists interested in establishing broader-range generalizations have devised quantitative methods of comparative analyses of configurations, which are treated as processes rather than events, and that would be suitable for this purpose (see, for example, Ragin 1987; Abbott 1992; Isaac 1997; Jensen 1997).

I wish to acknowledge the assistance of the following persons who served as important sources of information and offered their interpretations of different aspects of immigrant or African American relations in New York, Los Angeles, and Miami: Max Castro, Héctor Cordero-Guzmán, Nancy Foner, Guillermo Grenier, Philip Kasinitz, Peggy Levitt, Ivan Light, Pyong Min, Emily Rosenbaum, Ruben Rumbaut, Alex Stepick, Roger Waldinger, and Yu Zhou. I also thank the following people for assistance in the collection of data: Mary Fischer, Michael Jones-Correa, Michael Katz, Douglas Massey, John Mollenkopf, Jan Rath, Marta Tienda, and Richard Wright.

REFERENCES

Abbott, Andrew. 1992. "From Causes to Events: Notes on Narrative Positivism." *Sociological Methods and Research* 20(4): 428–55.
Abrams, Philip. 1982. *Historical Sociology*. Ithaca, N.Y.: Cornell University Press.

Alba, Richard, Nancy Denton, Shu-Yin Leung, and John Logan. 1995. "Neighborhood Change under Conditions of Mass Immigration: The New York City Region, 1970–1990." *International Migration Review* 29(3): 625–56.

Aminzade, Ronald. 1992. "Historical Sociology and Time." *Sociological Methods and Research* 20(4): 456–80.

Bailey, Thomas. 1987. *Immigrant and Native Workers: Contrasts and Competition.* Boulder, Colo.: Westview Press.

Bayor, Ronald. 1993. "Historical Encounters: Intergroup Relations in a 'Nation of Nations.'" *Annals of the American Academy of Political and Social Science* 530(November): 14–27.

Becker, Fred, and Milan Dluhy. 1998. "Fragmentation and the Erosion of Municipal Planning in Miami." *Research in Urban Policy* 7(1): 101–20.

Blalock, Hubert. 1967. *Toward a Theory of Minority-Group Relations.* New York: Wiley.

Blumer, Herbert. 1958. "Race Prejudice as a Sense of Group Position." *Pacific Sociological Review* 1(1): 3–7.

Bobo, Lawrence. 1991. "Social Responsibility, Individualism, and Redistributive Policies." *Sociological Forum* 6(1): 71–92.

Bobo, Lawrence, and Vincent Hutchings. 1996. "Perceptions of Racial Group Competition: Extending Blumer's Theory of Group Position to a Multiracial Social Context." *American Sociological Review* 61(6): 951–72.

Bonacich, Edna. 1973. "A Theory of Middleman Minorities." *American Sociological Review* 38(4): 583–94.

Borjas, George, and Richard Freeman. 1992. *Immigration and the Work Force.* Chicago: University of Chicago Press.

Bowie, Stan, and Alex Stepick. 1998. "Diversity and Division: Ethnicity and the History of Miami." *Research in Urban Policy* 7(1): 19–32.

Boyd, Robert. 1990. "Black and Asian Self-Employment in Large Metropolitan Areas: A Comparative Analysis." *Social Problems* 37(2): 256–74.

Bozorgmehr, Mehdi, Goerges Sabagh, and Ivan Light. 1996. "Los Angeles: Explosive Diversity." In *Origins and Destinies: Immigration, Race, and Ethnicity in America,* edited by Silvia Pedraza and Ruben Rumbaut. Belmont, Calif.: Wadsworth.

Brackman, Harold, and Steven Erie. 1995. "Beyond 'Politics by Other Means'? Empowerment Strategies for Los Angeles Asian Pacific Community." In *The Bubbling Cauldron,* edited by Michael Peter Smith and Joe Feagin. Minneapolis: University of Minnesota Press.

Browning, Rufus, Dale Marshall, and David Tabb, eds. 1984. *Racial Politics in American Cities.* New York: Longman.

Bryce-Laporte, Roy. 1987. "New York City and the New Caribbean Immigration." In *Caribbean Life in New York City: Sociocultural Dimensions,* edited by Constance Sutton and Elsa Chaney. New York: Center for Migration Studies.

Chang, Edward. 1994. "Jewish and Korean Merchants in African American Neighborhoods: A Comparative Perspective." In *Los Angeles: Struggles toward Multiethnic Community,* edited by Edward Chang and Russell Leong. Seattle: University of Washington Press.

Chang, Edward, and Russell Leong, eds. 1994. *Los Angeles: Struggles toward Multiethnic Community.* Seattle: University of Washington Press.

Charles, Carolle. 1992. "Transnationalism in the Construct of Haitian Migrants' Racial Categories of Identity in New York City." In *Towards a Transnational Perspective on Migration. Race, Class, Ethnicity, and Nationalism Reconsidered,* edited by Nina Glick Schiller, Linda Basch, and Cristina Blanc-Szanton. New York: New York Academy of Sciences.

Cheng, Lucie, and Yen Espiritu. 1989. "Korean Businesses in Black and Hispanic Neighborhoods: A Study of Intergroup Relation." *Sociological Perspectives* 32(4): 521–34.

Clark, William. 1996. "Residential Patterns: Avoidance, Assimilation, and Succession." In *Ethnic Los Angeles,* edited by Roger Waldinger and Mehdi Bozorgmehr. New York: Russell Sage Foundation.

Community Service Society. 1984. *The Changing Face of Poverty.* New York: Community Service Society.

Cordero-Guzmán, Héctor. 1994. "Changes in the Socio-Economic Conditions of the Puerto Rican Population in New York City between 1980 and 1990." Paper presented at the Puerto Rican Studies Association annual meeting, Boston (October 29).

———. 1999. "Queues and Leapfrogs: Differences in Education, Employment, and Earnings between Post-1965 Immigrants, U.S.-Born Non-Hispanic Whites, and U.S.-Born Minorities." Paper presented at the Population Association of America annual meeting. New York, March 25–27.

Crowder, Kyle. 1999. "Residential Segregation of West Indians in the New York/New Jersey Metropolitan Area: The Roles of Race and Ethnicity." *International Migration Review* 33(3): 79–113.

Fainstein, Susan, and Norman Fainstein. 1994. "Urban Regimes and Racial Conflict." In *Managing Divided Cities,* edited by Seamus Dunn. London: Ryburn.

Feldman, Stanley. 1988. "Structure and Consistency on Public Opinion: The Role of Core Beliefs and Values." *American Journal of Political Science* 32(2): 773–78.

Fernández-Kelly, Patricia, and Anna García. 1989. "Informalization at the Core: Hispanic Women, Homework, and the Advanced Capitalist State." In *Informal Economy,* edited by Alejandro Portes. Baltimore, Md.: Johns Hopkins University Press.

Foner, Nancy. 1987. "The Jamaicans: Race and Ethnicity among Migrants in New York City." In *New Immigrants in New York,* edited by Nancy Foner. New York: Columbia University Press.

———. 1998. "Towards a Comparative Perspective on Caribbean Migration." In *Caribbean Migration: Globalised Identities,* edited by Mary Chamberlain. London and New York: Routledge.

García-Zamor, Jean-Claude. 1998. "Social Servivce Delivery for Immigrants in Southeast Florida." *Research in Urban Policy* 7(1): 185–200.

Glazer, Nathan, and Daniel Patrick Moynihan. 1970. *Beyond the Melting Pot: The Negroes, Puerto Ricans, Jews, Italians, and Irish of New York City.* Cambridge, Mass.: MIT Press.

Grant, David, Melvin Oliver, and Angela James. 1996. "African Americans: Social and Economic Bifurcation." In *Ethnic Los Angeles,* edited by Roger Waldinger and Mehdi Bozorgmehr. New York: Russell Sage Foundation.

Grassmuck, Sherry, and Ramon Grosfoguel. 1997. "Geopolitics, Economic Niches, and Gendered Social Capital Among Recent Caribbean Immigrants in New York City." 40(3): 339–64.

Grassmuck, Sherry, and Patricia Pessar. 1991. *Between Two Islands: Dominican International Migration.* Berkeley: University of California Press.

———. 1996. "Dominicans in the United States: First- and Second- Generation Settlement." In *Origins and Destinies: Immigration, Race, and Ethnicity in America,* edited by Silvia Bedraza and Ruben Rumbaut. Belmont, Calif.: Wadsworth.

Grenier, Guillermo, and Max Castro. 1998. "The Emergence of an Adversarial Relation: Black-Cuban Relations in Miami, 1959–1998." *Research in Urban Policy* 7(1): 33–56.

Grenier, Guillermo, and Lisandro Pérez. 1996. "Miami Spice: The Ethnic Cauldron Simmers." In *Origins and Destinies: Immigration, Race, and Ethnicity in America,* edited by Silvia Pedraza and Ruben Rumbaut. Belmont, Calif.: Wadsworth.

Grenier, Guillermo, Alex Stepick, with Aline LaBorwit. 1994. "Grounding the Saturn Plant: Failed Restructuring in a Miami Apparel Plant." In *Newcomers in the Workplace,* edited by Louise Lamphere. Philadelphia: Temple University Press.

Guarnizo, Luis. 1997. "'Going Home': Class, Gender, and Household Transformation among Dominican Return Migrants." In *Carribean Cir-*

cuits: New Directions in the Study of Caribbean Migration, edited by Patricia Pessar. New York: Center for Migration Studies.

Hamermesh, Daniel, and Frank Bean, eds. 1998. *Help or Hindrance? The Economic Implications of Immigration for African Americans.* New York: Russell Sage Foundation.

Harris, Daryl. 1994. "Generating Racial and Ethnic Conflict in Miami: Impact of American Foreign Policy and Domestic Racism." In *Blacks, Latinos, and Asians in Urban America,* edited by James Jennings. Westport, Conn.: Praeger.

Harris, Fred, and Roger Wilkins. 1988. *Quiet Riots: Race and Poverty in the United States.* New York: Pantheon.

Henry, Charles. 1994. "Urban Politics and Incorporation: The Case of Blacks, Latinos, and Asians in Three Cities." In *Blacks, Latinos, and Asians in Urban America,* edited by James Jennings. Westport, Conn.: Praeger.

Herman, Michael. 1995. *A Tale of Two Cities: Testing Explanations for Riot Violence in Miami, Florida, and Los Angeles, California, 1992.* Washington, D.C.: American Sociological Association.

Higham, John. 1975. *Send These to Me: Jews and Other Immigrants in Urban America.* New York: Atheneum.

Huber, Joan, and William Form. 1973. *Income and Ideology: An Analysis of the American Political Formula.* New York: Free Press.

Isaac, Larry. 1997. "Transforming Localities: Reflections on Time, Causality, and Narrative in Contemporary Historical Sociology." *Historical Methods* 30(1): 4–13.

Isaac, Larry, and Larry Griffin. 1989. "Ahistoricism in Time-Series Analyses of Historical Processes." *American Sociological Review* 54(December): 873–90.

Jensen, Gary. 1997. "Time and Social History: Problems of Atemporality in Historical Analyses with Illustrations from Research on Early Modern Witch Hunts." *Historical Methods* 30(1): 46–57.

Johnson, James, Walter Farrell, and Chandra Guinn. 1997. "Immigration Reform and the Browning of America: Tensions, Conflicts and Community Instability in Metropolitan Los Angeles." *International Migration Review* 31(4): 1055–95.

Johnson, James, Melvin Oliver, and Lawrence Bobo. 1994. "Understanding the Contours of Deepening Urban Inequality: Theoretical Underpinnings and Research Design of Multi-City Study." *Urban Geography* 15(1): 77–89.

Jones-Correa, Michael. 1998. "Immigrants, Blacks, and Cities." Paper presented at the American Political Science Association annual meeting. Boston (September 2–6).

Joyce, Patrick. 1997. "A Reversal of Fortunes: Black Empowerment, Political Machines, and City Jobs in New York City and Chicago." *Urban Affairs Review* 32(3): 291–318.

Kalmijn, Mattijs. 1996. "The Socioeconomic Assimilation of Caribbean American Blacks." *Social Forces* 74(3): 911–30.

Kasinitz, Philip. 1992. *Caribbean New York: Black Immigrants and the Politics of Race.* Ithaca, N.Y.: Cornell University Press.

Kasinitz, Philip, and Jan Rosenberg. 1996. "Missing the Connection: Social Isolation and Employment on the Brooklyn Waterfront." *Social Problems* 43(2): 180–96.

Kasinitz, Philip, and Milton Vickerman. 1995. "Ethnic Niches and Racial Traps: Jamaicans in the New York Regional Economy." Paper presented at the Social Science History Association annual meeting. Chicago (November 18–21).

Katz, Michael. Forthcoming. *Redefining the Welfare State in America, 1980–1999.* New York: Metropolitan Books.

Kim, Claire Jean. 1996. "Cracks in the 'Gorgeous Mosaic': Black-Korean Conflict and Racial Mobilization in New York City." Ph.D. diss., Yale University, New Haven, Conn.

Kirschenman, Yoleen, and Kathryn Neckerman. 1991. "'We'd Love to Hire Them, But . . .' The Meaning of Race for Employers." In *The Urban Underclass,* edited by Christopher Jencks and Paul Peterson. Washington, D.C.: The Brookings Institution.

Kluegel, James, and Elliot Smith. 1986. *Beliefs about Inequality: Americans' Views of What Is and What Ought to Be.* New York: Aldine de Gruyter.

Lee, Heon Cheol. 1993. "Korean-Black Conflict in New York City: A Sociological Analysis." Ph.D. diss., Columbia University, New York.

Light, Ivan. 1998. "Immigrant Entrepreneurs in America: Koreans in Los Angeles." In *The Immigration Reader: America in a Multidisciplinary Perspective,* edited by David Jacobsen. New York: Blackwell.

Light, Ivan, Richard Bernard, and Rebecca Kim. 1999. "Immigrant Incorporation in the Garment Industry of Los Angeles." *International Migration Review* 33(3): 5–25.

Light, Ivan, and Edna Bonacich. 1989. *Ethnic Entrepreneurs.* Berkeley: University of California Press.

Light, Ivan, Hadas Har-Chui, and Kenneth Kan. 1994. "Black/Korean Conflict in Los Angeles." In *Managing Divided Cities,* edited by Seamus Dunn. London: Ryburn Publishing.

Light, Ivan, and Carolyn Rosenstein. 1995. *Race, Ethnicity, and Entrepreneurship in Urban America.* New York: Aldine de Gruyter.

Logan, John, and Richard Alba. 1999. "Minority Niches and Immigrant

Enclaves in New York and Los Angeles: Trends and Impacts." In *Immigration and Opportunity: Race, Ethnicity and Employment in the United States,* edited by Frank Bean and Stephanie Bell-Rose. New York: Russell Sage Foundation.

Logan, John, Richard Alba, and Thomas McNulty. 1994a. "The Racially Divided City: Housing and Labor Markets in Los Angeles." In *Managing Divided Cities,* edited by Seamus Dunn. London: Ryburn.

———. 1994b. "Ethnic Economies in Metropolitan Regions: Miami and Beyond." *Social Forces* 72(3): 691–724.

López, David, Eric Popkin, and Edward Telles. 1996. "Central Americans: At the Bottom, Struggling to Get Ahead." In *Ethnic Los Angeles,* edited by Roger Waldinger and Mehdi Bozorgmehr. New York: Russell Sage Foundation.

Massey, Douglas. 2000. "The Residential Segregation of Blacks, Hispanics, and Asians: 1970 to 1990." In *Immigration and Race Relations,* edited by Gerald Jaynes. New Haven, Conn.: Yale University Press.

Massey, Douglas, and Nancy Denton. 1987. "Trends in the Residential Segregation of Blacks, Hispanics, and Asians: 1970–1980." *American Sociological Review* 52(December): 802–25.

———. 1993. *American Apartheid: Segregation and the Making of the Underclass.* Cambridge, Mass.: Harvard University Press.

Min, Pyong Gap. 1996a. *Caught in the Middle: Korean Merchants in America's Multiethnic Cities.* Berkeley: University of California Press.

———. 1996b. "The Entrepreneurial Adaptation of Korean Immigrants." In *Origins and Destinies: Immigration, Race, and Ethnicity in America,* edited by Silvia Pedraza and Ruben Rumbaut. Belmont, Calif.: Wadsworth.

———. 1997. "Problems of Korean Immigrant Entrepreneurs." *International Migration Review* 31(4): 436–55.

———. 1998. *Changes and Conflicts: Korean Immigrant Families in New York.* Boston: Allyn and Bacon.

Mladenka, Kenneth. 1989. "Blacks and Hispanics in Urban Politics." *American Political Science Review* 83(1): 165–91.

Model, Suzanne. 1993. "The Ethnic Niche and the Structure of Opportunity: Immigrants and Minorities in New York City." In *The "Underclass" Debate: Views from History,* edited by Michael Katz. Princeton, N.J.: Princeton University Press.

———. 1995. "West Indian Prosperity: Fact or Fiction?" *Social Problems* 42(4): 535–53.

Mohl, Raymond. 1990. "On the Edge: Blacks and Hispanics in Metropolitan Miami since 1959." *Florida Historical Quarterly* 69(July): 37–56.

Mollenkopf, John. 1993. *A Phoenix in the Ashes: The Rise and Fall of the Koch Coalition in New York City Politics.* Princeton, N.J.: Princeton University Press.

Morales, Rebecca, and Paul Ong. 1993. "The Illusion of Progress: Latinos in Los Angeles." In *Latinos in a Changing U.S. Economy,* edited by Rebecca Morales and Frank Bonilla. Newbury Park, Calif.: Sage.

Navarro, Armando. 1994. "The South Central Los Angeles Eruption: A Latino Perspective." In *Los Angeles: Struggles toward Multiethnic Community,* edited by Edward Chang and Russell Leong. Seattle: University of Washington Press.

Olzak, Susan. 1992. *The Dynamics of Ethnic Competition and Conflict.* Stanford, Calif.: Stanford University Press.

Olzak, Susan, and Suzanne Shanahan. 1996. "Deprivation and Race Riots: An Extension of Spilerman's Analysis." *Social Forces* 74(3): 931–61.

Ong, Paul, and Janet Lawrence. 1992. "Pluralism and Residential Patterns in Los Angeles." Unpublished manuscript.

Ong, Paul, Kye Young Park, and Yasmin Tong. 1994. "The Korean-Black Conflict and the State." In *The New Asian Immigration in Los Angeles and Global Restructuring,* edited by Paul Ong, Edna Bonacich, and Lucie Cheng. Philadelphia: Temple University Press.

Ong, Paul, and Abel Valenzula. 1996. "The Labor Market: Immigrant Effects and Racial Disparities." In *Ethnic Los Angeles,* edited by Roger Waldinger and Mehdi Bozorgmehr. New York: Russell Sage Foundation.

Ortiz, Vilma. 1996. "The Mexican-Origin Population: Permanent Working Class or Emerging Middle Class?" In *Ethnic Los Angeles,* edited by Roger Waldinger and Mehdi Bozorgmehr. New York: Russell Sage Foundation.

Park, Kyeyoung. 1997. *The Korean American Dream.* Ithaca, N.Y.: Cornell University Press.

Pérez-Stable, Marifeli, and Miren Uriarte. 1997. "Cubans and the Changing Economy of Miami." In *New American Destinies,* edited by Darrell Hamamoto and Rodolfo Torres. New York: Routledge.

Pessar, Patricia. 1995. *A Visa for a Dream: Dominicans in the United States.* Boston: Allyn and Bacon.

Pessar, Patricia, ed. 1997. *Caribbean Circuits: New Directions in the Study of Caribbean Migration.* New York: Center for Migration Studies.

Portes, Alejandro. 1987. "The Social Origins of the Cuban Enclave Economy of Miami." *Sociological Perspectives* 30(4): 340–72.

———. 1995. "Children of Immigrants: Segmented Assimilation and Its

Determinants." In *The Economic Sociology of Immigration,* edited by Alejandro Portes. New York: Russell Sage Foundation.

Portes, Alejandro, and Alex Stepick. 1985. "Unwelcome Immigrants: The Labor Market Experience of 1980 (Mariel) Cuban and Haitian Refugees in South Florida." *American Sociological Review* 50(August): 493–514.

———. 1993. *City on Edge: The Transformation of Miami.* Berkeley: University of California Press.

Ragin, Charles. 1987. *The Comparative Method.* Berkeley: University of California Press.

———. 1994. *Contructing Social Research.* Thousand Oaks, Calif.: Pine Forge Press.

Razin, Erna, and Ivan Light. 1998. "Ethnic Entrepreneurs in America's Largest Metropolitan Areas." *Urban Affairs Review* 33(3): 332–60.

Reimers, Cordelia, and Howard Chernick. 1991. "Hispanic Employment in the Public Sector: Why Is It Lower Than Black?" In *Hispanics in the Labor Force,* edited by Edwin Meléndez, Clara Rodríguez, and Janis B. Figueroa. New York: Plenum.

Rieff, David. 1992. *Los Angeles Capital of the Third World.* New York: Simon & Schuster.

Rose, Peter. 1993. "'Of Every Hue and Caste': Race, Immigration, and Perceptions of Pluralism." *Annals of the American Academy of Political and Social Science* 530(November): 187–202.

Rosenbaum, Emily. 1996. "The Influence of Race on Hispanic Housing Choices: New York City, 1978–1987." *Urban Affairs Review* 32(2): 217–43.

Rosenberg, Mark. 1998. "The International Business Environment in Greater Miami." *Research in Urban Policy* 7(1): 67–78.

Rosenfeld, Michael, and Marta Tienda. 1999. "Mexican Immigration, Occupational Niches, and Labor-Market Competition: Evidence from Los Angeles, Chicago, and Atlanta, 1970–1990." In *Immigration and Opportunity: Race, Ethnicity, and Employment in the United States,* edited by Frank Bean and Stephanie Bell-Rose. New York: Russell Sage Foundation.

Rumbaut, Ruben. 1997. "Origins and Destinies: Immigration to the United States since World War II." In *New American Destinies,* edited by Darrell Hamamoto and Rodolfo Torres. New York: Routledge.

Sabagh, Georges, and Mehdi Bozorgmehr. 1996. "Population Change: Immigration and Ethnic Transformation." In *Ethnic Los Angeles,* edited by Roger Waldinger and Mehdi Bozorgmehr. New York: Russell Sage Foundation.

Sanjek, Roger. 1998. *The Future of Us All: Race and Neighborhood Politics in New York City.* Ithaca, N.Y.: Cornell University Press.

Sassen, Saskia. 1994. *Cities in a World Economy*. Thousand Oaks, Calif.: Pine Forge Press.

Scott, Allen. 1996. "The Manufacturing Economy: Ethnic and Gender Divisions of Labor." In *Ethnic Los Angeles*, edited by Roger Waldinger and Mehdi Bozorgmehr. New York: Russell Sage Foundation.

Shefter, Martin. 1988. "Political Incorporation and Containment: Regime Transformation in New York City." In *Power, Culture, and Place: Essays on New York City,* edited by John Mollenkopf. New York: Russell Sage Foundation.

Simon, Rita. 1993. "Old Minorities, New Immigrants: Aspirations, Hopes, and Fears." *Annals of the American Academy of Political and Social Science* 530(November): 61–71.

Soja, Edward, Rebecca Morales, and Goetz Wolff. 1989. "Urban Restructuring: An Analysis of Social and Spatial Change in Los Angeles." In *Atop the Urban Hierarchy,* edited by Robert Beauregard. Totowa, N.J.: Rowman and Littlefield.

Sonenshein, Raphael. 1993. *Politics in Black and White: Race and Power in Los Angeles*. Princeton, N.J.: Princeton University Press.

———. 1996. "The Battle over Liquor Stores in South Central Los Angeles: The Management of an Interminority Conflict." *Urban Affairs Review* 31(6): 710–37.

Stafford, Susan. 1987. "The Haitians: The Cultural Meaning of Race and Ethnicity." In *New Immigrants in New York,* edited by Nancy Foner. New York: Columbia University Press.

Stafford, Walter. 1991. "Racial, Ethnic, and Gender Employment Segmentation in New York City Agencies." In *Hispanics in the Labor Force,* edited by Edwin Meléndez, Clara Rodríguez, and Janis B. Figueroa. New York: Plenum.

Stepick, Alex. 1989. "Miami's Two Informal Economies." In *Informal Economy,* edited by Alejandro Portes. Baltimore, Md.: Johns Hopkins University Press.

———. 1994. "Miami: Capital of Latin America." In *Newcomers in the Workplace,* edited by Louise Lamphere, Alex Stepick, and Guillermo Grenier. Philadelphia: Temple University Press.

———. 1996. "Pride, Prejudice, and Poverty: Economic, Social, Political, and Cultural Capital among Haitians in Miami." In *Immigrants and Immigration Policy: Individual Skills, Family Ties, and Group Identities,* edited by Harrriet O. Duleep and Phadindra Wunnava. Greenwich, Conn.: JAI Press.

Stepick, Alex, and Guillermo Grenier. 1994a. "Brothers in Wood." In *Newcomers in the Workplace,* edited by Louise Lamphere. Philadelphia: Temple University Press.

————. 1994b. "The View from the Back of the House: Restaurants and Hotels in Miami." In *Newcomers in the Workplace,* edited by Louise Lamphere. Philadelphia: Temple University Press.

Thornton, Michael, and Robert Taylor. 1988. "Intergroup Attitudes: Black American Perceptions of Asian Americans." *Ethnic and Racial Studies* 11(4): 474–88.

Torres, Andres. 1995. *Between Melting Pot and Mosaic: African Americans and Puerto Ricans in the New York Political Economy.* Philadelphia: Temple University Press.

Torres, Andres, and Frank Bonilla. 1993. "Decline within Decline: The New York Perspective." In *Latinos in a Changing U.S. Economy,* edited by Rebecca Morales and Frank Bonilla. Newbury Park, Calif.: Sage.

Umemoto, Karen. 1994. "Blacks and Koreans in Los Angeles: The Case of LaTasha Harlins and Soon Ja Du." In *Blacks, Latinos, and Asians in Urban America,* edited by James Jennings. Westport, Conn.: Praeger.

Underwood, Katherine. 1997. "Ethnicity Is Not Enough: Latino-Led Multiracial Coalitions in Los Angeles." *Urban Affairs Review* 33(1): 3–27.

Valenzuela, Abel. 1997. "Compatriots or Competitors? Job Competition between Foreign- and U.S.-Born Angelenos." In *New American Destinies,* edited by Darrell Hamamoto and Rodolfo Torres. New York: Routledge.

Van Deburg, William, ed. 1997. *Modern Black Nationalism: From Marcus Garvey to Louis Farrakhan.* New York: New York University Press.

Vickerman, Milton. 1999. *Crosscurrents: West Indian Immigrants and Race.* New York: Oxford University Press.

Waldinger, Roger. 1995. "The 'Other Side' of Embeddedness: A Case-Study of the Interplay of Economy and Ethnicity." *Ethnic and Racial Studies* 18(3): 555–80.

————. 1996a. "From Ellis Island to LAX: Immigrant Prospects in the American City." *International Migration Review* 30(4): 1078–86.

————. 1996b. *Still the Promised City? African Americans and New Immigrants in Postindustrial New York.* Cambridge, Mass.: Harvard University Press.

————. 1996c. "Who Makes the Beds? Who Washes the Dishes? Black/Immigrant Competition Reassessed." In *Immigrants and Immigration Policy: Individual Skills, Family Ties, and Group Identities,* edited by Harriet Orcutt Duleep and Phanindra Wunnava. Greenwich, Conn.: JAI Press.

————. 1996d. "Ethnicity and Opportunity in Plural City." In *Ethnic Los Angeles,* edited by Roger Waldinger and Mehdi Bozorgmehr. New York: Russell Sage Foundation.

————. 1997. "Black/Immigrant Competition Reassessed: New Evidence from Los Angeles." *Sociological Perspectives* 40(3): 365–86.

Waldinger, Roger, and Mehdi Bozorgmehr, eds. 1996. *Ethnic Los Angeles*. New York: Russell Sage Foundation.

Waters, Mary. 1994. "Ethnic and Racial Identities of Second-Generation Black Immigrants in New York City." *International Migration Review* 28(4): 795–820.

————. 1999. Black Identities, West Indian Dreams, and American Realities. New York: Russell Sage Foundation.

Wilson, Thomas. 1998. "Fragmentation and Suburbanization in Metropolitan Miami." *Research in Urban Policy* 7(1): 217–29.

Yoon, In-Jin. 1997. *On My Own: Korean Businesses and Race Relations in America*. Chicago: University of Chicago Press.

Zenner, Walter. 1991. *Minorities in the Middle: A Cross-Cultural Analysis*. Albany: State University of New York Press.

Zephir, Flore. 1996. *Haitian Immigrants in Black America*. Westport, Conn.: Bergin and Garvey.

Zubrinsky, Camille, and Lawrence Bobo. 1996. "Prismatic Metropolis: Race and Residential Segregation in the City of Los Angeles." *Social Science Research* 25: 335–74.

—— Chapter 4 ——

Who Speaks for Women? Racial Exclusivity, Feminist Ideology, and the Dilemmas of Constituency

Robin Leidner

F EMINIST IDEOLOGY DEFINES the constituency of the contemporary women's movement extremely broadly: all women should benefit from the struggle, all could contribute to it, and none should feel excluded. The reality has been somewhat disappointing, especially with regard to racial diversity, and the difference between feminist organizations' desired constituencies and their actual participants is my subject. In addressing this question, I consider how feminist allegiance to participatory democracy affects the possibilities for building unity among women, particularly among women of different races and ethnic groups.

Diversity has been one of the most widely addressed themes in feminist theory and feminist politics in recent years. In the first giddy throes of sisterhood, second wave feminists, who were predominantly white and middle class, often assumed that they could speak for women as a whole (for example, Friedan 1963; Daly 1978; see also Buechler 1990; Echols 1989). Within a short time, the error of this stance was made abundantly clear, as lesbians, women of color, women from around the world, and other women who were not white, middle class, heterosexual, and American spoke up. They were angry at having been rendered invisible, and they argued that a true sisterhood could not emerge until their views of the world were valued and their concerns included on the feminist agenda (see Collins 1990; Combahee River Collective 1979; Dill 1983; hooks 1981, 1984; Moraga and Anzaldúa 1981).

At the level of theory and rhetoric, these arguments have been extremely successful (for example, Harding 1987; Ramazanoglu 1989; Jones 1993). Although claims about women that over-generalize from the perspective of the most privileged sectors have not disappeared entirely, they are no longer likely to go unchallenged. By and large, most feminists have accepted in principle that unity among women cannot be wished into existence, that multiple voices are crucial to successful politics and adequate theorizing, and that it is an arrogant mistake to think that one can arrive at the truth about women's position in the world merely through self-contemplation and discussion with similar others (Alperin 1990; Buechler 1990; Scott 1998), even though Spelman (1988) shows how racism may be reproduced within the rhetoric of inclusion.

THE EPISTEMOLOGY OF INCLUSION

The cogent critiques of women of color, and also the influence of postmodernist theorists suspicious of unitary stories, have sensitized feminists to the importance of diversity in theorizing and in politics. As Kathleen Jones (1993, 189) notes, "Shudders go down the feminist spine when someone accuses her of making definitive statements or arrogating to herself the power to speak in declarative sentences about anyone except herself . . . maybe even herself" (ellipsis in the original). Unfortunately, however, awareness of the hazards of exclusivity has not meant that solutions have been easy to implement (see Buechler 1990). Despite broader agendas and more diversified curricula, the tension between unity and diversity in feminism is still problematic, with racial inclusivity, in particular, remaining difficult to achieve.

In addressing the somewhat sore subject of the constituencies of the women's movement, one should not accept too hastily the familiar dismissive verdict that feminism is simply a middle-class white movement. As Barbara Ryan points out (1992, 125), this conclusion suggests that organizations devoted to improving the lives of women of color and of working-class women are not and were never part of the women's movement and downplays the strong support for feminist goals among those who are not themselves activists (see, for example, hooks 1981, 148; Mansbridge 1986, 15). It also ignores the contributions of many women of color and women of working-class origins to feminist organizations whose memberships are nonetheless predominantly white and middle class, and it dismisses the efforts these organizations have made to expand their agendas to reflect the concerns of a wider range of women (see also Buechler 1990, 150–51). In fairness, one should note, as does Buechler (1990, 169), that while "women's movements have always had difficulty transcending their white, middle-class roots . . . few movements have been better and many have been much worse at transcending (or even recognizing) such barriers."

Still, it is true that feminist aspirations to create organizations that reflect and respect the diversity of women have often fallen short, as both protestations from those excluded or treated badly and the mea culpas of other feminists testify (Davis 1990b; Jones 1993; Leidner 1993; Matthews 1989; Moraga and Anzaldúa 1981). Moreover, feminist efforts to overcome exclusionary practices have frequently been exceedingly painful, leaving legacies of mistrust, anger, and guilt. As Mansbridge and Yeatman (1991, 6) note,

> Many black feminists have written of their despair in trying to find a welcome place in existing feminist organizations with a predominantly white membership. Almost every major black feminist writer has some such story to tell, including bell hooks, Audre Lorde, Michelle Wallace, Alice Walker, Barbara Smith, and many whose works are less well known. Some black women adapted to these predominantly white organizations and worked within them for years. Others tried to shift the focus of the organization to reflect their own concerns and either met strong resistance or were told that they had better organize among black women. Still others, meeting a strong white dislike for confrontation and little understanding of their own experiences, were simply made to feel so uncomfortable that they left (see also Davenport 1981; hooks 1981; Lorde 1984; Walker 1983; Smith 1983; Wallace 1990).

Although speaking for a narrowly defined constituency is not problematic for many organizations and social movements, feminists hope to address the concerns of women of many backgrounds and perspectives. In fact, organizational legitimacy in the eyes of both members and external audiences may well depend in part on making sure that feminism does not speak, and does not appear to speak, only for the parochial interests of one subgroup of women. In short, the relative scarcity of women of color and working-class women in mainstream feminist organizations is problematic for other members of those organizations, because they want their movement to be for all women.

It is certainly common enough for ideologues to assert that they are speaking for a large mass of people, whether or not those people have indicated their support for the positions espoused. Movements have ideological ways of reconciling their broadly defined constituencies and their frequently meager numbers. For example, socialists in the United States have routinely had to explain why the working classes are overwhelmingly absent from their movement. The standard explanation, of course, is that the hegemony of the dominant classes causes workers to suffer from "false consciousness."

Feminists early on adopted a similar rationale to explain the embarrassing reality that huge numbers of women did not accept a feminist analysis of social life. "Their consciousnesses haven't been raised yet" was an appealing explanation for feminists who had themselves only recently experienced a radical transformation in worldview. This interpretation has been cast aside, however, as feminists have acknowledged that what they had believed was a thorough critique of oppression from the perspective of all women was in fact a partial vision reflecting the life experiences and concerns of only some women, relatively privileged ones at that. The feminist agenda, they came to see, was similarly incomplete (Echols 1989; Ferree and Hess 1985; Harding 1987; Jaggar 1983). Given feminist aspirations toward sisterhood—the wish to identify with, improve the lives of, and address the concerns of all women—feminist organizations have worked to increase the participation of underrepresented women, women's studies faculties have attempted to reformulate curricula to be more inclusive, and feminist theorists have wrestled with the difficulties of relinquishing a unitary vision (Harding 1987; Leidner 1991; Ryan 1992; Sirianni 1993b).

Feminist theory and ideology required that such efforts be

made. Much feminist thought and politics began from the premise that control of knowledge by men had produced limited and distorted understandings of the world and that control of resources by men had benefited men disproportionately. When women who felt that they were not being represented by the feminist movement used arguments that were identical in form to these (for example, Moraga and Anzaldúa 1981), principled feminists could hardly deny their validity. Over time, and under continued criticism, mainstream feminists largely came to accept that the concerns of lesbians, women of color, poor and working-class women, women outside of North America and Western Europe, homemakers, women with disabilities, and so on should all be regarded as feminist concerns.

For many feminists, moreover, such breadth of participation is not merely desirable, but essential, both to accurate understanding and to successful politics. Much feminist ideology has been underpinned by some version of epistemology that rejects the possibility of detached perception. Influential feminist theorists have developed various arguments to the effect that women have, or potentially can achieve, a distinctive perspective on reality (see Longino 1993). Some versions (for example, Flax 1983; Gilligan 1982) suggest that the female perspective is rooted in biology, in psychological development, or in widely shared experience of caregiving. Feminist standpoint theorists accept Hegel's idea that the slave has knowledge invisible to the master and apply Marxist ideas about attaining knowledge through struggle, pointing out that the experience of oppression is potentially a crucial source of insight. The oppressed have to know their oppressors as well as possible, have to conceal some types of knowledge about themselves, and have to understand how the world works more completely than those who are served. Their social location, or their active struggle to overcome their oppression, can help them to see through the mystifications of the dominant classes (Hartsock 1987; Jaggar 1983; Smith 1987).

If a distinct women's perspective arises from biology, near-universal female experience, or forms of oppression common to all women, then presumably there is a coherent women's standpoint, which any woman either already has or could achieve. Such an epistemology supports feminists who claim to speak for women as a whole. Versions of standpoint theory stressing the importance of social location and personal experience, however, suggest that there is no single women's standpoint (for example, Collins 1990; Stanley and Wise 1990), as does postmodern theory (Flax 1987; Weedon 1987).

Assuming that the latter position is correct, a number of different conclusions may be drawn. Some have been concerned that standpoint theory could lay the ground for a complete relativism that makes any claim to truth problematic (Hawkesworth 1989; Longino 1993). The argument that privilege blinds people to reality could be taken to suggest that those who are most oppressed are in the best position to perceive reality in an unbiased way, so that they can achieve the greatest access to truth (see Collins 1990, 207, for comment). Still others conclude that, although some standpoints are less distorted than others, any individual's standpoint provides only partial truth, giving insight into some aspects of reality, while obscuring others (Albrecht and Brewer 1990, 19). In that case, reality presumably could be approximated best by weighing knowledge drawn from many standpoints (Harding 1991; Stanley and Wise 1990). Postmodernism, with its distrust of essentialism and unitary thought, dampens the hope for any stable, all-encompassing vision, but strongly supports the impulse toward multivocality (Hekman 1990).

THE DILEMMAS OF INCLUSION

These epistemological concerns clarify why feminists must take claims of exclusion so seriously. Accepting that people who are white and middle class have benefited from prior colonialism or are otherwise privileged and have some stake in the mystifications that allow oppression to continue severely undercuts the grounds for resisting criticisms from those less privileged. Incorporating the insights of the most oppressed is crucial to arriving at an adequate understanding of reality, so one could argue that their priorities should guide the feminist agenda (see also Davis 1990a). Alternatively, the position that social locations provide only partial insights similarly undercuts the possibility that a group of privileged women could speak for all women and provides strong motivation to develop a movement in which no women are rendered invisible and no voices are excluded.

But how? Simply reaching out to members of underrepresented groups and encouraging them to join existing feminist organizations has not solved the problem (see, for example, Davis 1990b), for several reasons. First, women of color in particular assert that when they have tried to become participants they frequently have been treated disrespectfully or otherwise marginalized by white feminists (Davenport 1981; McKay 1993; Moraga and Anzaldúa 1981; Yamada 1981). Second, the organizations created by white middle-class feminists have evolved shared cultures that are likely to be unfamiliar, baffling, or sometimes even offensive to other women (for example, Matthews 1989).

Most important, though, is the ongoing reality of divergent priorities. If white middle-class feminists in the past took for granted that the feminist agenda they devised reflected the concerns of other women and would attract them to feminist activism, that expectation was unrealistic, indeed arrogant and condescending (Spelman 1988). Middle-class white feminists might well perceive that oppression based on gender is the fundamental problem facing them and that all women would benefit from its elimination. Those less privileged, however, can see that eliminating the forms of sexism targeted by these feminists would not in itself bring about their own empowerment or the empowerment of their communities. They have other concerns that are at least as pressing, and unless the agendas of feminist organizations change, they have limited incentive to join (see, for example, Buechler 1990; Christensen 1997; Dill 1983; García 1989; Giddings 1984; Joseph and Lewis 1981; King 1988; Lorde 1984).

Moreover, many women (including Latina, Asian American, African American, and white working-class women) perceive mainstream feminists as being harshly critical of their cultures without thoroughly understanding them and as promoting a divisiveness between men and women that undermines class-based, racial, or ethnic struggles (for example, Chow 1984; Collins 1990; García 1989). Even when such women support the goals of mainstream feminist organizations, they are unlikely to join if the costs include distancing themselves from their own communities and having their concerns treated as peripheral.

Feminist commitment to participatory democracy would seem to solve some of these problems. The desire to empower all women has led feminists to develop organizational practices that do not silence anyone and that enhance the power of those who are in the minority. One would hope that such practices would give women from underrepresented groups the opportunity to gain real power to shape the organizational agenda and culture. But these approaches have been problematic as well.

First, participatory democracy puts higher demands on participants' time, energy, and commitment than other forms of governance. Those with multiple responsibilities, multiple political commitments, and little ability to save time by paying for services face barriers to joining such demanding organizations and could be disadvantaged in gaining influence if they do join because of the limits to their involvement (Mansbridge 1973; Sirianni 1993b). The people who are most likely to perceive male domination as the major source of oppression in their lives, and therefore to put their energies into feminist activism rather than other political commitments, are white, middle-class women (see Buechler 1990; Spelman 1988). Moreover, they are more likely to have the leisure to devote themselves to "process" even when it slows down action. The high costs of democratic participation may therefore contribute to elitism and make it harder to build diverse movements (Phillips 1993).

Small feminist organizations have often used consensus decisionmaking to mandate participation and ensure that minority opinions are fully aired and taken into account. However, unless groups are relatively homogeneous, consensus is likely to be extraordinarily inefficient and often quite frustrating (Mansbridge 1980; Rothschild and Whitt 1986). Moreover, the process itself can create pressure to conform. As a result, this form of participatory democracy is unlikely to be suitable for diverse groups, and certainly not for large ones.

For larger organizations and polities, some form of special representation may be necessary if those in underrepresented groups are to gain more than token influence. Young (1989) makes the theoretical case for creating forms of "differential citizenship," acknowledging that the costs of participation disproportionately burden oppressed groups and that equalizing the voices of all participants does not ensure that the interests of disadvantaged minorities will be taken seriously. She recommends that polities provide support for the self-organization of such groups, ensure that their policy proposals are fully considered, and grant veto power over specific policies to groups that are uniquely affected by them. Her bold proposals would help oppressed minorities to exercise real power, but, as Sirianni (1993a) and Phillips (1993) each outline, they pose their own dangers.

The experience of the National Women's Studies Association, which has moved in the direction of differential citizenship, illustrates some of the problems with this version of participatory democracy (Leidner 1991, 1993). The designation of groups deserving of special representation is bound to be problematic, as new groups seek recognition and as the legitimacy of existing groups' claims of oppression changes over time. Moreover, basing political representation on identities reintroduces the problems of essentialism, creating a false appearance of unanimity within subgroups, undermining accountability, and predetermining which aspects of identity are politically pertinent. The most serious problem with the "strong" version of differential citizenship Young proposes is that it encourages what Phillips (1993, 136) calls a "politics of the enclave," locking people into narrow, specific concerns. Increasing Balkanization can generate conflict and resentment, blocking rather than facilitating the development of a wider sense of solidarity (Sirianni 1993a, 375; Phillips 1993, 150).

Scott's recent article (1998) describing two feminist organizations that have achieved a shift in the racial balance of both membership and leadership illustrates the degree of dedication to overcoming racism required to reorient an organization's culture and focus, but it also brings to light the inadequacy of race as a predictor of shared organizational politics. Scott describes two feminist service organizations, a battered women's shelter and a rape crisis center, in a large west coast city. Participants' awareness that services were not equally accessible to women of various racial-ethnic groups was a major impetus to both organizations' devising strategies for overcoming racial imbalances in staffing and leadership and for fighting racism within the organizations. In each case, achieving the desired changes required that members accept countering racism as a primary organizational goal.

The means chosen to accomplish this goal included a strong form of affirmative action, amounting to racial preferences in hiring, volunteer training programs targeted exclusively to women of color, and ongoing mandatory antiracism discussion groups for white women. These measures demonstrated the organizations' commitment to overcoming racism and empowering women of color, persuading many to devote their time and energy to organizations formerly dominated by whites. The racial demographics of the groups shifted substantially, such that women of color became the majority. Ultimately, white members who disagreed with the goal of undermining white privilege or the means of empowering women of color left the organizations, but some women of color who operated under the assumption that race was the best marker of potential allies came to feel betrayed by others of their own race who did not prove to be supportive, calling into question the viability of identity-based politics.

The success of these antiracist efforts demonstrates that significant shifts in power within feminist organizations are possible, particularly in service-oriented groups that operate on a scale where face-to-face interactions are possible. It is not clear, however, whether a comparable empowerment of women of color is possible in groups where white women are in the majority. Furthermore, for larger organizations with less ideological unanimity, forms of participatory democracy have not yet been developed to overcome the difficulties of building unity among diverse women. In fact, some existing or suggested forms themselves present barriers to the effective functioning of diverse organizations. An additional problem is that participatory democracy (along with feminist principles of solidarity and egalitarianism) generally increases the expectation that members' voices will be heard and their concerns taken into account. If members subsequently feel alienated or misused in spite of attempts at inclusiveness, their disappointment and resentment are magnified (see Riger 1984).

I am not suggesting that participatory democracy is the main barrier to building diverse feminist organizations, only that its principles have not yet provided a manageable way to overcome other barriers to the participation of women of color and working-class women. As Sirianni (1993b, 308) concludes, "A feminist theory of participation is confronted with its own set of perhaps irreducible paradoxes and permanent tensions."

RECOGNIZING VOICE, CULTIVATING LOYALTY, AND PREVENTING EXIT

In sum, a solution to the dilemma of predominantly white feminist organizations' actual membership being far less diverse than their ideal constituencies remains elusive. Democratic theory does not provide much guidance for dealing with this problem, since theorists typically either take the membership of a polity as a given and concern themselves with how best to represent those members or assume that inclusion is eagerly sought (for example, see Dahl 1990 [1970]; Walzer 1983). The situation here is that the polity wants to include people who do not choose to join. Like political parties and firms, feminist organizations and other social movement organizations must concern themselves with *attracting* participants and then dissuading them from leaving.

Albert Hirschman's ideas (1970, 1993) about voice, exit, and loyalty are helpful here. He analyzes voice and exit as two mechanisms that can allow organizations to recover from problems. When members voice their dissatisfactions, the leadership is given an opportunity to mend its ways and make changes that will satisfy these constituents. If voice is not available or proves unsuccessful, members can choose to leave the organization, and the pattern of exit provides the impetus and necessity for the leadership to make changes to prevent organizational disaster. Why haven't these mechanisms worked to overcome whatever problems have kept many feminist organizations from realizing their aspirations?

One immediate problem, of course, is that exit is available only to those who are already participants, and voice is most effective for them, too. The absence of desired members is the difficulty here, and efforts by privileged women to figure out for themselves what the concerns and priorities of women unlike themselves are have been subjected to scathing criticism, as have earnest requests for less privileged women to provide education to help others overcome racism or ignorance (Anzaldúa 1990, cited in Jones 1993, 227; McKay 1993; Spelman 1988; Yamada 1981).

However, women other than white, middle-class ones are present in many predominantly white organizations, sometimes even in leadership positions. They have made vigorous efforts to exercise voice, yet, for a variety of reasons, organizations have

frequently been unable to respond well enough to their dissatisfactions to keep them from leaving (see Mansbridge and Yeatman 1991, 6). The choice to exit, rather than to stay and continue
to try to change the faulty organization, is eased by the existence
of alternative organizations that can contribute to the empowerment of women of color and working-class women. In fact, feminists would be hard-pressed to dispute the legitimacy of the
choice to work in an organization of women from one's own
community or in a mixed-gender group (provided that one struggles with sexism there). It is possible that lesbians proved more
successful in forcing changes in the feminist agenda than heterosexual women of color and working-class women have because,
at least until the development of broad-based queer politics, the
choice to exit was less attractive than voice because of the paucity
of other bases for political action.

If exit can be a signal that prompts positive organizational
change under some circumstances, unfortunately that is not typically the case here. Despite recognition of the problems of exclusivity, predominantly white organizations are not likely to solve
those problems by themselves. Exit can promote recovery only
when the organization is able to figure out how to make the necessary changes and has the means to make them. In some situations, however, exit leads to further deterioration (see Hirschman
1970, 99–104), unless voice can be effectively exercised from outside the organization. In the case of feminist organizations, the
exit (or failure to join) of important constituents diminishes the
possibilities that predominantly white organizations will be able to
redefine their structures and agendas so as to attract a diverse
membership.

STRATEGIES FOR THE FUTURE

The foregoing, rather depressing discussion suggests that, while
women should continue trying to diversify predominantly white
feminist organizations, they will need to pursue other routes to
building a more diverse women's movement. Many writers have
suggested that coalitions and alliances are the most promising avenues for working toward unity, while allowing diversity to flour-

ish (Albrecht and Brewer 1990; Alperin 1990; Collins 1990; Fraser and Nicolson 1990; Joseph and Lewis 1981; Kaye/Kantrowitz 1986; Reagon 1983). Matthews (1989) gives a fairly encouraging example of the kind of autonomous, but interacting, organizations that are commonly recommended. Coalitions and alliances present us with new problems of representation, accountability, and leadership, however. Creating forms of participatory democracy that cross organizational boundaries is one challenge facing feminists.

Unity among diverse women, it is clear, cannot be an a priori basis for organization; it will have to be a hard-won accomplishment. In the meantime, predominantly white, middle-class feminist organizations are left with a problem of legitimacy. On whose behalf do they speak and act? The challenge remains to develop a realistic political practice that recognizes the limits to the vision and resources of any particular grouping of women, while still encouraging them to try to transcend those limits (for example, see Hansen 1990 [1986]).

I thank Gloria Gadsden, Kali Gross, Jane Mansbridge, Carol Mueller, and Carmen Sirianni for their advice and suggestions. A somewhat different version of this paper appears in *Identity Politics in the Women's Movement,* edited by Barbara Ryan (New York: New York University Press, 2001). An earlier version was presented at the thematic session "Women's Movements and Participatory Democracy," American Sociological Association annual meeting, Los Angeles (1994).

REFERENCES

Albrecht, Lisa, and Rose M. Brewer. 1990. "Bridges of Power: Women's Multicultural Alliances." In *Bridges of Power: Women's Multicultural Alliances,* edited by Lisa Albrecht and Rose M. Brewer. Philadelphia: New Society Publishers, in cooperation with the National Women's Studies Association.

Alperin, Davida J. 1990. "Social Diversity and the Necessity of Alliances: A Developing Feminist Perspective." In *Bridges of Power: Women's Multicultural Alliances,* edited by Lisa Albrecht and Rose M. Brewer.

Philadelphia: New Society Publishers, in cooperation with the National Women's Studies Association.

Anzaldúa, Gloria. 1990. *"En Rapport,* in Opposition: *Cobrando Cuentas a las Nuestras."* In *Making Face, Making Soul: Hacienda Caras, Creative and Critical Perspectives by Women,* edited by Gloria Anzaldúa. San Francisco: Aunt Lute Foundation Books.

Buechler, Steven M. 1990. *Women's Movements in the United States: Woman Suffrage, Equal Rights, and Beyond.* New Brunswick, N.J.: Rutgers University Press.

Chow, Esther Ngan-Ling. 1984. "The Development of Feminist Consciousness among Asian American Women." *Gender and Society* 1(3): 284–99.

Christensen, Kimberly. 1997. "With Whom Do You Believe Your Lot Is Cast? White Feminists and Racism." *Signs* 22(3): 617–48.

Collins, Patricia Hill. 1990. *Black Feminist Thought: Knowledge, Consciousness, and the Politics of Empowerment.* Boston: Unwin Hyman.

Combahee River Collective. 1979. "A Black Feminist Statement." In *Capitalist Patriarchy and the Case for Socialist Feminism,* edited by Zillah Eisenstein. New York: Monthly Review Press.

Dahl, Robert A. 1990 [1970]. *After the Revolution? Authority in a Good Society,* rev. ed. New Haven, Conn.: Yale University Press.

Daly, Mary. 1978. *Gyn/Ecology: The Metaethics of Radical Feminism.* Boston: Beacon Press.

Davenport, Doris. 1981. "The Pathology of Racism: A Conversation with Third World Wimmin." In *This Bridge Called My Back: Writings by Radical Women of Color,* edited by Cherrie Moraga and Gloria Anzaldúa. Watertown, Mass.: Persephone Press.

Davis, Angela. 1990a [1984]. "Facing Our Common Foe: Women and the Struggle against Racism." In *Women, Culture, and Politics.* New York: Vintage Books.

———. 1990b [1988]. "Let Us All Rise Together: Radical Perspectives on Empowerment for Afro-American Women." In *Women, Culture, and Politics.* New York: Vintage Books.

Dill, Bonnie T. 1983. "Race, Class, and Gender: Prospects for an All-Inclusive Sisterhood." *Feminist Studies* 9(1): 131–50.

Echols, Alice. 1989. *Daring to Be Bad: Radical Feminism in America, 1967–1975.* Minneapolis: University of Minnesota Press.

Ferree, Myra Marx, and Beth Hess. 1985. *Controversy and Coalition: The New Feminist Movement.* Boston: Hall/Twayne.

Flax, Jane. 1983. "Political Philosophy and the Patriarchal Unconscious: A Psychoanalytic Perspective on Epistemology and Metaphysics." In *Discovering Reality: Feminist Perspectives on Epistemology, Meta-*

physics, Methodology, and Philosophy of Science, edited by Sandra Harding and Merrill B. Hintikka. Dordrecht, the Netherlands: D. Reidel.

————. 1987. "Postmodernism and Gender Relations in Feminist Theory." *Signs* 12(4): 621–43.

Fraser, Nancy, and Linda Nicholson. 1990. "Social Criticism without Philosophy: An Encounter between Feminism and Postmodernism." In *Feminism/Postmodernism,* edited by Linda Nicolson. New York: Routledge.

Friedan, Betty. 1963. *The Feminine Mystique.* New York: Dell.

García, Alma. 1989. "The Development of Chicana Feminist Discourse, 1970–1980." *Gender and Society* 3(2): 217–38.

Giddings, Paula. 1984. *When and Where I Enter.* New York: Morrow.

Gilligan, Carol. 1982. *In a Different Voice.* Cambridge, Mass.: Harvard University Press.

Hansen, Karen V. 1990 [1986]. "Women's Unions and the Search for Political Identity." In *Women, Class, and the Feminist Imagination,* edited by Karen V. Hansen and Ilene J. Philipson. Philadelphia: Temple University Press.

Harding, Sandra, 1987. "Introduction: Is There a Feminist Method?" In *Feminism and Methodology,* edited by Sandra Harding. Bloomington: Indiana University Press.

————. 1991. *Whose Science? Whose Knowledge? Thinking from Women's Lives.* Ithaca, N.Y.: Cornell University Press.

Hartsock, Nancy C. M. 1987 [1983]. "The Feminist Standpoint: Developing the Ground for a Specifically Feminist Historical Materialism." In *Feminism and Methodology,* edited by Sandra Harding. Bloomington: Indiana University Press.

Hawkesworth, Mary E. 1989. "Knowers, Knowing, Known: Feminist Theory and Claims of Truth." *Signs* 14(3): 533–57.

Hekman, Susan. 1990. *Gender and Knowledge: Elements of a Postmodern Feminism.* Boston: Northeastern University Press.

Hirschman, Albert O. 1970. *Exit, Voice, and Loyalty.* Cambridge, Mass.: Harvard University Press.

————. 1993. "Exit, Voice, and the Fate of the German Democratic Republic: An Essay in Conceptual History." *World Politics* 45(2): 173–202.

hooks, bell. 1981. *Ain't I a Woman? Black Women and Feminism.* Boston: South End Press.

————. 1984. *Feminist Theory: From Margin to Center.* Boston: South End Press.

Jaggar, Alison M. 1983. *Feminist Politics and Human Nature.* Totowa, N.J.: Rowman and Allanheld.

Jones, Kathleen. 1993. *Compassionate Authority: Democracy and the Representation of Women*. New York: Routledge.

Joseph, Gloria, and Jill Lewis. 1981. *Common Differences: Conflicts in Black and White Feminism*. Garden City, N.Y.: Doubleday.

Kaye-Kantrowitz, Melanie. 1986. "To Be a Radical Jew in the Late 20th Century." In *The Tribe of Dina: A Jewish Women's Anthology*, edited by Melanie Kaye/Kantrowitz and Irena Klepfisz. Montpelier, Vt.: Sinister Wisdom Books.

King, Deborah H. 1988. "Multiple Jeopardy, Multiple Consciousness: The Context of a Black Feminist Ideology." *Signs* 14(1): 42–72.

Leidner, Robin. 1991. "Stretching the Boundaries of Liberalism: Democratic Innovation in a Feminist Organization." *Signs* 16(2): 263–89.

———. 1993. "Constituency, Accountability, and Deliberation: Democratic Innovation in a Feminist Organization." *NWSA Journal* 5(1): 263–89.

Longino, Helen G. 1993. "Feminist Standpoint Theory and the Problems of Knowledge." *Signs* 19(1): 201–12.

Lorde, Audre. 1984. *Sister Outsider*. Trumansburg, N.H.: Crossing Press.

Mansbridge, Jane. 1973. "Time, Emotion, and Inequality: Three Problems of Participatory Groups." *Journal of Applied Behavioral Science* 9: 351–68.

———. 1980. *Beyond Adversary Democracy*. Chicago: University of Chicago Press.

———. 1986. *Why We Lost the ERA*. Chicago: University of Chicago Press.

Mansbridge, Jane, and Gayle Yeatman. 1991. "Becoming a Feminist: African-American and White Experiences." Paper presented at the annual meeting of the Midwest Sociological Association. Des Moines, Iowa.

Matthews, Nancy. 1989. "Surmounting a Legacy: The Expansion of Racial Diversity in a Local Anti-Rape Movement." *Gender and Society* 3(4): 518–32.

McKay, Nellie Y. 1993. "Acknowledging Differences: Can Women Find Unity through Diversity?" In *Theorizing Black Feminisms: The Visionary Pragmatism of Black Women*, edited by Stanlie M. James and Abena P. A. Busia. London: Routledge.

Moraga, Cherrie, and Gloria Anzaldúa, eds. 1981. *This Bridge Called My Back: Writings by Radical Women of Color*. Watertown, Mass.: Persephone Press.

Phillips, Anne. 1993. *Democracy and Difference*. University Park: Pennsylvania State University Press.

Ramazanoglu, Caroline. 1989. *Feminism and the Contradictions of Oppression*. London: Routledge.

Reagon, Bernice Johnson. 1983. "Coalition Politics: Turning the Century." In *Home Girls—A Black Feminist Anthology,* edited by Barbara Smith. New York: Kitchen Table Press.

Riger, Stephanie. 1984. "Vehicles for Empowerment: The Case of Feminist Movement Organizations." In *Studies in Empowerment: Steps Toward Understanding and Action,* edited by Julian Rappaport, Caroline Swift, and Robert Hess. New York: Haworth Press.

Rothschild, Joyce, and J. Allen Whitt. 1986. *The Cooperative Workplace: Potentials and Dilemmas of Organizational Democracy and Participation.* Cambridge: Cambridge University Press.

Ryan, Barbara. 1992. *Feminism and the Women's Movement: Dynamics of Change in Social Movement Ideology and Activism.* New York: Routledge.

Scott, Ellen K. 1998. "Creating Partnerships for Change: Alliances and Betrayals in the Racial Politics of Two Feminist Organizations." *Gender and Society* 12(4): 400–23.

Sirianni, Carmen. 1993a. "Feminist Pluralism and Democratic Learning: The Politics of Citizenship in the National Women's Studies Association." *NWSA Journal* 5(3): 367–84.

———. 1993b. "Learning Pluralism: Democracy and Diversity in Feminist Organizations." In *Nomos XXXV: Democratic Community,* edited by John Chapman and Ian Shapiro. New York: New York University Press.

Smith, Barbara. 1983. "Introduction." In *Home Girls—A Black Feminist Anthology,* edited by Barbara Smith. New York: Kitchen Table Press.

Smith, Dorothy. 1987. *The Everyday World as Problematic.* Boston: Northeastern University Press.

Spelman, Elizabeth V. 1988. *Inessential Woman: Problems of Exclusion in Feminist Thought.* Boston: Beacon Press.

Stanley, Liz, and Sue Wise. 1990. "Method, Methodology, and Epistemology in Feminist Research Processes." In *Feminist Praxis: Research, Theory, and Epistemology in Feminist Sociology,* edited by Liz Stanley. London: Routledge.

Walker, Alice. 1983. *In Search of Our Mother's Gardens.* New York: Harcourt Brace Jovanovich.

Wallace, Michelle. 1990. "A Black Feminist's Search for Sisterhood." In *Invisibility Blues: From Pop to Theory.* New York: Verso.

Walzer, Michael. 1983. *Spheres of Justice: A Defense of Pluralism and Equality.* New York: Basic Books.

Weedon, Chris. 1987. *Feminist Practice and Poststructuralist Theory.* Oxford: Basil Blackwell.

Yamada, Mitsuye. 1981. "Asian Pacific American Women and Feminism."

In *This Bridge Called My Back: Writings by Radical Women of Color,* edited by Cherrie Moraga and Gloria Anzaldúa. Watertown, Mass.: Persephone Press.

Young, Iris. 1989. "Polity and Group Difference: A Critique of the Ideal of Universal Citizenship." *Ethics* 99(2): 250–74.

— Chapter 5 —

Race, Stratification, and Group-Based Rights

Ivar Berg

I N A RECENT review, Massey and Denton (1998) provide an ecological analysis of modern stratification research in the late
post–World War II era. They point out that recent demographic
and ethnographic studies of neighborhood effects afford us coherent and persuasive explanations for much of the residual variance
reported in studies of status attainment. Status attainment studies
blossomed in the fertile soil plowed by computer-assisted scholars
performing intergenerational, large-sample studies of the income
and socioeconomic status effects of cultural exposures and earnings experience of Americans whose opportunities are shaped by
the educational and other backgrounds of their families' senior
members.

Although Massey and Denton's points are well taken, use of
these two very different approaches *still* leaves us with much unex-
plained variance. One can hardly blame the losers for seeking to
gain group-based rights. The allocation of group-based rights, al-
legedly novel in the age of our now-waning commitment to affirmative action, cannot be readily linked statistically to the residential
and family background forces affecting new-age claimants to group-
based rights. They can, however, be considered in historical-institu-
tional terms, which clarifies the forces affecting haves and have nots
better than studies of human ecology and status attainment alone.

My analysis focuses on the vague but palpable institutional
forces, triggered over long periods of time by legislators and

115

courts, that have grouped people into classes or taxonomic categories that benefit greatly (or lose significantly) as a result of their prospects for reaping (or failing to reap) socioeconomic gains. Behind the circumstances of large numbers of status attainers, and behind both the sordid ghettos and gilded suburbs in which Americans of a given generation grow up, are constitutional and other legal-institutional developments that shape the prospects of different subsets of the population for gaining or being denied rights, privileges, and immunities.

A number of these formidable sorting and labeling forces have left legacies over multiple generations. Some of our forebears have broken out of such systems (such as the great-grandchild of slaves who became a Massachusetts senator or the son in a large, impoverished family who founded Standard Oil); many more will suffer (or enjoy) intergenerational echoes of placements accorded long ago to whole sociolegal categories.

The potential accumulations of human and social capital— terms that offend the humanist's sensibilities—of both individuals and aggregates of individuals are clearly influenced by standard variables of neighborhood and status attainment. Both of these, in turn, are touched heavily by public policies, especially by interventions both against and on behalf of grouped people. A large number of these interventions have had cumulative effects on most of us (and our kin) since 1789. A great many of us, at any given juncture, have been able to join in (or have been excluded from) "coverages" extended by Congress, which determines the list of prospective groups eligible for public endowments, licenses, access, or services; by the executive branch, via executive orders or other administrative laws and regulations; and by the courts, in what amount to the income and opportunity-distributing initiatives that affect the status, class location, and power-wielding capacity of people within differentially stratified subsets of present-day American society. Indeed, the inherited costs and benefits of numerous public initiatives visited on us via our forebears— and on respective associations such as tribal nations, age cohorts, genders, and other aggregations—figure prominently in shaping the odds that we ultimately will enjoy monopolies and suffrage rights, live in poor ghettos, be protected by tariffs or draft defer-ments, attend college, or be red-lined by the judgments of bankers and underwriters about risks.

Consider that immigration quotas favoring Scandinavians in the 1920s ultimately afforded me (and twenty-three other bilingual classmates out of my sixth-grade class of twenty-five in New York City) far more human capital dividends than were accorded to African Americans who moved to northern states from 1925 to 1939. Congress and the Immigration and Naturalization Service (INS) assured me, a Norwegian American, a 1920s version of Head Start through the favorable "institutional labeling" that New York teachers accorded my ethnic group. Ethnic blood lines were differentially and strictly ordered by the INS and thus were accorded differential access to immigration visas in an unequivocal ordering.

The experiences of today's populations in ghettos and suburbs, today's losers and winners, today's dropouts and Phi Beta Kappas come in large measure from groups that, earlier, were quite differentially favored. Some fell from grace in the New World, while others overcame their consignments and improved their lot. Of critical significance is the fact that early consignments allocated rights to many of today's haves and denials to our have nots. To the extent that critics of the status attainment model are correct about the relative significance of family background, they would be even more on target if they could factor in the legal status of forebears who gained, directly or derivatively, from group-based rights. If this were possible, they would indeed be able to account for a larger percentage of the variance in the status attainment process.

THE HISTORICAL LEGACY OF GROUP-BASED RIGHTS

Space does not permit a full treatment of the long-term process of "institutional labeling" and its correlates. Indeed, I focus only on two strategic examples of this process: the very long-term group rights of "corporate persons" and the widely questioned rights (starting in the late 1960s) of "protected groups" as defined by our affirmative action laws. Affirmative action is only the most recent of many historical efforts to enhance the claims of certain individuals-as-group-members in an effort to enhance their opportunities for mobility or other occupational benefits in our stratification system. A number of observers of the American corporation, a key unit in my discussion, have preceded me on this trail. Among modern social scientists, only Coleman (1982) and Patterson (1997) have offered longer or shorter monographic treatments, respectively, of the American corporation as a powerhouse of group rights (although Thurman Arnold did so in his 1937 classic, *The Folklore of Capitalism*).

The criticism of affirmative action that is grounded in misgivings about group rights gainsays the fact that most of our constitution's provisions apply, quite specifically and explicitly, to both natural and corporate persons—the latter being a legally worthy persona ficta, a distinction consistently ignored in debates over group versus individual rights, although it enjoys legal-historical blessings from the fifteenth century.

The omission is a serious one in sociological terms because it leads to a misspecification of the terms of debate. The fact that affirmative action appears to be on its last legs affords us an opportunity to consider an issue that should be high on the list of persons who study the sociology of knowledge, those specialists who could likely help us to understand why some well-established and, in many ways, productive ideas are intellectual orphans. Groups, after all, are basic units of study in social science, and social scientists increasingly honor their obligations to attend to institutional-historical forces.

The proponents of affirmative action are determined to undo injustices to persons who suffer from discrimination entirely or largely because they belong to disfavored groups, not because they are beyond merit's pale. Corporate persons, in contrast, are accorded large clusters of rights because legal interpretations by the courts group owners (groups of natural persons) collectively into legal entities—into persons—whatever their merits (or demerits).

From the earliest days of the republic, and consistent with a main theme of the Enlightenment, property owners have been conceived as the principal agents to be protected by the public laws protecting liberty. How better to protect property owners, given the logical identity established between liberty and property ownership, than to make large aggregates of owners into unfettered persons? I am not advancing a case either for or against affirmative action per se. I am only suggesting, very emphatically, that we embarked consciously and long ago on efforts to build group rights into the fabric of our constitutional-legal order, such that we both accorded and denied rights to groups even before our founding fathers submitted the constitution to the states for ratification. Group-based rights have been honored by our legal foundations in natural law and in common law and not less so by our system of constitutional law. Debates about the legitimacy of group-based rights, legitimacy in the formal Weberian sense, should inform both sides of the discussion, and antagonists ought to move on to other issues regarding affirmative action.

To either ignore or compartmentalize the facts about group rights in our history is to ignore the prospects for a full sociological analysis of a large segment of race relations and an equivalently large number of factors pertaining to racial components of our stratification system. A sociological discussion about group rights would be better directed to how *all* group rights (and what may logically be called group wrongs) are granted or denied, how they are distributed, and their intrinsic pros and cons. The allocation of rights (and wrongs) is immensely consequential for the distribution of advantages and disadvantages among subsets of the population, and group assignments figure prominently in the distribution of opportunities, subsidies, immunities, vulnerabilities, "shelters," incentives, and penalties. Group assignments, once again, include definitions of both the worthiness (merit) and the unworthiness (lack of merit) of natural persons.

Instead scholars consistently act and write as if protected group rights were problematically novel and unique and thus specifically vulnerable to and highly deserving of distaste or even contempt. The most telling fact is that *aggregates* of natural persons who own a stake in American corporations became *single, individual persons* under the law at a very early date. Until 1842 (in *Commonwealth v. Hunt*) a natural person who joined a union could be charged with the crime of conspiracy against the corporate person, whose property rights were held to be protected under the constitution. Corporations, representing property, benefited legitimately from group rights; unions, representing natural persons with grievances against corporate persons, lost out in the quest for group rights and, for many years thereafter, could be enjoined from taking disruptive actions against property owners. Although the conspiracy doctrine died in 1842, corporate persons were protected against human *actions* by the Sherman Anti-Trust Act, a circumstance that was tamed a bit by the Clayton Act of 1914, which held that workers were no longer commodities, in the terms of antitrust laws, over which union leaders could be conceived as the monopolistic owner-sellers. The obligation of employers to bargain with unions in good faith, however, was not confirmed until 1936, in the National Labor Relations Act, and the fines for unfair labor practices were so low that many firms (General Electric and, most scandalously, J. P. Stevens as depicted in the film *Norma Rae*) simply broke the laws with impunity. They still do.

The social construction of groups as persons under the law (and hence as legally deserving *or* undeserving members of corporate and noncorporate entities) is achieved through more or less arbitrary and adventitious public policies, of which there are many examples. Certain age qualifications and earnings histories, for example, make one an eligible payee for Social Security and Medicare benefits, although the character of aging has shifted dramatically; not many of us who were in our early twenties in 1950 thought there would be a market for anything like Viagra among septuagenarians. The study of cohort effects recognizes that, at all ages, Americans are younger, perhaps even in their sexuality, than their cohorts of 1910, 1920, 1930, and so on. A variety of clubs in professional sports (including those owned by one person) are accorded freedom from antitrust coverage because they are games, not businesses, and because they are putatively local, do not engage in interstate commerce, and protect their group immunity by dedicated support for congressional candidates.

Likewise, women and others were long denied voting rights in accordance with constitutional provisions established by our founders in favor of property-owning white males. More recently, college students with a "B" or better average were awarded legal status under selective service regulations that exempted them from the draft during our war with China and North Korea in 1950 to 1954 and during the Vietnam War in 1960 to 1975, even as World War II veterans (after considerable controversy) were awarded multiple benefits by the G.I. Bill of Rights.

Many more examples of group rights may be cited. Taxpayers with capital gains are graced with lower tax rates than those levied on earned incomes, as an incentive for investing in job-producing economic ventures. Homeowners may deduct interest payments on their mortgages from their income tax obligations. Homeowners on the nation's coastal waters, united and identified by nothing other than their interest in pretty but vulnerable locations, are entitled to low (that is, subsidized) federal insurance rates on structures endlessly and relentlessly exposed to the destruction of storm-driven tides. Many vetted rights—to practice law or medicine, to engage in hairdressing, to apply chemistry, to teach, to drive a car, or to operate a taxi—are likewise granted by public agencies to all who meet specified standards, some of them (like hairdressers and teachers) set by the practitioners themselves. However, these arrangements are ignored in decisions regarding the rights of protected groups in occupational contexts.

Today's groups considered to be protected under affirmative action have neither lately nor uniquely sought or won valuable considerations from the state. Millions of Americans enjoy protection from taxes, markets, and competition by virtue of one or another law. Generally, the beneficiaries do not know each other, any more than do members of protected groups defined under affirmative action. Those who are in favored occupations, who earn high incomes, and who enjoy public subsidies are typically represented and served by associations; just as the American Association of Retired Persons (AARP) strives to serve Americans over fifty, so the National Association for the Advancement of Colored People (NAACP) represents self-identified African Americans. It has been argued that rights have not, historically, been accorded by "blood," that is, by genetically inherited physical or biological attributes. However, the fact that the long-standing second-class citizenship of minorities is often referred to as an ascribed status, given to them by observers, is evidence that sociologists are no more blind to socially constructed imputations than were the enthusiasts who imposed Jim Crow's logics on southern blacks until 1964. Wealthy Americans, meanwhile, will no doubt try, again, to achieve even lower taxes on the inheritances left to sons and daughters who they quite understandably feel should be allowed to acquire family property without tax and other "discriminatory" encumbrances.

More apposite to the blood argument of affirmative action critics is the case that a majority of our founders reserved rights for blood-lined *whites*, coldly denying personhood to blood-lined slaves, as chattel or property, before their emancipation by a bloody Civil War. The Fugitive Slave Law, for example, made all persons aiding or abetting escaped slaves vulnerable to criminal violations of property rights; slave states earned extra representation in the House of Representatives for their "nonpersons" at the rate of three-fifths of a white representative for each black slave in 1789.

To be sure, we have denied as often as accorded rights by blood. Historically, grouped persons were the targets of prejudicial and bigoted malefactors of such structures. It is not logical and reasonable to argue, now, that some rights ought not be applied to persons as group members, while simultaneously denying rights to persons by socially constructing them as undeserving or suspicious (as when individual native-born Japanese American citizens on the west coast were sequestered in internment camps from 1942 to 1944).

Thus collections of persons have regularly and systematically been accorded or denied rights in the United States. In the present context, however, the most important grouped rights are those accorded to American corporations by treating them informally, at first, and formally, after 1819, as artificial persons or persona ficta. Corporations—conceived as aggregates of property owners and stockholders—were transmogrified into corporate persons, whose rights, privileges, immunities, and legal remedies came to match, in almost every respect, those the constitution granted to natural persons (twenty-two times in 1789 and in subsequent amendments). Whereas persona ficta was once a term of art, a rhetorical image, a useful metaphor, a compendious notion, after 1948 it became fully defined as a legal-technical term in the U.S. Code.

This transmogrification was highly inventive. In the case of minority rights and corporate rights, we are speaking not of a pair of competing natural persons, but of rights accorded to a fiction and rights claimed and sought by natural persons. It was, in the truest sense, an illustration of Ogburn's career-long interests in "social technology" as an invaluable element in the founding and growth of economic enterprises that we personalized corporations. Not only did corporate owners enjoy limited liabilities and perpetual organizational lives (yielding important incentives to save, invest, and generate more productive social structures), but they also came to enjoy the same benefits of protection against centralized political power as liberties guaranteed to natural persons by the Constitution, Bill of Rights, and successive amendments. It is not necessary to gainsay the rights of corporate persons when they may indeed have innumerable social returns as well as social costs. The point, in fairness, is that we should recognize both the costs and benefits attaching to *any* and all allocations of rights. I return to these benefits after a brief historical review of rights imputed to protected groups.

NATURAL RIGHTS AND THE ENLIGHTENMENT

The notion of the persona ficta first received attention in the work of writers on "natural rights" during the Middle Ages, a body of work that is part of our institutional legacy and on which embellishments were added by philosophers of the French and especially English Enlightenment. Locke, in particular, offered a detailed historical treatment of these intellectual movements with special reference to the concept of corporate personhood.

The basics of corporate personhood were adumbrated initially by natural law scholars who sought to derive authority for the Church and its substrata—its universities in particular—from "the rights of man" and to convey these rights to the larger body of Church leaders. This conveyance was referenced by later students of natural law under the widely popular rubric of concession theory. Universities, in need of governance, came next, followed by guilds. In all three instances, the socius was in need of the status of a corporate person, guided by a leader who retained authority to carry out socially needed duties in a way that later could be vetted by the Church, by princes and kings, and, in our own case, by our colonies and the states (Manent 1998).

Enlightenment writers were persistently concerned with the

rights of property holders. Indeed, they carefully and specifically identified freedom with property rights and the latter with natural law. Locke's position on the subject was very clear and greatly influenced our founders' favorable disposition toward organizations that were designed to help create value or wealth, the benefits from which they assumed would diffuse to larger communities. The concept of trickle-down economics, or what many liberal economists call "horse and sparrow economics," thus has a long and fairly glorious intellectual history. Alexander Hamilton (1791) was the one among our founders who wrote most carefully on the need of a democratic republic, for its stability, to have solid economic foundations.

Royal charters also were accorded to trading companies, endowing them with powers of governance. Indeed, most of our original colonial governments (and, later, our state governments) derived their authority, and indeed their initial *legitimacy*, directly from such corporate enterprises. The process of extending personhood was an evolutionary one guided by men of "right reason" with commitments to achieve reasonable ends.

In the United States, capitalist organizations (with absolutely no opprobrium implied by the term) were blessed early-on with substantial group-based rights, as urged and effected by Alexander Hamilton. His tract, *On Manufactures* (1791), inspired the very first substantive act of the new federal Congress: the Tariff Act of July 4, 1789, which effectively protected northern men of business (a nominal, but potent, group) at the expense of consumers and southern planters. The act embodied the concession theory of government and Locke's investment in the liberty of men of property to advance society's interests in political stability and thus in economic welfare.

The regional (and occupational) violence done to distributive justice by this act became a consequential grievance that was, in the late 1850s, attached to the South's opposition to the North's abolitionist movement. The attack on Fort Sumter, the triggering event of a bloody Civil War, was actually an attack on the tax collectors housed there under "Buchanan's Tariff," a tax that became effective only during Abraham Lincoln's early months in the White House. Put simply, pure price competition was rejected—that is, set aside (like jobs and contracts are set aside today under affirmative action)—in favor of infant industries. The federal guarantee of the face value of bonds, right after the tariff act, was likewise a set-aside for the speculators-cum-investors of the North at the expense of consumers and planters of the South. In return for the assumption of debt by the new central government, the national capital was relocated from Philadelphia to the "banks of the Potomac," close to Madison and Jefferson, to help them sell the assumption of debt to Virginia's taxpayers. Hamilton conceived of the idea, and the scion of the Philadelphia elite, Joseph Biddle, hosted the party at the City Tavern where the offer was made and accepted.

Given the antagonisms of so many American intellectuals toward "business" in the nineteenth century and afterward, it is ironic that the claims of corporate owners and directors (based on corporate personhood) were staked out by legal victories of the trustees of the University of Virginia, before the Revolution, and of Dartmouth College, in 1819. The juridical holdings in these two cases (involving the right to enter into enforceable contracts) were pronounced by the same person, John Marshall, first as a Virginia lawyer in the 1780s and later as chief justice of the Supreme Court. In the latter case, argued by Dartmouth alumnus Daniel Webster in 1819, the chief justice elevated the rights of natural persons, guaranteed in the constitution, in generic terms, to the trustees of Dartmouth as a *persona ficta* to enter into binding and enforceable contracts.

The precept quickly fed a stream of decisions that extended the legal rights of natural persons to their corporate "kin." Indeed, in 1948, Congress added Title I to Volume I of the United States code; thereafter the term "person," appearing in our laws, applied to natural persons, corporations, associations, and firms, unless the context of a given law specifically indicated otherwise. The claim, by critics of affirmative action, that group-based rights initiatives gratuitously and wrongly give *novel* rights to protected group members is not supported by historical fact.

Critics of affirmative action "compartmentalize" corporate *persona ficta* from other groups with rights by blessing (sensibly so) these agencies while damning by simply dismissing the member claims of affirmative action's protected groups. I use the word compartmentalize advisedly. One way to reduce the cognitive dissidence inherent in the logics of two valued group-based rights is to compartmentalize them. F. Scott Fitzgerald observed in *The Crack-up* (1936)—and I would agree—that we are an intelligent people because "the test of a first rate intelligence is the ability to hold two opposed ideas at the same time and still retain the ability to function."

Thoughtful students of stratification ought not to consider denying—or even "compartmentalizing"—the effects of according the same rights to natural and corporate persons, as the latter often involve huge aggregates of investors who count among their assets proprietary plants and equipment, patents, good will, cash, and organizational investments in corporate stocks and bonds, physical property, and public allowances such as trading licenses. These persona ficta earn public subsidies and gain access to hundreds of millions of acres of real property (through rights of way, which in the case of railroads, earned them twenty miles of developable land on either side of their tracks) and, for longer or shorter periods, dominant product market shares.

Even allowing that price competition has come, more and more, to discipline our once heavily oligopolized industries, we cannot lightly dismiss the enormous capacities of the Fortune 500's chief executive officers (CEOs) to relocate plants, to merge, to "offshore" and "outsource" jobs, to shut down plants, or to move to Thailand or Malaysia. The reciprocal of these rights are the damages thereby done, quite lawfully (and, perhaps in the long run, beneficially) to communities and employees. Indeed, the have nots among America's social strata include not a few "rightless" bystanders of the sometimes victimizing actions of corporate persons. The socioeconomic status of these bystanders can suffer whether they live in Scarsdale or Harlem, although the pains are not equally shared when, as Andrew Hacker (1965) once described, corporations in American society are "elephants dancing among the chickens." We may, some of us, dismiss the correlates and consequences of CEOs' decisionmaking options, but they may not be so lightly gainsaid by victims. And we may curse these persona ficta and deplore their deeds, but Americans do not, in *any* significant numbers, suggest that they do not have the right to make decisions they deem to be appropriate.

One may compartmentalize in polite discourse, of course, but such discourses in our deconstructed world do not effectively gainsay inequalities in the income allocated to labor and capital, whether or not one approves of collective bargaining and whether or not one approves of income inequalities. Indeed, many of us feel obliged to defend such inequalities. If so, the defense would be the same as the ways in which one may defend the practice of red-lining minorities into residential segregation or producing, as Massey and Denton (1996) have called it, "American Apartheid." Such defenses, attractive to many, simply do not come to grips with what others might identify as problematical justice, at the very least. Red-lined ghettos are produced, at bottom, not by multitudes of bigoted landlords and home sellers but by persona ficta with protected rights that sell (or deny) mortgages to developers and home buyers. The local hardware merchants of other times, bankrupted by a regional Home Depot store, have their rights, too, but Home Depot's rights are evidently more equal.

GROUP RIGHTS AND INDIVIDUAL MERIT

America's deployment of group rights is shot through with ironies involving racial and similar inequalities that dwarf those observed in reviews of the sometimes very serious misgivings of affirmative action's critics about these rights (see Skrentny 1996). Consider that Congress passed the fourteenth amendment—the equal rights amendment—to assist African Americans, predominantly ex-slaves, in gaining equality before the law. By the mid-twentieth century, however, corporations were citing this amendment in their unremitting, successful campaigns to undo state laws designed to protect workers (famously in 1905 in *Lochner v. New York*), consumers (famously in the 1873 slaughter house cases), as well as women and children. In *Lochner*, the Supreme Court's majority granted employers the right to exact sixty-hour work weeks from putatively complaisant workers who, the court's majority stated, were "equally free" to reject such terms of employment. Democracy, in these terms, meant little more than that we would have "equal sharing of miseries," as Winston Churchill so deftly put it at a White House Luncheon (June 26, 1954).

The score in the struggle between corporations and would-be

"progressive" states, acting to protect workers, on one side, and natural persons, on the other, is well over four hundred to one in favor of corporations' claims to protection under the fourteenth amendment (Mason and Garvey 1964). Champions of unfettered property rights continue, to this day, to damn Oliver Wendell Holmes's minority opinion, in *Lochner*, in which he offered the judgment that the Supreme Court's majority (by doing what conservative critics now damn as activism) elevated Spencer's *Social Dynamics* and Yale sociologist Charles Sumner's version of the economic doctrine of laissez-faire into law (Hofstadter 1944). Younger readers may not hear much about Spencer these days, nor about Sumner, but there was no doubt in the minds of these once-renowned sociologists about the legitimacy of corporate persons' rights and the marginal—indeed deplorable—claims of far too many natural persons against them. As Sumner put it, "Let it be understood that we cannot go outside of the alternative: liberty, inequality, survival of the fittest; not liberty, equality, survival of the unfittest. The former carries society forward and favors all its members; the latter carries society downwards and favors all its worst members" (Hofstadter 1944, 51). Sumner probably would be reassured that the cause of conventional capitalism has been served, in our time, by Herrenstein and Murray's consignment of Americans with low IQ scores to the *natural persons* "losers'" place at one end of a bell curve (1994).

Indeed, in 1979 the *Georgia Law Review* published a series of papers in which the contributors railed against sharing the group claims of corporations to constitutional rights with the claims of natural persons in quest of equality, quite along Sumner's lines. For the review's editor and most of the contributors, capitalism as we know it rewards the fit and only the fit, and the rest be damned. This social Darwinist theme lies just below the surface of many discussions of stratification. This theme was diluted, most effectively, to a palatable level in the approaches of the so-called functionalists, for whom systems of stratification represented the outcomes of social processes by which those whose efforts are most contributory to the theoretically putative "needs" of social systems earn the highest incomes (reflecting the effectiveness of these systems' divisions of labor in producing relevant goods and services—pornography, pollution, and prisons as well as penicillin, petri dishes, and prosthetics, among them).

Adam Smith (1937 [1776]) attributed income differences among the English, first, to differences in the costs and in the time needed for preparation to perform as professionals, artisans, or craftsmen and, second, to the "honor" accorded those whose efforts deserve the approbation of their inferiors. In modern times, the most trenchant formulation of the nuanced view of "fitness" was proffered by Davis and Moore (1945), who urged that the prerequisite functions of social systems are fulfilled by hierarchies of performers rewarded differentially among occupations arrayed in an income hierarchy. The major premise in the syllogism—that better-educated persons are more *meritorious* and hence earn higher pay—was that employers are inevitably rational economic men who would not pay differentially better wages to differentially educated persons unless they earned these higher wages *in perfectly competitive markets*. As Marx put it, in his preface to *Das Capital* (1906 [1867]), men of commerce do not do what they might prefer to do, but what they have to do in price-driven markets.

In the period since World War II we have come to simplify the social processes by which our system's needs for differentiated "fitness" are fulfilled by investing our formal educational apparatuses with the primary responsibilities for teaching neophytes and selecting from among them those who will fill the most skilled and the professional occupations. Dennison (in a comparative study of gross national product) and Schultz and Becker (in studies of U.S. income distribution) theorized, in 1962 to 1964, that educational systems generate human capital in quantities and qualities that match or exceed the contributions of physical capital to the products of nations and to the associated earnings of working Americans (see Berg 1999). The theory involved could not have been better sculpted with Occam's own razor: better-educated Americans earn more than their less-educated fellows because—the minor premise—they are more productive; we know they are more productive because rational employers pay them more—a second premise. Becker acknowledged his entire dependence here on the circumstantial evidence of education's statistical relationship to income.

The major premise in this tautology, already hinted at, is that employers would not pay Americans in excess of their marginal rates of productivity, an anchor point in neoclassical price theory. The sizable incomes that were allocated to college graduates during 1945 to 1960, in an economy where college-level jobs were multiplying very quickly, were taken to prove the human capital argument dispositively. The education boom beginning in 1945 has continued, with growing fanfare, into the present day, but the returns have dropped by half with the superabundance of college graduates and growing price competition that challenged our manufacturing sector's once oligopolistic structures from 1940 to 1979.

My own evidence on the issue (Berg 1970) was crude (although a good deal less so than Becker's) and later formed the basis for a well-known Supreme Court decision, according to George Cooper, a Columbia Law School colleague, who used my research in support of his client's claims in a landmark civil rights case (*Griggs v. Duke Power Co.*, 1971). My study afforded no confirmation of *productivity* differences among differentially educated persons whatever and suggested that marginal differences in *income* earned per unit of educational investment can reasonably be explained by market forces significantly tempered by managed prices. When the core of the economy (manufacturing) is substantially oligopolized, employers can reap somewhat higher earnings than possible under substantial price competition. In this way, they can pay college graduates pretty much what they choose to pay them. The study has been updated—which is to say, fully replicated—with similar conclusions by Livingstone (1998).

My contradictory findings left me skeptical of the widespread enthusiasm for human capital reasoning, a body of thought that came quickly to support the growing belief that college graduates offer more *merit* than less-educated workers! The merit business takes us to a critical point in a nominally democratic-egalitarian system: if we inevitably observe that the nexus of liberty and democratic equality yields economic inequality, as Tocqueville noted, then we also need mechanisms for rationalizing that inequality, as Tocqueville also recognized (Commager 1993). Educational achievements serve well as such a mechanism: the inequalities between

those of lower- and higher-income constitute precious "proxy"—
that is, indirect but necessarily circumstantial evidence—of differential worth or *merit*. In a society where an "aristocracy of talent"
is tolerable (famously to Thomas Jefferson and to William Jefferson Clinton), *illegitimate* authority with high pay is not tolerable
and becomes a source of popular disaffection. There is some sign
of this disaffection today, stimulated by reports of the stagnation
of four-fifths of Americans' income in juxtaposition with the ever-
growing shares of income by America's top 20 percent of earners.

That educational achievements may not only fail to bespeak
merit may be readily found in other *circumstantial* evidence par-
alleling that favored by human capitalists—namely, that the war in
China-Korea, the war in Vietnam, and the scandals of Watergate,
Contragate, and Monicagate were all the works of college, not
high school, graduates. It is just as problematic to derive merit
directly from education as it would be to blame education for the
miscreant behavior of our major and well-educated public leaders
during the major scandals of modern times. Circumstantial evidence may not be as persuasive as it was to Henry Thoreau, when
he recorded his suspicions in his *Journal*, November 11, 1850, that
his milkman watered his deliveries led him to conclude that "circumstantial evidence can be very compelling, as when we find a
trout in the milk." In the veritable sea of prose in human capital
studies, 1964 to 1999, we find a whale of a tautology.

I now address the group rights reprise with which the critics
of affirmative action confront its proponents. If better-educated
individuals are, by consensus at least, more meritorious than their
less-educated fellows, there is no clearly legitimate basis for grant-
ing rights to opportunities or jobs to persons-as-group members.
We might legitimately disallow overt, demonstrable discrimination
by one individual against another, of course, but state intervention
must stop there: there would be no preferences and no proportionate set-asides for individuals *based on membership in groups,
identified wrong-headedly as victims*, by misguided legislators or
by presidents who issue executive orders (Lyndon Johnson in
1968) or quota requirements (Richard Nixon in 1972) in support of
affirmative action. "Color blindness" should mark all distributive
processes, and the most meritorious will rise if only the state

would outlaw discrimination by *individuals against individuals* and if the opportunities were expanded for those willing to prepare themselves (through collegiate studies, for example) to compete not as members of labeled groups, but as one-on-one with all comers.

The fact is, however, that a great many Americans are indeed consigned to *individual* treatment informed by general perceptions of the groups with which we are inclined to identify them, groups from which a great many members are seen to be unfit or undeserving because they putatively have or lack merit: women until the constitution was amended, college students deferred from the draft, capital gains recipients who pay lower taxes than wage earners, or persons ages sixty-two or more who qualify for Social Security payments. Subsidies in bizarrely different amounts are available to corporate persons in different industries; veterans of diverse wars are eligible for diverse benefits; until 1994 professors (unlike persons in any other occupation) had to be retired during their seventieth year to protect the prospects and options of younger colleagues. One could go on and on about groups' gains and groups' losses, to include farmers, franchisers and franchisees, import licensees, patent holders, domestic producers, and polluters with rights to sell their quotas of pollution.

If innumerable persons are or were long *treated* as members of a group, for example, why do the critics of affirmative action reject only the group actions of "protected persons" seeking to *secure* rights? If natural persons are commonly consigned by social practice as well as law to a group associated with enduring disadvantages, why should we be surprised that they seek to undo their vulnerabilities? If, as charged, New Jersey's state troopers pursue African Americans on the Garden State Parkway because they are reminded that African Americans have disproportionately higher crime rates, why should African Americans not object to what is called racial profiling? As recently as January 1999 the Department of Agriculture admitted that African American farmers had regularly and systematically been denied crop price supports for many decades. Can we understand our stratification system fully, through either housing studies or status attainment studies, if the analytic models ignore a whole history of consignments to advantaged and disadvantaged groups by the logics that shape our laws regarding both natural and legal persons?

It should hardly surprise us that disadvantaged and vulnerable groups should seek an in-kind, group-shaped version of advantages when their rights as natural persons (specifically under the fourteenth amendment) have been systematically abridged for extraordinarily long periods or simply have been reallocated by the courts to corporate persons. Pole (1978, 183) offers reasonable estimates for anticipating such likelihoods:

> Within a few years of the Civil Rights Act of 1875, the Supreme Court took over the fortifications which the Democrats in Congress had failed to hold. Contrary to the expectations expressed by the court in the Slaughter House cases, the Fourteenth Amendment soon came to be applied as a matter of course to economic questions that had nothing to do with race; once it had been settled that corporations enjoyed the common law rights of persons, punitive or redistributionist forms of taxation and profit control were held to amount to unequal protection, and the amendment stood forth as the principal buttress. But the black minority received less considerate treatment. Beginning only three years after the passage of the act, a long series of cases deprived them of either the consolations of equality or the practice of protection.

Of all the efforts to reduce the imbalances wrought in favor of laissez-faire economics and the social Darwinian logic, one stands out: the angry response to the decision (*Griggs v. Duke Power Co.*, 1971, noted earlier) in which the Supreme Court held it unlawful to require high school degrees of African Americans for entry-level jobs or nominal promotions to positions in which whites had regularly been appointed without such degrees before 1965. If the results are discriminatory, the court held, these requirements are illegal unless employers can prove a "business necessity" (that is, the jobs are indeed performed better by those with more education). My own work bore, exclusively and entirely, only on this point in the case.

The company claimed that it had stopped such discrimination with the advent of the Civil Rights Act in 1965 and thereafter *both* whites and blacks needed high school diplomas. Given the historical exclusion of blacks from education in the South, however, the court held that what it regarded as the entirely gratuitous requirement of a high school degree produced "disparate treatment impact" that produced de facto inequality against blacks. Although critics argued that discrimination can only occur at the individual and not the group level, the fact was that several whites with no high school degree, hired before the Civil Rights Act of 1965, were in skilled jobs containing no blacks and that their rights to these jobs had been exclusive to whites under Jim Crow laws.

Critics nonetheless decried what they saw as the beginning of a quota system rooted in the stratified distribution of workers by race. Although this issue was gainsaid by Chief Justice Burger's holding for the unanimous court, critics continue to point out the disparate effects of the new legal requirements, favoring blacks, while defending the unequal *treatment* of disadvantaged African Americans before the Civil Rights Act on the grounds that it was, at the time, "legal," that is, blessed by Jim Crow. By this logic, and absent changes in jurisprudence in the period 1887 to 1991, Willie Griggs would, most certainly, have been a fifth-generation slave, not a plaintiff in a landmark civil rights case. I see the critics' position as an example of the hostility to group rights by those who neglect the long and full history of group rights in our republic, a history that is thoroughly informed by the logic of natural law and the adaptation of John Locke's writings on liberty and property, which gave stockholders full rights (virtually all those enumerated in the constitution) under the valuable rubric of persona ficta.

COLOR BLINDNESS

All the parties to the civil rights agenda—legislators as well as black leaders—argued in the 1960s that efforts to assure equal opportunity should be characterized by color blindness. As originally framed, there were to be no "preferences" based on "race." To this end President Lyndon Johnson signed Executive Order 11246 in 1967, implementing affirmative action guidelines requiring employers to set hiring goals and to construct timetables to diversify their workforces such that opportunities for protected groups would be created over a self-selected and reviewable timetable. Goals were to be established by comparing employers' needs for differentially educated employees with statistical distributions of persons in proximal and distal labor markets. Timetables were to be established on the bases of longitudinal plans for expansion or contraction and could take account of turnover rates based on historical experiences. Plans were to be updated and revised periodically, and compliance reviews were to be conducted periodically. Records (paper trails) of appointments and candidates were to be maintained so that compliance officers could assess whether or not hires were made, in good faith, to fulfill goals within the time plans set by employers. There were to be no quotas, however.

The executive order was first enforced in a reasonably energetic way in the fall of 1971. Some overzealous regional enforcement agencies pushed quotas on employers, and some nervous employers pushed quotas on themselves, knowing that they were not technically required to do so, in order to head off being debarred from receipt of federal funds. Employers had guaranteed rights, however, to contest the pressures of enforcement agents to apply quotas in the courts.

Later, in 1972, the Nixon administration shifted to favor quotas, a move that I believe, then and now, was a mistake. I see no difficulty with the earlier arrangements, although the burdensome paperwork was undeniably enormous. The only time a given "protected" job seeker would gain a "preference" was if he or she was *identically* qualified with a white male—a highly unusual circumstance if the search procedures had been carefully applied. There can be no color-blind searches where occupations are essentially bereft of protected group members. Where a given labor market segment does include protected group members, searches will be egalitarian if and only if employers are required to conduct open investigations of talent. If an organization's labor force is homogeneously white and male, in occupations where the external labor market is racially heterogeneous and protected persons are ignored, color blindness simply cannot be presumed.

With respect to college and graduate school admissions, most institutions have been careful to use conventional measurements (test scores and class rank as well as letters of recommendation and personal interviews) and to undertake careful assessments of students' interests in juxtaposition to institutional interests in students' potentialities as well as their financial needs. Admissions officers thus compute indexes of students' attractiveness in such a way that race and gender are among, but in no way the determining, "dispositive" variables.

With respect to college admissions, the most sophisticated study to date, that of Bowen and Bok (1998)—former presidents, respectively of Princeton and Harvard and both reputable students of human resources—indicates that highly qualified white males or females had about a 25 percent chance of being admitted to one of the eighteen elite colleges in their sample before affirmative action and that, as these schools began admitting qualified minorities, those prospects were reduced 3 percentage points. By January 1999, moreover, it was widely reported in the media that a minority male with a 4.0 academic average was rejected by the University of California at Berkeley. A fair-minded assessment of Bowen and Bok's evidence strongly suggests that affirmative action has worked with only very marginal statistical losses to long-favored majority students, losses far below those inflicted on ex-slaves by the systematically one-sided applications of the fourteenth amendment to corporate persons.

With respect to employment, the earnings of female college graduates rose slightly higher than the inflation rate from 1975 to 1995, whereas those of male college graduates rose slightly less and those of male high school graduates rose at rates substantially less than the rate of inflation. My own reading of Bureau of Labor Statistics reports suggests that women's better circumstances reflect an unmeasurable, but probably small, affirmative action dividend, and a return on their greater productivity. White males once earned returns of 11 percent, discounted over a lifetime, on investments in education, according to Becker's estimates (1964, ch. 1); many of these males were very often the beneficiaries of oligopolistic profits in the manufacturing sector. Females in 1995, by way of contrast, were paid in most sectors by employers who were generally driven by price competition; thus they were driven to pay more for productivity, as Becker and others supposed employers were driven in the 1950s. If, as the human capital theorists have urged from 1963 to the present, one should credit markets for wage allocations, one surely is obligated to take account of the degree of *price* competitiveness in markets, at a given period in time, in a theory rooted entirely in price theory.

In summary, I see no rationale for claiming color blindness in hires or admissions *where the searches for candidates have not been openly universalistic:* one cannot select among minorities and nonminorities in labor markets where minorities are present but where search procedures omit minorities. The virtual or total *absence* of minorities in a labor sector will occur from time to time, of course, in recognizably limiting cases. Finally, our total commitment to educational achievements as all-purpose measures of merit is poorly grounded in direct evidence. Although human capital studies are suggestive, they are based, as their architects duly note, entirely on circumstantial evidence such that wages are simultaneously both a result of education and a measure of productivity, a tautology that ought most emphatically not be admitted as objective evidence, under the law, of "merit."

CONCLUSIONS

Keeping the foregoing institutional history in mind, in addition to the findings of status attainment analysts and human ecologists, it is clear that a great many of today's winners represent the descendants of a great many persons who benefited from group-based rights before those rights became an issue under the rubric of affirmative action. Minorities thus have the heavy burden of now having to earn group rights that have long been accorded to majorities, including the ubiquitous status of persona ficta in a world in which minorities, as groups, are disfavored, for whatever reasons, by majorities. I thus urge a more systematic discussion, measurement, and analysis of *all* group-based rights with respect to a set of public interest standards. The group rights accorded minorities under recent affirmative action programs ought not to be treated as bizarre examples of modern legal novelties.

Although rapid economic growth without inflation will almost automatically reduce the temptations to discriminate, lowering the demand for "new-fangled" group-based rights, there remains the rub that rabid anti-inflationists (bond marketers, especially) will enforce slow-growth policies at the first sign (using their own favored and flawed measures) of inflation. Since inflation, at the moment, is virtually at zero (2.3 percent in July 2000) according to standard indicators, we cannot disallow the possibility of renewed fervor, in the near future, for a "sufficient" level of unemployment to control inflation. The "Philips Curve tradeoff," now raised to the status of a god-given regularity by the nomenclature of the "natural rate of inflation," is our old friend, laissez-faire economics, once again, except that now we *make* labor markets fit the interests of the investment communities that, perforce, call the tune. The tune they increasingly call, in their dirges, requires that we expend our minorities as soldiers in the war against inflation, enlisting them as casualties without affording them combat pay. If there are times when we need unemployment to control inflation, so be it, but we do not need to concentrate this unemployment disproportionately among African Americans and other minorities under the pretext that they are "less meritorious." As we fill our jails with the unemployed, let us recognize that a substantial number of African Americans who are now middle class owe their good fortune to the war on poverty and the federal and state jobs it created, and to the armed forces itself. Public works, in these critical events, are not all bad.

Next let us ponder a relatively neglected dimension of the baby boomers' concern about Social Security: they will soon be supported by a ratio of workers to retirees of three to one, compared with a current figure of seven or eight to one. Early in the new century, moreover, two of these three supporters will likely be minorities without any "dividends" from affirmative action! Baby boomers will gain little, as retirees, even with the investments of Social Security funds in the booming stock and securities market, without substantial upgrading of the potential productivity of young minorities.

Finally, let us keep in mind that the corporate persons who reduce their launching of toxic particulates into the air may currently sell their (property) "rights to pollute" to others who can afford to buy these credits more readily than they can afford the higher costs of technological improvements. Minority members on the welfare rolls, however, cannot sell their "sins" against popular sensibilities, even through public interest in controlling inflation by adequate levels of unemployment is a well-developed one, indeed. Now there is an irony.

In his volume, *Rituals of Blood,* Patterson (1998) resuscitates Daniel Patrick Moynihan's oft-condemned report *The Negro Fam-*

ily, a monograph published by the Department of Labor in the 1960s, in which the author urged "that slavery inflicted enduring psychological damage on black men" (Foner 1999, 12). I would join in Patterson's (1997) argument as follows: following slavery, there has been an expansion of group-based rights in which fewer blacks than whites share the legal blessing bestowed on corporate persons. The members of the large African American population who are not middle class suffer not only the legacies of slavery in their current circumstances but also the legacies that follow from their exclusion from long-vaunted group-based rights for others, natural and otherwise, to which affirmative action's critics wish to deny new claimants. With the waning of the public's commitment to affirmative action, these African Americans will be denied jobs (rather than the derivative benefits of group-based rights), but these rights will continue to be accorded to corporate employers. Therein lies a final, formidable irony.

REFERENCES

Arnold, Thurman W. 1937. *The Folklore of Capitalism.* New Haven, Conn.: Yale University Press.

Becker, Gary. 1964. *Human Capital.* New York: Columbia University Press.

Berg, Ivar. 1970. *Education and Jobs: The Great Training Robbery.* New York: Praeger.

———. 1999. "The Sociology of the Economics of Education." In *Education and Sociology: An Encyclopedia,* edited by David Levinson. New York: Garland Press.

Bowen, William G., and Derek Bok. 1998. *The Shape of the River: Long-Term Consequences of Considering Race in College and University Admissions.* Princeton, N.J.: Princeton University Press.

Coleman, James S. 1982. *The Asymmetric Society.* Syracuse, N.Y.: Syracuse University Press.

Commager, H. S. 1993. *Commager on Tocqueville.* Columbia, Mo.: University of Missouri Press.

Davis, Kingsley, and Wilbert E. Moore. 1945. "Some Principles of Stratification." *American Sociological Review* 10: 242–9.

Dennison, Edward F. 1962. *The Sources of Economic Growth in the United States.* New York: Committee for Economic Development.

Fitzgerald, F. Scott. 1936. *The Crack-up*. In *Familiar Quotations,* 16th ed. by John Bartlett. Boston: Little, Brown.

Foner, Eric. 1999. "The Crisis Is Within." *The New York Times Book Review,* February 12, 1999, p. 12.

Galbraith, John Kenneth. 1997 (1952). *American Capitalism: The Concept of Countervailing Power*. New Brunswick, N.J.: Transaction Press.

Georgia Law Review. 1979. "Perspectives on Rights." *Georgia Law Review,* special issue, 13(4).

Hacker, Louis, ed. 1965. *The Corporate Take-over*. Garden City, New York: Anchor Books.

Hamilton, Alexander. 1791. *Report on Manufactures*. In *The Reports of Alexander Hamilton,* edited by J. E. Cocke. From *The National Experience: A History of the United States,* 6th ed. 1985. Edited by John Blum, A. M. Schlesinger Jr., W. S. McFeely, et al. New York: Harcourt Brace Jovanovich.

Herrenstein, Richard J., and Charles Murray. 1994. *The Bell Curve: Intelligence and Class Structure in American Life*. New York: Free Press.

Hofstadter, Richard. 1944. *Social Darwinism in American Thought*. Philadelphia: University of Pennsylvania Press.

Livingstone, D. W. 1998. *The Education-Jobs Gap: Underemployment or Economic Democracy*. Boulder, Colo.: Westview Press.

Manent, Pierre. 1998. *The City of Man*. Princeton, N.J.: Princeton University Press.

Marx, Karl. 1906 (1867). *Das Capital*. 1st ed. New York: The Modern Library.

Mason, Alpheus T., and Gerald Garvey, eds. 1964. *American Constitutional History: Essays by Edward S. Corwin*. New York: Harper and Row.

Massey, Douglas S., and Nancy A. Denton. 1996. *American Apartheid: Segregation and the Making of the Underclass*. Cambridge, Mass.: Harvard University Press.

———. 1998. "Back to the Future: Rediscovering Neighborhood Context." Review Essay on *Neighborhood Poverty, Volumes I and II,* edited by Jeanne Brooks-Gunn, Greg J. Duncan, and Lawrence Aber. *Contemporary Sociology* 27(4): 570–73.

Moynihan, Daniel P. 1965. *The Negro Family: The Case for National Action*. Washington: U.S. Department of Labor, Department of Policy Planning and Research.

Patterson, Orlando. 1997. *The Ordeal of Integration: Progress and Resentment in America's "Racial" Crisis*. Washington, D.C.: Civitas/Counterpoint.

———. 1998. *Rituals of Blood: Consequences of Slavery in Two American Centuries.* Washington, D.C.: Civitas/Counterpoint.

Pole, Jack R. 1978. *The Pursuit of Equality in American History.* Berkeley: University of California Press.

Schultz, Theodore W. 1962. "Reflections on Investment in Man." *Journal of Political Economy,* part 2 October (supplement): 1-ff.

Skrentny, John D. 1996. *The Ironies of Affirmative Action: Politics, Culture, and Justice in America.* Chicago: University of Chicago Press.

Smith, Adam. 1937 [1776]. *The Wealth of Nations.* New York: Modern Library.

Tocqueville, Alexis de. 1961 [1835]. *Democracy in America.* 2 vols. New York: Schocken Books.

— Part II —

The Social Demography of Race

—— Chapter 6 ——

The Population
Dynamics of the
Changing Color Line

Tukufu Zuberi

A T THE DAWN of the twenty-first century, the problem of the
color line remains with us. The classification of humans into
races artificially imposes a formal nomenclature on the dynamic
patterns of physical variability. The boundaries of race are not fixed
and definite, because a member of one race can interbreed with
members of any other race, and our notions of race also change
over time. Racial classification is a tradition of convenience and is
used because it justifies racial stratification. In reality, the racial
composition of the United States has been anything but stable.
Assimilation and racial stratification define the dynamics of race.

In this chapter I examine the population dynamics of the
changing color line in the United States. I begin by briefly outlining the racial dynamics of assimilation and racial stratification and
then turn my attention to describing the color line and its evenness in the United States in the past and future. Finally, I discuss
the consequences that drawing a color line has had for the population of the United States.

RACIAL DYNAMICS

Assimilation and racial stratification are processes that take place
when racial populations are socially defined and come into con-

145

tact within a particular society. Assimilation is a gradual process in which one set of cultural traits and historical genealogies is relinquished and a new set is acquired through participation in the dominant mainstream culture. Racial stratification is the process of using race as a factor in the allocation of resources and power in a society and is a barrier to full assimilation into the dominant culture. Both assimilation and racial stratification can operate simultaneously.

The classical model of assimilation is described by a melting pot model, which assumes that immigrants arrive with a relative disadvantage vis-à-vis mainstream America (see Taeuber and Taeuber 1965; Burgess 1967; Park 1967 [1925]). They are culturally distant and distinct and lack communication skills. Thus immigrants are initially clustered, or segregated, near the core of the city. The passage of time, however, brings a withering of ethnic differences, and socioeconomic advancement translates into residential mobility and assimilation. In the United States the three principal forms of assimilation are through residential integration, intermarriage, and the racial classification of children. In each of these types of assimilation, the African American has been uniquely excluded.

To comprehend the population dynamics of the color line therefore requires an understanding of racial stratification (McDaniel 1995; Bashi and McDaniel 1997). Racial stratification implies that different ethnic groups assimilate into particular races, and ethnic assimilation occurs among groups once considered ethnically different. For example, immigrants from Nigeria and Ghana have assimilated into the African American race, and immigrants from Sweden and Ireland have assimilated into the European American race. In the racial assimilation of an ethnic group, physical distinctions are overshadowed by the myth of cultural and historical similarities. Likewise, Asians do not come to the United States as Asians, they arrive as Chinese, Japanese, and Indians. Migrants from Latin America do not come to the United States as Latinos, they come as Mexicans and Cubans. Ethnicity and race are confounded in the United States by history and by the legacy of dichotomous physical distinctions that were necessary to justify racial slavery and colonization. Whiteness identifies European-origin populations in the United States despite the fact that they come from a variety of nations and cultures. Likewise, the physical distinction of blackness identifies African Americans no matter what their national origins.

The racial stratification perspective defines race as a socially constructed concept. Racial differences evoke somatic images that are related to social differences. Often these social differences are based on the concepts of ethnocentrism and social intolerance. Ethnocentrism is a social attitude that focuses on the virtue of a group's history and culture. It pits "us" against the "others" and is important for group glorification and solidarity. Social intolerance is social displeasure or resentment against a group that refuses to conform to the established practice and beliefs of a social group. A racially differentiated society that is characterized by both ethnocentrism and social intolerance is racially stratified (Cox 1948).

In the United States this process has been extremely important in the creation of the "white race." In the racial assimilation of an ethnic group, physical distinctions are overshadowed by the myth of cultural and historical similarities. Assimilation requires that the subordinate group recognize myths of historical similarities and accept the dominate group's culture and historical predisposition. The classic case of this kind of assimilation is the Irish in the United States (Smedley 1993; Allen 1994). A similar form of assimilation occurred among African immigrants to the United States, although African slaves were in no position to perpetuate their own national or tribal identities. Rather, they were forced to accept their designation as black or African. Unlike the Irish, the African population continues to be racially stratified within the United States. In fact, the racial stratification of the African-origin population continues to be a major element of racial classification within American society.

As a concept, race requires the existence of two or more distinct races. Race relations refer to contact between different racial groups. Ethnic relations are governed by processes of assimilation, and race relations are governed by processes of racial stratification. Ethnic relations refer to the social interaction of two populations distinguishable on the basis of their culture and historical genealogy; the importance of physical differences is not insurmountable. In the United States, contact between two distinct ethnic groups initially may be governed by race relations. Given *time* and *favorable social conditions*, however, physical differences are given decreasing significance, a common historical genealogy is adapted, and the subordinate group's culture is assimilated into the dominant culture.

DESCRIBING THE COLOR LINE

Changes in racial composition result from a combination of differential fertility and mortality, net immigration, and rules of racial classification. Differentials in fertility and mortality, or more specifically natural increase, had a significant effect on the early racial composition of the U.S. population. However, since the twentieth century differentials in the rates of natural increase have had a relatively small influence on the racial distribution of the population. The most significant factor affecting racial distribution within the United States is racial classification.

In the United States all births, deaths, and immigrants are racially classified. Racial classification and immigration have had a particularly strong effect on the social conceptualization of race in the United States. Figure 6.1 presents the changing racial composition of the United States from 1630 to 2050. The racial composition of the population of the Americas has been generally dominated by immigration from Europe, Asia, and Africa. In fact, it is the arrival of immigrants that created the racial composition and began the process of racial stratification in the United States.

Historically, the most distinguishing feature of the racial composition of the Americas has been the growth of the African and European populations and the decline of the American Indian population. Immigration from Europe and Africa initiated the process. From 1630 to 1700, enslaved Africans and European immigrants dominated inputs to the changing racial composition of North America, a period also highlighted by the decline of the Native American population. The decline of the Native American population resulted initially from their high rates of mortality and thereafter from high rates of immigration from Africa and Europe. European immigrants and their descendants have dominated the racial makeup of the U.S. population since the eighteenth century. In 1810 the European population accounted for about 73 percent of the total population. By 1930 the European population accounted for more than 88 percent of the total.

The rate of natural increase has not been the driving force in the recent changes in the racial distribution of the population. For example, since 1900 the African-origin population has consistently made up about 12 percent of the total population. This has been so even though the natural increase of the African American population is twice that of the European-origin population. This discrepancy resulted in part from the high rate of immigration from Europe.

The growth of the Asian and Latino populations through immigration from 1950 onward has been equally important, but the sudden appearance of the Latino population also reflects the acceptance around 1965 of a new classification—Hispanic—in contemporary debates about race and ethnic difference. It is difficult to estimate the actual size of the Latino population for the period before 1950. Common ancestral ties to Spain and Latin America do not necessarily imply an underlying cultural unity among Latinos (Bean and Tienda 1987), and Mexicans, Puerto Ricans, Cubans, and Dominicans continue to remain distinct populations with discernable characteristics (Willette 1982). Historically, however, the majority of pre-1950 Latinos were counted as white, and thus they are found in the pre-1950 European population in figure 6.1.

Beginning in the nineteenth century, the American Indian and African proportion of the population underwent a long decline that lasted until the 1940s. It was most notable for the American Indian population, which did not begin to recover in its proportionate distribution until the 1970s, although its population decline ended around 1880. Although in some localities of the South, Africans outnumbered Europeans in the sixteenth and seventeenth centuries (Wood 1975), nationwide their share stood at 20 percent in 1810. Like American Indians, the relative share of African Americans underwent a steady decline in the succeeding century, falling to around 10 percent in the 1920s and remaining there through the 1960s.

For the most part, these declines in relative size stemmed from a combination of European immigration and exceptionally high rates of mortality within the American Indian and African populations. Another reason for the decline in the African population is

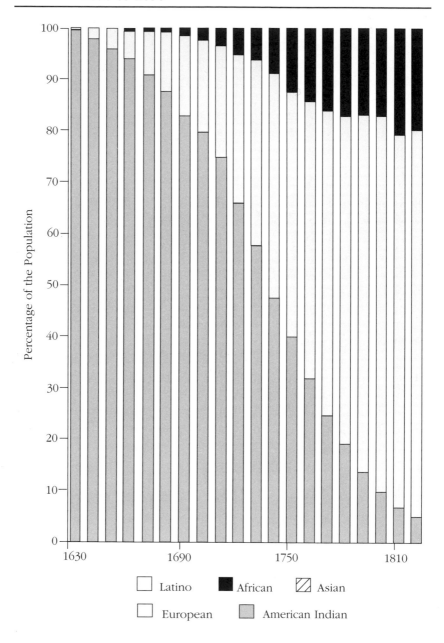

FIGURE 6.1 **Racial Distribution in the United States by Year, 1630 to 2050**

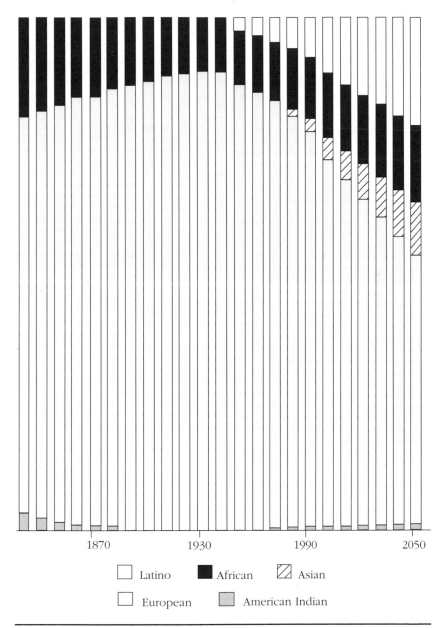

1870   1930   1990   2050

□ Latino   ■ African   ▨ Asian

□ European   ▨ American Indian

Sources: Willette et al. 1982; U.S. Bureau of the Census 1991, 1992; Thornton and Marsh-Thornton 1981; Barringer et al. 1993; Eblen 1974; Coale and Rives 1973; Hollman 1993; Robinson et al. 1993; Bogue 1985; Coale and Zelnik 1963; and Siegel 1974.

that the legal slave trade to the United States ended in 1808, just as the European rate of immigration was increasing. European immigration increased steadily throughout the nineteenth century, reaching record levels in the period between 1880 and 1914. In reaction to the massive entry of "unassimilable" southern and eastern Europeans early this century, Congress imposed a restrictive national-origins quota system in the early 1920s that limited the total number of immigrants, favored those from northern and western European nations, and virtually banned the entry of Asians and Africans.

The Hart-Celler Immigration Act of 1965 replaced this discriminatory national-origins system. This act set quotas of twenty thousand per country and supported occupational skill preferences. As a result, the number of immigrants from Asia and Latin America increased substantially. Around 1950 the Latino and Asian populations began to increase their relative proportions of the population substantially, with the Latino population experiencing the most proportionate growth. Following the Great Depression, immigration from Europe declined, never to revive again, and by 1990 the European-origin population accounted for less than 20 percent of the total (Jasso and Rosenzweig 1990, table 1.2).

Changes in the racial distribution of the population have been concentrated in the western and southern regions of the United States. Figure 6.2 presents the racial distribution of the 1990 population by region. The concentration in the West and South are a result of the historical experience of racial dynamics in the United States and the ports-of-entry for the recent waves of Asian and Latino immigrants. African Americans continue to be concentrated in the South. Latinos, Asians, and Native Americans tend to be concentrated in the West.

THE COLOR LINE IN THE TWENTY-FIRST CENTURY

The past racial composition of the United States has important implications for the twenty-first century. Figure 6.1 also presents the projected population percentages by race for the next fifty years. The proportion of the population that is descended from Europe has been declining since the 1930s. In fact, the European

FIGURE 6.2 **Racial Distribution in the United States by Region, 1990**

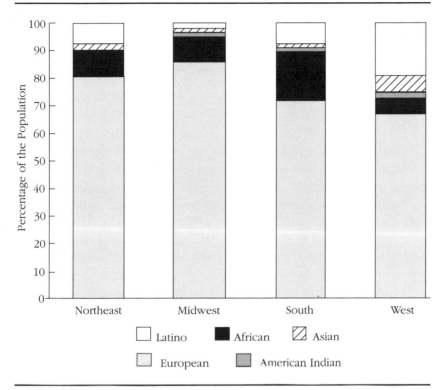

Source: U.S. Bureau of the Census 1992.

American population is projected to experience an absolute population decline after 2030. During the next sixty years the U.S. population is projected to grow more slowly than ever before, yet the racial distribution of the population is projected to change more dramatically. The non-European-origin populations are projected to dominate future population growth (Ahlburg 1993). Although the future composition of the population depends on many factors that are not necessarily taken into account in population projections, it is clear that the relative demographic importance of Europeans will decline over the next century.

If the current demographic trends and racial conceptualizations hold, minority groups will account for more than 47 percent of the population by 2050 (see figure 6.1). By the middle of the next century, the Latino, African, and American Indian populations could double their 1990 size. Given current levels of intermarriage among Asians, Latinos, and American Indians, the proportion of the population with multiple ancestry probably will increase. How these multiracial individuals are racially classified will have an important impact on the future of the color line.

Children are the best indicator of future trends in the composition of the color line. The racial composition of today's school-age population suggests that the future will be dramatically different. Children, working-age adults, and the elderly are affected differently by the dynamics of racial composition. Figure 6.3 presents the projected number of children between the ages of five and eighteen by their anticipated racial and ethnic identification. As with the general population, the child population will become more multiracial and multiethnic. However, among children the shift from a majority- to a minority-dominated population is projected to occur around 2030. Under current conditions, enrollment in elementary school (ages five to eleven) and middle school (ages twelve and thirteen) will increase to 47.8 million by 2050, 13.4 million more than the 34.4 million in 1995. High school (ages fourteen to seventeen) enrollments will rise from 14.7 million in 1995 to 21.2 million in 2050. Students of color will make up the majority of enrollments in elementary through high school.

Population aging poses a problem for old-age entitlement programs, such as federal expenditures on Social Security and Medicare. The fiscal viability of these entitlement programs is determined substantially by the ratio of people above the age of sixty-five to people in the working ages. Although a surplus is now being built up on the books of Social Security, both Social Security and Medicare are pay-as-you-go programs. Figure 6.4 presents what is projected to happen to the dependency ratio in the future. The dependency ratio is defined as the ratio of people above age sixty-five and below age eighteen to people in the working ages (nineteen to sixty-four).

The dependency ratio is projected to increase, especially for the elderly. This is why social policy is becoming increasingly concerned with the problems of an aging population. The growth of the diversity of the population has implications for the nature of aging in American society. As the population ages, the number of

FIGURE 6.3 **Future Racial Distribution in the United States, Ages Five to Eighteen**

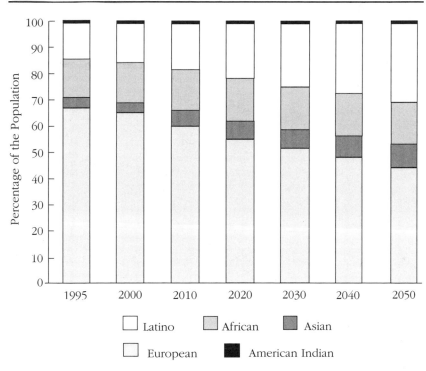

Source: U.S. Bureau of the Census 1992.

working people of color will increase. The future of America is a future of diversity. And the diversity of the United States will consist of an ever-more-diverse young population. The majority of the population sixty-five years and older will be of European origin (69 percent) in the year 2050; however, the majority (around 57 percent) of the children eighteen years and younger will be people of color (U.S. Bureau of the Census 1992).

THE EVENNESS OF THE COLOR LINE

Routine racial classification started at the same time as the national census, which categorized the population by occupation, place of birth, citizenship, and race, among other characteristics. Today,

FIGURE 6.4 **Dependency Ratio in the United States, 1995 to 2050**

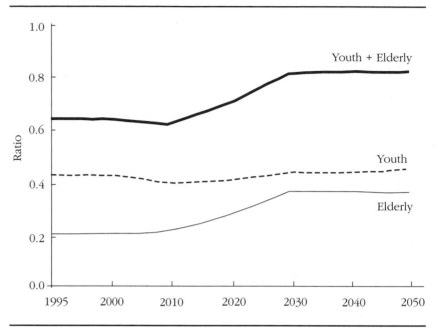

Source: U.S. Bureau of the Census 1992.

the public is served a steady diet of statistics and demographic analysis—often differentiated by race. These findings are accepted as the result of scientific methods of data collection and believed to be politically neutral. Racial classification is not benign, however. The social meaning of race affects *how* we interpret quantitative representations of racial reality. In measuring the color line, I assume that race is not benign, but an indicator of racial stratification. Fluctuations in the color line indicate the persistence, not the degree, of racial stratification.

The magnitude of the color line can be seen as the amount of racial diversity present in a population. Population diversity is the distribution of persons along a continuum of homogeneity to heterogeneity with respect to a defining characteristic or variable. This basic idea has many applications in demography. Within this context a better way of seeing the color line is by using an index to suggest the magnitude of possible interracial contact. Racial diversity is a function of *racial abundance* (the number of races in the population) and *racial evenness* (the evenness with which the individuals in the population are distributed among these racial categories). Abundance and evenness are not necessarily positively correlated. It is possible for increases in racial evenness to accompany decreases in racial abundance. Racial diversity is an aspect of community structure, not the importance of various groups to the community. It does not exist as an intrinsic characteristic of a population but is a result of both social and biological processes. The social definition of racial diversity depends on the nature of racial classification and racial stratification.

The racial index of diversity (RID) provides an unbiased estimator of the probability that two individuals chosen at random and independently from the population will be found to belong to the same group. If we consider a population in which each individual belongs to one racial group, and let $n_1 \ldots n_i$ be the number of individuals in the various groups (so that $\Sigma n_i = N$), then RID can be defined as a measure of the concentration of racial classifications within the population. I define RID as

$$\left[1 - \frac{\Sigma\, n_i(n_{i-1})}{N(N-1)} \right] \Big/ 1 - (1/i) \qquad (6.1)$$

This equation works because $0.5N(N-1)$ is the number of pairs in the population, and $0.5\Sigma n(n-1)$ is the number of pairs drawn from the same racial group in the population. The RID generally increases as smaller populations increase in size, and it decreases as the largest population increases in size. For small samples RID might be slightly greater than 1; however, larger populations will converge toward a value of 1.0. The RID is constrained between 0 and 1 to describe the actual level of diversity as a proportion of the maximum level possible with the specified number of races. When a population has an even racial distribution, the RID will equal 1.0, and when population is homogeneous, the measure will equal 0.0. This measure, like most diversity measures, is an abstraction of reality, because both spatial distributions and encounters between individuals are nonrandom events. However, within the limits of their assumptions, diversity measures socially significant processes.

FIGURE 6.5 **Racial Index of Diversity in the United States, 1630 to 2050**

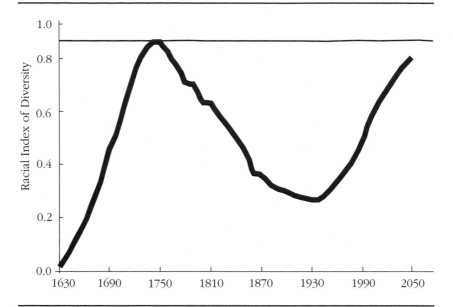

Sources: Willette et al. 1982; U.S. Bureau of the Census 1991, 1992; Thornton and Marsh-Thornton 1981; Barringer et al. 1993; Eblen 1974; Coale and Rives 1973; Hollman 1993; Robinson et al. 1993; Bogue 1985; Coale and Zelnik 1963; and Siegel 1974.

Figure 6.5 presents the RID from 1630 to 2050 for the United States. From the fifteenth century to the beginning of the nineteenth century, there was a massive transfer of populations from Africa and Europe to North America. In the middle of the eighteenth century, the European-origin population became the largest population. This is indicated in figure 6.5 by the decline in the RID during the eighteenth century. In the nineteenth and first half of the twentieth century, this transfer continued for European-origin populations; however, the immigration of large numbers of Africans to North America stopped after 1860. In the past fifty years we have witnessed a massive new transfer of populations to North America, particularly the United States, from Asia, Latin America, and the Caribbean. These new streams of immigrants have resulted in increasing diversity. If current trends continue, the U.S. population will be more diverse than ever before.

Figure 6.6 presents the racial index of diversity by region for

FIGURE 6.6 **Racial Index of Diversity in the United States by Region, 1990**

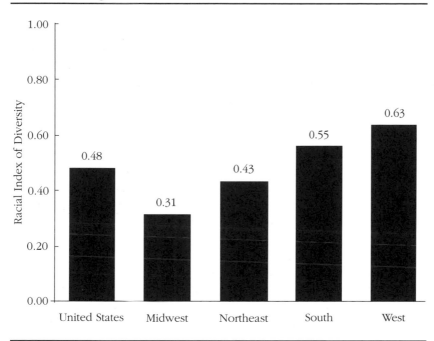

Source: U.S. Bureau of the Census 1992.

the United States. The West and South are the most racially diverse regions of the United States. The Midwest is the least-diverse area in the United States. The concentration of Asians and Latinos in the West and of Africans in the South yields less diversity in the Midwest and Northeast. A small number of states within these regions have populations with all of the four largest racial groups (namely Asians, Africans, Europeans, and Latinos) represented in large numbers: California, New York, Texas, and Illinois.

RECENT IMMIGRATION AND THE RACIAL INDEX OF DIVERSITY

The United States is often thought of as a refuge for immigrants, and the criteria by which immigrants are absorbed into U.S. society embody some of our essential values. Immigrants arrive in the United States and are subjected to its system of racial stratification. This process has had a tremendous effect on U.S. immigration policies and on the racial classification of individuals within the population. The United States has consistently attempted to regulate the racial and ethnic composition of the immigrant population as part of its national immigration policy (Hutchinson 1981, 478–91). Race, national origin, and ethnicity always have been fundamental aspects of the selection of immigrants permitted to enter and settle in the United States.

Throughout U.S. history, the underlying policy seems to have been to maintain the racial composition of the national population, or at least to maintain the white population's majority. This policy found its fullest expression in the national-origins quota system for the allocation of immigrant visas. This policy excluded certain populations on the basis of region of origin. For example, the Asiatic Barred Zone Act of 1917 excluded various national populations from Asia. This exclusion did not end until 1952, when quotas for Asians were established on the basis of race or ancestry rather than birthplace. Another less drastic example was the use of more selective policy instruments to curb the immigration of southern and eastern Europeans. The Immigration Act of 1952 also introduced occupational skills preferences.

The Hart-Celler Immigration Act attempted to eliminate the racially preferential nature of immigration legislation before 1965. The stated purpose of the house bill was "the elimination of the national-origins system as the basis for the selection of immigrants to the United States" (Hutchinson 1981). Before this act, the vast majority (more than 80 percent) of all legal immigrants to the United States were from Europe. Since 1965, the proportion of immigrants from Europe has declined substantially, while the proportions from the Americas and Asia have increased. Asians now dominate the legal immigrant population; however, the magnitude of undocumented immigration is substantial, and most illegal immigrants come to the United States from Latin America.

Immigrants from Asia, Latin America, and the Caribbean conceptualize racial identity in a way that is quite different from the bipolar racial categories of the United States (Denton and Massey 1989; Barringer, Gardner, and Levin 1993). For example, Mexicans have a racial continuum that runs from white to red, not from white to black as in Puerto Rico. Furthermore, the Puerto Rican continuum from white to black is different from the bipolar conceptualization in the United States. The Puerto Rican continuum may have more to do with culture than skin color (see Rodríguez and Cordero-Guzmán 1992). Racial identification for Asians may not be based on a color continuum and may have more to do with social and political exigencies than with color (Espiritu 1992). For immigrants from the non-Hispanic Caribbean, Africa, and Europe, racial identification within the United States is clearly rooted in the history of the United States and these other geographical areas. Black immigrants from the Caribbean and Africa enter the United States as African Americans and experience the United States as other African Americans. Immigrants from Europe enter the United States as European Americans. It is a social transformation for their children and grandchildren to become white.

Euiopean immigrants at the turn of the century experienced a similar transformation in racial conceptualization. European ethnic groups were integrated into the European-derived white population of the United States and eventually came to employ their ethnic identity as an option rather than an ascribed status (Waters 1990; Hout and Goldstein 1994). Immigrants must modify their actions to coincide with their host society's concept of racial stratification or face social isolation and dislocation. In the United States racial groups are power groups, which stand culturally or racially as potential or actual antagonists.

Racial polarization is accepted by the native-born population regardless of race and has been important in identification of the new wave of immigrants. Immigrants from the Caribbean and Latin America have had to conform their notions of who is black and who is white to the prevailing racial conceptualizations of the United States (see Denton and Massey 1989). Immigrants from the Asian and Latin American countries have been lumped together by the larger society as "Asians" and "Latinos," regardless of national origin, and these groups have, in turn, used this social ascription as a basis for forming a community of interest (Espiritu 1992). This identity formation is a continuation of the dynamics of racial classification in the United States. In the 1940s, the League of United Latin American Citizens fought against Mexicans in

Texas being classified as "colored," pressuring politicians and government enumerators to classify them as white.

However race in the United States has been defined conventionally or legally, in reality it is a dynamic concept where, racially, each person may be located on a continuum between white and black. The new wave of Asian and Latin America immigrants are challenging this definition. For example, in the 1990 census, a majority of the ten million people who chose the "other, not specified" race category rather than one of the specified categories were Latino. More than 50 percent of the Latino population answered "other" on the race question (McDaniel 1995). This makes racial classification of the population difficult and projections by race suspect.

Indeed, the Latino population may be a sign of the future. The dynamic character of racial classification among immigrants from Latin America has implications for our measurement of RID. Figure 6.7 graphically presents these implications. If we consider the Latino population as a single race, then the diversity within the United States will reach the highest levels ever. However, if we consider the Latino population as part of the existing system of racial classification (white, black, and so forth), then racial diversity will increase, but more modestly than generally anticipated.

The diversity within the so-called minority population is complicated by the problems of racial classification. How racial groups are socially classified has a tremendous influence on the racial composition observed by any scholar. The two principal problems in racially classifying Latinos arise from the large percentage of Latinos who are immigrants and the different racial classifications they carry with them from their countries of origin. Many Latinos coming to the United States would be classified as white in the their country of origin. In fact, most Latino immigrants classified themselves as racially white within the United States prior to 1980 (McDaniel 1995). In 1960 and 1970, more than 95 percent of the immigrants from Latin America were classified as white, and in 1980 the Census Bureau broadened its racial classifications to allow the Latino population to indicate their "Spanish" race (McDaniel 1995). Although the Census Bureau eliminated the "Spanish" race category in 1990, immigrants from Latin America continued to classify themselves as other than black or white.

FIGURE 6.7 **Racial Index of Diversity in the United States by Race of Latino Population, 1630 to 2050**

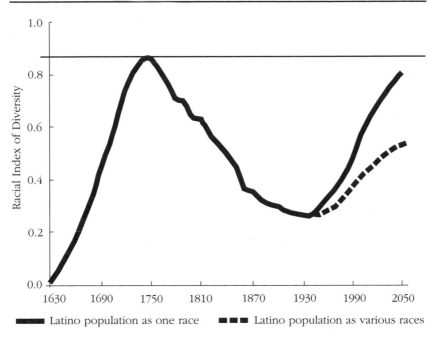

Sources: Willette et al. 1982; U.S. Bureau of the Census, 1991, 1992; Thornton and Marsh-Thornton 1981; Barringer et al. 1993; Eblen 1974; Coale and Rives 1973; Hollman 1993; Robinson et al. 1993; Bogue 1985; Coale and Zelnik 1963; and Siegel 1974.

A FINAL WORD

The United States provides an excellent example of how historical origins and race are interrelated in racially stratified societies. Racial data have been used in many ways. For example, the U.S. constitution directed enumerators to count three racial groups in the census: whites, the enslaved Africans as "three-fifths" of a person, and civilized Native Americans. Since then, the census has facilitated the development and public awareness of social statistics and demography, and now the public is served a steady diet of racial data. Racial data are necessary for viewing the effects of racial prejudice on socioeconomic status and individual well-being.

Researchers employ observational records to define abstract concepts like race. The researchers or the subject (as in self-administered surveys or censuses) can make the observation; however, the researchers and the purpose of their study determine the meaning of the record. This is how empirical research reifies race. If we have records of racial classification, the population of races rather than the population of persons is open to statistical investigation; yet in social statistics it is always a mistake to think of a population of races as a genetic population. A population of races in this sense is a statistical concept based on a crude system of measurement that has been politically constructed.

We must demystify aspects of currently accepted notions of racial statistics by showing the extent to which this research has been shaped by extrinsic factors such as the interests and social position of particular writers and debated issues long since forgotten. Most research on race has not yet come to terms with the full range of problems to which the idea was originally addressed, and, in this way, we may be led to new ideas or to new applications by returning to the source of the idea.

I have argued that race is a social construct. I have attempted to graph what this construct looks like historically. Within this construct, the person of color does not exist outside of his or her otherness (Fanon 1967; Gordon 1995). The belief in race as real is what makes race real in its social consequences. Nevertheless, we should question how and why we believe race is real. My desire is not to diminish the social significance of race, but to bring into view the reality of the color line, the reality of the experience of race. If race existed only on its condition of being believed, its life may have ceased long ago.

It is in the collective belief that humans are divided into races, built into the experience of everyday life, that the idea of the color line to which we are subordinate gains its place in the real world. In order to change, or eliminate, the color line, we must change not merely our own thinking but also the social conditions of everyday life.

We are not born as members of a racial group. The conflicts between racial groups cannot be explained in terms of fixed invariables like biological identity. Otherwise the problems of the color line would always be the same at all times and places; further, there would never be any solution to racial conflict except through a change in that which is permanently fixed. The solution to racial conflict must be sought through a change in how we view and practice race and a change in how race is used to maintain the color line.

REFERENCES

Ahlburg, Dennis A. 1993. "The Census Bureau's New Projections of the U.S. Population." *Population and Development Review* 19(1): 159–74.

Allen, Theodore W. 1994. *The Invention of the White Race.* Vol. 1: *Racial Oppression and Social Control.* New York: Verso.

Barringer, Herbert, Robert W. Gardner, and Michael J. Levin. 1993. *Asians and Pacific Islanders in the United States.* New York: Russell Sage Foundation.

Bashi, Vilna, and Antonio McDaniel. 1997. "A Theory of Immigration and Racial Stratification." *Journal of Black Studies* 27(5): 668–82.

Bean, Frank D., and Marta Tienda. 1987. *The Hispanic Population of the United States.* New York: Russell Sage Foundation.

Bogue, Donald J. 1985. *Population of the United States: Historical Trends and Future Projections.* New York: The Free Press.

Burgess, Ernest W. 1967 [1925]. "The Growth of the City." In *The City,* edited by Robert E. Park, Ernest W. Burgess, and Roderick D. McKenzie. Chicago: University of Chicago Press.

Coale, Ansley J., and Norfleet Rives. 1973. "A Statistical Reconstruction of the Black Population of the United States, 1880–1970: Estimates of the Numbers by Age and Sex, Birth Rates and Total Fertility." *Population Index* 39(1): 3–36.

Coale, Ansley J. and Melvin Zelnik. 1963. *New Estimates of Fertility and Population in the United States.* Princeton, N.J.: Princeton University Press.

Cox, Oliver C. 1948. *Caste, Class, and Race: A Study in Social Dynamics.* New York: Doubleday.

Denton, Nancy A., and Douglas S. Massey. 1989. "Racial Identity among Caribbean Latinos." *American Sociological Review* 54(5): 790–808.

Eblen, Jack. 1974. "New Estimates of Vital Rates of the United States Black Population during the 19th Century." *Demography* 11(2): 301–19.

Espiritu, Yen Le. 1992. *Asian American Pan-Ethnicity: Bridging Institutions and Identities.* Philadelphia: Temple University Press.

Fanon, Frantz. 1967. *Black Skin, White Masks.* New York: Grove Press.

Gordon, Lewis R. 1995. *Fanon and the Crisis of European Man: An Essay on Philosophy and the Human Sciences.* New York: Routledge.

Hout, Michael, and Joshua R. Goldstein. 1994. "How 4.5 Million Irish Immigrants Became 40 Million Irish Americans." *American Sociological Review* 59(1): 64–82.

Hutchinson, Edward P. 1981. *Legislative History of American Immigration Policy: 1798–1965.* Philadelphia: University of Pennsylvania Press.

Jasso, Guillermina, and Mark R. Rosenzweig. 1990. *The New Chosen People: Immigrants in the United States.* New York: Russell Sage Foundation.

McDaniel, Antonio. 1995. "The Dynamic Racial Composition of the United States." *Daedalus* 124(1): 79–98.

Park, Robert E. 1967 [1925]. "The City." In *The City,* edited by Robert E. Park, Ernest W. Burgess, and Roderick D. McKenzie. Chicago: University of Chicago Press.

Robinson, Gregory, Bashir Ahmed, Prighwis Das Gupta, and Karen Woodrow. 1993. "Estimates of Population Coverage in the 1990 United States Census Based on Demographic Analysis." *Journal of the American Statistical Association* 88(423): 1,061–71.

Rodríguez, Clara E., and Héctor Cordero-Guzmán. 1992. "Placing Race in Context." *Racial and Ethnic Studies* 15(4): 523–41.

Siegel, Jacob. 1974. "Estimates of Coverage of the Population by Sex, Race, and Age in the 1970 Census" *Demography* (February): 7.

Smedley, Audrey. 1993. *Race in North America: Origin and Evolution of a Worldview.* Boulder, Colo.: Westview Press.

Taeuber, Karl, and Alma F. Taeuber. 1965. *Negroes in Cities.* Chicago: Aldine.

Thornton, Russell and Joan Marsh-Thornton. 1981. "Estimating Prehistoric American Indian Population Size for United States Area: Implication for the Nineteenth Century Population Decline and Nadir." *American Journal of Physical Anthropology* 55: 47–53.

U.S. Bureau of the Census. 1991. "The Hispanic Population in the United States: March 1990." *Current Population Reports.* Washington: U.S. Government Printing Office.

———. 1992. "Population Projections of the United States, by Age, Sex, Race and Hispanic Origin: 1992–2050." *Current Population Reports,* P25–1092. Washington: U.S. Government Printing Office.

———. 1993. "U.S. Population Estimates by Age, Sex, Race, and Hispanic Origin: 1980 to 1991." *Current Population Reports,* P25–1095. Washington: U.S. Government Printing Office.

Waters, Mary C. 1990. *Ethnic Options: Choosing Identities in America.* Berkeley: University of California Press.

Willette, JoAnne. 1982. *The Demographic and Socioeconomic Characteristics of the Latino Population in the United States: 1950–1980.* Washington: U.S. Department of Health and Human Services and Population Reference Bureau.

Willette, JoAnne, Robert Haupt, Carl Haub, Leon Bouvier, and Cary Davis. 1982. "The Demographic and Socioeconomic Characteristics of the Hispanic Population in the United States: 1950–1980." Report to the Department of Health and Human Services, Development Associates, Inc. and Population Reference Bureau, Inc., January 18, table 1 and 2.

Wood, Peter H. 1975. "More Like a Negro Country: Demographic Patterns in Colonial South Carolina, 1700–1740." In *Race and Slavery in the Western Hemisphere: Quantitative Studies,* edited by Stanley L. Engerman and Eugene D. Genovese. Princeton, N.J.: Princeton University Press.

—— Chapter 7 ——

The African American Population, 1930 to 1990

Irma T. Elo and Samuel H. Preston

U NDERSTANDING THE DEMOGRAPHY of the African American population is not a matter of looking up data in official government
reports. Official data are plagued by incompleteness and inac-
curacy—in more technical terms, by errors in coverage and content.
These errors impede a reliable assessment of the social, economic,
and health conditions of the African American population.

To date there has been only one effort to provide a comprehensive assessment of African American demography, and that
was published a quarter century ago (Coale and Rives 1973).
Since that time, new data and new methods (most of them developed for use in Third World countries) have become available,
permitting a fresh appraisal. The U.S. Bureau of the Census has
taken advantage of some of these new resources in its efforts to
assess census undercounts. Ironically, these efforts at demographic reconstruction ignore one of the most important sources
of demographic information, the census itself. In this chapter, we
summarize results of our project to reconstruct African American
demography during the period from 1930 to 1990.

DATA ON AFRICAN AMERICANS

The United States was the last industrial country to implement a
nationwide system of birth and death registration. The routine col-

168

lection of annual death statistics did not begin until 1900, the birth registration area was not established until 1915, and it was not until 1933 that all states had been admitted to both the national birth and death registration areas. The laggard region was the South, where the vast majority of African Americans lived in early decades of the twentieth century (U.S. Bureau of the Census 1939, 1–2).

Unfortunately, completion of the registration system did not mean an end to incomplete counts. Underregistration of African American births remained substantial as late as 1950 (Shapiro and Schachter 1952). It was not until the mid-1960s that birth registration was estimated to be nearly complete among both African Americans and whites (98.0 percent for African Americans and 99.4 percent for whites; see U.S. Bureau of the Census 1973). Recent revisions in the estimated extent of underregistration of African American births in the 1930s and 1940s illustrate the remaining uncertainties in the early record, and these uncertainties carry forward on a cohort basis to contemporary counts of older African Americans (Robinson 1991; Robinson et al. 1993).

High omission rates of African Americans in the decennial censuses throughout this century affect all demographic assessments of the African American population, including levels of mortality and fertility. The Census Bureau's program to estimate the completeness of decennial census counts for various age, sex, and racial groups has found consistently high rates of census undercount for African Americans, especially males (Robinson et al. 1993). Such undercounts not only have implications for analyses of demographic processes but also raise important questions about equity in congressional representation and in the allocation of federal funds to localities.

Errors in coverage appear smaller in death statistics, except in the case of infants. A death certificate is required for burial, providing a strong incentive for registration: fewer than 1 percent of deaths went unregistered as early as 1967 (Shryock and Siegel 1973, 391). Another source of doubt in estimates of African American mortality, in addition to census undercount, is the poor quality of age reporting in both death statistics and censuses, particularly at older ages (Coale and Kisker 1990; Elo and Preston 1994; Kestenbaum 1992). Age misreporting also affects estimates of old-age mortality based on Social Security and Medicare data (Elo and Preston 1994; Preston et al. 1996). The unreliability of age data for elderly African Americans undoubtedly reflects the fact that many of their births were never registered.

Errors in African American demographic data are readily demonstrated through a simple consistency test. Figure 7.1 compares the population enumerated in a census, by age, to the expected population in that age group in the previous census, allowing for intercensal deaths and migration. A ratio of 1.0 indicates perfect consistency among the data sources. Deviations from 1.0, in turn, can result from underenumeration in one or both censuses, underregistration of deaths, or misreporting of age in any or all data sources (Condran, Himes, and Preston 1991). The expected size of a cohort at the second census can be obtained by subtracting cohort deaths from the size of the cohort at the first census and then adjusting for intercensal migration. The ratio of actual to expected population is calculated from the enumerated population in the second census and the expected population at that census.

The patterns of deviation shown in this figure for African American women are similar to those for African American men (which are not shown). The most notable inconsistencies are at ages sixty-five to seventy-four, particularly at the censuses from 1940 to 1960, and at the oldest ages in each of the intercensal decades. The excess of enumerated relative to expected persons at ages sixty-five to seventy-four is most likely related to incentives to overstate age that were created by enactment of the Social Security legislation in the mid-1930s (U.S. Bureau of the Census 1946). At older ages, the size of the enumerated population in the second census tends to fall below the expected population at that census, as indicated by ratios that fall below 1.0.

This pattern could result from underregistration of deaths at older ages. More likely, however, it reflects the overstatement of ages in the census relative to death statistics (Elo and Preston 1994). Other evidence that points to similar data errors includes inconsistencies in the reporting of age on death certificates and records for the same individuals in the 1960 census of population (National Center for Health Statistics 1968; Kitagawa and Hauser 1973), as well as differences between mortality rates estimated from vital statistics and census information and those from Medi-

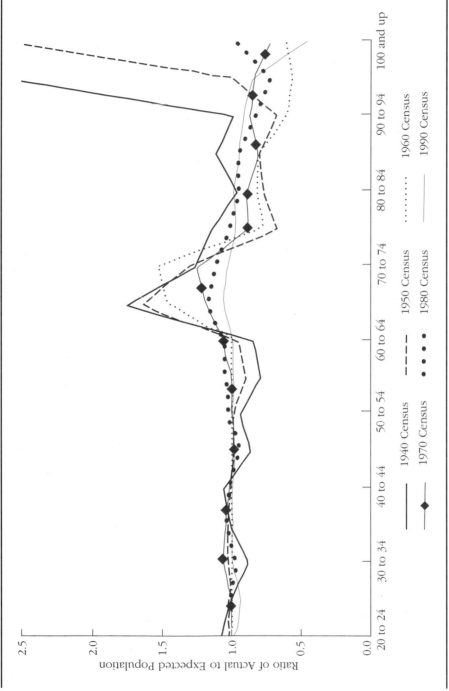

FIGURE 7.1 Ratio of Actual to Expected Census Population, African American Females, 1940 to 1990

1940 Census   1950 Census   1960 Census

1970 Census   1980 Census   1990 Census

Ratio of Actual to Expected Population

20 to 24   30 to 34   40 to 44   50 to 54   60 to 64   70 to 74   80 to 84   90 to 94   100 and up

Source: Elo and Preston 1994.

care data (Coale and Kisker 1990), Social Security data (Bayo 1972; Kestenbaum 1992), insurance records (Zelnik 1969), and extinct-generation procedures (Elo and Preston 1994).

Another potential problem in reconstructing the African American population arises from inconsistencies in the reporting of race on vital certificates and census records. Fortunately, there seems to be a high degree of consistency in the reporting of African American status on race questions. A study linking death certificates with the 1960 census of population finds, for example, that for 98.2 percent of African Americans the same race was reported on the death certificate as in the census record; the net difference was only 0.3 percent (National Center for Health Statistics 1969). A more recent study linking records from twelve current population surveys (CPS) with the national death index for the period 1979 to 1985 finds a similarly high correspondence in the reporting of race among African Americans: in 98.2 percent of cases the same race was reported on the death certificate as in the CPS record, with a net difference of just 0.4 percent (Sorlie, Rogot, and Johnson 1992). Studies linking census and CPS records further show that the reporting of race is highly consistent for African Americans (see U.S. Bureau of the Census 1964, 1975).

Slightly larger inconsistencies appear to exist in the reporting of race on birth and infant death certificates, however. Hahn, Mulinare, and Teutsch (1992) find that 4.3 percent of infants classified as black at birth were assigned a different race on the death certificate in linked birth-infant death data for the United States in the period 1983 to 1985. The net difference was −1.9 percent. An increase in interracial marriages in recent years has further increased the potential for inconsistent reporting of race for the offspring of such marriages on death certificates and on birth and census records (for example, Robinson and Gist 1992; Harrison and Bennett 1995). Such inconsistencies did not lead to notable discrepancies in earlier decades.

Errors present in vital statistics and census data have led to important misconceptions regarding some key features of African American demography. Data problems pose obvious difficulties for establishing valid estimates of African American death rates at the oldest ages, which consistently are estimated to have been lower than those of whites throughout the twentieth century (for example, Bayo 1972; National Center for Health Statistics 1985; U.S. Bureau of the Census 1946; Zelnik 1969). The crossover to lower African American than white mortality at older ages has provided empirical underpinnings for suggestion that a "survival of the fittest" mechanism is operating in old-age mortality (Manton and Stallard 1981; Manton, Stallard, and Vaupel 1981). Because African Americans were subject to exceptionally adverse health conditions earlier in the century, it is plausible that the more vulnerable members of a cohort died at younger ages, with only the most robust surviving to old age. Evidence from other populations, however, suggests that cohorts subject to severe health conditions in early life also experience elevated mortality in later life (Coale and Kisker 1986; Elo and Preston 1992; Mosley and Gray 1993).

African American mortality estimates are also affected by the census undercount. Because omission rates are much higher for men than for women, especially in young adulthood and at middle age, excess male mortality at these ages can be exaggerated if the denominator in the construction of death rates is not corrected for census undercount. The census undercount of reproductive-age women can also bias estimates of age-specific fertility rates. Estimation of fertility is further complicated by underregistration of births in the first half of the century and, in recent years, by a potential mismatch in the racial classification of births and women in the census.

Somewhat surprising, the available data for African Americans have not been fully exploited. The most obvious gap is the absence of life tables for African Americans between the decennial life tables of 1939 to 1941 and 1969 to 1971. These tables are available only for whites and nonwhites. Although the vast majority of the nonwhite population during this period was African American, the differences in mortality rates between African Americans and other nonwhites, such as Japanese and Chinese, were substantial (for example, Kitagawa and Hauser 1973; Barringer, Gardner, and Levin 1993), and thus the experience of nonwhites is not strictly applicable to African Americans. The absence of a continuous series of mortality estimates and the presence of errors in vital statistics and census data for African Americans make it impossible to assess accurately the evolution of mortality in this population during the twentieth century.

ANALYTIC STRATEGY

To fill this void, we attempt to reconstruct the demography of the African American population during the period from 1930 to 1990. Our purpose is to construct a consistent set of estimates of age- and sex-specific death and birth rates, as well as estimates of age and sex distribution of the population at various census dates. These series are designed to correct data errors present in vital statistics and censuses. Our analytic strategy proceeds as follows:

(1) We correct the official series of deaths for age misreporting by conducting a matching study of ages at death on death certificates in 1980 and 1985. The sample of death certificates is matched on a case-by-case basis to records for the same individuals in censuses of 1900, 1910, and 1920 and to Social Security records for these same individuals.

(2) The pattern of age misreporting uncovered in the matching study is extended backward in time by reference to an empirical relation established between age misreporting and literacy.

(3) Birth and infant death series are corrected for underregistration using results from analyses by the U.S. Census Bureau (Robinson et al. 1993). Because the racial classification of births is based on the race of the father, we slightly modify the series for the analysis of age-specific fertility rates by reclassifying births by race of the mother.

(4) Using corrected data on deaths by age and births, we estimate the true population by age and sex at censuses from 1930 to 1990 using one of three techniques. For the oldest cohorts, we employ extinct-generation methods, estimating the size of cohorts by counting the subsequent number of corrected deaths in the cohort. For the youngest cohorts, we estimate the size at census by using the corrected birth series and subtracting cohort deaths, employing the estimated death series and esti-

mated net intercensal migration. For the intermediate cohorts, we employ an age-period-cohort model of census counts.

The consistent series of births, deaths, and census counts produced by these steps then provides the basis for estimates of fertility and mortality. Our series differs from those of the Census Bureau by extending estimates further backward in time, by introducing deaths corrected for age misreporting, and by integrating actual census counts directly into the estimation framework (in the last step).

QUALITY OF AGE REPORTING
ON DEATH CERTIFICATES

Our correction of vital statistics data on deaths for age misreporting is based on the results of a record-linkage study aimed at identifying the true ages at death of African Americans reported as dying at ages sixty-five and older in 1985. We match a national sample of decedents to records of the Social Security Administration and to U.S. censuses of 1900, 1910, and 1920 (that is, when these individuals were children or young adults). Of the 5,262 death certificates in our sample, we successfully link 4,968 records to at least one of the two sources; a three-way linkage is achieved for 2,657 records, or 50.5 percent of the entire sample of death certificates (Preston et al. 1996).

Our results confirm that age misreporting on death certificates among elderly African Americans poses a serious problem in estimating mortality at older ages. Only 47.6 percent of deaths linked to early census records and 65.7 percent of those linked to Social Security records exhibit age agreement in the two sources. In both cases, ages on the death certificate are found to be too young, on average, and age agreement is worse for women than for men. Relative to early census age, for example, 40.4 percent of the women had a death certificate age that was too young compared with 32.4 percent of the men. In contrast, age at death was overstated on the death certificate for only 15.1 percent of the women and 16.9 percent of the men (Preston et al. 1996). Our results are consistent with the findings from the 1960 study linking death certificates with census records, which also reveals systematic underreporting of age on the death certificate relative to the age on the matching census record (National Center for Health Statistics 1968). Similarly, Kestenbaum (1992) finds that ages at death for African Americans reported on 1987 death certificates from Texas and Massachusetts were more frequently understated than overstated in relation to ages on Social Security records.

Many factors undoubtedly contribute to the widespread misreporting of age at death and net age understatement. As noted, most elderly African Americans were born in the South, where birth registration was inadequate or nonexistent and literacy levels were low. Both the availability of birth certificates and higher levels of literacy significantly improve age reporting (Elo et al. 1996; Hill et al. 1997). It also has been suggested that the concept of chronological age lacks salience among elderly African Americans and that the esteem associated with advanced age is lower among African Americans than some other groups (Peterson 1990). Interviews with elderly African Americans conducted in Philadelphia further suggest a vanity motive for age understatement, especially among women (Clarke, Hill, and Riddley 1995). The understatement of age on death certificates may also simply reflect the informant's failure to advance the decedent's age at each birthday. Age accuracy requires periodic updating, and errors of omission lead to understatement of age.

Despite the tendency for ages to be understated on death certificates relative to census and Social Security records, we find that too many deaths in vital statistics were registered above age ninety-five, as shown in figure 7.2. The excess above age ninety-five may appear surprising in light of the tendency for age on the death certificate to be understated. This apparent paradox occurs when age misreporting takes place in both directions and the age distribution declines rapidly with age. Even though the net direction of age misreporting is downward, more deaths can be transferred inappropriately into an age category from below than are transferred out of it to a younger age group. Exactly this type of mechanism is operating in vital statistics data on deaths for African Americans, as seen in table 7.1 at census ages ninety to ninety-

TABLE 7.1 **Weighted Joint Distribution of the Number of Deaths, by Age at Death on the Death Certificate and That Implied by an Early Census Record**

Age on Death Certificate	Calculated Age at Death (Census)										Total
	60 to 64	65 to 69	70 to 74	75 to 79	80 to 84	85 to 89	90 to 94	95 to 99	100 to 104	105 to 109	
60 to 64	353.12	75.68	10.55	16.81							456.16
65 to 69	16.82	379.03	90.92	13.43	3.47						503.68
70 to 74		15.44	421.77	88.06	23.05	5.66	1.55				555.53
75 to 79		3.10	26.53	390.63	84.81	14.64	3.19				522.91
80 to 84		2.72	3.14	25.31	314.98	75.01	15.25	2.55			438.95
85 to 89				3.28	13.34	223.87	34.14	4.04	0.47		279.13
90 to 94			0.75		1.47	21.13	115.79	8.41			147.55
95 to 99						6.31	15.56	39.33	1.09		62.29
100 to 104					0.94		5.14	4.79	7.24	0.11	18.23
105 to 109									1.58	2.70	4.28
110 and up								0.63	0.63		1.27
Total	369.94	475.98	553.66	537.52	442.06	346.63	190.62	59.75	11.02	2.81	2,990.00

Source: Preston et al. 1996.

FIGURE 7.2 **Ratio of Number of Deaths by Age on Death Certificates to Those in Two Other Sources: Three-Way Matched Sample**

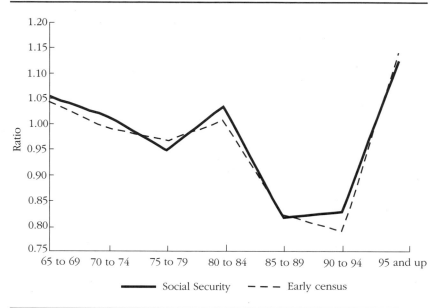

Source: Preston et al. 1996.

four and ninety-five to ninety-nine. At both census ages, many more deaths were transferred downward than upward. Yet because deaths at ninety to ninety-four were far more numerous, close to twice as many deaths were transferred upward from the census age ninety to ninety-four to the death certificate age ninety-five to ninety-nine (15.56) than were transferred downward from the census age ninety-five to ninety-nine to the death certificate age ninety to ninety-four (8.41).

The 1985 age misreporting matrix shown in table 7.2 also provides the basis for correcting the vital statistics data on deaths at younger ages and during prior decades. The substantial amount of age misreporting among persons ages sixty-five to sixty-nine and ages seventy to seventy-four (shown in table 7.2) suggests that age misreporting is likely to occur at younger ages as well. We cannot, however, examine such age misreporting using the 1920 census of population, the latest census for which census manuscript records

TABLE 7.2 **Age Reporting Propensities Based on Three-Way Match of Death Certificates, Social Security Records, and Early Census Records, 1985**

	Percentage Reporting in Five-Year Age Bracket That Is					
Final Age	Two Below Final Age Bracket	One Below Final Age Bracket	Same Age Bracket	One Above Final Age Bracket	Two Above Final Age Bracket	Total Number of Deaths
Females						
65 to 69	—	9.93	89.14	0.93	0.00	170.4
70 to 74	6.42	10.88	81.31	1.02	0.37	217.3
75 to 79	4.63	13.31	80.60	0.93	0.53	236.7
80 to 84	6.72	13.50	77.57	1.76	0.45	195.9
85 to 89	4.12	24.05	67.62	3.06	1.15	182.3
90 to 94	9.23	14.29	68.91	5.93	1.64	107.2
95 to 99	11.79	7.27	75.07	4.86	1.01	37.9
100 and up	0.00	10.72	72.27	17.01	0.00	9.7
Males						
65 to 69	—	11.45	85.38	2.55	0.62	256.6
70 to 74	1.48	11.28	85.01	1.50	0.74	269.7
75 to 79	1.89	11.12	82.07	4.55	0.37	258.2
80 to 84	3.85	9.71	85.23	1.21	0.00	175.9
85 to 89	3.03	11.96	79.59	3.12	2.30	115.3
90 to 94	7.67	10.32	72.28	6.13	3.60	58.6
95 to 99	5.38	9.69	83.55	0.00	1.38	12.7
100 and up	0.00	0.00	63.13	36.87	0.00	3.8

Source: Preston et al. 1998.
Note. Structural zero

were available. Instead, we take advantage of the finding that age misreporting is significantly associated with levels of literacy (Elo et al. 1996; Hill et al. 1997).

Specifically, we estimate patterns of age misreporting at younger ages as a function of the proportion of persons in his or her sex, state of birth, and birth cohort who completed zero to four years of schooling by fitting a multinomial logit model to observations in our sample of three-way matches (death certificate-early census-Social Security) at ages seventy and above. Using the estimated coefficients of this equation together with the proportion of individuals who completed zero to four years of schooling in the person's state of birth and cohort by sex, we predict age-misreporting propensities in 1985 at ages forty to forty-four, forty-five to forty-nine, and fifty to fifty-four. Misreporting propensities at ages fifty-five to fifty-nine and ages sixty to sixty-four are linearly interpolated between those at ages fifty to fifty-four and those at ages sixty-five to sixty-nine in our original matrix. We further assume that age forty is a barrier to age misreporting; that is, there are no transfers across this boundary and no misreporting below this age (Preston et al. 1998, appendix).

It is not reasonable to assume that age misreporting was the same in 1985 as in decades prior to the 1980s. Educational levels, for example, were much lower during earlier decades, and it is reasonable to expect that age misreporting problems would increase as we go further back in time. To reconstruct misreporting matrixes for earlier periods all the way back to 1930, we cannot rely on the relatively small range of variation in levels of aggregate schooling observed in the 1980s; improvements in schooling levels were so rapid that out-of-sample extrapolation would be required for all years before 1970. Instead, we obtain information on the literacy level of the mother of each decedent age eighty-five and older in our three-way-match sample from census manuscript records. We select this age interval because literacy levels are lowest and age misreporting is most frequent at the oldest ages.

On the basis of this sample, we estimate a multinomial logistic equation predicting age-reporting propensities as a function of mother's literacy. We then employ the estimated coefficients and estimated changes in the average level of mother's literacy by age to estimate changes in the age misreporting matrix back in time. These misreporting matrixes are then used to relate the observed number of deaths in five-year age groups to the estimated true number of deaths by five-year time blocks back to 1930. We make these adjustments beginning at age forty to forty-four up to the age interval one hundred and above (see Preston et al. 1998). The corrected death distributions are then used to reconstruct the size of the African American population by age and sex at each of the census dates and to estimate mortality from 1935 to 1990.

THE AFRICAN AMERICAN POPULATION
BY AGE AND SEX

The next step in our reconstruction is to estimate the true size of the African American population by sex and five-year age groups at census dates beginning in 1930 and extending to 1990. The building blocks in our analyses are the enumerated populations by age and sex in each census, cohort deaths corrected for age misreporting, estimated numbers of births from 1935 to 1990, and estimates of net intercensal migration. In addition to correcting the death series for age misreporting, we assume that infant deaths are underregistered by the same percentage as births. This assumption differs from that employed by the Census Bureau, which assumes that underregistration of infant deaths is half as great as underregistration of births.

As noted, we employ the most recent estimates of African American births prepared by the Census Bureau (Robinson et al. 1993). We also rely on Census Bureau estimates of net intercensal migration, except that we modify the bureau's series by our own estimates of migration among the African American, Puerto Rican–born population. Our estimates are designed to take account of both net migration between Puerto Rico and the United States and changes in racial classification of Puerto Rican–born individuals in the various censuses (see Elo and Preston 1994).

We employ a varied set of estimation techniques, depending on the cohort for which estimates are being sought. Table 7.3 shows the cells for which population estimates are made. For the cells in the upper-right-hand corner, we follow the Census Bureau and use classic demographic analysis with some modifications in the input data (Himes and Clogg 1992). For cells identified in the lower-left-hand corner of table 7.3, we construct cohort size using the extinct-generation method (Vincent 1951). For a cohort all of whose members have died, this method estimates the size of the cohort at a particular age by adding together all recorded deaths to the cohort subsequent to that age. Since we have reconstructed the death series with care, we believe that estimates of cohort size that can be derived exclusively from deaths are more reliable than estimates based on census counts.

TABLE 7.3 Cells for Which Population Estimates Are Sought

Age	Census Date						
	1930	1940	1950	1960	1970	1980	1990
0 to 4	$N_{1,1}$	$N_{1,2}$	$N_{1,3}$	$N_{1,4}$	$N_{1,5}$	$N_{1,6}$	$N_{1,7}$
5 to 9	$N_{2,1}$	$N_{2,2}$	$N_{2,3}$	$N_{2,4}$	$N_{2,5}$	$N_{2,6}$	$N_{2,7}$
10 to 14	$N_{3,1}$	$N_{3,2}$	$N_{3,3}$	$N_{3,4}$	$N_{3,5}$	$N_{3,6}$	$N_{3,7}$
15 to 19	$N_{4,1}$	$N_{4,2}$	$N_{4,3}$	$N_{4,4}$	$N_{4,5}$	$N_{4,6}$	$N_{4,7}$
20 to 24	$N_{5,1}$	$N_{5,2}$	$N_{5,3}$	$N_{5,4}$	$N_{5,5}$	$N_{5,6}$	$N_{5,7}$
25 to 29	$N_{6,1}$	$N_{6,2}$	$N_{6,3}$	$N_{6,4}$	$N_{6,5}$	$N_{6,6}$	$N_{6,7}$
30 to 34	$N_{7,1}$	$N_{7,2}$	$N_{7,3}$	$N_{7,4}$	$N_{7,5}$	$N_{7,6}$	$N_{7,7}$
35 to 39	$N_{8,1}$	$N_{8,2}$	$N_{8,3}$	$N_{8,4}$	$N_{8,5}$	$N_{8,6}$	$N_{8,7}$
40 to 44	$N_{9,1}$	$N_{9,2}$	$N_{9,3}$	$N_{9,4}$	$N_{9,5}$	$N_{9,6}$	$N_{9,7}$
45 to 49	$N_{10,1}$	$N_{10,2}$	$N_{10,3}$	$N_{10,4}$	$N_{10,5}$	$N_{10,6}$	$N_{10,7}$
50 to 54	$N_{11,1}$	$N_{11,2}$	$N_{11,3}$	$N_{11,4}$	$N_{11,5}$	$N_{11,6}$	$N_{11,7}$
55 to 59	$N_{12,1}$	$N_{12,2}$	$N_{12,3}$	$N_{12,4}$	$N_{12,5}$	$N_{12,6}$	$N_{12,7}$
60 to 64	$N_{13,1}$	$N_{13,2}$	$N_{13,3}$	$N_{13,4}$	$N_{13,5}$	$N_{13,6}$	$N_{13,7}$
65 to 69	$N_{14,1}$	$N_{14,2}$	$N_{14,3}$	$N_{14,4}$	$N_{14,5}$	$N_{14,6}$	$N_{14,7}$
70 to 74	$N_{15,1}$	$N_{15,2}$	$N_{15,3}$	$N_{15,4}$	$N_{15,5}$	$N_{15,6}$	$N_{15,7}$
75 to 79	$N_{16,1}$	$N_{16,2}$	$N_{16,3}$	$N_{16,4}$	$N_{16,5}$	$N_{16,6}$	$N_{16,7}$
80 to 84	$N_{17,1}$	$N_{17,2}$	$N_{17,3}$	$N_{17,4}$	$N_{17,5}$	$N_{17,6}$	$N_{17,7}$

Source: Preston et al. 1998.

For cohorts in the middle of table 7.3, for which neither extinct-generation estimates nor estimates from demographic analysis are available, we employ an age-period-cohort model of census counts to estimate the true size of these cohorts. In contrast to demographic analysis or extinct-generation methods, which ignore census counts altogether, this procedure uses census counts themselves as the basis for estimation. It takes advantage of the fact that multiple observations are available on the size of a cohort across different censuses. By examining census counts for particular cohorts in successive censuses, it identifies systematic errors associated with age and census date and develops a single preferred estimate of cohort size at each census date. Further detail on these procedures can be found in the appendix to this chapter.

The results of these analyses produce new estimates of census counts by sex and five-year age groups from ages zero to eighty-four for each of the censuses from 1930 to 1990, as shown in table 7.4. We derive these estimates by subtracting intercensal deaths and adding intercensal net migration by cohort to the estimates of initial cohort size that are developed through one of the three methods described earlier and in the appendix (births, extinct-generation methods, and the age/period/cohort model). Our estimates for 1990 provide, in general, strong confirmation of the Census Bureau's estimates of census undercount in that year.

Table 7.5 compares estimates of total census undercount based on our reconstructions with those of Coale and Rives (1973) and the Census Bureau for all censuses for which these estimates overlap. On the one hand, for each census, our estimates of census undercount are much lower than those made by Coale and Rives, especially in earlier censuses and for females. On the other hand, our estimates are surprisingly close to those prepared by the Census Bureau, even though the methods used are very different. The value added by our estimates is thus greatest for the earlier years of the series, where we have employed new methods that take advantage of information not available to Coale and Rives. At the same time, we provide independent validation of the Census Bureau's estimates, while extending the range of reconstructions to one additional census and eight additional five-year birth cohorts.

The sex ratios implied by our reconstructed populations are shown in table 7.6. The principal oddity of these ratios is the high masculinity of the population at ages thirty and above in 1930, a pattern that is carried forward on a cohort basis to subsequent censuses. It is unusual to encounter such high masculinity in populations in which migration is not an important factor of population change. The implication is that adult death rates for females were very high relative to those of males in years prior to 1930.

Some confirmation of this tendency is provided by cause-of-death life tables for U.S. nonwhites in 1920. Females had higher death rates than males at all ages from fifteen to sixty-nine, with the difference in annual death rates reaching four per one thousand between ages fifty-five and sixty-four (Preston, Keyfitz, and Schoen 1972, 740–43). The probability of surviving from age fifteen to age sixty-five was 11.5 percent higher for males than for females, although this discrepancy is probably overstated by relative census undercount of males. Females showed an exceptionally high death rate from maternal causes: a fifteen-year-old woman had a 3.1 percent chance of dying from maternal causes

TABLE 7.4 Reconstructed African American Population by Age and Sex, 1930 to 1990

Age Group	1930	1940	1950	1960	1970	1980	1990
Females							
0 to 4	720,240	708,329	1,020,113	1,442,354	1,334,938	1,330,438	1,582,400
5 to 9	726,194	678,408	795,577	1,254,685	1,466,426	1,312,450	1,448,000
10 to 14	674,132	700,009	697,041	1,010,904	1,445,952	1,354,967	1,355,946
15 to 19	676,140	709,472	672,115	792,179	1,265,582	1,497,661	1,350,429
20 to 24	619,694	642,294	687,433	690,356	1,022,656	1,472,919	1,389,281
25 to 29	595,268	628,901	684,700	660,474	803,147	1,287,133	1,526,851
30 to 34	498,619	568,668	613,497	670,326	694,098	1,035,511	1,494,002
35 to 39	450,945	542,557	594,538	662,118	655,249	803,269	1,290,351
40 to 44	370,906	442,129	527,567	583,099	651,356	684,900	1,025,452
45 to 49	297,612	393,162	491,028	554,232	628,773	632,943	784,031
50 to 54	220,571	310,544	385,877	478,336	539,668	613,007	656,080
55 to 59	165,306	235,179	333,580	428,946	499,646	577,977	591,259
60 to 64	119,568	164,861	249,541	317,657	411,427	478,242	550,126
65 to 69	77,177	113,063	174,565	261,873	337,300	417,490	489,118
70 to 74	46,659	70,821	105,482	169,460	213,165	309,356	371,133
75 to 79	32,804	39,246	62,537	103,232	166,111	217,737	285,576
80 to 84	21,089	19,932	33,464	52,749	88,770	110,940	176,573
Total	6,312,924	6,967,575	8,128,655	10,132,980	12,224,264	14,136,940	16,366,608

Males

Age							
0 to 4	714,479	713,733	1,032,372	1,461,510	1,355,039	1,361,051	1,626,465
5 to 9	724,015	675,594	802,974	1,263,306	1,481,589	1,340,881	1,485,669
10 to 14	672,783	691,569	700,019	1,020,578	1,461,328	1,371,378	1,385,916
15 to 19	677,492	707,355	664,559	790,868	1,257,330	1,497,019	1,368,438
20 to 24	617,215	644,326	668,739	675,644	950,698	1,436,545	1,375,121
25 to 29	583,958	633,825	672,425	645,148	777,070	1,248,365	1,503,643
30 to 34	505,600	566,471	605,348	651,169	671,164	998,456	1,464,046
35 to 39	472,233	529,842	593,422	644,617	624,994	768,696	1,235,916
40 to 44	391,700	443,073	520,655	571,312	618,028	651,997	965,218
45 to 49	314,844	404,244	473,893	547,820	596,462	590,216	727,564
50 to 54	238,162	318,053	375,021	462,430	509,254	555,587	598,088
55 to 59	187,869	238,095	326,240	398,215	465,394	510,287	517,766
60 to 64	133,504	170,232	241,526	287,317	365,977	408,610	456,391
65 to 69	81,782	122,537	165,563	230,868	283,744	340,591	379,762
70 to 74	49,155	73,240	99,576	143,272	158,264	229,552	266,171
75 to 79	32,014	36,857	59,120	81,815	112,357	148,347	186,014
80 to 84	19,308	17,624	28,474	39,806	55,855	49,661	94,179
Total	6,416,113	6,986,770	8,029,926	9,915,695	11,744,547	13,507,239	15,636,367

Source: Preston et al. 1998.

TABLE 7.5 **Estimated Percentage of African Americans Omitted from Various Censuses by Sex, 1930 to 1990**

Census Year	Males			Females		
	Present Estimates[a]	Census Bureau Estimates	Coale and Rives	Present Estimates[a]	Census Bureau Estimates	Coale and Rives
1930	8.9	—	12.9	4.6	—	12.1
1940	10.5	10.9	13.9	5.6	6.0	11.5
1950	9.3	9.7	12.4	5.0	5.4	9.0
1960	8.4	8.8	10.6	4.1	4.4	7.0
1970	8.8	9.1	10.4	3.7	4.0	5.4
1980	7.0	7.5	—	1.2	1.7	—
1990	8.2	8.5	—	2.8	3.0	—

Source: Preston et al. 1998. For the Census Bureau estimates, Robinson et al. 1993; for Coale and Rives estimates, Coale and Rives 1973.
Notes: — Not available.
[a]Ages zero to eighty-four.

before age fifty. The authenticity of this high masculinity is suggested by the 1930 census itself. Despite the possibility of higher undercounts for males, the census enumerated 16.8 percent more males than females in the age range forty-five to sixty-four (U.S. Bureau of the Census 1989, 16).

A useful by-product of our age-period-cohort model is the estimation of age and period effects of census completeness (the αs and τs in equations 7A.1 to 7A.3; see the appendix). We convert these coefficients into estimated proportions omitted by age and period shown in figures 7.3 and 7.4. As is shown in figure 7.3, relative to ages ten to fourteen, where the omission rate is arbitrarily set to zero to allow identification of the model, younger children of both sexes had higher estimated omission rates. Thereafter, females had a relatively flat pattern of age effects up to age sixty-four. Males, in contrast, had very high relative omission rates at ages twenty to forty-nine. This general pattern is not surprising since it has been uncovered using other methods as well (Robinson et al. 1993). Both sexes show negative relative omission rates—suggesting large relative overcounts—at ages sixty-five to sixty-nine and above. It is likely that this pattern reflects age mis-

TABLE 7.6 **Sex Ratios Based on Reconstructed Populations, African Americans, 1930 to 1990**

Age Group	1930	1940	1950	1960	1970	1980	1990
0 to 4	0.992	1.008	1.012	1.013	1.015	1.023	1.028
5 to 9	0.997	0.996	1.009	1.007	1.010	1.022	1.026
10 to 14	0.998	0.988	1.004	1.010	1.011	1.012	1.022
15 to 19	1.002	0.997	0.989	0.998	0.993	1.000	1.013
20 to 24	0.996	1.003	0.973	0.979	0.930	0.975	0.990
25 to 29	0.981	1.008	0.982	0.977	0.968	0.970	0.985
30 to 34	1.014	0.996	0.987	0.971	0.967	0.964	0.980
35 to 39	1.047	0.977	0.998	0.974	0.954	0.957	0.958
40 to 44	1.056	1.002	0.987	0.980	0.949	0.952	0.941
45 to 49	1.058	1.028	0.965	0.988	0.949	0.932	0.928
50 to 54	1.080	1.024	0.972	0.967	0.944	0.906	0.912
55 to 59	1.136	1.012	0.978	0.928	0.931	0.883	0.876
60 to 64	1.117	1.033	0.968	0.904	0.890	0.854	0.830
65 to 69	1.060	1.084	0.948	0.882	0.841	0.816	0.776
70 to 74	1.053	1.034	0.944	0.845	0.742	0.742	0.717
75 to 79	0.976	0.939	0.945	0.793	0.676	0.681	0.651
80 to 84	0.916	0.884	0.851	0.755	0.629	0.448	0.533
Total	1.016	1.003	0.988	0.979	0.961	0.955	0.955

Source: Preston et al. 1998.

reporting among older persons, a problem alluded to in our earlier discussion.

The census effects, presented in figure 7.4, show a trend that is toward improving census coverage for both sexes, but that is faster for females than for males. The 1990 census appears less complete than the 1980 census, an inference also made by the Census Bureau (Robinson et al. 1993). The 1930 census, while having an above-average level of incompleteness, appears to have been more complete than the 1940 census. The census effects are not direct estimates of the undercount in a particular census, which depends as well on age-specific omission rates combined with the age distribution of the population, which are shown in table 7.7. Despite the trend toward improved coverage for males between 1940 and 1980, the estimated census undercount for males is very similar in 1990 and 1930. Little improvement in male enumeration completeness is evident over this sixty-year period.

FIGURE 7.3 **Estimated Multipliers of Census Counts, by Age**

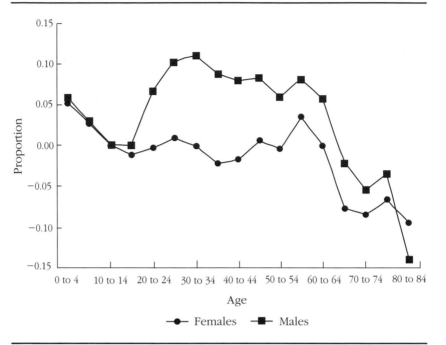

Source: Preston et al. 1998.

AFRICAN AMERICAN MORTALITY

The reconstruction of the size of the African American population by age and sex at each census from 1930 to 1990, together with our reconstructed death series, provides the basis for a consistent set of estimates of African American mortality over time. Age- and sex-specific death rates and life tables are constructed for five-year intervals from the period 1935 to 1940 through the period 1985 to 1990. This series fills an important gap in the official series, which lacks life tables for the African American population between 1940 and 1970. It also is the only series to establish consistency between deaths and census counts.

We estimate death rates at ages one to four through ages eighty to eighty-four in a conventional manner by combining all deaths in a five-year age group for a given five-year time block

FIGURE 7.4 Estimated Multipliers of Census Counts, by Census

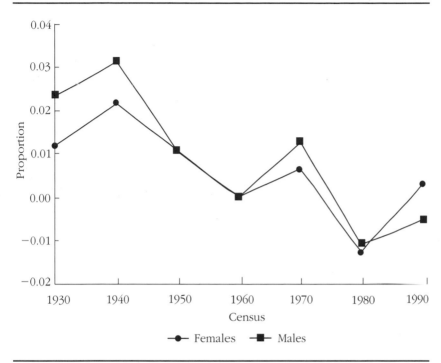

Source: Preston et al. 1998.

and by dividing the sum by an estimate of person-years at risk. Our estimates of infant mortality are obtained directly from births and deaths corrected for underregistration. To derive age-specific death rates at the highest ages, ages eighty-five to ninety-nine, we fit a linear function to the relationship between the logit of estimated age-specific death rates at ages forty-five to forty-nine through eighty to eighty-four and the logit of age-specific death rates taken from a standard age pattern of mortality (for further detail, see Elo 2001). As the standard, we use a model age pattern of mortality developed by Himes, Preston, and Condran (1994). We calculate life tables for each five-year period with MortPak, a life table program developed by the U.N. Population Division (United Nations 1990).

Table 7.8 summarizes estimated life expectancies at given ages in our new life tables. We graph age-specific death rates on a log-

TABLE 7.7 Estimated Census Omission Rates by Age and Sex, African Americans, 1930 to 1990

Age	1930	1940	1950	1960	1970	1980	1990
Females							
0 to 4	0.1396	0.1142	0.0777	0.0567	0.0906	0.0833	0.0817
5 to 9	0.0506	0.0407	0.0342	0.0464	0.0648	0.0517	0.0747
10 to 14	0.0669	0.0438	0.0281	0.0263	0.0285	0.0126	0.0404
15 to 19	0.0303	0.0492	0.0594	0.0449	0.0338	−0.0059	0.0048
20 to 24	−0.0494	−0.0043	0.0287	0.0689	0.0464	0.0249	0.0241
25 to 29	0.0392	0.0210	0.0273	0.0441	0.0396	0.0312	0.0458
30 to 34	0.1012	0.0768	0.0308	0.0100	0.0124	0.0097	0.0309
35 to 39	−0.0222	0.0355	−0.0237	0.0142	−0.0009	0.0025	0.0196
40 to 44	0.0604	0.0617	0.0451	0.0072	−0.0054	−0.0066	0.0114
45 to 49	−0.0324	0.1236	0.0985	0.0363	0.0405	0.0021	0.0199
50 to 54	−0.0306	0.1392	0.0853	0.0698	0.0152	−0.0240	0.0135
55 to 59	0.1822	0.1921	0.2464	0.0821	0.0608	0.0088	0.0175
60 to 64	0.0888	0.1407	0.2312	0.0856	0.0284	−0.0197	−0.0063
65 to 69	0.0617	−0.2803	−0.2062	0.0127	−0.0382	−0.0699	−0.0203
70 to 74	−0.0342	−0.1171	−0.0589	−0.0229	−0.0895	−0.0671	−0.0377
75 to 79	0.0999	−0.0663	−0.0339	−0.0558	0.1296	−0.0800	−0.0675
80 to 84	0.1439	−0.0912	−0.0187	0.0408	0.0374	−0.1291	−0.0757
Total, 0 to 84	0.0463	0.0561	0.0503	0.0406	0.0370	0.0122	0.0281

Males

0 to 4	0.1434	0.1289	0.0858	0.0659	0.0993	0.0892	0.0862
5 to 9	0.0599	0.0472	0.0501	0.0523	0.0694	0.0568	0.0768
10 to 14	0.0725	0.0437	0.0293	0.0289	0.0362	0.0132	0.0416
15 to 19	0.1197	0.1092	0.1047	0.0615	0.0432	-0.0022	-0.0014
20 to 24	0.1019	0.1461	0.1511	0.1558	0.1151	0.0859	0.0553
25 to 29	0.1418	0.1644	0.1258	0.1492	0.1529	0.1228	0.1204
30 to 34	0.1745	0.1740	0.1450	0.1331	0.1528	0.1201	0.1326
35 to 39	0.0873	0.1270	0.1000	0.1156	0.1344	0.317	0.1146
40 to 44	0.1326	0.0966	0.0982	0.1091	0.1194	0.1246	0.1008
45 to 49	-0.0277	0.1385	0.1129	0.1230	0.1272	0.1212	0.1137
50 to 54	-0.1668	0.1098	0.0616	0.1184	0.0987	0.0870	0.1133
55 to 59	0.0707	0.1296	0.1882	0.0811	0.1295	0.0819	0.1116
60 to 64	-0.0001	0.0938	0.1941	0.0973	0.0852	0.0543	0.0838
65 to 69	-0.0144	-0.2404	-0.1509	0.0061	0.0224	0.0233	0.0503
70 to 74	-0.0368	-0.1447	-0.0907	-0.0565	-0.1624	-0.0230	0.0496
75 to 79	0.0862	-0.0869	-0.1029	-0.1535	0.0209	-0.0318	0.0393
80 to 84	0.2044	-0.0601	-0.0853	-0.0027	-0.0512	-0.5124	-0.0443
Total, 0 to 84	0.0890	0.1047	0.0928	0.0836	0.0878	0.0702	0.0820

Source: Preston et al. 1998.

scale for females in figure 7.5. The results for males are similar. Our series of age-specific death rates is somewhat erratic, more so as we go further back in time when the reconstructions of our death series are more vulnerable to error. We do not attempt to smooth our estimates; instead, we simply present the rates as calculated. These rates also form the basis of the life table estimates presented in table 7.8. We believe that these estimates provide the best available basis for examining trends in African American mortality during the twentieth century. They are based on population and death series that are consistent with one another, that incorporate estimates of census undercount and of underregistration of births and infant deaths, and that correct for age misreporting in death statistics.

As is evident in the table, life expectancy at birth increased substantially for both African American men and women between 1935 to 1940 and 1985 to 1990, although male gains lagged behind those of females. Life expectancy at birth increased 19.5 years (from 54.3 to 73.8 years) for women and 14.3 years (from 51.6 to 65.9 years) for men during this period. Improvements in health conditions were particularly pronounced during the first ten years of our series for both sexes. Life expectancy rose 7.9

TABLE 7.8 **Estimated Life Expectancy at Birth and Age Sixty-Five, African American Females and Males, 1935 to 1990**

	Females		Males	
Time Period	e_0	e_{65}	e_0	e_{65}
1935 to 1940	54.33	12.20	51.60	10.94
1940 to 1945	58.10	12.73	55.43	11.33
1945 to 1950	62.25	13.58	59.13	12.03
1950 to 1955	64.76	13.94	60.72	11.99
1955 to 1960	66.28	14.39	61.82	12.06
1960 to 1965	66.96	14.59	61.78	11.76
1965 to 1970	67.75	14.65	61.14	11.57
1970 to 1975	69.62	15.36	62.01	12.01
1975 to 1980	72.15	16.26	64.29	12.50
1980 to 1985	73.30	16.55	65.78	12.90
1985 to 1990	73.85	16.91	65.92	13.13

Source: Elo 2001.

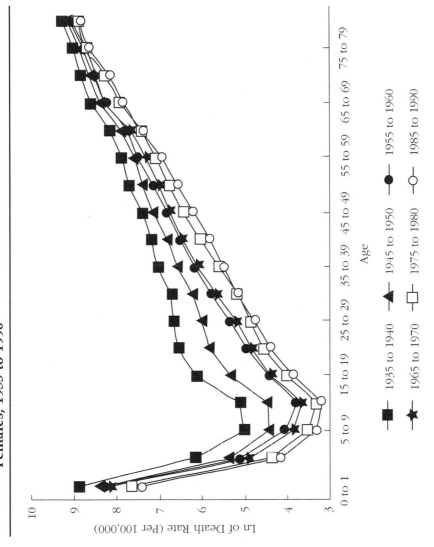

FIGURE 7.5 Log of Age-Specific Death Rates (Per 100,000), African American Females, 1935 to 1990

Source: Elo 2001.

years for women and 7.5 years for men between the period 1935 to 1940 and the period 1945 to 1950, representing about 40 percent of the total increase for women and more than 50 percent for men. Thereafter, improvements in health conditions more consistently benefited women.

The more rapid gains in life expectancy among women than men can be explained largely by trends in age-specific death rates at young adult and older ages. Child mortality, the probability of dying by age five, $q(5)$, and mortality between ages five and fifteen exhibited rather parallel declines for both sexes (figure 7.6). Above age fifteen, however, mortality decline clearly favored women. Sex-specific declines in death rates during young adulthood and middle age ($_{45}q_{15}$, the probability of dying between age fifteen and sixty) began to diverge in the mid-1950s. Subsequently, male mortality in this age range increased during the 1960s before resuming its downward course in the late 1970s, while female mortality continued to decline after briefly stagnating in the late 1960s.

In the latter half of the 1980s, mortality decline again slowed down in young adulthood and middle age, particularly among men. An increase in male death rates between ages fifteen and forty was a major contributing factor. Although age-specific death rates for women between ages fifteen and thirty-five also increased in the late 1980s relative to the first half of the decade, these increases were smaller than for men (see also Kochanek, Maurer, and Rosenberg 1994). Similarly, improvements in health conditions at the oldest ages ($_{25}q_{60}$, the probability of dying between ages sixty and eighty-five) clearly favored women. Throughout the period, female mortality continued to decline, while reductions in male mortality at the oldest ages were confined to the first and last decades covered by our estimates.

These sex differences in mortality decline led to dramatic changes in sex mortality differentials. Figure 7.7 graphs the ratio of male to female death rates by age over the period. While excess female mortality in the youngest reproductive ages was apparent in 1935 to 1940, by the end of the period an extreme male excess in mortality emerged at young adult ages. Although health conditions clearly improved during this period for both men and women, as shown in table 7.8, the more rapid improvements for women after age fifteen were translated into some striking changes in sex differentials in mortality.

Unfortunately, there is no series to which our estimates are directly comparable. As noted, many of the official life tables for the period under review pertain to the nonwhite rather than the African American population, and life tables for five-year periods have not been prepared either for African Americans or for nonwhites. In table 7.9, we compare our life expectancy estimates with those in official life tables centered on census years for which life tables for African Americans have been prepared, for the most recent five-year period covered by our series, and for nonwhites when life tables for African Americans are not available. To make our estimates comparable to the decennial life tables, we take the average of the life table values for the adjacent five-year periods, except in 1985 to 1990 when the value is taken directly from the 1985 to 1990 life table. In this case, the U.S. life table estimates refer to the average of the values taken from official tables for 1985 and for 1989 to 1991 (National Center for Health Statistics 1988, 1997a).

The first of these comparisons centers on the census taken in 1940. For males, the life expectancy at birth in the official life table was 52.3 years compared to our estimate of 53.5. For females, the respective values were 55.6 and 56.2 (table 7.9). Thus we estimate that mortality conditions during the earlier years were somewhat more favorable than previous estimates would suggest. The most likely source of this disparity is that we have corrected for census underenumeration; no such correction was made in construction of the 1939 to 1941 decennial life table (U.S. Bureau of the Census 1946). Toward the end of the series, the two estimates are more similar, especially for women.

In the latter half of the 1980s, life expectancy at birth for African American males based on the 1985 and the 1989 to 1991 life tables was 64.9 years compared to our estimate of 65.9. The respective figures for females were 73.6 and 73.8. We continue to estimate a somewhat higher life expectancy at birth for African Americans than what the official estimates would imply (table 7.9). The disparities are larger for men than for women, which is explained at least in part by the higher census omission rates for males than for females, a tendency for which we have corrected,

FIGURE 7.6 Decline in Mortality by Selected Age Groups, African American Females and Males, 1935 to 1990

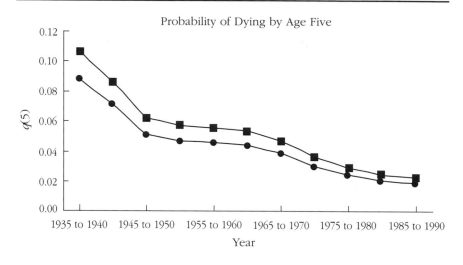

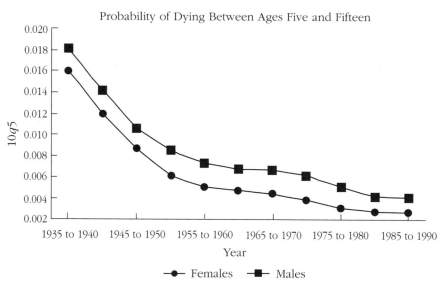

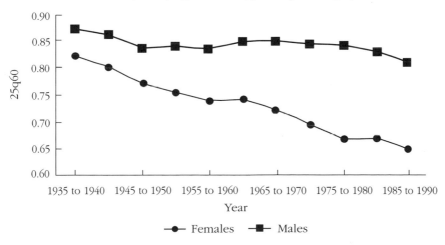

Probability of Dying Between Ages Fifteen and Sixty

Probability of Dying Between Ages Sixty and Eighty-Five

Source: Elo 2001.

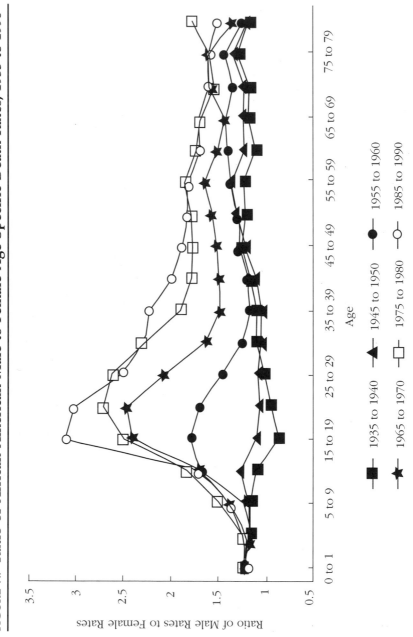

FIGURE 7.7 Ratio of African American Male to Female Age-Specific Death Rates, 1935 to 1990

Ratio of Male Rates to Female Rates

Age

1935 to 1940   1945 to 1950   1955 to 1960
1965 to 1970   1975 to 1980   1985 to 1990

0 to 1   5 to 9   15 to 19   25 to 29   35 to 39   45 to 49   55 to 59   65 to 69   75 to 79

Source: Elo 2001.

TABLE 7.9 Life Expectancy at Birth and Age Sixty-Five: Our Estimates and U.S. Life Table Estimates, African Americans and Whites

Year	African American Females Our Estimate[a]	African American Females U.S. Life Tables[b]	White Females U.S. Life Tables[b]	African American Males Our Estimate[a]	African American Males U.S. Life Tables[b]	White Males U.S. Life Tables[b]
1939 to 1941						
e_0	56.22	55.56	67.29	53.52	52.26	62.81
e_{65}	12.47	13.93	13.56	11.14	12.21	12.07
1949 to 1951[c]						
e_0	63.51	62.70	72.03	59.93	58.91	66.31
e_{65}	13.76	14.54	15.00	12.01	12.75	12.75
1959 to 1961[c]						
e_0	66.62	66.47	74.19	61.80	61.48	67.55
e_{65}	14.49	15.12	15.88	11.91	12.84	12.97
1969 to 1971						
e_0	68.69	68.32	75.49	61.58	60.00	67.94
e_{65}	15.01	15.67	16.93	11.79	12.53	13.02
1979 to 1981						
e_0	72.73	72.88	78.22	65.04	64.10	70.82
e_{65}	16.41	17.13	18.55	12.70	13.29	14.26
1985 to 1990						
e_0	73.85	73.64	79.10	65.92	64.91	72.29
e_{65}	16.91	17.19	18.90	13.13	13.30	14.93

Source: Table 7.8 and National Center for Health Statistics 1954a, 1964, 1975, 1985, 1997a; U.S. Bureau of the Census 1946; Elo 2001.
[a] An average of life table values for adjacent five-year periods, except in 1985 to 1990 when the value is taken from the life table calculated for this period.
[b] Decennial life tables, except values for 1985 to 1990 are taken as the average of life table values available for 1985 and for 1989 to 1991.
[c] For nonwhites.

but official series have not. The differences between our estimates for African Americans and those for nonwhites in 1949 to 1951 and 1959 to 1961 exhibit a similar pattern. Because African Americans made up the vast majority of nonwhites during these years, the nonwhite life tables largely reflect the mortality experience of African Americans.

At older ages, however, our mortality estimates are higher than the official figures. In every year for which a comparison is made, our value of life expectancy at age sixty-five is lower than that in the official life table, with the differences being greater in earlier than later periods (table 7.9). The most likely reason for the disagreement is that we have corrected the age distribution of deaths for age misreporting at older ages. We also have corrected for an apparent inflation of census counts at ages sixty-five and above.

Sources of Increase in Survivorship

These mortality trends are an important indicator of the social and economic conditions facing African Americans during this century. Many factors undoubtedly contributed to improvements in health conditions over time and to deviations from the generally downward trend in mortality. Although our purpose is to document rather than explain mortality conditions of the African American population, we briefly highlight some of the factors that probably have contributed to the trends described.

The declines in infant and child mortality during the early years of our series were particularly important to gains in life expectancy (figure 7.6). Improvements in obstetrical practices and continued advances made in the fight against childhood infectious diseases were instrumental in promoting the health of infants and children. According to our estimates, child mortality, $q(5)$, fell 42 percent for both sexes between the period 1935 to 1940 and the period 1945 to 1950, or at an annual rate of about 5 percent. Although child mortality began to fall shortly after the turn of the century, our results suggest that this decline accelerated during the 1940s. Ewbank (1987) estimates that child mortality in the African American population began to fall around 1905 and fell 3.4 percent a year between 1920 and 1940.

During the 1940s, a growing number of African American births were being delivered in hospitals or by physicians. The percentage of African American births that took place in hospitals increased from 27 percent in 1940 to 58 percent in 1950, while the percentage of deliveries attended to by midwives and others fell from 49 to 28 percent. These gains were initially more rapid in urban areas and regions outside the South (National Center for Health Statistics 1954b). At the same time, continued advances in medical technology, such as the introduction of sulfa drugs in the late 1930s and penicillin in the early 1940s, provided new tools to combat childhood infectious diseases.

Child care practices also improved in response to public health campaigns aimed at educating mothers in the care of their infants and young children. These campaigns, first introduced in the major urban areas around the turn of the century, reached a growing segment of the population by the 1930s (Condran and Preston 1994). Health-related activities undertaken by the Works Progress Administration and the expanding role of the Children's Bureau in assisting states to develop maternal and infant health care services facilitated the spread of knowledge of health care practices in the African American community (McBride 1991). In an era of officially sanctioned segregation, activities undertaken by African Americans themselves under the auspices of the National Negro Health Week were particularly important. This health education campaign, established by Booker T. Washington in 1915, led to the creation of many permanent health councils at the local level that carried out public health activities throughout the year.

These efforts received a significant boost in 1932 when the U.S. Public Health Service established the Office of Negro Health and also took over the administration of the National Negro Health Week. Subsequently, the number of communities that organized health-related activities under the auspices of this program grew rapidly. In 1925, 140 communities reported such activities. By 1935, this number had grown to 2,200, peaking at 12,500 in 1945 (Smith 1995, 70). The Office of Negro Health was abolished in 1950 in response to calls for integrated public health activities (Smith 1995; McBride 1991).

In more recent years, declines in infant and child mortality were influenced by factors such as continued progress against childhood infectious diseases and improvements in medical practices associated with childbirth. The discovery of surfactant and the increased use of corticosteroids, for example, improved survival rates at all gestational ages and birthweights (Luke et al. 1993; Kliegman 1995). In addition, educational advances, improvements in economic circumstances, and improved access to health care services by African American women contributed to declines in infant and child mortality. An important event in increasing access to health services by poor African American women was the passage of Medicaid legislation in the mid-1960s (Davis et al. 1987).

One of the most notable features of the mortality trends described is the change in the relative mortality differentials between men and women, particularly at young adult ages. In the period 1935 to 1940, female death rates were higher than male death rates between ages fifteen and twenty-four, and sex differentials were relatively small throughout the reproductive ages (figure 7.7). We noted earlier that adult female death rates must have been high relative to those of males in earlier decades of this century to produce the high male-female ratios identified in our population reconstructions.

Ewbank (1987) suggests that high female mortality during reproductive ages had been a long-standing characteristic of African American mortality and cites as evidence excess female deaths at ages ten to forty-four recorded in the censuses of 1870, 1880, and 1900. While deaths from maternal causes were undoubtedly one of the key factors responsible for this excess, mortality from respiratory tuberculosis also played a role. Deaths from respiratory tuberculosis in registration states in 1920, for example, were higher among nonwhite women than nonwhite men at ages ten to thirty-four (Preston, Keyfitz, and Schoen 1972). The mortality experience of the industrial policyholders of the Metropolitan Life Insurance Company also reveals excess female mortality from tuberculosis at ages ten through twenty-four among "colored" policyholders in 1931 to 1935 (Dublin and Lotka 1937).

By 1945 to 1950, however, the female excess in death rates at all ages had disappeared (figure 7.7). Improvements in obstetrical practices, which played a role in the decline in child mortality, also undoubtedly reduced mortality from maternal causes. In addition, the continued rapid decline in mortality from respiratory tuberculosis benefited both men and women. Age-standardized death rates from this disease at ages one to seventy-four fell, for example, 41 percent among males and 45 percent among females between the periods 1931 to 1935 and 1941 to 1945 among "colored" industrial policyholders of the Metropolitan Life Insurance Company, although female death rates at the early reproductive ages remained above those of males (Dublin 1948, ch. 3, table 2). During this period, mortality from other infectious diseases, such as parasitic diseases, influenza, and pneumonia, also fell rapidly at all ages (Crimmins 1981).

The subsequent deterioration in health conditions for adult men in the 1960s and early 1970s and the widening of sex differentials in mortality were not atypical. Similar patterns have been documented for white Americans and for most developed countries. In most cases, mortality declines were accompanied by a substantial increase in the sex differential in mortality at adult ages (Crimmins 1981; United Nations 1982; Waldron 1993; Zhang, Sasaki, and Kesteloot 1995). An examination of cause-specific death rates shows that higher mortality for men from causes such as heart disease, lung cancer, and intentional and unintentional injuries were the major contributing causes for these differentials (Crimmins 1981; Waldron 1993). In 1989 to 1991, death rates from heart disease, cerebrovascular diseases, and cancer also contributed to the excess male mortality among African Americans.

Age-standardized death rates at ages forty-five and above for males from these causes were 31 to 90 percent above the rates for females (Elo and Preston 1997). Higher male mortality from these causes, in turn, was related to factors such as sex differences in past smoking habits, men's greater exposure to occupational hazards, and the protective effects of female sex hormones for heart disease (Waldron 1993; Zhang, Sasaki, and Kesteloot 1995). Deaths from intentional and unintentional injuries, in turn, played a large role in sex differentials at younger ages. Death rates from motor vehicle–related injuries, homicide, and legal interventions were consistently three to five times higher for African American males than females at ages fifteen to forty-four during the latter half of the twentieth century (National Center for Health Statistics 1997b, tables 46, 47).

Social and economic trends affecting the African American population also may have contributed to the observed trends in sex differentials in African American mortality. Annual earnings of African American women improved more rapidly than those of African American men in recent decades, although for both groups increases in earnings stagnated during the 1980s (Blau and Beller 1992). It also appears that African American men suffer particularly high death rates in some urban environments. Geronimus et al. (1996), for example, estimate that a fifteen-year-old male in Harlem had only a 37 percent chance of surviving to age sixty-five, while the probability for a fifteen-year old female was 65 percent. Preston, Hill, and Drevenstedt (1998) suggest that African American males more generally paid a high penalty for rural to urban migration during the twentieth century. The authors find that African American men who grew up on farms were twice as likely to survive to advanced age as men who did not; such differentials were markedly less for African American women. The authors suggest that at least a part of this male differential may be due to the fact that African American men who grew up on farms may have been more likely to be farmers themselves and thus be spared the higher mortality of urban black males. In addition, it may be that some part of the sex differentials below age sixty-five was related to access to health care. Subsidized medical insurance coverage is more readily available for poor African American women than men through the Medicaid program. More poor women than poor men qualify for Medicaid through their participation in the Aid to Families with Dependent Children program (Elo and Preston 1996).

Racial Differences in Mortality

Although African American mortality declined substantially during the twentieth century, it consistently exceeded that of white Americans. Racial disparities in death rates were already receiving public attention during the early decades of this century and gained prominence during the 1930s and 1940s with the New Deal's focus on societal inequalities. Several government agencies and private organizations sponsored studies of racial disparities in health and mortality. The National Health Survey of 1935 to 1936, which collected information on morbidity by socioeconomic status, for example, focused attention on high rates of debilitating conditions among African Americans and on racial inequalities in access to health services in rural Georgia (Holland and Perrott 1938; Mott and Roemer 1948). Two volumes on the mortality experience of the industrial policyholders of the Metropolitan Life Insurance Company demonstrated racial disparities in mortality at all ages (Dublin and Lotka 1937; Dublin 1948). Other studies highlighted the role of economic deprivation in producing excess mortality among African Americans relative to whites (for example, Britten 1934; Britten, Brown, and Altman 1940; see also Krieger and Fee 1996), a focus that remains central to discussions of racial disparities in health and mortality to the present day.

Although African American death rates have remained well above those of whites, some progress has been made toward narrowing the racial gap in overall mortality. The racial difference in life expectancy at birth, for example, declined from 9.3 years in 1940 to 5.8 years in 1980 for males and from 11.1 to 5.5 years for females (table 7.9). During the 1980s, however, this favorable trend reversed for males and slowed down for females. Kochanek, Maurer, and Rosenberg (1994) attribute this reversal to trends in mortality from homicide and human immunodeficiency virus (HIV) infection and to sharper declines in heart disease mortality for whites than for African Americans. The findings for the 1980s may be related to a general widening in social class differentials in mortality among males (Kochanek, Maurer, and Rosenberg 1994). Two recent studies have uncovered a widening in educational differentials in mortality for males since 1960 (Preston and Elo 1995; Feldman et al. 1989). Such trends have been more favorable for women (Preston and Elo 1995). The deterioration in economic circumstances among African Americans relative to whites in the 1980s is also likely to have played a role (Bound and Freeman 1992; Blau and Beller 1992).

Many analysts have sought to explain racial disparities in mortality by differences in socioeconomic status. Most studies that have examined the contribution of social class to racial differences at adult and older ages have found that the inclusion of a standard set of socioeconomic variables eliminates most, if not all, of the excess mortality among African Americans (for example, Preston and Taubman 1994; Smith and Kington 1997). The ability of these variables to account for racial differences appears, however, to be related to the age range under consideration. At higher ages, where racial differences in death rates narrow, social and economic differentials explain more of the smaller gap. They are less successful at younger ages (Elo and Preston 1996) and typically fail to explain racial differences in birth outcomes (for example, Starfield et al. 1991; Cramer 1995; Parker, Schoendorf, and Kiely 1994; Hummer 1993). Added to the possible causes for racial disparities in health and mortality in recent years is an emphasis on the possible contributions of racism, stress, and psychosocial factors (Williams 1990; James 1993) and factors associated with the racial differences in one's immediate living environment (Geronimus et al. 1996; LeClere, Rogers, and Peters 1997; Roberts 1997). The relative importance of each of these domains and their possible interactions are yet to be fully established.

AFRICAN AMERICAN FERTILITY

Our fertility estimates are based on the age-specific estimates of the African American female population and the Census Bureau's birth series, except that we have modified the birth series to adjust the classification of births from the race of the father to the race of the mother. These adjustments make a very small difference in the early years of the birth series, but they become progressively more important over time. In 1968, for example, the estimated ratio of "mother-rule" to "father-rule" births was 0.9890 compared to 0.9637 in 1989 (Robinson and Gist 1992).

These procedures provide an estimate of the total number of births born to African American women for each of the census years between 1935 and 1990. We allocate these births by five-year age groups of the mother by using the age distribution of births available in vital statistics data published by the National Center for Health Statistics. These data pertain to the African American population except in 1935 to 1936 and 1960 to 1963, when they are based on births classified as "other races" or nonwhites. Under these rules, a mother's race was used to assign the child's race only if the father was white, the mother was Hawaiian, or the father's race was missing from the birth certificate (National Center for Health Statistics 1993). We do not believe that this difference in the racial classification of births has a substantive impact on the allocation of the birth series by the age of the mother and thus on the estimates presented here.

We estimate age-specific fertility rates by five-year age groups for five-year time blocks from the period 1935 to 1940 to the period 1985 to 1990. To do so, we take all births to women in a given age group during the five-year time period in question and then divide this sum by averaging the population in the given age interval at the beginning and end of the time period in question and multiplying this average by five. In addition to age-specific fertility rates, we present the total fertility rate for each of the five-year periods in question, which are obtained as follows: TFR = $5 \times \Sigma_n f_x$ where $_n f_x$ refers to an age-specific fertility rate in a given age interval. The total fertility rate is the average number of children that would be born to a woman who survived to the end of her childbearing period and bore children according to the age-specific fertility rates of a particular period.

These estimates are presented in table 7.10 and figures 7.8 to 7.10. They provide a consistent series of fertility estimates for the period that takes into account estimates of census undercounts and underregistration of births. In addition, this is the first series of African American fertility in which the racial classification of births is based on the race of the mother.

The age pattern and trends in fertility in this series are similar to those documented previously in official statistics. Fertility levels were low in the late 1930s and early 1940s, coinciding with the depression and World War II, and high during the baby boom years following the war.

The total fertility rate rose from a low of 2.5 in 1935 to 1940 to a peak of 4.4 in the late 1950s, declining thereafter until the 1980s (figure 7.10). In 1985 to 1990, we estimate the total fertility rate to be 2.23. Although African American fertility is estimated to be consistently higher than white fertility throughout the period, the trends in total fertility rates were very similar (Linder and Grove 1943; Grove and Hetzel 1968; Ventura et al. 1998). In 1985 to

TABLE 7.10 Estimated Age-Specific Fertility Rates, per One Thousand Women, and Total Fertility Rate, African Americans, 1935 to 1990

Year	Age of the Mother								Total Fertility Rate
	10 to 14	15 to 19	20 to 24	25 to 29	30 to 34	35 to 39	40 to 44	45 to 49	
1935 to 1940	3.18	108.23	150.04	104.94	66.21	50.74	17.08	2.87	2.52
1940 to 1945	3.73	118.79	162.89	111.55	75.33	48.96	16.37	2.01	2.70
1945 to 1950	4.40	136.52	202.60	143.15	90.59	58.56	17.38	1.99	3.28
1950 to 1955	4.83	155.80	246.93	183.87	115.99	65.46	19.55	1.67	3.97
1955 to 1960	4.55	160.42	280.50	207.89	134.41	74.26	20.62	1.63	4.42
1960 to 1965	3.96	138.29	262.61	200.75	130.34	71.02	20.96	1.47	4.15
1965 to 1970	4.41	135.28	199.57	139.66	88.84	50.29	15.86	1.15	3.18
1970 to 1975	5.02	123.49	159.12	105.37	63.72	32.74	9.79	0.70	2.50
1975 to 1980	4.49	102.49	136.78	99.59	54.77	24.12	6.39	0.43	2.15
1980 to 1985	4.03	95.11	134.48	100.24	58.47	23.09	5.21	0.30	2.10
1985 to 1990	4.38	101.16	143.13	104.41	61.94	25.60	4.97	0.26	2.23

Source: Elo 1998.

FIGURE 7.8 African American Age-Specific Fertility Rates, 1930 to 1960

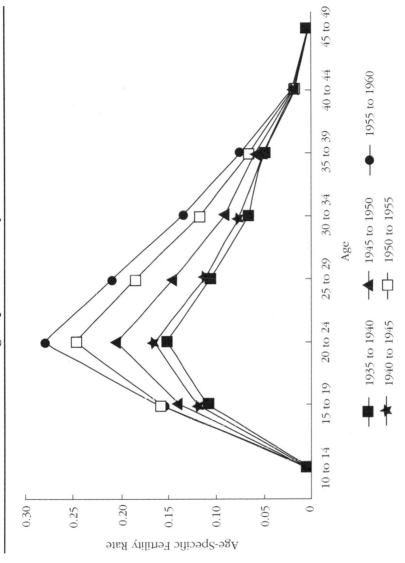

Source: Elo 1998.

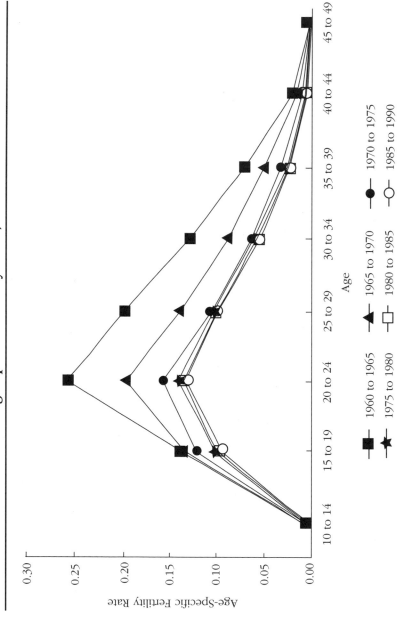

FIGURE 7.9 African American Age-Specific Fertility Rates, 1960 to 1990

Source: Elo 1998.

FIGURE 7.10 African American Total Fertility Rate, 1935 to 1990

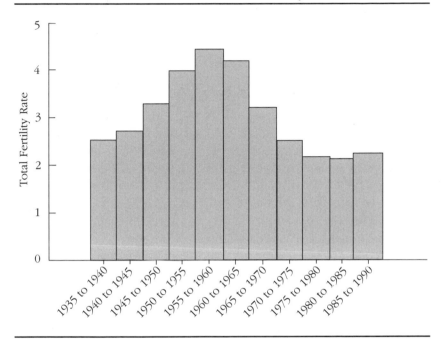

Source: Elo 1998.

1990, the black total fertility rate of 2.23 children per woman was 22 percent above that (1.83) of white women (the total fertility rate for whites is calculated as the average of rates in 1985 to 1989; see Ventura et al. 1998, table 4). This differential does not seem consistent with widespread public images of high black fertility that is driving a rapid increase in the percentage of the population that is black. In the most recent projections of the Census Bureau, the percentage of the population that is African American will only grow from 12.6 percent in 1995 to 15.4 percent in 2050 (U.S. Bureau of the Census 1996, table J).

The public focus on African American fertility may owe less to its overall level than to the context in which it takes place. Despite falling birth rates, the rapid rise in the proportion of African American births that take place outside the confines of marriage and the possible consequences of growing up in single-parent households for children's well-being have driven much of the recent public debate on welfare reform. Although births outside of marriage have increased for both African Americans and whites, the percentage of children born out of wedlock remains much higher among African Americans. As Smith, Morgan, and Koropeckyj-Cox (1996, 141) point out, "In the early 1960s, only one black child in four, and less than one white child in 20, was born out of wedlock. By the early 1990s, two out of every three African American children, and close to one white child in four, were born to unmarried mothers." The rapid rise in out-of-wedlock births among teen mothers since the 1960s has added to these concerns (Furstenberg 1991). Unfortunately, these debates often neglect the factors that have contributed to these trends.

While fertility levels fluctuated during recent decades, the age pattern of fertility exhibited much less variation. Age-specific fertility rates rose sharply through the teenage years to their highest level at ages twenty to twenty-four, a pattern that persisted throughout the period. At the youngest ages, African American fertility rates were well above white rates, with the racial patterns converging at older ages. Not only were age-specific fertility rates higher than white rates at young reproductive ages, but the age at which fertility rates peak was earlier among African Americans than whites, a racial difference that persisted throughout the period (results not shown).

Several explanations have been suggested for the early fertility among African Americans, including factors such as contraceptive failure, unintended consequences of satisfying sexual desires combined with an earlier age at sexual maturity, diminished parental supervision of teenagers, reduced costs of childrearing through sharing of responsibilities among several adults, and role models and neighborhood context (Forste and Tienda 1996). Geronimus (1986, 1987, 1996) has added spark to this debate by suggesting that early fertility among African Americans represents a rational response to rapidly deteriorating health conditions among poor African American women.

The fertility estimates presented in table 7.10 and figures 7.8 to 7.10 are not substantively different from those previously published. In general, they tend be slightly lower than official figures. The sources of these disparities are related to adjustments in birth underregistration, which has a greater impact in earlier years, corrections for census undercount, and the adjustment in the racial classification of births. Our estimates are slightly below those of Coale and Rives (1973) prior to 1950, slightly higher between 1950 and 1965, and lower again in the late 1960s.

SUMMARY

Every population deserves an accurate rendering of its conditions. Supplying reliable demographic information about the African American population has proven difficult because of serious flaws in the basic data. The United States was the last developed country to complete its birth and death registration system, and it was even later in achieving complete counts of births and deaths. This tardiness has contributed to considerable uncertainty about age among older African Americans, a factor that thwarts the application of conventional demographic tools. In addition, censuses have systematically failed to count large fractions of African American males.

We have made a major effort to identify the extent of these problems and to overcome them. Our procedures have produced age-specific series of deaths, births, and population counts that are internally consistent and that extend continuously throughout the period 1930 to 1990. They are at considerable variance with a historical series produced by Coale and Rives, but more consistent with a truncated series of population counts produced by the U.S. Census Bureau.

The corrections for census undercounts have produced higher values of life expectancy than official estimates, but less improvement over the period covered. Additional corrections for age misreporting in death statistics, together with corrections for census undercounts, produce life expectancy estimates at age sixty-five that are lower than those in official sources. African American mortality declined rapidly for both men and women during the first fifteen years covered by our estimates, from 1935 to 1950, and improved steadily thereafter for women. Male mortality during the young adult years and middle age has proven far less malleable since mid-century, producing exceptionally high ratios of male to female mortality at these ages. In fact, one of the most disturbing aspects of the mortality trends documented here is the slow decline in African American male mortality. In the latter half of the 1980s, the life expectancy at birth for African American men, 65.9 years, was lower than that for white men, 66.3 years, in 1949 to 1951 (National Center for Health Statistics 1954a). The widening of the gender gap in life expectancy among African Americans was also more pronounced than among whites during the latter half of the twentieth century. Although a fully satisfactory explanation for these sex differences is lacking, past smoking habits, occupational differences, and more rapid improvements in economic circumstances for African American women than men in recent decades are likely to have played some role.

While African Americans have benefited from advances in medical technology and improvements in living standards, the racial gap in life expectancy at birth continues to be substantial. In the late 1980s, there was a difference of 7.4 years in life expectancy at birth for African American and white men and a difference of 5.3 years for African American and white women. Inequalities in socioeconomic status between African Americans and whites explain some, but not all, of this disparity. Further studies of factors that account for the mortality trends documented here are desperately needed.

The age pattern of African American fertility was remarkably steady during the period covered, invariably peaking in the age range twenty to twenty-four. The average number of children per woman reached 4.42 in the midst of the baby boom and fell to less than half of this value, 2.10, in 1980 to 1985. While the volume of fertility fluctuated in close correspondence to that of the white population, the age pattern of African American fertility became increasingly distinctive.

APPENDIX

Age-period-cohort model and estimates of census populations. Our age-period-cohort model estimates the true size of each cohort using information on the observed populations at each census and deaths and net migrations to each cohort between census dates.

We model errors in census counts through a multiplicative model containing an age effect and a period (or census-specific) effect. The model can be written as follows:

$$E(C_{it} \mid i,t,j) = \alpha_j \tau_t X_{it} = \alpha_j \tau_t (\gamma_i - D_{it}) \qquad (7A.1)$$

where C_{it} is the observed number of people enumerated in cohort i in the census taken at time t; j refers to the age group occupied by cohort i at census t; α_j captures age-specific variation in census coverage; τ_t captures time-specific variation in coverage; γ_i denotes the true size of cohort i; and D_{it} refers to the cumulative deaths and net migrations in cohort i between its first appearance and time t. The model can be expressed equivalently as:

$$C_{it} = \alpha_j \tau_t (\gamma_i - D_{it}) + \epsilon_{it} \qquad (7A.2)$$

where ϵ_{it} is a residual with a mean zero conditional on age, time period, and cohort.

The second specification suggests that model parameters can be estimated using nonlinear least squares. In particular, one can obtain consistent estimates of the parameters α, τ, and γ by minimizing the objective function:

$$SSE = \sum_{it} [C_{it} - \alpha_j \tau_t (\gamma_i - D_{it})]^2 \qquad (7.A3)$$

with respect to the parameters α_j, τ_t, γ_i.

We use extinct-generation estimates to fix the initial size of cohorts ages thirty-five to thirty-nine and eighty to eighty-four in 1930 (Vincent 1951). In the upper-right-hand corner of table 7.3, we fix cohort size based on the Census Bureau's birth series, together with our corrected intercensal death series. The age-period-cohort model thus estimates the initial cohort size for cohorts born between 1895 and 1935. We further impose a sex ratio constraint on each of these cohorts. We obtain parameter estimates and heteroskedasticity-consistent standard errors (Huber 1967) by using a nonlinear least squares procedure written in the GAUSS programming language.

This research was supported by Grant AG10168 from the National Institute of Aging. We would like to thank Mark Hill, Ira Rosenwaike, Tim Cheney, and many others at the University of Pennsylvania who made important contributions to this research. We also would like to give special thanks to Greg Robinson of the U.S. Bureau of the Census and Bert Kestenbaum of the Social Security Administration who provided invaluable assistance throughout this project.

REFERENCES

Barringer, H. R., R. W. Gardner, and M. J. Levin. 1993. *Asian and Pacific Islanders in the United States. The Population of the United States in the 1980s*. Census Monograph Series. New York: Russell Sage Foundation.

Bayo, F. R. 1972. "Mortality of the Aged." *Transactions of the Society of Actuaries* 24: 1–24.

Blau, F. D., and A. H. Beller. 1992. "Black-White Earnings over the 1970s and 1980s: Gender Differences in Trends." *Review of Economics and Statistics* 74(2): 276–86.

Bound, John, and R. B. Freeman. 1992. "What Went Wrong? The Erosion of Relative Earnings and Employment among Young Black Men in the 1980s." *Quarterly Journal of Economics* 107(1): 201–32.

Britten, R. H. 1934. "The Relation between Housing and Health." *Public Health Reports* 49(4): 1301–13.

Britten, R. H., J. E. Brown, and Isidore Altman. 1940. "Certain Characteristics of Urban Housing and Their Relation to Illness and Accidents: Summary of Findings of the National Health Survey." *Milbank Memorial Fund Quarterly* 18(1): 91–113.

Clarke, Averil Y., Mark Hill, and Cathleen Riddley. 1995. "Conceptions of Age and Age Accuracy among Elderly African Americans: An Ethnographic Inquiry." Unpublished manuscript. Philadelphia: Population Studies Center, University of Pennsylvania.

Coale, A. J., and E. E. Kisker. 1986. "Mortality Crossovers: Reality or Bad Data?" *Population Studies* 40(3): 389–401.

———. 1990. "Defects in Data on Old-Age Mortality in the United States: New Procedures for Calculating Mortality Schedules and Life Tables at the Highest Ages." *Asian and Pacific Population Forum* 4(1): 1–31.

Coale, A. J., and N. W. Rives. 1973. "A Statistical Reconstruction of the

Black Population of the United States, 1880–1970: Estimates of True Numbers by Age and Sex, Birth Rates, and Total Fertility." *Population Index* 39(1): 3–36.

Condran, G. A., C. L. Himes, and Samuel H. Preston. 1991. "Old-Age Mortality Patterns in Low-Mortality Countries: An Evaluation of Population and Death Data at Advanced Ages, 1950 to the Present." *Population Bulletin of the United Nations* 30: 23–60.

Condran, G. A., and Samuel H. Preston. 1994. "Child Mortality Differences, Personal Health Care Practices, and Medical Technology: The United States, 1900–1930." In *Health and Social Change in International Perspective,* edited by L. C. Chen, Arthur Kleinman, and N. C. Ware. Cambridge, Mass.: Harvard University Press.

Cramer, J. C. 1995. "Racial and Ethnic Differences in Birth Weight: The Role of Income and Financial Assistance." *Demography* 32(2): 231–47.

Crimmins, Eileen. 1981. "The Changing Pattern of American Mortality Decline, 1940–77, and Its Implications for the Future." *Population and Development Review* 7(2): 229–54.

Davis, Karen, Marsha Lillie-Blanton, Barbara Lyons, Fitzhugh Mullan, Neil Powe, and Diane Rowland. 1987. "Health Care for Black Americans: The Public Sector Role." *Milbank Quarterly* 65 (supp. 1): 213–47.

Dublin, L. I. 1948. *Health Progress, 1936 to 1945: A Supplement to Twenty-Five Years of Health Progress.* New York: Metropolitan Life Insurance Company.

Dublin, L. I., and A. J. Lotka. 1937. *Twenty-Five Years of Health Progress: A Study of the Mortality Experience among the Industrial Policy Holders of the Metropolitan Life Insurance Company, 1911 to 1935.* New York: Metropolitan Life Insurance Company.

Elo, Irma T. 1998. "African American Mortality and Fertility since 1935." Working Paper Series 98–23. University of Pennsylvania, Population Aging Research Center, Philadelphia.

———. 2001. "New African American Life Tables from 1935–40 to 1985–90." *Demography* 38(1): 97–114.

Elo, Irma T., and Samuel H. Preston. 1992. "The Effect of Early Life Conditions on Adult Mortality: A Review." *Population Index* 58(2): 186–212.

———. 1994. "Estimating African-American Mortality from Inaccurate Data." *Demography* 31(3): 427–58.

———. 1996. "Educational Differentials in Mortality: United States 1979–1985." *Social Science and Medicine* 42(1): 47–57.

———. 1997. "Racial and Ethnic Differences in Mortality at Older Ages." In *Racial and Ethnic Differences in the Health of Older Americans,* edited by L. G. Martin and B. J. Soldo. Washington, D.C.: National Academy Press.

Elo, Irma T., Samuel H. Preston, Ira Rosenwaike, Mark Hill, and Timothy Cheney. 1996. "Consistency of Age Reporting on Death Certificates and Social Security Records among Elderly African Americans." *Social Science Research* 25(3): 292–307.

Ewbank, Douglas. 1987. "History of Black Mortality and Health before 1940." *Milbank Quarterly* 65 (supp. 1): 100–28.

Feldman, J. J., D. M. Makuc, J. C. Kleinman, and Joan Cornoni-Huntley. 1989. "National Trends in Educational Differentials in Mortality." *American Journal of Epidemiology* 129 (5): 919–33.

Forste, Renata., and Marta Tienda. 1996. "What's Behind Racial and Ethnic Fertility Differentials?" In *Fertility in the United States: New Patterns and New Theories,* edited by J. B. Casterline, R. D. Lee, and K. A. Foote. *Population and Development Review* 22 (supplement).

Furstenberg, Frank F., Jr. 1991. "As the Pendulum Swings: Teenage Childbearing and Social Concern." *Family Relations* 40(2): 127–38.

Geronimus, A. T. 1986. "The Effects of Race, Residence, and Prenatal Care on the Relationship between Maternal Age to Neonatal Mortality." *American Journal of Public Health* 76(12): 1416–21.

———. 1987. "On Teenage Childbearing and Neonatal Mortality in the United States." *Population and Development Review* 13(2): 245–79.

———. 1996. "Black/White Differences in the Relationship of Maternal Age to Birthweight: A Population-based Test of the Weathering Hypothesis." *Social Science and Medicine* 42(4): 589–97.

Geronimus, A. T., John Bound, T. A. Waidmann, M. M. Hillemeier, and P. B. Burns. 1996. "Excess Mortality among Blacks and Whites in the United States." *New England Journal of Medicine* 335(21): 1552–58.

Grove, R. D., and A. M. Hetzel. 1968. *Vital Statistics Rates in the United States 1940–1960.* Washington: U.S. Government Printing Office.

Hahn, R. A., Joseph Mulinare, and S. M. Teutsch. 1992. "Inconsistencies in Coding of Race and Ethnicity between Birth and Death in U.S. Infants." *Journal of the American Medical Association* 267 (2): 259–63.

Harrison, R. J., and C. E. Bennett. 1995. "Racial and Ethnic Diversity." In *State of the Union: America in the 1990s.* Vol. 2: *Social Trends,* edited by Reynolds Farley. New York: Russell Sage Foundation.

Hill, M. E., Samuel H. Preston, Irma T. Elo, and Ira Rosenwaike. 1997. "Age-Linked Institutions and Age Reporting among Older African Americans." *Social Forces* 75(3): 1007–30.

Himes, C. L., and C. C. Clogg. 1992. "An Overview of Demographic Analysis as a Method for Evaluating Census Coverage in the United States." *Population Index* 58(4): 587–607.

Himes, C. L., Samuel H. Preston, and G. A. Condran. 1994. "A Relational Model of Mortality at Older Ages in Low Mortality Countries." *Population Studies* 48(2): 269–91.

Holland, D. F., and G. St. J. Perrott. 1938. "Health of the Negro." *Milbank Memorial Fund Quarterly* 16(1): 5–38.

Huber, P. J. 1967. "The Behavior of Maximum Likelihood Estimates under Non-Standard Conditions." In *Proceedings of the Fifth Berkeley Symposium on Mathematical Statistics and Probability,* vol. 1. Berkeley: University of California Press.

Hummer, R. A. 1993. "Racial Differences in Infant Mortality in the U.S.: An Examination of Social and Health Determinants." *Social Forces* 72(2): 529–54.

James, S. A. 1993. "Racial and Ethnic Differences in Infant Mortality and Low Birth Weight: A Psychosocial Critique." *Annals of Epidemiology* 3(2): 130–36.

Kestenbaum, Bert. 1992. "A Description of the Extreme Aged Population Based on Improved Medicare Enrollment Data." *Demography* 29(4): 565–80.

Kitagawa, E. M., and P. M. Hauser. 1973. *Differential Mortality in the United States: A Study in Socioeconomic Epidemiology.* Cambridge, Mass.: Harvard University Press.

Kliegman, R. M. 1995. "Neonatal Technology, Perinatal Survival, Social Consequences, and the Perinatal Paradox." *American Journal of Public Health* 85(7): 909–13.

Kochanek, K. D., J. D. Maurer, and H. M. Rosenberg. 1994. "Why Did Black Life Expectancy Decline from 1984 through 1989 in the United States." *American Journal of Public Health* 84(6): 938–44.

Krieger, Nancy K., and Elizabeth Fee. 1996. "Measuring Social Inequalities in Health in the United States: A Historical Review, 1900–1950." *International Journal of Health Services* 26(3): 391–418.

LeClere, F. B., R. G. Rogers, and K. D. Peters. 1997. "Ethnicity and Mortality in the United States: Individual and Community Correlates." *Social Forces* 76(1): 169–98.

Linder, F. E., and R. D. Grove. 1943. *Vital Statistics Rates in the United States, 1900–1940.* Washington: U.S. Government Printing Office.

Luke, B., C. Williams, J. Minogue, and L. Keith. 1993. "The Changing Pattern of Infant Mortality in the U.S.: The Role of Perinatal Factors and Their Obstetrical Implications." *International Journal of Gynecology and Obstetrics* 40(3): 199–212.

Manton, K. G., and Eric Stallard. 1981. "Methods for Evaluating the Het-

erogeneity of Aging Processes in Human Populations Using Vital Statistics Data: Explaining the Black/White Mortality Crossover by a
Model of Mortality Selection." *Human Biology* 53(1): 47–67.

Manton, K. G., Eric Stallard, and J. W. Vaupel. 1981. "Methods for Comparing the Mortality Experience of Heterogenous Populations." *Demography* 18(3): 389–410.

McBride, David. 1991. *From TB to AIDS: Epidemics among Urban Blacks
since 1900.* Albany: State University of New York Press.

Mosley, W. H., and Ronald Gray. 1993. "Childhood Precursors of Adult
Morbidity and Mortality in Developing Countries: Implications for
Health Programs." In *The Epidemiological Transition: Policy and
Planning Implications for Developing Countries,* edited by James N.
Gribble and Samuel H. Preston. Washington, D.C.: National Academy
Press.

Mott, F. D., and M. I. Roemer. 1948. *Rural Health and Medical Care.*
New York: McGraw-Hill.

National Center for Health Statistics. 1954a. *United States Life Tables,
1949–51.* Vital Statistics of the United States, Special Reports, vol. 41,
no. 1. Washington: U.S. Government Printing Office.

———. 1954b. *Vital Statistics of the United States 1950,* vol. 1. Washington: U.S. Government Printing Office.

———. 1964. *United States Life Tables, 1959–61,* vol. 1, no. 1. Washington, D.C.: Public Health Service.

———. 1968. *Comparability of Age on the Death Certificate and Matching Census Record, United States: May–August 1960.* Vital and Health
Statistics, series 2, no. 29. Washington, D.C.: Public Health Service.

———. 1969. *Comparability of Marital Status, Race, Nativity, and Country of Origin on the Death Certificate and Matching Census Record,
United States: May–August 1960.* Vital and Health Statistics, series 2,
no. 34. Washington, D.C.: Public Health Service.

———. 1975. *U.S. Decennial Life Tables for 1969–71,* vol. 1, no. 1.
DHEW Publication (HRA)75-1150. Washington: U.S. Government
Printing Office.

———. 1985. *U.S. Decennial Life Tables for 1979–81,* vol. 1, no. 1.
DHHS Publication (PHS) 85-1150-1. Washington: U.S. Government
Printing Office.

———. 1988. *Vital Statistics of the United States, 1985.* Vol. 2, sec. 6: *Life
Tables.* DHHS Publication (PHS) 88–1104. Washington: U.S. Government Printing Office.

———. 1993. *Vital Statistics of the United States 1989.* Vol. 1: *Natality.*
Washington: U.S. Government Printing Office.

———. 1997a. *U.S. Decennial Life Tables for 1989–91.* Vol. 1, no. 1:

United States Life Tables. DHHS Publication PHS-98-1150-1. Washington: U.S. Government Printing Office.

———. 1997b. *Health, United States, 1996–97 and Injury Chartbook.* Washington: U.S. Government Printing Office.

Parker, J. D., K. C. Schoendorf, and J. L. Kiely. 1994. "Association between Measures of Socioeconomic Status and Low Birth Weight, Small for Gestational Age, and Premature Delivery in the United States." *Annals of Epidemiology* 4(4): 271–78.

Peterson, J. W. 1990. "Age of Wisdom: Elderly Black Women in Family and Church." In *The Cultural Context of Aging,* edited by Jay Sokolowsky. New York: Bergin and Garvey.

Preston, Samuel H., and Irma T. Elo. 1995. "Are Educational Differentials in Adult Mortality Increasing in the United States?" *Journal of Aging and Health* 7(4): 476–96.

Preston, Samuel H., Irma T. Elo, Andrew Foster, and Haishan Fu. 1998. "Reconstructing the Size of the African American Population by Age and Sex, 1930–1990." *Demography* 35(1): 1–21.

Preston, Samuel H., Irma T. Elo, Ira Rosenwaike, and Mark Hill. 1996. "African American Mortality at Older Ages: Results of a Matching Study." *Demography* 33(2): 193–209.

Preston, Samuel H., Mark Hill, and Greg Drevenstedt. 1998. "Childhood Conditions That Predict Survival to Advanced Ages among African Americans." *Social Science and Medicine* 47(9): 1231–46.

Preston, Samuel H., Nathan Keyfitz, and Robert Schoen. 1972. *Causes of Death: Life Tables for National Populations.* New York: Seminar Press.

Preston, Samuel H., and Paul Taubman. 1994. "Socioeconomic Differences in Adult Mortality and Health Status." In *The Demography of Aging,* edited by Linda Martin and Samuel H. Preston. Washington, D.C.: National Academy Press.

Roberts, E. M. 1997. "Neighborhood Social Environments and the Distribution of Low Birthweight in Chicago." *American Journal of Public Health* 87(4): 597–603.

Robinson, J. G. 1991. *Error in the Birth Registration Completeness Estimates.* 1990 Decennial Census Preliminary Research and Evaluation Memorandum 74. Washington: U.S. Bureau of the Census.

Robinson, J. G., Bashir Ahmed, Prithwis Das Gupta, and Karen A. Woodrow. 1993. "Estimation of Population Coverage in the 1990 United States Census Based on Demographic Analysis." *Journal of the American Statistical Association* 88(423): 1061–79.

Robinson, J. G., and Y. J. Gist. 1992. "The Effect of Alternative Race Classification Rules on the Annual Number of Births by Race: 1968–

1989." Presented at the annual meetings of the Population Association of America. Denver.

Shapiro, Sam, and Joseph Schachter. 1952. "Birth Registration Completeness in the United States, 1950." *Public Health Reports* 67(6): 513–24.

Shryock, H. S., and J. S. Siegel. 1973. *The Methods and Materials of Demography,* vol. 2, rev. ed. Washington: U.S. Bureau of the Census.

Smith, H. L., S. P. Morgan, and Tanya Koropeckyj-Cox. 1996. "A Decomposition of Trends in the Nonmarital Fertility Ratios of Blacks and Whites in the United States, 1960–1992." *Demography* 33(2): 141–51.

Smith, James P., and Raynard S. Kington. 1997. "Race, Socioeconomic Status, and Health in Later Life." In *Racial and Ethnic Differences in the Health of Older Americans,* edited by L. G. Martin and B. J. Soldo. Washington, D.C.: National Academy Press.

Smith, S. L. 1995. *Sick and Tired of Being Sick and Tired: Black Women's Health Activism in America, 1890–1950.* Philadelphia: University of Pennsylvania Press.

Sorlie, P. D., Eugene Rogot, and N. J. Johnson. 1992. "Validity of Demographic Characteristics on the Death Certificate." *Epidemiology* 3(2): 181–84.

Starfield, Barbara, Sam Shapiro, Judith Weiss, Kung-Yee Liang, Knut Ra, David Paige, and Xiaobin Wang. 1991. "Race, Family Income, and Low Birth Weight." *American Journal of Epidemiology* 134 (10): 1167–74.

United Nations, Department of International Economic and Social Affairs. 1982. *Levels and Trends of Mortality since 1950.* New York: United Nations.

———. 1990. *MortPak and MortPak-Lite Upgrades: Version 3.0 of the United Nations Software Packages for Mortality Measurement.* New York: United Nations.

U.S. Bureau of the Census. 1939. *Vital Statistics of the United States 1937. Part 1: Natality and Mortality Data for the United States Tabulated by Place of Occurrence with Supplemental Tables for Hawaii, Puerto Rico, and the Virgin Islands.* Washington: U.S. Government Printing Office.

———. 1946. *United States Life Tables and Actuarial Tables, 1939–1941.* Washington: U.S. Government Printing Office.

———. 1964. *Accuracy of Data on Population Characteristics as Measured by CPS-Census Match.* 1960 Census of Population and Housing: Evaluation and Research Program. Series ER 60, no. 5. Washington: U.S. Government Printing Office.

———. 1973. *Test of Birth Registration Completeness 1964 to 1968.* Census of Population and Housing: 1970 Evaluation and Research Program PHC(E)-2. Washington: U.S. Government Printing Office.

———. 1974. *Estimates of Coverage of Population by Sex, Race, and Age: Demographic Analysis.* 1970 Census of Population and Housing: Evaluation and Research Program PHC(E)-4. Washington: U.S. Government Printing Office.

———. 1975. *Accuracy of Data for Selected Population Characteristics as Measured by the 1970 CPS-Census Match.* 1970 Census of Population and Housing: Evaluation and Research Program. Washington: U.S. Government Printing Office.

———. 1989. *Historical Statistics of the United States: Colonial Times to 1970,* part 1. White Plains, N.Y.: Kraus International Publications.

———. 1996. *Population Projections of the United States by Age, Sex, Race, and Hispanic Origin: 1995 to 2050.* Current Population Reports P25-1130. Washington: U.S. Government Printing Office.

Ventura, S. J., J. A. Martin, S. C. Curtin, and T. J. Mathews. 1998. *Report of Final Natality Statistics, 1996.* Monthly Vital Statistics Report, vol. 46, no. 11 (supplement). Washington: U.S. Government Printing Office.

Vincent, P. 1951. "La mortalité des vieillards." *Population* 6: 181–204.

Waldron, Ingrid. 1993. "Recent Trends in Sex Mortality Ratios for Adults in Developed Countries." *Social Science and Medicine* 36(4): 451–62.

Williams, D. R. 1990. "Socioeconomic Differentials in Health: A Review and Redirection." *Social Psychology Quarterly* 53(2): 81–99.

Zelnik, Melvin. 1969. "Age Patterns of Mortality of American Negroes, 1900–02 to 1959–61." *Journal of American Statistical Association* 64(326): 433–51.

Zhang, X. H., S. Sasaki, and H. Kesteloot. 1995. "The Sex Ratio of Mortality and Its Secular Trends." *International Journal of Epidemiology* 24(4): 720–29.

—— Chapter 8 ——

The Fading Dream: Prospects for Marriage in the Inner City

Frank F. Furstenberg Jr.

IN ITS SHORT history, America has had many periods in which dramatic changes have occurred in the family. However, the final third of the twentieth century has to stand as one of the most remarkable of all. Within a span of merely three decades, we have moved from an era when the vast majority of women were wed by their early twenties to the present time when only a small minority marry by then. This change has been especially marked for black women, who during the middle of this century were about as likely to enter marriage as were white women. In 1960, 75 percent of black women and 85 percent of white women were married by the age of twenty-five, and all but 2 percent of black women had entered wedlock by age forty-five compared to 1 percent of whites (Carter and Glick 1976).

Demographers now project that at least a quarter of all black women now in their twenties will never marry at all (compared to about 10 percent of whites; see Bennett, Bloom, and Craig 1989; Cherlin 1992; Saluter 1996). Of those who do marry, the great majority can expect unstable unions, and many who separate will not reenter marriage even if they form a second union. Furthermore, almost all experts think that the retreat from marriage is likely to continue for the foreseeable future. If trends of nonmarital childbearing are any indication of the confidence that African Ameri-

224

cans place in marriage, the prognosis for revitalization is poor (Driscoll et al. 1999; Foster and Hoffman 1996; Pagnini and Rindfuss 1993). These aggregate figures, moreover, conceal sharp socioeconomic differences. Among the very poor, the proportion who will ever marry is much lower. To my knowledge, no one has made any projections for very recent cohorts of inner-city residents, but it is probably safe to predict that not much more than half of the very poor will ever marry.

Why has marriage lost its grip as a social form? No simple explanation fits all the available evidence. In a certain sense it is tautological to point to values about the importance of marriage as an explanation. Yet the loss of confidence in marriage is a very real phenomenon, especially among low-income populations (Anderson 1993; Cherlin 1996; Edin 1998; Sullivan 1993). Surely some of these changes have to do with the everyday experiences of children growing up in a world where few marriages ultimately endure (Furstenberg, Sherwood, and Sullivan 1992).

These broader marriage trends are mirrored in a thirty-year longitudinal study I have conducted in Baltimore, Maryland, following the lives of a cohort of adolescent mothers and their children. Back in the 1960s when the teen parents in my study first became pregnant, I asked a series of questions about marriage expectations. Virtually all expected to wed, and the great majority did so. More than half were married by their early twenties, and by their mid-forties more than three in four had wed, nearly half to the father of their child. This propensity to marry—often to the child's father—was the prevailing pattern in the 1960s (O'Connell and Moore 1981; Ventura 1987).

Among the next generation of young parents—the daughters of the teen mothers who were in my original study—the practice was very different (Furstenberg, Levine, and Brooks-Gunn 1990). Slightly more than a third of the female offspring became parents in their teens, but hardly any of the women married. Even by their early twenties, only 14 percent of the second-generation teenage moms had wed, and just 4 percent of the young women who were not yet mothers were married. Of course, these youths were following the popular regime of postponing marriage; nevertheless, inner-city youths displayed an extreme model of this new prototype of family formation.

This chapter considers why African American youths are reluctant to marry, and why they have difficulty forming and maintaining stable partnerships, even when they continue to hold on to the ideal of marriage. Various hypotheses have been proposed to account for the decline in marriage among African Americans. I begin by mentioning briefly the most prominent explanations offered by several disciplines for why blacks are less inclined to marry or remain married when they do wed. The theories developed by economists, demographers, and sociologists provide a useful backdrop against which to compare the first-hand accounts offered by the youths that I interviewed.

EXPLANATIONS FOR THE DECLINE IN MARRIAGE

In the 1960s, Moynihan (1965) was one of the first to observe that rates of marriage began to decline and the incidence of nonmarital childbearing began to rise steeply simultaneously with the unemployment of black males. Since then, many economists and sociologists have argued that the institution of marriage is bolstered when men and women trade resources—money and time—and by specialization between the sexes (Becker 1991; Fuchs 1983; Cherlin 1996; Goldscheider and Waite 1991). Under these conditions, males are expected to perform the role of the "good provider," and women are expected to manage the domestic sphere. This gender-based division of labor was never completely operative in the black community, however (Mare and Winship 1991). By necessity, if not preference, black women participated in the labor force much earlier than white women (Garfinkel and McLanahan 1986). Whatever glue was provided by economic exchange thus had a distinctive mixture long before men's economic position was compromised by the massive loss of industrial jobs that occurred in the second half of this century (Wilson 1996).

The declining position of black men in the labor force is linked indirectly to a second explanation for racial differences in marriage patterns: blacks form a separate marriage market circumscribed by racial segregation, and, within this market, marriageable males are in short supply (Darity and Myers 1984; Lichter, LeClere, and McLaughlin 1991; Wu 1996). During the 1960s, the age structure of the population favored males of marriageable age. More recently, high rates of mortality and morbidity associated with stressful life conditions, along with incarceration, have substantially reduced the number of black males available as attractive mates, and some of the relatively few desirable men marry outside their race, further decreasing African American women's chances of finding a partner.

Finally, some historians and anthropologists argue that African Americans are culturally disinclined toward strong marriage. The relatively weak commitment to marriage is sometimes viewed as a cultural pattern imported from Africa and at other times as a survival strategy. The first group of scholars regards this kinship pattern as deeply rooted in Afro-centric cultural traditions that were maintained and perhaps elaborated on during slavery (Morgan et al. 1993). The second group of scholars views culture in a more immediate sense—as a recent adaptation to persistent poverty, in which reliance on close kin represents a way of coping with disadvantage (Stack 1974). From either perspective, the marginal economic position of males contributes to a predisposition to rely on generational ties rather than marital bonds as a primary source of support (Cherlin 1992).

Typically researchers present these explanations as competing ways of accounting for racial differences in family formation, but they need not be viewed as rival theories. Indeed, some scholars contend that they may well work in tandem to produce the large racial differences in marriage practices described earlier. Much of the evidence that I present here seems to reinforce this position, revealing how economic, cultural, and biographical experiences are interwoven in everyday life. To treat these conditions as separate elements and attempt to measure their distinctive contributions dismisses their *compound* effect, which creates an especially powerful effect on family formation.

I do not wish to claim that the in-depth discussions that I and my collaborators have conducted over the past several years, with several dozen youths and their families, provide a secure purchase for explaining the sources of marriage patterns in the inner city. Nonetheless, these first-hand accounts are useful in interpreting evidence derived from demographic surveys.

In the course of many far-ranging conversations about male-female relations, I learned what inner-city youths look for in intimate relationships and what they usually find. These representations about relationships helped me to see more clearly why marriage is so much more precarious in the inner city today than it was even thirty years ago. Although I attempted to draw general conclusions about the sources and consequences of marriage beliefs in the inner city, I did not find consensus or uniformity among the people that I interviewed. Men and women have different perspectives, opinions change over time as youths move from late adolescence to early adulthood, and views differ depending on family history and social location. These sources of variation tell us a lot about why marriage practices are changing.

THE CULTURE OF GENDER DISTRUST

In the spring of 1991, I conducted a focus group with eight young mothers who were members of my original study. The women were assembled to talk about the men who had fathered their children and, in some cases, who had gone on to take their place as the children's daddies. The discussion began with each group member giving a short history of her relationship with the father of their child (or, in some cases, of their children). The tales of disappointment accumulated as we went around the room (see Furstenberg 1995). At several points, a general discussion of men's failures in relation to women and children ensued, and eventually the talk turned to marriage itself. All eight women in the group were or had been in serious relationships, and most had given serious thought to the issue. Only one woman was married at the time, although several were living in more or less stable unions; others were in or between relationships.

As is evident from the following transcript of a passage from their conversation, opinions were divided about the desirability of marriage and, even more so, about their own prospects for finding a suitable mate or a reliable partner:

> *Robin:* You talk about marriage a lot, but I don't know when it's time. I really don't. We've been together for about ten years, and I still don't know.

Georgia (who is planning to marry soon): It's something you work at.

Robin: It's not me. More so, it's him, and I don't know what it is about men, but they got that tendency. They want to run . . . How old are you going to be when you get that running out? And, I don't want to be in a relationship, and he leaves me . . . I don't know.

Leisha (nodding her head): I'm scared of marriage. I'm very scared of marriage. We've mentioned it . . . I've seen too many marriages that just flop, you know. I have an aunt that her marriage lasted for five months.

Leisha went on to explain that her friend has a goal of where he wants to be when he gets married: he doesn't want to be struggling economically, adding, "He thinks a conflict would come, and we would be arguing over money and stuff like that." She told the group that she agrees with him but still asks herself, "If you lose your job, then what?" She and her friend had been going back and forth, one feeling uncertain and the other feeling more ready. "We—like he—mentioned [getting married] to me once or twice, and I told him I didn't know. Then he decides that he just wanted to wait for a while to do it till he gets that goal on track."

Georgia, who had lived with the father of her second child for three years, admitted that she has the same sorts of reservations, explaining that her concerns grow when she looks at other people's marriages, particularly her mother's:

And then I looked at my grandparents. They have been married for fifty-six years. So I go like . . . That's one reason to get married. So we are going to get married after I have the baby . . . The thing is you never know when it's time to do it. You just know you want to do it. You don't know exactly when. It's just something that just has to be worked out.

Her resolution of this dilemma seemed to ignite a reaction from among several others who feel less prepared than she to assume the risks. Tanisha, who had been seeing the father of her child on and off for a number of years, chimed in,

I don't have time for other relationships. Right now I just moved, and I'm working two jobs. And then came the baby. That's all I have time for right now.

Angie shook her head in agreement and insisted that she's "not getting married or nothing. I'm just cautious in all relationships. I

don't want to get too close." Wanda Jackson, who had been taking all of this in quietly, was asked how she feels about getting
married. Her succinct reply was "No."

At this point, I turned to Karen, the one woman in the group
who had been stably wed since her child was born. She asserted
that she was not forced into marriage, noting, "We loved each
other, and we wanted to get married." One of the women said,
supportively, "That's nice." Karen explained that, although she
was not even seventeen when she got married, she is not scared
and has been happily married for six years. The others in the
group were incredulous. Karen retorted that she cannot understand why they are so scared. At this, Robin King tried once again
to explain why she is so ambivalent about marriage:

> Well, really I think I'm too young. And then once I look at my age, I figure,
> well, I'm not getting any younger. And, it's just like you said—based on
> other people's relationships. My sister got married Christmas day. It did not
> go a whole year before she got a divorce . . . Close to home like, you
> know, it really scares me. Then my mother was married for two years, and
> her and my father were separated for eighteen years, and I'm like—Uh-uh.
> I don't want to.

Karen insisted again that she should stop looking at other people's marriages, and Robin rejoined, "But that's what scares me."
"If you hadn't broken up after ten years," Karen questioned,
"shouldn't you be able to get married?" Robin said that she does
not need the paper and then added to her list of reservations:

> He still acts like a baby . . . I mean he acts just like another of my children,
> you know. Got to treat him just like you treat women and children.

Karen conceded this point, agreeing that "I think that's all men . . .
they want to be pampered." Several women jumped in to complain that men are just spoiled. They are unwilling and unfit to
help out with the children. On this point there was some dissent
among a couple of the women who cited cases of men they know
who have been raised to help out, even a few who are willing to
"change the diapers." I was prompted to ask, "How many men are
like that?" A chorus of responses to my questions suggested that
these exceptional men are few in number. "One in ten," someone

replied. Another concurred: "You just can't find them. They just aren't around."

Were it not for the dozens of interviews that I conducted after this session, I might be inclined to treat this brief exchange with more circumspection. However, in interviews with nearly twenty women, I was often reminded of this conversation. When I interviewed several women in the group again later on, I was told that the conversation about men resumed in the car during the ride home. Complaints about men and a broader distrust of men are the stock and trade of everyday conversation among most of the women with whom I spoke. It seems that many poor black women, like those who participated in the focus group, subscribe to a set of related beliefs about men that have implications for how they think about long-term relationships and marriage in particular. Despite some variation in beliefs, a common set of views emerged from the interviews I conducted:

- *Men are immature.* Most women think that men are ill-prepared to enter serious relationships. In one form or another, I heard a lot about men's immaturity, especially their need to "run" before they settle down.
- *Men are spoiled.* Frequently, I was told that men are spoiled from an early age. Too little is expected of them, and they are not trained to be responsible; they are allowed to be self-indulgent and to grow up with selfish attitudes.
- *Men are not self-reliant.* Many women, as we heard in the group, think that men are incapable of taking care of themselves. They are like children who need to be managed, and most do not do their fair share.
- *Men are controlling.* I heard a lot about how possessive men can be when they get into relationships. They expect to get their own way and expect women to cater to their needs. Worse, they are suspicious and jealous of their partners.
- *Men are unreliable.* Related to their immaturity, I was often told that men cannot be relied on in relationships. They cannot be trusted to be faithful, and many cannot even be counted on to provide for their families.

This interconnected set of beliefs about men leads most women with whom I spoke to be very wary about relationships. They enter relationships expecting them to fail, and their sensitivity to the failings of men leads many to monitor relationships closely, looking for early warning signals of distress. The kind of discussion that I heard in the focus group is familiar to all the women with whom I spoke: they have been told about men's failings from early childhood, they have learned about these failings from painful experience, and they continually swap stories that reinforce this "culture of distrust" with family and friends. In the words of one woman, "My mother brought me up like that. You don't depend on a man. You have to be strong because he could leave you today or tomorrow."

Women thus are trained to be vigilant and are always looking for signs of distress or reassurance. Even in functioning and relatively permanent unions, women retain a large share of distrust about their long-term prospects. Whether right or wrong, they seem to expect men to demonstrate the qualities that they have been led to fear will show up in time. Sociologists might describe this pattern as a form of "anticipatory socialization." In sum, marriage represents a terrifying role transition for African American women, who believe that men are likely to let them down.

As I learned from the focus group, there is no easy way of assessing readiness for marriage. Economic security is certainly a prime indicator, and a relatively low proportion of black men are in a position to demonstrate their commitment through a capacity for steady and secure earnings. Current employment does not eliminate the pervasive question "what if?" that so many women feel about their partners' economic futures. It is hard to be confident of men's economic security when women themselves are not confident of the job market. After all, even those who are currently employed could lose their jobs.

Employment is a necessary, but not a sufficient, condition for marriage. According to focus group discussions, men may be stable providers, but they are often untrustworthy in other respects. Many women are unwilling to give up their autonomy for a man, feeling that men are too controlling and possessive. Men expect more than they are prepared to give in return, as I was often told:

Just because we're women, that don't mean we can do it. I mean superwoman and stuff. It's just, he feels as though I'm the woman. I'm the mother.

I'm supposed to do this. He supposed to do . . . go to work and bring home the money.

Cohabitation becomes a strategy for managing this uncertainty. Women make a conditional commitment, permitting them the opportunity to test a relationship, but the test often serves only to feed their doubts as relationships suffer the wear and tear that come from living stressful lives.

Even if somewhat hedged, marriage still remains an ideal for many women. Although it was common to hear of failed marriages, most of the women in my study spoke reverently about the marriages that have survived. These marriages become the yardstick against which the prospects for current relationships are judged. Inner-city youths are as likely as the rest of us to conjure up images of the good old days when marriages were stable and men and women respected and relied on one another. The small number of parents, uncles, and aunts, as well as the larger number of grandparents, who maintain stable relationships surely provide role models, but they also arouse uncertainties about whether it is possible to measure up to past standards:

It seems like today more kids are raising themselves because you have more single parents than it used to be back in the days. And it's a difference when two parents are raising a child as opposed to one.

In a paradoxical way, the scarcity of surviving marriages—both good and not-so-good unions—inflates the ideal of marriage. As stable marriages become more rare in reality, they become ever more idealized. Stable marriages require exceptional men. The ideal of marriage is thus preserved but is reserved for men who are exceptional: unusually reliable and uncommonly trustworthy. Karen, though she confessed that she has to baby her husband, is something of an exception in not adhering to the culture of distrust with respect to men. She later confided to me that most of the women in the group are too hard on men.

In the course of my study, I also spoke to a number of men and solicited their views on the issue of marriage. Although I did not convene a focus group, numerous one-on-one conversations with low-income black males, some of whom were partners of women I had spoken to earlier, yielded a fairly consistent, and equally unattractive, view of women:

- *Women expect too much of men.* Most men say that women are too hard on them and expect too much. They complain particularly about women's harsh judgments of their motives and their family commitments.
- *Men need their freedom.* Many men speak about needing a period of freedom before they can settle down. They need to get the "running out of their system." Women do not seem to understand that men have to have an outside life.
- *Women do not trust men to be faithful.* According to men, women are jealous and fearful that they will become involved with other relationships. Men sometimes talk about the extreme lengths that women go to check up on them.
- *Women are spoiled.* Women want to be taken care of and indulged by men. They demand lavish attention and are materialistic, looking for gifts as an expression of men's interests in them.
- *Women do not respect men.* Some men feel that women do not treat them with proper deference; rather, women denigrate them and do not grant them the respect they need to be good husbands. Too many women want to control the relationship.

SOURCES OF GENDER DISTRUST

It is easy to see in this set of overlapping beliefs a convergence of views between men and women. Some of the men's complaints about women are the mirror image of women's criticisms about men, whereas others reflect the same concerns that women have about men. These divergent perspectives exemplify what might be called a "culture of gender distrust," a system of beliefs that is deeply rooted in the economic and social structure of inner-city communities. Men's marginal and uncertain position in the labor market contributes greatly to the lack of confidence that both genders feel about men's uncertain role as coprovider. Indeed, *all* of the women I spoke with expect to share the economic responsibility of raising a family. Although some women are sympathetic to the difficulty men have in finding stable employment and spoke of the discrimination that black males face in the labor market, others are not so understanding.

Working women who are struggling to make ends meet often feel impatient about men's reluctance to find or stay in low-income jobs. As a result, they view men as lazy and irresponsible about meeting their obligations. It is not surprisingly that men are defensive about the criticisms leveled by their partners or former partners. They often spoke about the frustrations they face when looking for work, the rejections, and the slights experienced on the job. A number of men that I spoke with felt that women do not appreciate their efforts to deal with the injuries inflicted in the workplace and their legitimate concerns about maintaining their dignity.

Men's poor position in the labor market has a direct effect on relationships and the prospect of marriage. Women rarely remain in relationships with unstable providers, and chronically unemployed men generally are unable to settle down. Rather, they move in and out of short-term relationships, exhausting the patience of women who feel exploited and ill-cared for by them. As Wilson (1987) has argued so perceptively, the absence of stable employment affects the patterning of men's routines. The high premium placed on freedom from domestic responsibility is partly a product of the unpredictability of work life, prolonging the period of youthfulness. Women refer to men's resistance to settling down as proof of their immaturity and selfishness or see a prolonged period of "getting the running out of their system."

Men, perceiving the unattractive alternatives for work and sometimes the absolute lack of alternatives, come to define their marginal position in the labor force as having certain privileged or desirable features. The absence of routines preserves their freedom and extends their manliness by allowing peer play. Settling down can only occur when a man holds a stable job, and in the meantime he may indulge his need to get out on the streets. As one man told me,

> I think there are things that you need to get out of your system before you get married. Every guy between the ages of high school till they reach

early—maybe twenty-three—have a little playing. Go out and have fun. Hang around with the guys.

This view is consistent with that of a woman experiencing difficulties in her relationship with her child's father. As she explained,

He's not ready to settle down. He wants his cake and eat it too . . . why should he have to settle down right now if that's not what he wants to do?

The secondary effects of unemployment, chronic or episodic, are equally consequential in maintaining the culture of gender distrust. Men with poor employment prospects or those whose jobs disappear are more likely to rely on illegitimate means of making a living. They are more likely to use drugs and alcohol to excess, and they more frequently become violent and excessively controlling in their relations with women. Both women and men often attribute the downfall of their relationship to economic uncertainty or, at least, to economic pressures. As two female respondents put it,

He had come home, and he didn't have a job, so he wasn't like doing his part or nothing like that . . . but we were still together. So finally, I couldn't take it anymore so I just, you know, "go play . . . do what you want to do." He didn't really take care of his responsibilities. He was out all of the time. He was work[ing], and he wasn't. His money wasn't coming into the house . . . It didn't work, so I moved back home with my parents.

Negative definitions accompany negative behavior, and the distrust of men consequently spreads and grows, leading women to adopt a suspicious view of the other sex. It is easy to see how this suspicion, in turn, becomes a part of men's sense that women in general treat them unfairly and regard them with undue distrust. Women are attentive to signs of unreliability in men, and men know it. These public definitions occur against a backdrop of biographical experience that feeds the culture of gender distrust. As witnessed in the focus group discussion, it is common for inner-city youths to invoke memories of the past to explain their reservations about current relationships. Virtually everyone with whom I spoke has witnessed painful dealings between their parents or other close family members. These memories seem to frame their fears about the present, fueling their doubts about their own capacity or the capacity of their partners to repeat history (Furstenberg 1995). Thus the excessively high rate of family instability creates fear, if not an expectation of failure, in forming stable unions.

Neither the sources nor the consequences of gender distrust just described are unique to inner-city black youths. The perception that men are more selfish and less trustworthy or that women are demanding and suspicious can be found in all segments of our society. More youths in the middle class are growing up these days with a family history of unstable relations and are acquiring experience from informal unions that may undermine a sense of trust in the opposite sex. However, the strength and pervasiveness of these convictions assume a qualitatively different character in a context where the conditions promoting gender distrust are unusually strong and pervasive.

Ordinarily inner-city youths encounter economic conditions that undercut the ability of couples to count on a secure income. Women's confidence in men, and men's confidence in themselves as reliable providers, thus undermines an inner-city couple's ability to imagine a predictable future. The wariness created by economic uncertainty is continually reinforced by everyday experience. The high rate of failure in relationships—both past and present—contributes heavily to the lack of confidence that men and women have in forming stable unions.

Explanations of low marriage rates and high levels of instability that separate economic and cultural sources into discrete and separate "variables" ignore the inextricable ways in which these components become fused in a system of beliefs, expectations, and practices that destabilize relations between men and women in the inner city. While for some purposes, it may be useful to examine the relative weight of economic and cultural contributions to the marriage patterns of black Americans, such exercises, in fact, run the risk of distorting the reality as it is experienced by those whose behaviors we attempt to explain from afar.

Consider the case of Leisha, one of the women in the focus group who expressed deep reservations about marriage. Leisha has been living periodically with a male friend for several years who is the father of her two younger children. He is a reliable provider, holding down two jobs. According to Leisha, he is also a good man who has few bad habits and has willingly become a daddy to her oldest child. But Leisha's response to his unusually high commitment to her and the children is to wonder about the security of the current arrangement. What will happen if he loses one of his jobs? The father of Leisha's oldest child was a reliable partner for a couple of years until he lost his job. So the value of present commitments is discounted in the future.

The discounting occurs only partly for economic reasons. Leisha admitted that she is suspicious of his motives for other reasons. Leisha and her friend have little time to spend together. Although they sometimes talk things over, she is not so sure that he understands her needs or desires. She insists that neither of them wanted the last two pregnancies, but each expected the other to take responsibility for preventing it from happening. Based on that experience and other misunderstandings in the past, Leisha is not so certain she can trust him. She acknowledged that her lack of confidence in men probably comes from watching her mother fail in a succession of relationships. Leisha is disinclined to rely too much on a man's good intentions. She is looking to see if these intentions are demonstrated in behavior. Nevertheless, her partner's better-than-average behavior still does not allay her fears that the relationship will eventually fail.

How useful is it to separate the strands of individual and collective experience figuring in Leisha's assessment of the future prospects of her relationship? Is it even possible to disentangle the web of economic, interpersonal, and cultural conditions that contribute to Leisha's doubts about the viability of marriage? Are we prepared to rule out the significance of economic influences even when her partner has been a stable provider? Do we want simply to say that she and her partner have problems communicating? Does it not make more sense to see those problems as emanating at least in part from an economic context where many other men have failed to support their families? This setting gives rise to a culture reflecting innumerable incidents in which men and women frequently disappoint each another. And can we separate these disappointments from the history of family experience that itself cumulates into a widespread expectation that most relationships do not survive?

SOURCES OF DIFFERENTIATION

The reluctance of many men and women to enter marriage or even marriage-like relationships may be determined simultaneously by economic, cultural, and interpersonal conditions that mutually reinforce each other in a system that, if not distinctive to, is at least characteristic of the inner city. What I have referred to as the culture of gender distrust is widely shared by most of the young people to whom I spoke. A number of these young adults do not see marriage in their immediate plans, and others do not plan to marry even in the indefinite future. We must take care not to fashion a crude stereotype by assuming that all, or even most, inner-city youths subscribe to a common set of beliefs and a common code of behavior. It is important to resist the temptation to treat inner-city youths as an undifferentiated population.

In fact, the focus group uncovered a range of opinion among young mothers, a population that might be expected to have the most negative views toward marriage. Several of the women, such as Angie and Wanda, seem to have given up on men or, at least, on the prospect of men as stable partners. Others, such as Robin and Leisha, while expressing uncertainties, continue to hold out the hope that their relationship might develop into a permanent arrangement. These women continue to define marriage as desirable even though they harbor doubts that they will realize their dreams. More rare in this group of young mothers, but more common in the larger sample of participants, are women like Karen who are convinced that marriage is both preferable and attainable.

The men with whom I spoke are similarly located along a spectrum anchored at one end by those who regard marriage as undesirable and unattainable and at the other by those who have or are about to wed. Falling in between are the counterparts to Leisha—men who contemplate marriage or at least think it is a desirable status, but who are unsure that they ever will be in a position to marry.

It would be wrong to think of these commitments as permanently fixed in the minds of my informants. Some of the people I interviewed situate themselves differently over time. Opinions about marriage were more tentative in the first interviews (conducted when the youths were approaching adulthood), as they regarded marriage as something far off and spoke about it more abstractly:

> I guess because my parents never got married, it was always a dream of mine that I would get married, have a house, have a couple of kids, you know, that was my dream.

By their mid-twenties, however, their views had begun to crystallize, although not to the extent that they were impervious to future experience. Beliefs about marriage were still incompletely internalized, subject to revision depending on their life options and experience (see Gerson 1985 for a similar argument). In this respect, thinking about marriage reflects and responds to developmental trajectories that cannot be foreseen. Indeed, the uncertainty of men's and women's economic futures and the corresponding availability or lack of availability of marriageable partners complicate the process of establishing fixed scenarios of family formation.

Consistent with this high level of uncertainty about their future prospects, most of the young people whom I interviewed seem to operate with several alternative scripts about marriage. Most hold out hope that the right person might come along and that they might be ready to marry, if that were to happen. At the same time, many regard the possibility of marriage warily. Depending on the phrasing of the question, the context in which it is posed, current circumstances, and, no doubt, who is asking them, respondents are capable of producing quite varied reactions to the idea of marriage.

In fact, many hold ambivalent or conflicting views about the chances they will marry or the desirability of marriage. By holding a set of inconsistent, if not contradictory, views, inner-city youths are prepared for all eventualities. At the same time, their uncertain sentiments help to explain behavioral choices that appear to be inconsistent or irrational with respect to their goals. Notions of rationality fit most neatly when individual preferences are strong and relatively fixed. When objectives are fluid, behavior is as likely to determine preferences as the reverse. Uncertainty about options produces what appears from the outside to look like "aimless" behavior or high levels of risk taking. But seemingly irrational actions may actually reveal the uncertainty surrounding objectives that may be unattainable. This is why, as I have argued elsewhere, we need a theory of "rationalized choice," one that takes account of the capacity of human beings to make sense of their behaviors in contrast to behaving in sensible ways (Furstenberg 1998).

More than a few of the women with whom I spoke and several of the men in this study claimed that they are staying out of relationships altogether. Like discouraged workers who stop looking for a job, these nonseekers have removed themselves from the marriage market and are investing themselves emotionally in their work, children, or community, which is not to say that the right circumstance or person might not draw them back into a relationship.

Most youths have adopted a wait-and-see attitude that keeps their options open. They enter relationships, but they are not looking to marry, at least for the present. A few are in marriage-like relationships, wavering back and forth on whether to increase the level of commitment. Many have moved in and out of unions in hopes of finding a satisfying and more permanent arrangement. They are acutely aware of the low odds of finding a good partner and establishing a lasting bond.

Finally, a sizable minority of those to whom I spoke expressed a definite intention to marry or were about to do so. These youths, while aware of and concerned about the risks of entering marriage, tend to hold more conventional or mainstream views about family formation and are more committed to marriage as a social institution. To describe their beliefs as traditional is something of an oversimplification because many of those who had already married did so after living together or because of a pregnancy. While often understanding of others' choices, they expressed a strong preference for marriage. They usually did so out of religious convictions or because they were brought up to believe that children are better off when they are raised by both of their parents.

This spectrum of opinion appears to be linked in part to the social position of the youths and their families. Often, but not invariably, those with the greatest skepticism toward marriage are from the most disadvantaged families, and nearly all of those with the most conventional views about marriage are from relatively secure backgrounds. But the connection between social position and beliefs about marriage appears to be more than a simple association between belief and a family's income, education, or position in the labor market.

A family's economic status is generally created and maintained by a complex set of social conditions. Youths from better-off families are more likely to have grown up in families with two parents (although not always two biological parents). In part, then, notions about the viability of marriage reflect their biographical experience; regardless of parental economic status or marital stability, their family networks include a higher proportion of working and middle-class members and of stable families. Thus youths who subscribe to more conventional attitudes about marriage come from families with more access to resources and more exposure to models of marital success:

> I mean, I wouldn't want to be home full-time, no, but I like keeping house and being a wife and everything that comes with it . . . [I grew up with steady father figure]. What I wanted was both of them [father and child] to be together because all my friends had both their parents home with them. It seems like their life was going much better. They had a role model. What I try to base it on is an example, my grandparents, my father's parents, they have been together for forty-seven years . . . and they always were close family . . . I try to follow them, use them as an example.

Privilege and the social experiences associated with it imperfectly account for these youths' views and choices about marriage. Overlapping, and perhaps underlying, the social experience that differentiates more and less advantaged families is the belief system of the families themselves. Family subcultures, which are connected to a variety of institutions beyond the family, exert a powerful influence on youths' ideas. In particular, conventional notions of marriage are often carried forward within families actively involved in religious institutions and part of a broader religious community.

Nonetheless, neither social connectedness nor personal religious involvement adequately explains the full range of differentiation that I detected in beliefs and practices related to marriage.

These explanations give too little weight to the role of individuals in interpreting and shaping their experiences. In talking to young people, I was impressed by the large differences even among youths who are seemingly in similar circumstances. Thus individuals take an active part in choosing options among the available alternatives. In this sense, individuals play an important part in putting together their beliefs about marriage and relationships. In doing so, of course, they reflect on their own experiences and use them to justify one course of action or another. They are not merely passive receivers but creators of their culture and circumstances.

Allowing for a sense of agency in the formation of beliefs about marriage is entirely consistent with a recognition that individuals are greatly constrained by their current social circumstances, access to cultural beliefs, and past experiences. These conditions delimit the way young people approach relationships with the opposite sex. Their expectations are shaped by initial experiences, and these experiences often force youths to revise their expectations.

CONCLUSIONS

I am skeptical that any single explanation for the recent retreat from marriage is sufficient to account for the loss of confidence that inner-city youths feel in the institution itself or for their inability to form stable unions. Instead, I contend that the separate explanations are, in fact, inextricably interconnected. Economic uncertainties help to make marriage a less desirable, predictable, and permanent social form. Children learn to be wary of expecting relations to work out. Those apprehensions are reinforced during adolescence as both men and women experience fleeting and often unsatisfactory relationships. A culture of gender distrust emerges as men and women increasingly live in separate spheres. The cultural climate of the urban poor creates extravagant fantasies and expectations, bitter disappointments and discontents, and a reliance on maternal kin. Each of these conditions, in turn, renders the conjugal unit less dependable and sturdy as a social form. This culture of distrust is not unique to African Americans, nor is it uniformly shared by those at the bottom of the social ladder. However, life in the inner city creates fertile conditions for breeding suspicions about marriage that reside elsewhere in our society, often in a less potent form. Marriage is an elusive ideal for the disadvantaged. Young parents—whether they are teenagers or in their twenties—are reluctant to enter marriage unless job prospects for men improve and unless young couples acquire reasonable skills of cooperating in family endeavors. It is unlikely that young people will be talked into marriage when their everyday experience tells them it is a bad bet.

REFERENCES

Anderson, Elijah. 1993. "Sex Codes and Family Life among Poor Inner-City Youths." In *Young Unwed Fathers: Changing Roles and Emerging Policies,* edited by R. I. Lerman and T. J. Ooms. Philadelphia: Temple University Press.

Becker, Gary S. 1991. *A Treatise on the Family.* Cambridge, Mass.: Harvard University Press.

Bennett, Neil G., David E. Bloom, and P. H. Craig. 1989. "The Divergence of Black and White Marriage Patterns." *American Journal of Sociology* 95(2): 692–722.

Carter, Hugh, and Paul C. Glick. 1976. *Marriage and Divorce: A Social and Economic Study,* rev. ed. Cambridge, Mass.: Harvard University Press.

Cherlin, Andrew J. 1992. *Marriage, Divorce, Remarriage,* rev. ed. Cambridge, Mass.: Harvard University Press.

———. 1996. *Public and Private Families: An Introduction.* New York: McGraw-Hill.

Darity, William A., and Samuel L. Myers. 1984. "Does Welfare Dependency Cause Female Headship? The Case of the Black Family." *Journal of Marriage and the Family* 46(4): 765–79.

Driscoll, Anne K., Gesine K. Hearn, V. Jeffrey Evans, Kristin A. Moore, Barbara W. Sugland, and Vaughn Call. 1999. "Nonmarital Childbearing among Adult Women." *Journal of Marriage and the Family* 61(1): 178–87.

Edin, Kathryn. 1998. "Why Don't Poor Single Mothers Get Married (or Remarried)?" Paper presented at the Russell Sage Foundation, New York.

Farley, Reynolds, and Walter R. Allen. 1987. *The Color Line and the Quality of Life in America.* New York: Russell Sage Foundation.

Foster, E. Michael, and Saul D. Hoffman. 1996. "Nonmarital Childbearing in the 1980s: Assessing the Importance of Women 25 and Older." *Family Planning Perspectives* 28(3): 117–19.

Fuchs, Victor R. 1983. *How We Live: An Economic Perspective on Americans from Birth to Death.* Cambridge, Mass.: Harvard University Press.

Furstenberg, Frank F., Jr. 1995. "Fathering in the Inner City: Paternal Participation and Public Policy." In *Fatherhood: Contemporary Theory, Research, and Social Policy,* edited by William Marsiglio. Thousand Oaks, Calif.: Sage Publications.

———. 1998. "When Will Teenage Childbearing Become a Social Problem? The Implications of Western Experience for Developing Countries." *Studies in Family Planning* 29(2): 246–53.

Furstenberg, Frank F., Jr., Judith A. Levine, and Jeanne Brooks-Gunn. 1990. "The Daughters of Teenage Mothers: Patterns of Early Childbearing in Two Generations." *Family Planning Perspectives* 22(2): 54–61.

Furstenberg, Frank F., Jr., K. E. Sherwood, and Mercer L. Sullivan. 1992. *Caring and Paying: What Fathers and Mothers Say about Child Support.* Report prepared for Manpower Demonstration Research Corporation Project, Parents' Fair Share Demonstration. New York: Demonstration Research Corporation Project.

Garfinkel, Irving, and Sara S. McLanahan. 1986. *Single Mothers and Their Children: A New American Dilemma.* Washington, D.C.: Urban Institute Press.

Gerson, Katherine. 1985. *Hard Choices: How Women Decide about Work, Career, and Motherhood.* Berkeley: University of California Press.

Goldscheider, Frances K., and Linda Waite. 1991. *New Families, No Families: The Transformation of the American Home.* Berkeley: University of California Press.

Lichter, D. T., F. B. LeClere, and D. K. McLaughlin. 1991. "Local Marriage Markets and the Marital Behavior of Black and White Women." *American Journal of Sociology* 96(4): 843–67.

Mare, Robert D., and Christopher Winship. 1991. "Socioeconomic Change and the Decline of Marriage for Blacks and Whites." In *The Urban Underclass,* edited by Christopher Jencks and Paul E. Peterson. Washington, D.C.: Brookings Institution.

Morgan, S. Philip, Antonio McDaniel, Andrew Miller, and Samuel H. Preston. 1993. "Differences in Household and Family Structure at the Turn of the Century." *American Journal of Sociology* 98(4): 799–828.

Moynihan, Daniel P. 1965. *The Negro Family: The Case for National Ac-*

tion. Washington: U.S. Department of Labor, Department of Policy Planning and Research.

O'Connell, Martin, and M. J. Moore. 1981. "The Legitimacy Status of First Births to U.S. Women Aged 15–24, 1939–1978." In *Teenage Sexuality, Pregnancy, and Childbearing*, edited by Frank F. Furstenberg Jr., Richard Lincoln, and Jane A. Menken. Philadelphia: University of Pennsylvania Press.

Pagnini, D. L., and R. R. Rindfuss. 1993. "The Divorce of Marriage and Childbearing: Changing Attitudes and Behavior in the United States." *Population and Development Review* 19(2): 331–47.

Saluter, A. F. 1996. *Marital Status and Living Arrangements: March 1994*. Current Population Reports Series P20-484. Washington: U.S. Government Printing Office.

Stack, Carol B. 1974. *All Our Kin*. New York: Harper and Row.

Sullivan, Mercer L. 1993. "Young Fathers and Parenting in Two Inner-City Neighborhoods." In *Young Unwed Fathers: Changing Roles and Emerging Policies*, edited by R. I. Lerman and T. J. Ooms. Philadelphia: Temple University Press.

Ventura, S. J. 1987. "Trends in Marital Status of Mothers at Conception and Birth of First Child: United States, 1964–66, 1972, and 1980." *Monthly Vital Statistics Report* 36 (2), supp. DHHS publication 87-1120. Hyattsville, Md.: Public Health Services.

Wilson, William J. 1987. *The Truly Disadvantaged*. Chicago: University of Chicago Press.

———. 1996. *When Work Disappears: The World of the New Urban Poor*. New York: Knopf.

Wu, Lawrence L. 1996. "Effects of Family Instability, Income, and Income Stability on the Risk of a Premarital Birth." *American Sociological Review* 61(3): 386–406.

—— Chapter 9 ——

Quality of In-Patient AIDS Care: Does Race Matter?

Linda H. Aiken and Douglas M. Sloane

A HEALTH GAP persists in the United States by income, race, and ethnicity. The health gap is widest for African Americans, whose life expectancy is 6.6 years less than that of whites (National Center for Health Statistics 1998). Blacks experience a pattern of elevated death rates compared to whites for thirteen of the fifteen leading causes of death (Williams 1998). For infant mortality—a benchmark measure often used to evaluate the social well-being of populations—the rate of blacks is more than twice that of whites. Hispanics have lower death rates for heart disease and cancer than do non-Hispanics, but higher mortality rates for conditions such as diabetes, cirrhosis, and homicide, as well as elevated rates for a number of infectious diseases including HIV and AIDS (Williams 1998).

Disparities in access to health care have long been assumed to be responsible, in part, for poorer health outcomes among disadvantaged minority populations. Over the latter half of the twentieth century, substantial gains were made in extending health insurance coverage to low-income and minority populations principally through the Medicare program for the elderly and disabled and the Medicaid program for the poor (Aiken and Bays 1984; Freeman et al. 1987, 1990). Indeed expanded health insurance contributed to narrowing long-standing gaps in the use of health services between whites and others (Davis 1975; Mechanic and Aiken 1989a). In 1963 the proportion of blacks who saw a

247

physician regularly was 18 percent lower than the proportion of whites, but by 1982 this gap had been almost eliminated (Blendon et al. 1989). Although real parity in access to medical care would result in blacks having substantially higher use of medical services than whites because of their higher burden of illness, there is little doubt that expanded health insurance coverage for the elderly and the poor has helped to narrow the racial gap in the use of medical services (Blendon et al. 1989; Physician Payment Review Commission 1997).

In recent years, the number of uninsured Americans has been on the rise, reversing a twenty-year period of improving insurance coverage. Of minority adults ages eighteen to sixty-four, 31 percent did not have health insurance in 1995, compared with 14 percent of white adults of the same age. Half of all minority adults were uninsured at some point within the past two years (Commonwealth Fund 1995). Health insurance in the United States is related to steady, full-time employment in manufacturing, a shrinking sector of the economy, and in the higher-income segments of the service industry, where minorities are underrepresented. Welfare reform has added more minority women and children to the ranks of the uninsured, as the jobs that former welfare recipients obtain are unlikely to include employer health insurance benefits comparable to Medicaid coverage.

Although the high numbers of adults and children without health insurance in the United States are an important factor in differential access to medical care, health insurance does not guarantee access to medical services of high quality (Dutton 1986). Because health outcomes continue to vary substantially by race even among those with health insurance, researchers have increasingly turned their attention to studies that aim to understand whether quality of medical care varies by race and, if so, how and why. A growing body of evidence suggests that even after gaining access to the health care system, racial disparities are common in the receipt of potentially beneficial technologies and medical interventions (Yergan et al. 1987). Despite universal health insurance coverage provided by Medicare to elderly Americans, the patterns of service use differ for blacks and whites (Kahn et al. 1994). Black Medicare beneficiaries living in poor urban areas receive substantially fewer medical care services than others, and they are more than twice as likely to receive routine care in emergency room settings. Emergency room settings do not provide continuity of care or health promotion and disease prevention services characteristic of mainstream primary medical care settings, and they are less effective in treating chronic illnesses that burden the poor and undermine their functioning in everyday life (Physician Payment Review Commission 1997; St. Peter, Newacheck, and Halfon 1992). Blacks are about half as likely as whites to receive intervention therapy for coronary artery disease, but blacks with diabetes are substantially more likely to have amputations than whites. These differentials are not explained by differences in the severity of illness at the point of medical consultation (Ford and Cooper 1995; Peterson et al. 1994; Ayanian et al. 1993; Whittle et al. 1993). Likewise, racial differences in the use of Medicare for restorative procedures such as total hip replacement persist even when correction is made for income differences (Gornick et al. 1996).

Two principal explanations have been advanced to explain racial differences in the patterns of medical care and outcomes once access to the medical care system has been achieved (Dutton 1978). One focuses on racial discrimination in medical decisionmaking and institutional racism (Hummer 1996). An example is reluctance of physicians to offer the most effective AIDS drugs to HIV-infected patients whose lifestyles they presume will prevent adherence to the complex regimens required for successful control of the virus. A second hypothesis is that minorities receive poorer-quality medical care because they tend to use a subset (and in many ways a *different* set) of medical institutions and facilities than the general population and that these institutions are less likely to offer the full range of treatments or the best quality of care. Support for this explanation is found in the work of Smith (1998, 1999) and others (Waitzman and Smith 1998) documenting the effect of race- and income-related residential patterns on the use of medical care facilities. Smith (1998) finds substantial racial segregation of hospitals in the United States and argues that racial disparities in health would be even greater were it not for the significantly higher probability that the urban poor will receive care in high-quality teaching hospitals.

In summary, there is plentiful evidence of persistent racial inequities in health that derive at least in part from differential access to medical care. Racial minorities, and particularly blacks, in comparison to whites are more likely to lack health insurance coverage, receive fewer health services in relation to their burden of illness, receive care in a more limited range of settings and types of institutions, and receive less-intensive services, fewer technologically advanced treatments, and fewer restorative interventions. In the remainder of this chapter, we focus on the fourth point—the effect of race on the content of care once access to the health system has been attained.

RACE AND OUTCOMES OF IN-PATIENT AIDS CARE

The results reported here are part of an ongoing study to assess how the organization of in-patient hospital care affects outcomes for AIDS patients (Aiken et al. 1997). The study was motivated by debate over the consequences of segregating patients from socially marginalized groups with highly stigmatized and potentially communicable diseases from other hospitalized patients and mainstream health care providers. The establishment of dedicated AIDS units in hospitals, in contrast to most specialty units, resulted as much from a perceived need to protect non-AIDS patients and hospital staff as to provide the best possible specialty care (Fox, Aiken, and Messikomer 1990; Aiken et al. 1999). Indeed, effective treatments and AIDS specialists—two essential elements for in-patient specialty care units—were in short supply when most specialized AIDS units were established. Other notable examples of isolating stigmatized patients, including those with mental illnesses, have resulted in poor quality of care (Mechanic and Aiken 1989b). Thus many advocates for people with AIDS opposed early dedicated AIDS units in many locations on the assumption that the quality of care would be stigmatizing and isolating to the patients, yielding outcomes of poorer quality.

Our study of in-patient AIDS care focuses primarily on how the outcomes are related to whether care is provided in dedicated AIDS units or in conventional medical units where AIDS patients are interspersed among patients with other diagnoses. For comparison, we also study outcomes for AIDS patients in three hospitals that are known to provide excellent nursing care, but that do not have specialized AIDS units. These hospitals are known as "magnet" hospitals for their success in attracting and retaining nurses (Aiken and Sloane 1997). Evidence previously reported indicates that patients in dedicated AIDS units and magnet hospitals are more satisfied with the quality of their care than are patients in general medical units in conventional hospitals (Aiken, Sloane, and Lake 1997). Moreover, patients in magnet hospitals and those in dedicated AIDS units—particularly those in dedicated units who had access to an AIDS specialist—have significantly lower mortality than the other patients (Aiken et al. 1999). Having found that dedicated AIDS units have distinct benefits, therefore, it is important to understand whether blacks and whites have equal access to them.

In this chapter we investigate whether there are racial differences in patient satisfaction and mortality among hospitalized AIDS patients and whether the differences in these outcomes are, at least in part, attributable to differences in the settings in which the patients are hospitalized. In addressing these questions, we expand our consideration of patient care to include not only whether patients are cared for in magnet hospitals and whether they are in dedicated AIDS units, but also whether the hospitals are public or private. Taking the latter into account represents our attempt to investigate the effect of institutional segregation on the nature of AIDS services available to minorities. We also consider whether type of health insurance—public or private—affects care or outcomes. Most AIDS patients are now covered by some form of insurance for in-patient hospital services because of medical assistance and Medicaid policies, so the absence of insurance coverage is not an issue for study.

DATA AND METHODS

Given the sensitivity of AIDS research and its complex human subjects requirements (including, in some states, laws governing access to subjects and information), we have worked to construct an unusually rich database on in-patient AIDS care. We obtained high-quality, comprehensive data from twenty hospitals in eleven

U.S. cities, including detailed information on 1,304 AIDS patient admissions (involving 1,205 different patients) and 955 of the nurses who cared for them. Our patient population is almost identical to the national AIDS population in terms of sex, race, ethnicity, and category of HIV transmission.

Hospital Sample

A regionally stratified representative sample of urban hospitals with dedicated AIDS units in cities with a high incidence of AIDS was matched with a group of comparable hospitals without dedicated units. The universe of hospitals with dedicated AIDS units was defined by a census conducted by *Modern Healthcare* (Taravella 1989), which identified forty hospitals with dedicated AIDS units in operation at the end of 1988. Because the distribution of AIDS is concentrated in specific urban areas, we restricted our study to hospitals located in one of the twenty-five cities with the highest cumulative total of AIDS cases as of April 1988. For-profit, HMO (Health Maintenance Organization)-owned hospitals, veterans hospitals, and hospitals with AIDS units of less than ten beds were excluded from consideration. Twenty-two hospitals with dedicated units met our criteria for inclusion.

Ten of the twenty-two eligible hospitals were selected for the study in such a way as to include public and private hospitals and teaching and nonteaching hospitals in all regions of the country, on the basis of the availability of a suitable comparison hospital. This sampling strategy enhanced the diversity and representativeness of both the nurse and patient samples. Specifically, this sampling frame assured diversity in the demographic and HIV transmission categories of patients with AIDS and diversity in the demographic, educational, and employment characteristics of staff nurses. The ten hospitals with dedicated units were matched with ten hospitals without dedicated units on the basis of hospital characteristics and patient mix.

The two nursing units with the highest average number of AIDS patients were selected for study at each of the twenty hospitals, for a total of forty nursing units. For hospitals with a dedicated unit, the multiple-diagnosis nursing unit with the highest average number of AIDS patients was selected; for the matched control hospitals, the two nursing units with the highest average number of AIDS patients were chosen. This design yielded eleven dedicated units and twenty-nine scattered-bed units (one hospital in New York had two dedicated units and no scattered-bed unit).

Patient Sample

We sampled every consecutive AIDS patient admitted to these study units after a designated date who met eligibility criteria (that is, a diagnosis of AIDS and a minimum stay in the unit of three days), with the aim of obtaining data from seventy-five patients in each of the dedicated AIDS units and twenty-five patients in each of the scattered-bed units. Due to the small number of AIDS patients in some of the scattered-bed units, the twenty hospitals admitted an eligible cohort of 1,392 patients, slightly fewer than the 1,500 patients we had planned. Roughly 2 percent of patients refused to participate, and another 4 percent were missed by data collection error. Ultimately, medical records were collected for 1,304 patient admissions involving 1,205 different patients. Data collection errors were held to a minimum by cross-checking the on-site research nurses' logs of eligible patients with the patient admission logs kept by unit personnel. Patients' medical records were extracted twice (at the beginning and end of a hospital stay) to create an admissions and discharge measure of the severity of illness. Extensive data about patients and their hospital stays were collected from medical records, discharge abstracts, and bill summaries. The data included patients' demographic characteristics, category of HIV transmission, type of health insurance, results of the physical exam for admission, laboratory results, nurses' clinical assessments, diagnosis and procedure codes, length of stay, destination at discharge, in-patient mortality, and hospital charges.

Our design called for interviews with a subset of twenty-five patients per unit from the consecutively accrued full sample. The sampling frame for the subset of patient interviews consisted of eligible patients who were mentally and physically able to be interviewed, as judged by the research nurse on each unit. The research nurse in each hospital kept a prospective record of AIDS admissions, and when the three-day minimum was satisfied he or she approached the patient to obtain written consent. Of the 1,205 patients in the full sample, 222 (18 percent) were not interviewed because they were admitted to units on which targets had been reached, 110 (9 percent) were not interviewed because of poor physical or mental status, and 14 (1 percent) were not or could not be approached for an interview (because they denied their diagnosis or were transferred on the third day of their stay before the research nurse approached them). Of the 859 potentially eligible patients, actual eligibility was uncertain for 137 (16 percent) of the patients because research staff records were inadequate.

Of the remaining 722 patients, 594 (82 percent) were interviewed, 11 percent refused, 5 percent were missed after one or more attempts, and less than 2 percent could not be interviewed due to language barriers. Patients interviewed did not differ significantly from patients not interviewed, except that those who were not interviewed were in decidedly poorer health than patients who were interviewed. The patient interviews provided information on satisfaction with nursing care, process of care measures (for example, continuity of nursing care, discharge planning, and counseling regarding life-sustaining measures), experience with and preferences about dedicated AIDS units, functional ability, and hospitalization history. In the analyses reported here, we only use data associated with first admissions to avoid problems of double-counting.

The Nurse Sample

The core sampling frame for nurses consisted of all registered or licensed practical nurses who worked at least sixteen hours a week in the forty study units. For this sampling frame we collected demographic and employment characteristics, nursing degree, and designation from the head nurse. Of the 955 nurses who met these criteria, 820 (86 percent) responded to the nurse questionnaire. The twenty-one-page questionnaire included sections gathering background characteristics (sociodemographic characteristics, education, nursing experience, and job variables), clinical autonomy, job satisfaction, work-related stress, burnout, social support, knowledge of HIV transmission and infection, perceived risk of HIV infection, attitude and behavior toward AIDS patients, and use of universal precautions with blood and body fluids. The nurse data collection instruments also allowed us to derive indicators of the organizational attributes of the hospitals and hospital units we sampled.

Measures

The primary patient outcome measures used in this chapter are thirty-day mortality indicators and expressed satisfaction with nursing care. Thirty-day mortality was measured from time of admission to the hospital and was obtained from hospital records for patients discharged dead or thirty days after admission and from a search of vital records, subsequent hospital admission files, and Equifax records for patients discharged less than thirty days after admission. Patient satisfaction with nursing care was measured using a twenty-one-item scale drawn from the previously validated LaMonica-Oberst Patient Satisfaction scale (LaMonica et al. 1986) and items developed by the investigators that were pertinent to AIDS patients.

The primary factors of interest to us were the patient's race (obtained from patient interviews and medical records) and hospital setting. We distinguished hospitals along several dimensions: whether they were public or private, whether they had been designated as a magnet hospital, and whether they had dedicated AIDS units. Among the hospitals with designated AIDS units, we further distinguished between those units that were dedicated to AIDS treatment and those that were conventional scattered-bed units.

In investigating the effects of these factors, we sought to control for a large number of patient, hospital, and unit characteristics. The characteristics with significant or sizable effects on either mortality or patient satisfaction were retained and included in the models described in this chapter. Relevant patient characteristics included severity of illness (measured using a global Activities of Daily Living [ADL] scale, the Severity Classification for AIDS Hospitalizations [SCAH] index, and the Clinical AIDS Prognostic Staging [CAPS] measure); type of insurance (private, public, or none); the most likely mode of AIDS transmission (homosexual sex or intravenous drug use); and whether their attending physician was part of an AIDS specialty service. The hospital characteristics that turned out to have significant effects were the extent to which nurses had control over their practice environment (obtained by summing responses from nurse survey items that were part of the Nurse Work index) and the percentage of nurses on the unit who were white.

RESULTS: RACE AND AIDS CARE

Table 9.1 shows that the hospitals and units represented in our study are quite different in the racial composition of AIDS patients found in them. Magnet hospitals (all of which were private) and other private hospitals have larger percentages of white patients (and smaller percentages of black patients) than the public hospitals in our study. The magnet hospitals in our study also have lower percentages of Hispanic patients, although the percentage of Hispanic patients in the other private hospitals is similar to that in public hospitals.

Blacks represent roughly one-third of the AIDS patient sample in the ten hospitals with dedicated AIDS units (which we refer to in the tables as AIDS hospitals) and in the ten hospitals without dedicated AIDS units (which we call non-AIDS hospitals). There are, however, higher percentages of whites and lower percentages of Hispanics in hospitals with dedicated AIDS units than in non-AIDS hospitals. Among patients in the hospitals with dedicated AIDS units, both blacks and Hispanics are less prevalent in the dedicated AIDS units than in the conventional scattered-bed units. Thus it appears that blacks have difficulty gaining access to private hospitals generally, while Hispanics have difficulty gaining access only to magnet hospitals. It appears too that whereas neither blacks nor Hispanics have a problem gaining access to hospitals with dedicated AIDS units, both groups are more likely, in hospitals that have such units, to be in scattered-bed units than in dedicated AIDS units.

What motivates our interest in the racial composition of different types of hospitals and units is the fact that these settings can differ substantially in terms of patient outcomes. Table 9.2 provides descriptive information on how patients' race, and the hos-

TABLE 9.1 **Racial or Ethnic Composition of Patients in Different Kinds of Hospitals and Units (Percentage of Patients)**

Type of Hospital or Unit	White	Black	Hispanic
Type of hospital			
Public (*n* = 421)	38.5	38.7	22.8
Magnet (*n* = 158)	74.1	19.6	6.3
Other private (*n* = 610)	47.9	30.7	21.5
AIDS hospital (*n* = 693)	43.6	31.6	24.8
Non-AIDS hospital (*n* = 496)	54.2	32.7	13.1
Type of unit (in AIDS hospitals)			
Dedicated AIDS unit (*n* = 582)	46.4	30.6	23.0
Scattered-bed unit (*n* = 111)	28.8	36.9	34.2

Source: Authors' compilation.
Note: Tabulation excludes sixteen patients whose race is missing or other.

pital settings in which they find themselves, are related to satisfaction with the quality of their nursing care and to the likelihood of dying within thirty days of admission.

Patient satisfaction clearly varies by race and setting. White AIDS patients are more satisfied with their care than blacks or Hispanics. AIDS patients in magnet hospitals are more satisfied than those in other private hospitals and those in public hospitals (although patients in the latter two categories do not appear to differ much from one another). Patients in hospitals that have dedicated AIDS units are more satisfied than those in other hospitals, and, among the former, those in dedicated AIDS units are more satisfied than those in scattered-bed units.

To the extent that there are any overall racial differences in thirty-day mortality, they appear to be slight and to favor the minority patients. Roughly 14 percent of the white patients, 12 percent of the black patients, and 11 percent of the Hispanic patients die within thirty days of admission. These differences are small relative to differences across settings. Before controlling for other factors that vary across settings, we find that a substantially lower percentage of AIDS patients in magnet hospitals, and a slightly lower percentage of AIDS patients in other private hospitals, die within thirty days of admission. Although patients in hospitals

TABLE 9.2 **Patient Satisfaction and Thirty-Day Mortality by Patient's Race and Ethnicity, Type of Hospital, and Type of Unit**

Characteristic	Mean Patient Satisfaction	Percentage Dead Within Thirty Days
Patient race or ethnicity		
White (n = 306 patients, 538 records)	65.1	13.6
Black (n = 177 patients, 355 records)	61.1	12.1
Hispanic (n = 103 patients, 219 records)	59.4	11.4
Type of hospital		
Public (n = 188 patients, 385 records)	61.3	15.3
Magnet (n = 94 patients, 150 records)	68.1	6.0
Other private (n = 306 patients, 580 records)	62.3	12.6
AIDS hospital (n = 283 patients, 656 records)	63.0	12.8
Non-AIDS hospital (n = 211 patients, 309 records)	60.4	15.5
Type of unit (in AIDS hospitals)		
Dedicated AIDS unit (n = 210 patients, 552 records)	64.4	13.4
Scattered-bed unit (n = 73 patients, 104 records)	59.1	9.6

Source: Authors' compilation.
Note: The numbers in parentheses refer to the numbers of patients in each category for which we have survey data (first number) and medical records indicating a date of death (second number).

with dedicated AIDS units have lower mortality than those in other hospitals, thirty-day mortality is lower in the scattered-bed units than in the dedicated AIDS units.

In our multivariate analyses of patient satisfaction and thirty-day mortality, we fit a series of regression models, beginning with baseline models that estimate racial differences when other variables are ignored and then moving on to models that reestimate racial differences after controlling for other patient characteristics, including the severity of their illness, likely mode of HIV transmission, and type of insurance; differences in satisfaction and mortality across hospitals and hospital units; and characteristics of the hospital units themselves, including the percentage of nurses who are white and the extent to which they have control over their environment.

For both outcomes, we allow for differences across hospitals and units by using dummy variables that contrast public versus private hospitals, magnet versus nonmagnet hospitals, hospitals with AIDS units versus hospitals without AIDS units, and, among those hospitals with dedicated AIDS units, the actual AIDS units versus conventional scattered-bed units. We also introduce interaction terms to allow the public versus private hospital effects to vary across AIDS hospitals and non-AIDS hospitals and to allow the AIDS versus conventional unit effect to vary across public and private hospitals. The dummy variables for hospital settings employed in the models are those that emerge as statistically significant or sizable enough to warrant scrutiny, either before or after controlling for the other factors in the models.

Table 9.3 shows coefficients for ordinary least squares (OLS) regressions predicting patient satisfaction. Model one includes the dummy variables to contrast black and Hispanic patients with white patients. Consistent with what we saw in table 9.2, both blacks and Hispanics have significantly lower satisfaction than whites (by roughly 4 and 6 points, respectively), and race by itself accounts for 7 percent of the variance in patient satisfaction. Model two introduces other patient characteristics (severity of illness, measured by global ADL, homosexuality as the likely mode of HIV transmission, and type of insurance). Although higher illness severity, in this model, is unrelated to patient satisfaction, homosexual patients and patients with private insurance are more satisfied with their care than other patients. Controlling for those differences accounts in part for the racial differences in satisfaction, although the latter remain significant and sizable in this second model.

In model three we introduce four dummy variables to distinguish differences in hospital settings that were found to be significant. The first three of these variables indicate magnet hospitals, AIDS hospitals (both public and private), and public non-AIDS hospitals, with the reference category being private non-AIDS

TABLE 9.3 **Regression Coefficients Describing the Effects of Race, In-Patient Setting, and Other Factors on Patient Satisfaction**

	Model			
Characteristic	(1)	(2)	(3)	(4)
Patient race or ethnicity				
Black	−4.05**	−1.85**	−0.93	−0.72
Hispanic	−5.65**	−3.79**	−2.78**	−2.22**
Other patient characteristics				
Severity of illness		−0.61	−0.65	−0.88
Homosexual		3.99**	2.69**	−2.08**
Private insurance (versus none)		1.82*	0.23	−0.07
Public insurance (versus none)		0.88	−0.78	−1.13
Type of hospital or unit				
Magnet			5.72**	0.99
AIDS hospital			−0.75	−2.24
Public non-AIDS hospital			−2.21**	−2.26*
AIDS unit			4.31**	2.85*
Other unit characteristics				
Percentage white nurses				0.04**
Nurse control				0.43**
Adjusted R^2	0.07	0.11	0.18	0.20

Source: Authors' compilation.
Note: Patient satisfaction is measured using a twenty-one-item scale based on the Lamonica-Oberst Patient Satisfaction scale.
*p less than 0.10.
**p less than 0.05.

hospitals. The fourth dummy contrasts dedicated AIDS units with conventional units in AIDS hospitals. The coefficients for these dummy variables suggest that patients in magnet hospitals have significantly higher satisfaction than those in other private non-AIDS hospitals; patients in the public and private AIDS hospitals have somewhat lower satisfaction than those in the private non-AIDS hospitals; patients in public non-AIDS hospitals have significantly lower satisfaction than those in private non-AIDS hospitals; and patients in dedicated AIDS units of AIDS hospitals have higher satisfaction than those in private non-AIDS hospitals. These differences across hospital settings account further for the racial differences in satisfaction. The black-white difference is reduced to a single point and is insignificant, once hospital setting is controlled, whereas the Hispanic-white difference drops from 3.8 points to 2.8 points but remains statistically significant. Moreover, it appears that differences in hospital settings account for the difference in satisfaction between patients with private health insurance and others.

Model four, finally, introduces two other characteristics of the hospital units: the percentage of white nurses and the extent to which nurses control their practice environment. We had thought the former might interact with patients' race in affecting their satisfaction, although supplemental analyses (not shown) involving the use of interaction terms provided no evidence of such an effect. The percentage of white nurses does, however, significantly increase satisfaction across all patients. Moreover, the introduction of the nurse control variable in model four accounts entirely for the difference between magnet hospitals and other private non-AIDS hospitals and accounts substantially for the difference between dedicated AIDS units and the scattered-bed units in the hospitals that had both type of units.

Table 9.4 shows coefficients for logistic regression models used to predict thirty-day mortality among sample patients. Model one includes, as before, dummy variables contrasting black and Hispanic with white patients. As we saw in table 9.2, both minority groups have lower odds of dying within thirty days than whites, although the differences are not significant. Model two introduces a number of patient characteristics that affect mortality, most notably illness severity. All three measures of severity—the ADL and CAPS as well as the SCAH scales—have sizable and significant effects on mortality, with the ADL measure having an effect that is nearly double the size of the other two measures. While mortality appears to be unaffected by type of insurance, whether or not the patient has a specialist physician (which characterizes roughly a third of patients in the dedicated AIDS units, but fewer than 1 percent of other patients) has a pronounced effect on thirty-day mortality. Patients with specialist care display odds of dying that are lower than others by a factor of 0.47. Once these background variables are controlled, the odds of dying within thirty days are *greater* for blacks and Hispanics than for whites, although only the latter difference is statistically significant.

Although there is no significant main effect of intravenous (IV) drug use, that factor interacts significantly with whether or not the

TABLE 9.4 **Odds Ratios from Logistic Regression Models Describing the Effects of Race, In-Patient Setting, and Other Characteristics on Thirty-Day Mortality**

Characteristic	Model			
	(1)	(2)	(3)	(4)
Patient race or ethnicity				
Black	0.88	1.12	1.05	1.04
Hispanic	0.83	1.89*	1.87*	2.19**
Other patient characteristics				
Global ADL scale		2.75**	2.73**	2.90**
CAPS scale		1.59**	1.57**	1.59**
SCAH scale		1.72**	1.71**	1.66**
Intravenous drug use		0.72	0.76	0.77
AIDS specialty service		0.47**	0.47**	0.43**
Private insurance (versus none)		1.13	1.29	1.19
Public insurance (versus none)		0.95	1.02	0.97
Hispanic and intravenous drug use		0.17**	0.16**	0.15**
Type of hospital or unit				
Magnet			0.37**	0.30**
AIDS hospital			0.54	0.71
AIDS unit			1.26	0.96
Other unit characteristics				
Percentage white nurses				1.01
Nurse control				0.93
Generalized R^2	0.00	0.24	0.26	0.26

Source: Authors' compilation.
*p less than 0.10.
**p less than 0.05.

patient is Hispanic. Net of all other factors, Hispanic patients who are not IV drug users have higher odds of dying than do white patients who are not IV drug users. That is, among patients who are not IV drug users, Hispanics are roughly 1.9 times as likely to die within thirty days as whites. Among IV drug users, however, Hispanic patients display lower odds of dying within thirty days than whites, by a factor of $1.89 \times 0.17 = 0.32$.

Model three indicates that the Hispanic-white difference in the odds of dying is not greatly affected by controlling for hospital setting. In fitting these models to describe mortality differences, we do not include a dummy variable to represent the public/private difference, since no difference is found either prior to or after controlling other factors. Here, because we enter dummy variables for magnet hospitals, AIDS hospitals, and AIDS units, the referent category becomes non-AIDS, nonmagnet hospitals.

Relative to patients in the latter hospitals, those in magnet hospitals have significantly and substantially lower odds of dying within thirty days. The odds of dying in that period in magnet hospitals are only a third of what they are in other non-AIDS hospitals. Patients in AIDS hospitals also have somewhat lower odds of dying than patients in non-AIDS hospitals, by a factor of 0.54, although the difference is insignificant. Moreover, patients in dedicated AIDS units have a somewhat higher likelihood of dying than other patients, although here too the difference is insignificant.

In model four, we add the other unit characteristics (percentage of white nurses and nurses' control over the practice environment) that affect satisfaction and account partly for the racial differences in satisfaction. Neither is significant in this model, nor are a number of others we tested (like the skill mix of nurses and nurse-patient ratios).

DISCUSSION

Our findings are consistent with the few other studies that have examined race and AIDS care. Although we did not examine racial differences in the use of therapies and drugs, several other studies have documented large racial differences in drug use in outpatient AIDS care (Moore et al. 1994). Blacks infected with HIV use drugs to prevent *Pneumocystis carinii* pneumonia (PCP) less often than infected whites, even after adjusting for differences in health insurance (Piette et al. 1993). In a single-hospital study that predates our larger multiple-hospital project, Fahs et al. (1992) finds that women, older patients, and blacks are less likely to be cared for in specialized AIDS units than whites, a finding that is similar to ours. Bennett et al. (1995) study racial differences in AIDS hospital care in five cities and conclude that racial factors do not appear to be an important determinant of the intensity of diagnostic or therapeutic care among patients who are hospitalized with PCP but that variations in care are attributable largely to differences in health insurance and characteristics of the admitting hospital.

Our study of AIDS care is not designed in a way that permits us fully to explore all the dimensions of access to care that are important in determining the disparate effects of race. The major limitation is that we know nothing about the accessibility problems of people with AIDS who do not find their way into hospitals. Our sample is not representative of the entire population of people hospitalized with AIDS. Nonetheless, it is drawn systematically from hospitals in urban AIDS epicenters and probably represents a reasonable approximation of the status of urban in-patient AIDS care in 1990 to 1991.

Our findings suggest, as might be expected, that race remains a significant factor in determining the characteristics of the admitting hospital. Blacks constitute a higher percentage of AIDS patients in public hospitals than in private hospitals, and blacks and Hispanics both constitute a considerably smaller percentage of AIDS patients in magnet and exemplary private hospitals than in other private hospitals or public hospitals, a finding supporting Smith's (1999) contention that hospital care in the United States remains segregated by race. From the perspective of both organizational sociology and public policy, our findings suggest that public hospitals can achieve outcomes as good as most private hospitals if they implement organizational innovations such as dedicated AIDS units. In fact, early in the AIDS epidemic, New York State policymakers anticipated that dedicated AIDS units would be beneficial and provided hospitals' financial incentives to develop such units.

Our finding that black and Hispanic patients have a lower probability of entering dedicated AIDS units is of concern since we have established that these units have beneficial health outcomes. It is difficult to separate the effects of race in our study from the effects of HIV risk group. We have shown elsewhere (Aiken et al. 1999) that homosexuals and IV drug users are distributed very differently across types of hospitals and units. Most homosexuals with AIDS are white, while injecting drug users and individuals with high-risk heterosexual partners are disproportionately black and Hispanic. The gay community is generally better organized and has more information about AIDS care than other groups. More homosexuals also request a specific unit, and those who do are likely to request a dedicated AIDS unit. Thus homosexuals self-select into dedicated AIDS units. We are still concerned, however, that the lower representation of minorities may represent discrimination against blacks and Hispanics. Another explanation might be that homosexuals self-select into units known to contain other homosexuals and out of other units. Whatever the case, it is clear that entry into dedicated AIDS units and to magnet hospitals is not random and not without consequences.

REFERENCES

Aiken, Linda H., and K. D. Bays. 1984. "The Medicare Debate: Round One." *New England Journal of Medicine* 311(18): 1196–1200.

Aiken, Linda H., Eileen T. Lake, Julie A. Sochalski, and Douglas M. Sloane. 1997. "Design of an Outcomes Study of the Organization of Hospital AIDS Care." *Research in the Sociology of Health Care* 14: 3–26.

Aiken, Linda H., and Douglas M. Sloane. 1997. "Effects of Specialization and Client Differentiation on the Status of Nurses: The Case of AIDS." *Journal of Health and Social Behavior* 38(3): 203–22.

Aiken, Linda H., Douglas M. Sloane, and E. T. Lake. 1997. "Satisfaction with Inpatient AIDS Care: A National Comparison of Dedicated Units and Scattered-Beds." *Medical Care* 35(9): 948–62.

Aiken, Linda H., Douglas M. Sloane, Eileen T. Lake, Julie A. Sochalski, and A. L. Weber. 1999. "Organization and Outcomes of Inpatient AIDS Care." *Medical Care* 37(8): 760–72.

Ayanian, J. Z., I. S. Udvarhelyi, C. A. Gatsonis, C. L. Pashos, and A. M. Epstein. 1993. "Racial Differences in the Use of Revascularization Procedures after Coronary Angiography." *Journal of the American Medical Association* 269(20): 2642–46.

Bennett, C. L., R. D. Horner, R. A. Weinstein, G. M. Dickinson, J. A. DeHovitz, S. E. Cohn, H. A. Kessler, Jeffrey Jacobson, M. B. Goetz, Michael Simberkoff, Dave Pitrak, G. W. Lance, S. C. Gilman, and M. F. Shapiro. 1995. "Racial Differences in Care among Hospitalized Patients with *Pneumocystis Carinii* Pneumonia in Chicago, New York, Los Angeles, Miami, and Raleigh-Durham." *Archives of Internal Medicine* 155(15): 1586–92.

Blendon, R. J., Linda H. Aiken, H. E. Freeman, and C. K. Corey. 1989. "Access to Medical Care for Black and White Americans." *Journal of the American Medical Association* 261(2): 278–81.

Commonwealth Fund. 1995. *National Comparative Survey of Minority Health Care.* New York: Commonwealth Fund.

Davis, Karen. 1975. "Equal Treatment and Unequal Benefits: The Medicare Program." *Milbank Memorial Fund Quarterly* 53(4): 449–88.

Dutton, D. B. 1978. "Explaining the Low Use of Health Services by the Poor: Costs, Attitudes, or Delivery Systems?" *American Sociological Review* 43(3): 348–68.

———. 1986. "Social Class, Health, and Illness." In *Applications of Social Science to Clinical Medicine and Health Policy,* edited by Linda Aiken and David Mechanic. New Brunswick, N.J.: Rutgers University Press.

Fahs, Marianne C., George Fulop, J. J. Strain, H. S. Sacks, Charlotte Muller, P. D. Cleary, James Schmeidler, and Barbara Turner. 1992. "The Inpatient AIDS Unit: A Preliminary Empirical Investigation of Access, Economic, and Outcome Issues." *American Journal of Public Health* 82(4): 576–78.

Ford, E. S., and R. S. Cooper. 1995. "Implications of Race/Ethnicity for Health and Health Care Use." *Health Services Research* 30(1, part 2): 237–52.

Fox, R. C., Linda H. Aiken, and Carla Messikomer. 1990. "The Culture of Caring: AIDS and the Nursing Profession." *Milbank Memorial Fund Quarterly* 68 (S2): 226–56.

Freeman, H. E., Linda H. Aiken, R. J. Blendon, and C. R. Corey. 1990. "Uninsured Working-Age Adults: Characteristics and Consequences." *Health Services Research* 24(6): 811–23.

Freeman, H. E., R. J. Blendon, Linda H. Aiken, S. Sudman, C. F. Mullinix, and C. R. Corey. 1987. "Americans Report on Their Access to Care." *Health Affairs* 6(1): 6–8.

Gornick, M. E., P. W. Eggers, T. W. Reilly, R. M. Mentnech, K. L. Fitternman, L. E. Kuchen, and B. C. Vladeck. 1996. "Effects of Race and Income on Mortality and Use of Services among Medicare Beneficiaries." *New England Journal of Medicine* 335(11): 791–99.

Hummer, R. A. 1996. "Black-White Differences in Health and Mortality: A Review and Conceptual Model." *Sociological Quarterly* 37(1): 105–25.

Kahn, C. L., M. L. Pearson, E. R. Harrison, K. A. Desmond, W. H. Rogers, L. V. Rubenstein, R. H. Brook, and E. B. Keeler. 1994. "Health Care for Black and Poor Hospitalized Medicare Patients." *Journal of the American Medical Association* 271(15): 1170–74.

LaMonica, E. L., M. T. Oberst, A. R. Madea, and R. M. Wolf. 1986. "Development of a Patient Satisfaction Scale." *Research in Nursing and Health* 9(1): 43–50.

Mechanic, David, and Linda H. Aiken. 1989a. "Access to Health Care and Use of Medical Care Services." In *Handbook of Medical Sociology,* edited by Howard Freeman and Sol Levine. New York: Prentice-Hall.

————. 1989b. "Lessons from the Past: Responding to the AIDS Crisis." *Health Affairs* 8(3): 16–32.

Moore, R. D., David Stanton, Ramana Gopalan, and R. E. Chaisson. 1994. "Racial Differences in the Use of Drug Therapy for HIV Disease in an Urban Community." *New England Journal of Medicine* 330(11): 763–68.

National Center for Health Statistics. 1998. *Health, United States, 1998.* Hyattsville, Md.: National Center for Health Statistics.

Peterson, E. D., S. M. Wright, Jennifer Daley, and G. E. Thibault. 1994. "Racial Variation in Cardiac Procedure Use and Survival Following Acute Myocardial Infarction in the Department of Veterans Affairs." *Journal of the American Medical Association* 271 (15): 1175–80.

Physician Payment Review Commission. 1997. *Factors Related to the Access Problems of Vulnerable Medicare Beneficiaries: Annual Report to Congress.* Washington: U.S. Government Printing Office.

Piette, John D., Vincent Mor, Kurt Mayer, Sally Zierler, and Thomas Wachtel. 1993. "The Effects of Immune Status and Race on Health Service Use among People with HIV Disease." *American Journal of Public Health* 83(4): 510–14.

Smith, D. B. 1998. "The Racial Segregation of Hospital Care Revisited: Medicare Discharge Patterns and Their Implications." *American Journal of Public Health* 88(3): 461–63.

————. 1999. *Health Care Divided: Race and Healing a Nation.* Ann Arbor: University of Michigan Press.

St. Peter, R. F., P. W. Newacheck, and Neal Halfon. 1992. "Access to Care for Poor Children: Separate and Unequal?" *Journal of the American Medical Association* 267(20): 2760–64.

Taravella, S. 1989. "Reserving a Place to Treat AIDS Patients in the Hospital." *Modern Healthcare* 19(6): 32–37.

Waitzman, N. J., and K. R. Smith. 1998. "Separate but Lethal: The Effects of Economic Segregation on Mortality in Metropolitan America." *Milbank Quarterly* 76(3): 341–73.

Whittle, Jeff, Joseph Conigliaro, C. B. Good, and R. P. Lofgren. 1993. "Racial Differences in the Use of Invasive Cardiovascular Procedures in the Department of Veterans Affairs Medical System." *New England Journal of Medicine* 329(9): 621–27.

Williams, D. R. 1998. "Race and Health." Paper presented at the Kansas Conference on Health and Its Determinants. Wichita, Kansas (April 20–21).

Yergan, J., A. B. Flood, J. P. LoGerfo, and Paula Diehr. 1987. "Relationship Between Patient Race and the Intensity of Hospital Services." *Medical Care* 25(7): 592–603.

—— Part III ——

The Social
Ecology of Race

—— Chapter 10 ——

Socioeconomic Status and Segregation: African Americans, Hispanics, and Asians in Los Angeles

Camille Zubrinsky Charles

R ACIAL RESIDENTIAL SEGREGATION is arguably the "structural linch-pin" of American race relations (Bobo 1989; Pettigrew 1979). Analyses of 1980 census data show that in sixteen large metropolitan areas—including Los Angeles—African Americans were hypersegregated from whites, exhibiting extreme isolation across at least four of five standard indicators (Massey and Denton 1989). Although some modest improvement occurred between 1980 and 1990, blacks remain highly segregated from whites and substantially more isolated than either Asians or Hispanics (Farley and Frey 1994). Among larger metropolitan areas, however, Los Angeles showed the largest decrease in black-white segregation between 1980 and 1990 (Farley and Frey 1994; Harrison and Weinberg 1992). Despite these gains, according to recent work by Denton (1994), Los Angeles remains one of the nation's hypersegregated cities for African Americans.

Some researchers challenge the view that uniquely potent levels of antiblack prejudice and discrimination contribute to higher levels of black segregation from whites, opting instead for

271

explanations that emphasize objective socioeconomic disparities. For example, a number of econometric analyses emphasize factors such as differences in economic status, job location, and tastes as contributing to racial residential segregation (Leven et al. 1976). Proponents of this perspective view racial residential segregation as the rational outcome of well-documented economic disparities between racial groups (Galster 1988).

There is a body of research to suggest that this is, in fact, the case for Hispanic and Asian Americans. Both groups exhibit low to moderate levels of segregation from whites. As Hispanic and Asian socioeconomic status improves, segregation from whites decreases (Denton and Massey 1989; Massey and Mullan 1984; White 1986; Massey and Fong 1990; Alba and Logan 1993). Research in this area also shows that blacks, unlike other groups, are not able to translate socioeconomic gains into improved residential mobility. Kain (1986) finds that the proportion of high-income blacks living in Cleveland and Chicago area suburbs is actually lower than the proportion of low-income whites residing in these suburbs. Massey and Denton (1987, 1992) conclude that black-white segregation is in no way connected to either real or perceived socioeconomic disparities. Finally, Galster (1988) concludes that, at best, socioeconomic disparities account for only a small portion of black-white segregation. All of these results are consistent with findings from studies using census data from 1970 (Pascal 1967; Hermalin and Farley 1973; Taeuber 1976; Schnare 1977) as well as from 1980 (Kain 1986, 1987; Farley 1986; Darden 1987). In each of these cases, researchers conclude that there is little or no relationship between socioeconomic status and black residential segregation from whites.

Despite the consistency of these results over time and across metropolitan areas, there is good reason to revisit the role of socioeconomic class status in understanding racial residential patterns using Los Angeles as a case study. First, and possibly most important, Los Angeles provides the opportunity for a multiethnic analysis of whites, blacks, Hispanics, and Asians in a single metropolitan area, something lacking in previous research. Moreover, changes to the 1990 public use files from the census allow multivariate household analysis within a single metropolitan area that has been divided into substantially more areas than was the case in previous research. In the analysis that follows, relatively simple, but effective, statistical methods similar to those used in previous studies (Pascal 1967; Taeuber 1976; Schnare 1977; Farley 1986; Kain 1986) are used to examine the contribution of various socioeconomic characteristics to residential segregation in Los Angeles.

DATA AND METHODS

Historically, explorations of the relationship between socioeconomic class characteristics and racial residential segregation fall into two categories. One of these is *indirect standardization*, a technique used to "redistribute" the population of a metropolitan area based on income or housing cost and then compute expected segregation indexes based on the assumption that one of these factors is the only cause of residential segregation. This expected level of segregation is compared to actual segregation to determine the amount of segregation that can be explained by differences in income or the cost of housing (Farley 1995). The alternative method is simply to separate a population into categories of income or housing cost and to compute segregation indexes within each of those categories. Again, these within-category segregation indexes are compared to actual levels of segregation. If segregation within categories of income or housing cost is similar to actual levels of segregation, it can be concluded that these factors are not important to understanding residential segregation; if within-category segregation is lower than actual segregation, income or housing cost is concluded to be an important socioeconomic factor (Farley 1995).

To some extent, these analyses have been limited, usually controlling for a single socioeconomic factor (for example, income *or* housing cost) and ignoring a vast array of household characteristics known to influence decisions regarding residential location. Kain (1986) is one of few exceptions, employing indirect standardization using several household and economic factors to define 384 different socioeconomic categories. His analysis only considers black-white segregation, however. I seek to address this limitation, employing indirect standardization with four socioeconomic factors—family type, family size, income, and age of head—to examine the role of income and household structure in maintaining residential patterns in Los Angeles County.

Specifically, I employ data from the 1990 Public Use Microdata Sample (PUMS) 5 percent file to predict the segregation levels that would be observed for blacks, Hispanics, and Asians if residential patterns were determined solely on the basis of income and household structure, not race or ethnicity. This methodology is similar to that used in earlier studies for other cities (Pascal 1967; Taeuber and Taeuber 1965; Taeuber 1976), particularly the work of Kain (1986).

The unit of geography is the Public Use Microdata Sample Area (PUMA), which is a census-defined area with a minimum of one hundred thousand residents. These areas are substantially larger than tracts and are designed to provide detailed information for relatively small areas, while at the same time maintaining confidentiality. A single PUMA never includes both central city and suburban areas, and noncentral cities are never broken into separate PUMAs (thus all of Long Beach is one PUMA). They are typically geographically contiguous, unless this would require violating one of the other guidelines. In the Los Angeles–Long Beach Primary Metropolitan Statistical Area (PMSA), only one PUMA is seriously fragmented, so I have included all PUMAs in the analysis to cover the entire county.

This unit of geography is nonetheless substantially larger than the tract-level data used in most analyses of residential segregation (for example, Denton and Massey 1989; Massey and Denton 1989): Los Angeles County has fifty-eight PUMAs compared with 1,642 census tracts. As a result, indexes of dissimilarity calculated from fifty-eight PUMAs will be lower than those normally discussed for Los Angeles County because the unit of aggregation is much larger (for a discussion of this effect, see Van Valey and Roof 1976). Still, differences in the degree of residential segregation experienced by each racial group resemble those calculated from tract-level data. Table 10.1 compares segregation measures (dissimilarity indexes) computed for both PUMAs and tracts in the Los Angeles metropolitan area. As can be seen, even at this scale of aggregation black-white segregation remains high enough to be characterized as extreme (Massey and Denton 1989; Denton 1994), and segregation among Hispanics and Asians is more accurately characterized as moderate.

TABLE 10.1 **Index of Dissimilarity Computed Between Whites and Blacks, Hispanics, and Asians Using Two Geographic Units: Census Tracts and PUMAs in the Los Angeles Metropolitan Area, 1990**

Geographic Unit	Blacks	Hispanics	Asians
Tracts	0.728	0.611	0.463
PUMAs	0.613	0.458	0.344
Difference	−0.115	−0.153	−0.118

Source: U.S. Bureau of the Census (1990a).

Despite this drawback, these data provide an improvement over previous work, most notably that of Kain (1986). Because Kain's methodology employs a total of four sociodemographic characteristics, his analysis is more robust than those that employ only a single factor. However, the fifty-eight PUMAs that constitute Los Angeles County are more than double the number of areas used in Kain's analysis of Chicago and Cleveland (twenty-three and seventeen geographic areas, respectively). Given that the index of dissimilarity decreases as the unit of geography increases, Kain's findings would be strengthened by having a larger number of areas (that is, a smaller unit of geography). Thus this analysis improves on a sizable body of research, providing a more robust test of the relationship between socioeconomic factors and segregation by combining a large number of controls with data for a single metropolitan area.

Using information on type and size of family, age of household head, and income, I define 270 household types for white, black, Hispanic, and Asian households in Los Angeles County. There are two categories for family type (families with and without children under eighteen); five categories for family size (one, two, three, four to five, and more than five members); five income categories (less than $15,000, $15,000 to $28,339, $28,340 to $43,499, $43,500 to $66,999, and more than $67,000); and six age of head categories (less than twenty-five, twenty-five to thirty-four, thirty-five to forty-four, forty-five to fifty-four, fifty-five to sixty-four, and sixty-five and older). Although the cross-classification of these categories yields a total of 300 cells, only 270 are valid (since all of the categories that involve one-person households and children under eighteen are by definition empty). All of these factors affect neighborhood choices regardless of race and are used in other analyses, particularly that of Kain (1986).

From these categories, I compute two distributions for household type: the distribution of the four racial groups across the 270 household types and the distribution of household types across the fifty-eight PUMAs in Los Angeles County. The next step is to compute the predicted racial composition for each of the fifty-eight PUMAs. This is done by multiplying the proportion of each racial group conforming to a particular household type, a^e_{ik}, by the proportion of all households of that type, h_{ik}. If 25 percent of the households of type I in Los Angeles County are Asian, for example, and 1 percent of all households in a given PUMA are type I, the product of these two figures is 0.0025, or the proportion of the household-based neighborhood that would be comprised of Asian families of type I households. This process is repeated for each household type and each racial category. Finally, summing within racial categories across the 270 household types produces the racial composition of each PUMA if allocated on the basis of household structure and income. (These are household distributions, not "person" distributions, so whites are overrepresented.)

RESULTS

Whites live in substantial numbers throughout Los Angeles County, irrespective of social class, suggesting that a great deal of white residential choice is explained by socioeconomic factors. The clear exceptions to this pattern are areas with heavy concentrations of minorities—particularly blacks and Hispanics. For example, the percentage of white households in East Los Angeles and Huntington Park is less than 10 percent. These are among several areas of traditional Hispanic settlement in Los Angeles County; East Los Angeles is also known as a lower-income community with heavy Hispanic gang activity. Pico Rivera–Montebello (24.6 percent), Puente–West Puente (25.8 percent), Vernon–Bell–Bell Gardens (18.6 percent), and San Gabriel (21.5 percent) are also areas with heavy Hispanic settlement, contrasted by white settlement that is roughly half the proportion of their total population share of 40.8 percent (Turner and Allen 1992).

The remaining communities characterized by low percentages of white households are the three areas that, together, make up South Central Los Angeles and Compton. Taken together, white households average slightly more than 4 percent of the total population in these areas. These communities have historically been the residential centers of the African American community. The restructuring of the Los Angeles economy over the past two decades, however, has negatively affected these areas, transforming what were once thriving working- and middle-class communities into impoverished areas rife with crime and gang activity and devoid of economic opportunities and many of the services needed to conduct day-to-day life (such as grocery stores, banks, and gas stations; see Johnson et al. 1992). These communities have emerged as transitional residential areas for the large influx of Mexican and Central American immigrants—probably due to the low cost of housing—who often cram several families into single-family dwellings (Skerry 1993).

Unlike white households, black households are extremely underrepresented in a substantial proportion of the areas, constituting less than 5 percent of households in thirty-two of the fifty-eight areas (55.2 percent). The areas of underrepresentation include the more desirable, middle- and upper middle-class communities that tend to be majority-white: the historically conservative communities of Burbank–San Fernando, where black households constitute only 1.3 percent of the population, while white households constitute 71.6 percent; Glendale, where an even lower 1.1 percent of all households are black and 73.2 percent of households are white; the area that includes the trendy community of Santa Monica (2.4 percent black households and 86.5 percent white households); and the section of the City of Los Angeles that includes Bel Air, Pacific Palisades, Encino, and Sherman Oaks, which is overwhelmingly populated by white households (91.5 percent), with black households making up only 1.6 percent.

Black households are also severely underrepresented in areas with heavy concentrations of Asian and, to some extent, Hispanic households. In the Monterey Park–Rosemead area, black households are less than 1 percent of the population. In the mid-1980s, Monterey Park emerged as the first majority-Chinese suburb in North America (Davis 1990). However, there is still a sizable number of Hispanic households in this area (32.7 percent). Black households also constitute less than 1 percent of all households in the overwhelmingly Hispanic East Los Angeles, as well as the majority-Hispanic communities of El Monte and Pico Rivera–Montebello.

In stark contrast to the even distribution of white households throughout middle- and upper-middle-class portions of Los Angeles is the extreme concentration of black households in a small number of areas, irrespective of income or other sociodemographic characteristics. Black households exceed 50 percent of the total population in only five of the fifty-eight areas in Los Angeles County: Inglewood and the surrounding unincorporated areas (56.6 percent), a community with both middle- and lower-income housing and part of the new "Black Westside" (Davis 1990); Compton (64.6 percent), once a thriving working-class community, now known for having one of the highest per capita murder rates in the county; and the three areas that make up South Central Los Angeles (57.0, 69.2, and 60.9 percent, respectively), another community that has become associated with crime, drugs, gang activity, civil unrest, and lack of economic opportunity.

Hispanics are much less likely than blacks to be underrepresented: in only one instance do they represent less than 5 percent of an area's population, and, again, this is the portion of the city of Los Angeles that is home to the very rich—Bel Air and Pacific Palisades—and is overwhelmingly white (92 percent). Yet Hispanics also represent a larger share of the county's total population than do blacks—a full 37.8 percent according to the 1990 census (Turner and Allen 1992). In twenty-two of fifty-eight areas (37.9 percent), the proportion of Hispanic households is less than half of their share of the total population. Like blacks, many of the areas of Hispanic underrepresentation are overwhelmingly white, middle-class and upper-middle-class (at least) communities: Beverly Hills, West Hollywood, Marina del Rey, Santa Clarita, La Verne-Claremont, Palos Verdes, Santa Monica, and parts of the San Fernando Valley. Likewise, Hispanic households are overrepresented in areas of traditional Hispanic settlement (Pico Rivera–Montebello, East Los Angeles, Huntington Park, Hacienda Heights) as well as in the areas that were previously majority-black communities: South Central Los Angeles and Compton.

Finally, Asian households are heavily concentrated in the Monterey Park–Rosemead–South San Gabriel area (44.5 percent). Recall that Monterey Park was North America's first majority-Chinese suburb and home to a sizable Japanese community (Davis 1990). Other areas of Asian overrepresentation include the communities of Alhambra and South Pasadena in the San Gabriel Valley, as well as their upscale, old-money neighbor, San Marino. With few exceptions, Asians follow a pattern similar to that of white households, in that areas with sizable Asian populations tend to have extremely small black populations.

Racial Composition Predicted by
Income and Household Composition

I now turn to racial composition predicted by income and household structure and expected measures of segregation. The most obvious difference between actual and predicted racial residential segregation is found among black households, where the differences are striking: the black-white segregation index drops to a low 0.110, a difference of -0.503 (see table 10.2). This decline far exceeds the 1980 to 1990 change of less than 0.10 and is consistent with previous research on the relationship between racial residential segregation and socioeconomic status. Simply put, there is no relationship between the two for black Americans. If black households were distributed throughout the Los Angeles area on the basis of socioeconomic characteristics alone, black-white residential segregation would be roughly 5.5 times lower than it actually is (see table 10.2). Class resources most emphatically are not the reason for high black concentration in just a few areas and severe underrepresentation in others. Rather, we must take seriously the persistent salience of race—factors such as prejudice and negative stereotypes and housing market discrimination—and the potential role of in-group preferences among residents of Los Angeles County.

TABLE 10.2 **Actual and Predicted Levels of Black, Hispanic, and Asian Residential Segregation from Whites in the Los Angeles Metropolitan Area, 1990**

Index of Dissimilarity	Blacks	Hispanics	Asians
Actual	0.613	0.458	0.344
Predicted	0.110	0.191	0.087
Difference	−0.503	−0.267	−0.257
Ratio	5.572	2.398	3.954

Source: U.S. Bureau of the Census (1990a).

For all fifty-eight areas, black households are *always* within 2.5 percentage points of their actual share of the total population (10.5 percent). The areas where black households would still make up less than 10.5 percent of the population are among the most expensive in Los Angeles County: part of the City of Los Angeles that includes Bel Air and Pacific Palisades (8.1 percent), part of the San Fernando Valley (8.8 percent), West Los Angeles (8.5 percent), and Redondo Beach–Manhattan Beach–Palos Verdes–Rolling Hills (8.2 percent). This suggests that, on the whole, the composition of black households is similar to that of the general population. Table 10.3 summarizes the distribution of whites, blacks, Hispanics, and Asians across the sociodemographic characteristics used in this analysis. These results indicate that black household characteristics are no longer distinctive from those of whites and that households of blacks are, in fact, similar to those of the overall population.

Like blacks, Asians show a marked decline in segregation under the predicted model (from 0.344 to 0.087, a difference of −0.257). Only twice does the percentage of Asian households fall more than 2 percentage points below the total Asian population, and, again like blacks, these both occur in very expensive, upscale sections of Los Angeles (the area that includes Beverly Hills, in addition to Bel Air, Sherman Oaks, Encino, and Pacific Palisades). Asian households are also far less likely to be overrepresented in the predicted model than any of the other groups. For instance, under the predicted model, black households are overrepresented in twenty-eight of the fifty-eight areas (48 percent), and whites are overrepresented in almost 70 percent of the areas.

TABLE 10.3 Distribution of Household Characteristics by Race and Ethnicity in the Los Angeles Metropolitan Area

Characteristic	Whites	Blacks	Hispanics	Asians
Mean	0.251	0.431	0.647	0.483
Standard deviation	0.430	0.490	0.480	0.500
Family size				
1	0.305	0.267	0.093	0.141
2	0.360	0.257	0.155	0.222
3	0.151	0.187	0.159	0.188
4 to 5	0.160	0.215	0.338	0.330
5+	0.023	0.073	0.254	0.118
Mean	2.32	2.78	4.26	3.40
Standard deviation	1.31	1.72	2.33	1.82
Household income				
Less than $15,000	0.157	0.312	0.236	0.173
$15,000 to 28,339	0.171	0.229	0.275	0.177
$28,340 to 43,499	0.191	0.189	0.224	0.192
$43,500 to $66,999	0.217	0.158	0.171	0.230
$67,000+	0.264	0.111	0.093	0.228
Mean	$53,806	$33,304	$33,696	$48,128
Standard deviation	$49,292	$30,763	$27,194	$41,063
Age of household head				
Less than 25	0.034	0.049	0.080	0.037
25 to 34	0.194	0.220	0.314	0.230
35 to 44	0.210	0.231	0.265	0.292
45 to 54	0.164	0.180	0.156	0.199
55 to 64	0.149	0.142	0.100	0.126
65+	0.249	0.177	0.085	0.116
Mean	50	47	41	45
Standard deviation	17.4	16.3	14.4	14.4
Number of cases	77,540	14,871	36,802	13,543

Source: U.S. Bureau of the Census (1990a).
Notes: (Children under eighteen years; 1 = yes).

Conversely, Asian households are overrepresented only three times, and the degree of overrepresentation is very small: in the predominantly Asian community of Monterey Park (10.9 percent), the majority-Hispanic area of La Puente–West Puente (10.8 percent), and the Rowland Heights–Diamond Bar area (11.3 percent).

Therefore, like blacks, it appears that the residential distribution of Asian households in Los Angeles has little to do with socio-economic factors.

The decrease in Asian-white segregation under the predicted model is not the largest among the three groups. However, because Asians begin as the group least segregated from whites, they end up with the lowest absolute index—an extremely low 0.087. Thus, as is true for blacks, differential socioeconomic status cannot explain the bulk of Asian residential segregation: Asian households would be nearly four times less segregated if households were distributed on the basis of income and household structure. This is not to say that we can *immediately* conclude that anti-Asian sentiment *is* the primary factor behind the pattern—quite the contrary, as we know that whites have more positive stereotypes of Asians and are more willing to share residential space with them than with *either* blacks or Hispanics (Bobo and Zubrinsky 1996; Zubrinsky and Bobo 1996; Charles 2000). Rather, the distribution probably reflects the fact that the Asian population is overwhelmingly composed of recent immigrants, and we know that immigrant status also acts to influence residential decisions: research suggests that recent immigrants tend to have higher segregation rates than more established group members. This outcome could reflect both improved social status and cultural adaptation (Ong, Lawrence, and Davidson 1992; Massey and Fong 1990; Alba and Logan 1993).

Hispanics are the only group that remains moderately segregated (0.191) after redistributing households by income and household composition, suggesting that Hispanic household characteristics differ markedly from those of the other groups. An examination of household characteristics by race (table 10.3) suggests that this is, in fact, the case. Hispanic households are substantially more likely to have children under eighteen, to have younger heads, and to be significantly larger than all other groups. Hispanic segregation, therefore, can be understood, to some extent, by differential socioeconomic status. Again, this is consistent with a growing body of research that clearly demonstrates a decline in segregation with increased socioeconomic status among Hispanics (Denton and Massey 1989; Massey and Fong 1990; Massey and Denton 1992). Another possible factor is, again, the large number of recent immigrants within the Hispanic community of Los Angeles. As with Asians, it is important to consider not only the possibility of anti-Hispanic attitudes among whites but also a possible self-segregation process among Hispanics, at least among newer arrivals.

Under the predicted model, which distributes households on the basis of income and household characteristics, Hispanics, like all other groups, are distributed more evenly throughout the Los Angeles area, with fewer instances of severe underrepresentation. In no area are Hispanic households less than 10 percent of the total population, and only about 21 percent of the areas are less than 20 percent Hispanic. Hispanic households increase for areas like Glendale (where the Hispanic share doubles to 21.6 percent) and Val Verde–Santa Clarita (an increase of 10.5 percent). Similarly, Hispanic concentration is much less severe in areas such as East Los Angeles (-50.1 percent), Walnut–Huntington Park (-29.3 percent), South Gate–Lynwood (-24.6 percent), and La Puente–West Puente (-24.9 percent). The number of Hispanic households in traditionally black areas like Carson-Inglewood and South Central Los Angeles remains relatively stable and includes an increase in Compton ($+10.21$ percent).

Finally, redistributing white households on the basis of income and household composition substantially increases the population of white households in South Central, Inglewood, Compton, East Los Angeles, and Monterey Park—the traditional areas of minority concentration that are nearly devoid of white households in reality. Still, their household share in the more expensive (and traditionally white) areas approximates reality, and white households exceed their proportion of the general population in nearly 70 percent of Los Angeles County's local areas (forty of fifty-eight PUMAs).

CONCLUSIONS

Overall, this multiethnic, multivariate analysis of the relationship between socioeconomic differences and racial residential segregation in Los Angeles is consistent with previous research on other cities (including Long Beach; see White 1986). For the most part,

the previous research has been limited to analyses of one group—
blacks or Hispanics or Asians—and based on categories within a
single socioeconomic variable (for example, income or housing
cost). Exceptions to the former include Massey and Fong (1990);
exceptions to the latter include Kain (1986), whose analysis provides the model for the current study. Using detailed data from the
1990 census 5 percent public use file and information on income,
household type, size, and age of head, these results provide the
most comprehensive analysis to date of the relevance of these
factors for black, Hispanic, and Asian residential segregation for a
single metropolitan area.

As expected, white households are distributed in substantial
numbers throughout Los Angeles County, regardless of socioeconomic class. The clear and unmistakable exception to this pattern is the scarcity of white households in areas of high minority
concentration—particularly those with high concentrations of
blacks and Hispanics. In East Los Angeles, Compton, and parts of
South Central Los Angeles, white households are less than 5 percent of the total population. In the more affluent portion of South
Central that includes the middle-income black suburb of Baldwin
Hills, white households are still less than 8 percent of the population. In contrast, 21.5 percent of households are white in the traditionally Chinese and Japanese suburb of Monterey Park–Rosemead (44.5 percent Asian households). Under the predicted
model, there is an eightfold increase in white households for East
Los Angeles, Compton, and the eastern portion of South Central
Los Angeles, and a whopping thirty-fold increase in another portion of South Central Los Angeles. The two-fold increase in white
households in Monterey Park–Rosemead pales in comparison.

At the other extreme, black households are concentrated in a
very small number of areas. Moreover, this is true irrespective of
their socioeconomic resources. The areas of severe black concentration are generally characterized as low-income, ghetto communities, rife with drugs, crime, and violence (South Central Los Angeles and Compton). Black-white residential segregation is nearly
six times the level it would be if black households were distributed strictly on the basis of income and household characteristics.

In sum, Los Angeles remains a hypersegregated city for blacks
(Massey and Denton 1989; Denton 1994). Members of this group

consistently express preferences for neighborhoods with substantial integration with whites, overwhelmingly for reasons of racial harmony (Farley et al. 1978, 1993, 1994; Bobo 1989; Pettigrew 1973). Yet consistent with the findings of Massey and Denton (1987, 1993) and Kain (1986), low-income white households are more likely to be located in desirable, middle-class (predominantly white) areas than are affluent black households. Given these preferences, their consistency over time, and the persistent, extreme degree of black-white segregation, the near-disappearance of segregation when socioeconomic characteristics are held constant leaves only one conclusion: black-white segregation cannot be understood in terms of disparities in socioeconomic resources, and, therefore, the continuing significance of race must be taken seriously.

A more substantial fraction of Hispanic-white residential segregation can be tied to socioeconomic disparities. After "redistributing" Los Angeles County households on the basis of these characteristics, Hispanics are the only group that remains moderately segregated from whites. Still, under the predicted model, Hispanic-white segregation is 2.4 times lower than actual levels. This is consistent with previous research on Hispanic segregation from whites (Denton and Massey 1989; Massey and Fong 1990; Alba and Logan 1993). Hispanic households stand out as being significantly larger, as being more likely to have children under eighteen living at home, and as having younger heads. Despite an average household income roughly equal that of blacks, these other differences leave Hispanic households at an economic disadvantage.

Given these differences in household composition, the logical conclusion is that socioeconomic disparities account for a meaningful portion of Hispanic-white segregation. Still, differences in immigrant status, not considered here, make it reasonable to suggest the possibility of a self-segregation process, particularly among the more recent arrivals, that also influences Hispanic residential patterns.

The lack of a relationship between socioeconomic class characteristics and residential patterns for Asian households is a bit of a surprise. Contrary to existing research (Massey and Fong 1990; White 1986), these factors do not account for a substantial portion of residential isolation for Asians in Los Angeles. A comparison of household characteristics supports this finding: despite some differences in average household size and age of head, Asian households have incomes that ought to allow them to translate socioeconomic resources into greater residential mobility.

Asian-white segregation in Los Angeles County—and elsewhere—is already substantially lower than both black and Hispanic segregation from whites. As is the case for black households in Los Angeles, redistributing the population by income and household characteristics all but eliminates the already moderate degree of residential segregation experienced by Asians. Again, it is realistic to assert that understanding the role of immigrant status could be crucial to understanding Asian-white segregation. Given that socioeconomic factors are important for Hispanics, but not for Asians, it seems even more likely that a self-segregation process among Asians (again, particularly among more recent arrivals) plays a significant role in predicting their residential patterns. Like Hispanics, Asians are largely a community of recent immigrants. Moreover, and again like Hispanics, Asian immigrants speak different languages and have cultural patterns that differ from those of their new "host" country (Portes and Rumbaut 1990). Still, relative to both blacks and Hispanics, Asian households are largely integrated, yet socioeconomic differences tell us little about Asian residential segregation.

Minimally, these results add to a large body of research over several decades and many cities that consistently illustrates the inability of blacks to turn socioeconomic gains into greater residential mobility. For the first time, analysis suggests the absence of a relationship between economic resources and residential locations for Asians as well. However, it is important to bear in mind that, in the Los Angeles case, differences in immigrant status must be taken seriously as factors contributing to residential patterns among both Asians and Hispanics. Taken together, these results lend credence to the notion that factors such as prejudice and discrimination, ethnocentrism, or something as simple as inaccurate information about the housing market explain the lion's share of persistent racial residential segregation.

REFERENCES

Alba, Richard D., and John R. Logan. 1993. "Minority Proximity to Whites in Suburbs: An Individual-Level Analysis of Segregation." *American Journal of Sociology* 98(6): 1388–1427.

Bobo, Lawrence. 1989. "Keeping the Linchpin in Place: Testing the Multiple Sources of Opposition to Residential Integration." *International Review of Social Psychology* 2(3): 305–23.

Bobo, Lawrence, and Camille L. Zubrinsky. 1996. "Attitudes toward Residential Integration: Perceived Status Differences, Mere In-Group Preference, or Racial Prejudice?" *Social Forces* 74(3): 851–81.

Charles, Camille Zubrinsky. 2000. "Neighborhood Racial Composition Preferences : Evidence from a Multiethnic Metropolis." *Social Problems* 47(3): 379–407.

Darden, Joe T. 1987. "Choosing Neighbors and Neighborhoods: The Role of Race in Housing Preference." In *Divided Neighborhoods: Changing Patterns of Racial Segregation,* edited by Gary A. Tobin. Newbury Park, Calif.: Sage.

Davis, Mike. 1990. *City of Quartz.* New York: Vintage Books.

Denton, Nancy A. 1994. "Are African Americans Still Hypersegregated?" In *Residential Apartheid: The American Legacy,* edited by Robert Bullard, Charles Lee, and J. Eugene Grigsby. Los Angeles: UCLA Center for Afro-American Studies.

Denton, Nancy A., and Douglas S. Massey. 1989. "Racial Identity among Caribbean Hispanics: The Effect of Double Minority Status on Residential Segregation." *American Sociological Review* 54(5): 790–808.

Farley, John E. 1986. "Segregated City, Segregated Suburbs: To What Extent Are They Products of Black-White Socioeconomic Differentials?" *Urban Geography* 7(2): 164–71.

———. 1995. "Race Still Matters: The Minimal Role of Income and Housing Cost as Causes of Housing Segregation in St. Louis, 1990." *Urban Affairs Review* 31(2): 244–54.

Farley, Reynolds, and William H. Frey. 1994. "Changes in the Segregation of Whites from Blacks during the 1980's: Small Steps toward a More Integrated Society." *American Sociological Review* 59(1): 23–45.

Farley, Reynolds, Maria Krysan, Tara Jackson, Charlotte Steeh, and Keith Reeves. 1993. "Causes of Continued Racial Residential Segregation in Detroit: 'Chocolate City, Vanilla Suburbs' Revisited." *Journal of Housing Research* 4(1): 1–38.

Farley, Reynolds, Howard Schuman, Suzanne Bianchi, Diane Colasanto, and Shirley Hatchett. 1978. "A 'Chocolate City, Vanilla Suburbs': Will the Trend toward Racially Separate Communities Continue?" *Social Science Research* 7(1): 319–44.

Farley, Reynolds, Charlotte Steeh, Maria Krysan, Tara Jackson, and Keith Reeves. 1994. "Stereotypes and Segregation: Neighborhoods in the Detroit Area." *American Journal of Sociology* 100(3): 750–80.

Galster, George C. 1988. "Residential Segregation in American Cities: A Contrary Review." *Population Research and Policy Review* 7(2): 93–112.

Harrison, Roderick J., and Daniel H. Weinberg. 1992. "Changes in Racial and Ethnic Residential Segregation 1980–1990." Paper prepared for the American Statistical Association meetings. Boston (August).

Hermalin, Albert I., and Reynolds Farley. 1973. "The Potential for Residential Integration in Cities and Suburbs: Implications for the Busing Controversy." *American Sociological Review* 38(5): 595–610.

Johnson, James H., Jr., Clyzelle K. Jones, Walter C. Farrell Jr., and Melvin L. Oliver. 1992. "The Los Angeles Rebellion: A Retrospective View." *Economic Development Quarterly* 6(4): 356–72.

Kain, John F. 1986. "The Influence of Race and Income on Racial Segregation and Housing Policy." In *Housing Desegregation and Federal Policy,* edited by John M. Goering. Chapel Hill: University of North Carolina Press.

———. 1987. "Housing Market Discrimination and Black Suburbanization in the 1980s." In *Divided Neighborhoods: Changing Patterns of Racial Segregation,* edited by Gary A. Tobin. Newbury Park, Calif.: Sage Press.

Leven, Charles L., James T. Little, Hugh O. Nourse, and R. Read. 1976. *Neighborhood Change: Lessons in the Dynamics of Urban Decay.* Cambridge, Mass.: Ballinger.

Massey, Douglas S., and Nancy A. Denton. 1987. "Trends in the Residential Segregation of Blacks, Hispanics, and Asians." *American Sociological Review* 52(6): 802–25.

———. 1989. "Hypersegregation in U.S. Metropolitan Areas: Black and Hispanic Segregation along Five Dimensions." *Demography* 26(3): 373–92.

———. 1992. "Residential Segregation of Asian-Origin Groups in U.S. Metropolitan Areas." *Social Science Research* 76(4): 170–77.

———. 1993. *American Apartheid.* Cambridge, Mass.: Harvard University Press.

Massey, Douglas S., and Eric Fong. 1990. "Segregation and Neighborhood Quality: Blacks, Hispanics, and Asians in the San Francisco Metropolitan Area." *Social Forces* 69(1): 15–32.

Massey, Douglas S., and Brendan P. Mullan. 1984. "Processes of Hispanic and Black Spatial Assimilation." *American Journal of Sociology* 89(4): 836–73.

Ong, Paul M., and Janette R. Lawrence, with Kevin Davidson. 1992. "Pluralism and Residential Patterns in Los Angeles." Unpublished paper. School of Architecture and Urban Planning, University of California, Los Angeles.

Pascal, H. A. 1967. *The Economics of Housing Segregation.* Santa Monica, Calif.: Rand Corporation.

Pettigrew, Thomas F. 1973. "Attitudes on Race and Housing: A Social Psychological View." In *Segregation in Residential Areas,* edited by A. H. Hawley and V. P. Rock. Washington, D.C.: National Academy of Sciences Press.

———. 1979. "Racial Change and Social Policy." *Annals of the American Academy of Political and Social Science* 441: 114–31.

Portes, Alejandro, and Ruben G. Rumbaut. 1990. *Immigrant America: A Portrait.* Berkeley and Los Angeles: University of California Press.

Schnare, Ann B. 1977. *Residential Segregation by Race in U.S. Metropolitan Areas: An Analysis across Cities and over Time.* Washington, D.C.: Urban Institute.

Skerry, Peter. 1993. *Mexican Americans: The Ambivalent Minority.* Cambridge, Mass.: Harvard University Press.

Taeuber, Karl E. 1976. "The Effect of Income Redistribution on Racial Residential Segregation." *Urban Affairs Quarterly* 4(1): 5–15.

Taeuber, Karl E., and Alma F. Taeuber. 1965. *Negroes in Cities: Residential Segregation and Neighborhood Change.* Chicago: Aldine.

Turner, Eugene, and James P. Allen. 1992. *An Atlas of Population Patterns in Metropolitan Los Angeles and Orange Counties.* Northridge: California State University Department of Geography.

U.S. Bureau of the Census. 1990a. *Census of Population and Housing.* Washington: U.S. Government Printing Office.

———. 1990b. "Public Use Microdata Sample 5 Percent File." Machine-readable database. Washington: U.S. Government Printing Office.

Van Valey, Thomas L., and Wade Clark Roof. 1976. "Measuring Residential Segregation in American Cities: Problems of Intercity Comparison." *Urban Affairs Quarterly* 11(4): 453–61.

White, Clay. 1986. "Residential Segregation among Asians in Long Beach: Japanese, Chinese, Filipino, Korean, Indian, Vietnamese, Hawaiian, Guamanian, and Samoan." *Social Science Research* 70(4): 266–67.

Zubrinsky, Camille L., and Lawrence Bobo. 1996. "Prismatic Metropolis: Race and Residential Segregation in the City of Angels." *Social Science Research* 25(4): 335–74.

—— Chapter 11 ——

Do Racial Composition and Segregation Affect Economic Outcomes in Metropolitan Areas?

Janice F. Madden

THERE IS EXTENSIVE evidence that African Americans earn less than members of other groups, even after controlling for measurable differences in credentials. Partly as a consequence, they are more likely to reside in poor households than whites. Although there is general agreement that these racial differences exist, there is considerable debate about the reasons for them. On the one hand, African Americans may earn less and live in poorer households because they experience current discrimination in the labor market. On the other hand, these racial differences may arise from unmeasured differences in credentials, motivation, and interests that are rooted in different histories, including past discrimination. Both current labor market discrimination and racial histories may contribute to present racial differences in economic outcomes, and sorting out the importance of each is critical to alleviating racial disparities.

It is also well established that African Americans who live in racially segregated neighborhoods earn less and are more likely to reside in poor households than those living in racially integrated areas. Many researchers and policymakers have argued that racial segregation in housing contributes to poor economic outcomes for African Americans, including higher unemployment, lower wages, and inferior schools and housing (see Massey and Denton 1993). There is abundant evidence that ghetto residents not only have lower incomes but also are more likely to be victims of crime, to drop out of high school, and to experience higher mortality than African Americans who do not reside in ghettos. Although the correlation between these outcomes is widely accepted, there are real questions about the causal connections. Two hypotheses have been advanced to explain how residential segregation causes lower incomes.

John Kain (1968) argues that a "spatial mismatch" between workers' residences and job sites increases unemployment among urban ghetto residents. He hypothesizes that housing discrimination restricts African Americans to inner-city ghettos that, in turn, inhibit their ability to obtain employment in the suburbs, where metropolitan job growth is concentrated. The resulting spatial mismatch is thought to account for at least part of the higher unemployment rates and lower earnings of African Americans in metropolitan areas. Kain's analysis of employment and residential data from Detroit and Chicago leads him to conclude that housing discrimination reduced nonwhite employment by nine thousand in Detroit and twenty-four thousand in Chicago in the 1950s.

William Julius Wilson's (1987) work on the urban underclass argues that the social isolation of ghetto residents has increased in recent years, as middle-class African Americans have moved increasingly into suburban and more integrated, higher-income neighborhoods. Wilson argues that the social isolation produces increasing unemployment, decreasing earnings, lower household income, and escalating social pathologies among ghetto residents beyond those that would have occurred in neighborhoods with a more economically and socially diverse population.

As with the spatial mismatch hypothesis, the underclass hypothesis attributes some of the unfavorable labor market and income outcomes for ghetto residents to housing discrimination, but the underlying mechanisms differ. For Wilson, it is the socioeconomic climate of the neighborhood (for example, the lack of employed persons to serve as role models or informants about job opportunities and the presence of disruptive persons who increase crime and make the provision of services more difficult) and not its physical distance from job sites that contributes to higher unemployment, lower earnings, and lower household incomes of ghetto residents.

Reviews of empirical research testing these two hypotheses yield no consensus on their validity. Ihlanfeldt (1992), Kain (1992), and Holzer (1991) all document the lack of consensus with respect to spatial mismatch, whereas Jencks and Mayer (1990) document the lack of consensus on the urban underclass hypothesis. The lack of agreement arises from the inherent difficulties in conducting empirical research on these issues. Manski (1993), for example, argues that it is very difficult, if not impossible, to obtain reliable empirical measurements of neighborhood effects on individual or household behavior.

A major problem is that the observed correlation between neighborhood of residence and economic outcomes does not establish cause and effect. People may live in ghettos because they have not succeeded in the labor market, or they may not succeed in the labor market because they live in ghettos. Another problem is that impediments to the optimal matching of workers with jobs (that is, ghettos, racial segregation, or income segmentation) may hurt everyone's economic opportunities—both residents of poor areas and residents of richer areas or both African Americans and whites—because these phenomena reduce overall productivity in the local labor market. If that is the case, then simple comparisons of ghetto residents with nonghetto residents or of whites with African Americans do not quantify the economic losses from racial segregation and income segmentation.

In summary, although the correlation between racial segregation and poor job outcomes is well established for individuals, there is no agreement on the mechanisms that account for the association. There has been even less study of the connections between racial composition, income segmentation, and socioeconomic outcomes for all participants in the local labor market. A few studies have documented lower median incomes and greater levels of income inequality and poverty for metropolitan statistical areas (MSAs) with more African Americans (see Farbman 1975; Danziger 1976; Nord 1980a, 1980b; Garofalo and Fogarty 1979), but none has examined the effects of various forms of income segmentation. Establishing the relationships between racial composition, income segmentation, and metropolitan-wide economic outcomes offers important evidence for determining the underlying *causal* connections among race, neighborhood, and outcomes at the individual level.

THINKING ABOUT COMPOSITION, SEGREGATION, AND SEGMENTATION

In this section, I propose a way to distinguish the racial income differentials arising from current discrimination from those arising from differential productivity (the legacy of past discrimination). Assume that there is no underemployment or unemployment for workers with skills more than the lowest level. Wage levels for those with above the lowest skill, then, adjust to create full employment. Assume further that mandated minimum-wage levels or fringe benefits result in above-market compensation for the lowest-skill workers. As a result, not all lowest-skill workers are employed; some experience periodic unemployment.

Now consider how the overall income distribution within an MSA is affected by changes in racial composition if African American workers are less productive than others or if African American workers are equally productive but subject to (current) discrimination.

If African Americans are less productive, then they are more likely to be in the lowest-skill group and to have lower incomes. The racial composition of the MSA, then, affects the shape of the distribution of worker skills (and productivity) within the MSA. The lower tail of the distribution is thicker for MSAs with more African Americans. Thus MSAs that are 25 percent African American have more low-income households than MSAs that are 5 percent African American. As there are more African Americans in an MSA, there are more workers in the lowest-skill group, resulting in higher poverty rates and greater income inequality.

If African Americans are as skilled as other workers, but are subject to (current) discrimination, they are more likely to be placed in the lowest-wage positions and to experience greater unemployment than are similarly skilled whites. In this case, the underlying distribution of worker skills (or productivity) within the MSA is *not* affected by racial composition. While African Americans are more likely to be assigned to the lowest jobs (high unemployment and low income), there are the same number of lowest-skill jobs in MSAs with more African Americans as in those with fewer. MSAs with populations that are 25 percent African American thus have the same proportion of lowest-skill jobs (and poverty and income inequality) as those that are otherwise similar but with populations that are 5 percent African American. With current discrimination in the labor market, race determines *who* receives low versus high pay, or it assigns persons to inferior positions in the distribution of income or output, but it does not affect total output or the distribution of worker skills. While African Americans would be disproportionately among the poor, there would be no association between racial composition of an MSA and the proportion of the population in poverty or receiving lower incomes in an MSA.

There are other plausible scenarios in which current discrimination might directly influence the overall distribution of production, and therefore poverty or income inequality. There is no scenario for which systematic productivity differences by race would not imply differences in income distribution that are associated with racial composition. Therefore, if racial composition does not affect the equality of income distribution, then current discrimination is the *more likely* explanation for income differences by race.

Now consider how variations in the extent of segmentation within MSAs might affect income inequality or poverty. Segmentation is any barrier that spatially separates metropolitan residents and reduces geographic mobility. These barriers may arise from political boundaries, racial boundaries, or other social constructs that create artificial boundaries. For the same reasons discussed for skill level, if segmentation *lowers* productivity (causes inferior job outcomes), it is more likely to shape the overall distribution of income within the MSA than when it is the *result* of the residential sorting of workers based on income or race (that is, it produces the effect of inferior job outcomes). There are three relevant forms of segmentation to consider:

- *Segmentation of local governments.* The more fragmented is metropolitan government (the greater the number of municipalities in the MSA), the smaller is the central city government relative to its suburban counterparts, and the greater is the potential for low-income or minority groups to become isolated within local governments that have lower taxing capacities and that consequently provide lower levels of public goods such as education, sanitation, and crime control.
- *Residential segregation by race.* The more racially segregated are an MSA's residential neighborhoods, the greater is the likelihood of spatial mismatch between workers and jobs, and consequently the greater is the likelihood that urban underclass neighborhood effects occur.
- *Suburbanization of jobs.* In the United States, jobs have been moving from central cities into suburbs and beyond for the past thirty years. Much of this migration is a response to earlier shifts in the residential location of the workforce (that is, the suburbanization of residences), but for those areas where jobs are moving out faster than the workforce, central city residents are more likely to be isolated from jobs and to experience problems in commuting to work within the MSA.

METHODOLOGY

An analysis that measures how racial composition and segmentation are correlated with the distribution of outcomes, such as income or earnings, using macro or economy-wide data can provide evidence on the direction of causality between these characteristics and outcomes. How should the aggregate economy be defined for such an analysis? In this study, I use metropolitan statistical areas, which are defined by the U.S. Bureau of the Census in terms of counties (except for New England, where they are defined in terms of cities and towns). An area is an MSA if it includes at least one city of at least fifty thousand inhabitants or if it includes a census-defined urbanized area of at least fifty thousand inhabitants and a total MSA population of at least one hundred thousand. The outlying counties included in an MSA are defined based on their commuting patterns to the central city and their population density, and the boundaries are defined in such a way that they constitute individual economies. In this chapter, I analyze whether MSA characteristics, including racial composition, extent of residential segregation by race, and other measures of governmental or labor market segmentation, affect a variety of labor market outcomes.

Although MSAs offer a large number of observations that permit a statistical analysis of the correlates between racial composition, segregation, and economic outcomes, cross-sectional studies raise a set of inevitable difficulties. There are likely to be many underlying differences between any two metropolitan areas at the same point in time, and many, probably most, of these differences are difficult to measure. These differences may be correlated with racial composition or segmentation, and they also may affect job outcomes. Consider, for example, the case of MSAs dominated by a large research university (such as Urbana, Illinois, or Gainesville, Florida). These MSAs have different educational, migration, and labor force participation characteristics and a different age structure than other MSAs of similar size and regional location. They also have a disproportionate share of households and earners with relatively low income for their educational attainment. These incomes are low because household members, often working at least part time, are pursuing a degree or supporting a family member who is pursuing a degree. Their incomes will rise later, but, for most, at a different location. A study examining the effects of race, segmentation, income, or earnings inequality in these MSAs, without taking note of this unique situation, would underestimate the effects of education and labor force participation on income and poverty. It would be very misleading.

Although some of these MSA characteristics can be measured, in a large cross-sectional analysis it is difficult to measure subtleties, such as amenities or disamenities that affect subgroups of workers. A study using MSAs as the unit of observation therefore must develop a methodology that controls for unobserved differences between MSAs that are correlated with the outcome variables. In this study, I compare *changes* in MSA outcomes over a decade. I assume, then, that unobserved differences between MSAs affect the *absolute level* of an outcome (such as poverty or income inequality) but do not affect the relationships between *changes* in characteristics and in outcomes over the decade. I assume, then, that a change in characteristics has a fixed effect on a change in outcomes across all MSAs.

In this case, I analyze whether MSAs with more African Americans and with higher levels of racial segregation and job or governmental segmentation have higher poverty rates, higher concentrations of poverty in the central city, and greater income and wage inequality. I estimate an equation to measure the systematic relationships between changes in a metropolitan area's racial composition and segmentation or segregation and changes in its poverty rate and income inequality. Specifically,

$$\Delta POV_j = \alpha_0 + \alpha_1 \Delta \% AA_j + \alpha_2 \Delta \% LIVCEN_j + \alpha_3 \Delta \% WORK/ \quad (11.1)$$
$$LIVECEN_j + \alpha_4 \Delta SEGINDEX_j + \alpha_5 \ OTHCHAR_j + \varepsilon_j$$

where ΔPOV_j is a measure of the change in the distribution of income or earnings, where change is the difference between the 1990 and the 1980 rate divided by the 1990 rate. Various indexes are analyzed, including the change in the personal poverty rate, the concentration of MSA poverty in the city, the change in the Gini coefficient for household income, and the change in the quintile share of income in the metropolitan area.

Key explanatory variables include $\Delta \% AA_j$, the change in the proportion of households in MSA j that are African American; $\Delta \% LIVCEN_j$, the change in the proportion of MSA residents who live in the central city (reflecting the extent of local governmental segmentation in the metropolitan area); $\Delta \% WORK/LIVCEN_j$, the change in the ratio of the percentage of MSA workers who work in the central city to the percentage of residents who live in the central city (reflecting the tightness of the labor market for central city residents relative to suburban residents); $\Delta SEGINDEX_j$, the change in the dissimilarity index of racial residential segregation for MSA j; and $\Delta OTHCHAR_j$, the change in other demographic, skill, locational, and labor market characteristics. ε_{ji} is an error term.

Demographic variables represented among "other characteristics" include the mean number of persons per household, the proportions of households headed by women and persons over age sixty-five, the share of population that moved into the MSA in the last five years, and the proportions of households with multiple earners and no earners. Skill characteristics in the *OTHCAR* vector include median education and the Gini coefficient for the distribution of educational attainment among persons ages twenty-five and above. Locational characteristics include the MSA mean household income and total population size, while labor market characteristics include the employment-to-population ratio and the Gini coefficient for earnings of wage and salary workers in the MSA. The Gini coefficient on earnings provides a precise control for the effects of the earnings structure of the local labor market. The *OTHCAR* vector also includes a dummy variable indicating whether the MSA is in the South Central region as well as the 1980 level of the variable from which the dependent variable, a rate of change, is computed.

DATA AND BASIC TRENDS

Equation 11.1 is estimated using data from the 5 percent Public Use Micro Samples (PUMS) of the 1980 and the 1990 U.S. censuses. These data permit the computation of measures of the inequality of earnings across individuals and of income across households or families for the 182 largest MSAs in 1980 and 1990 (those among the two hundred largest at *both* census dates). Table 11.1 reports basic data on racial composition, segregation, economic and political structure, income inequality, and poverty for these U.S. metropolitan areas.

The first panel summarizes the demographic and physical structure of the MSAs. Over the decade there was an increase in the average representation of African Americans among metropolitan residents, which went from 9.2 percent in 1980 to 11.0 percent in 1990. The relatively large standard deviations indicate the tremendous range of variation in racial composition across metropolitan areas. In 1990 Jackson, Mississippi, had the largest African American representation at 51 percent, and Provo, Utah, had the lowest, with no measurable representation.

American metropolitan areas are highly segregated by race, although there was a slight decrease in segregation over the de-

TABLE 11.1 **Racial and Structural Characteristics and Mean Inequality and Poverty for 182 MSAs in 1979 and 1989**

Variable	1979	1989	Percentage Change
Racial and structural characteristics*			
Percent African American	0.092	0.110	0.279
	(0.085)	(0.100)	(0.372)
Black-white segregation index	0.691	0.651	−0.058
	(0.116)	(0.114)	(0.053)
Tightness of city versus suburban labor market			0.032
			(0.155)
Measures of income distribution and poverty			
Gini coefficient for household income	0.374	0.412	0.106
	(0.026)	(0.026)	(0.049)
Gini coefficient for all wages and salaries	0.453	0.466	0.027
	(0.020)	(0.027)	(0.033)
Poverty rate	0.117	0.127	0.093
	(0.040)	(0.050)	(0.191)
Central city poverty/MSA poverty	1.412	1.533	0.067
	(0.396)	(0.504)	(0.070)

Source: Based on author's calculations using the Five Percent Public Use Micro Sample of the 1980 and 1990 U.S. Censuses.
Note: Numbers in parentheses are standard errors.
*Demographic characteristics are for April 1980 and 1990; income data are for 1979 and 1989.

cade. In 1980 the index of segregation in the average MSA was 0.691, indicating that 69.1 percent of African Americans (or of whites) would have to change their neighborhood of residence for race not to matter in residential location. By 1989 this percentage had declined to 65.1 percent. As with racial composition, the variation across MSAs is notable. Fort Wayne, Indiana, was the most segregated MSA in 1990, with a segregation index of 0.91, and Santa Cruz, California, was the least segregated, with an index of 0.40. In the average MSA, segregation decreased about 6 percent.

The economic structure and the extent of segmentation in local government also vary across MSAs. One simple measure of local government segmentation is the proportion of the metropolitan population that lives in the central city. As the percentage increases, there is less segmentation because more of the population receives government services from, and pays taxes to, the largest local government in the area. The proportion of metropolitan residents in the central city changed little over the decade, with an average of 40.7 percent in 1980 and 41.0 percent in 1990. Lincoln, Nebraska, was the least governmentally segmented MSA, with 89 percent of the population in the central city, and Benton Harbor, Michigan, was the most segmented, with only 8.1 percent of the MSA population in the central city.

A measure of the health of the central city economy (and local government) is the proportion of the metropolitan area's jobs that are located in the central city relative to the city's proportion of metropolitan residents. Increasing income and preferences for larger homes and lots may increase the attraction of suburban residential areas, decreasing the central city's share of metropolitan residents. If the city maintains or increases its relative share of jobs, however, then the central city economy remains strong and jobs become relatively more accessible to central city residents. Also the spatial mismatch effects of residential segregation are weaker if jobs are more centralized. Although there was a slight decrease in the central city's share of residents in the average MSA during the decade, there was an increase in the proportion of jobs relative to residents in MSAs. The average central city had a 3.2 percent increase in its ratio of jobs to residents, with the greatest increases (53.8 percent) occurring in South Bend, Indiana, and the largest losses occurring in Charleston, South Carolina (-44.3 percent).

The next panel in table 11.1 presents means and the standard errors for MSA measures of household income, wages and salaries, and poverty rates. The Gini coefficient measures the difference between the actual distribution and a completely equal distribution of income or earnings and ranges between zero and one. If all incomes are the same, there is no difference between the actual and equal distributions, and the Gini coefficient is zero. At the other extreme, if all income is received by only one person or household, the Gini coefficient is one.

These data show increasing inequality and poverty in metropolitan areas and an increasing concentration of poverty in the central cities of these areas. In 1979 the average MSA had a Gini coefficient of 0.374 for household income and 0.453 for individual wages and salaries. By 1989 both coefficients had grown (to 0.412 for household income and 0.466 for wage and salary income), reflecting increased inequality within U.S. metropolitan areas. Although the Gini for household income was lower than that for wage and salary income at both dates, household income inequality grew faster than wage and salary inequality over the decade.

There is also substantial variation across metropolitan areas, as well as between cities and suburbs within metropolitan areas, in another important measure of income distribution: the poverty rate. As shown in the table, 11.7 percent of persons in the average MSA had incomes below the poverty line in 1979, and this figure grew to 12.7 percent in 1989. The highest MSA poverty rate in 1989 (35.2 percent) was in McAllen, Texas, and the lowest poverty rate for an MSA with a central city occurred in Stamford, Connecticut, at 6.3 percent. The poverty rates within central cities have exceeded both the national rate and the total rate for their MSAs for some time. Poverty rates in the central cities averaged 15.9 percent in 1979 and 18.5 percent in 1989, growing from 141.2 percent of the MSA rate to 153.3 percent in 1989. The difference between the average central city rate and the rate for its metropolitan area grew 6.7 percent over the decade.

EFFECTS OF COMPOSITION, SEGREGATION, AND SEGMENTATION

Table 11.2 reports the results of regressing various measures of MSA inequality on changes in racial composition, residential segregation by race, and economic structure, controlling for the other variables described in the previous section. These results show how racial segregation and political and economic segmentation of MSAs are associated with changes in Gini coefficients for household income, with changes in poverty, and with changes in the concentration of poverty in the central city in the 182 metropolitan areas between 1979 and 1989. A negative coefficient indicates that the variable operates to *decrease* inequality, poverty, and concentration, whereas a positive coefficient means that it works to *increase* these variables. Table 11.2 reports unstandar-

TABLE 11.2 Effect of Changes in Racial and Urban Characteristics on Change in Household Income Inequality in 182 Metropolitan Areas, from 1979 to 1989

Variable	Inequality of Household Income		Poverty Rate		Central City/MSA Poverty Rate	
	Basic Model	Full Model	Basic Model	Full Model	Basic Model	Full Model
Percentage African American						
Regression coefficient	−0.011	−0.003	−0.101	−0.017	0.034	0.029
t-statistic	(−1.40)	(−0.53)	(−2.41)	(−0.61)	(2.07)	(1.63)
Beta coefficient	−0.083	−0.026	−0.191	−0.032	0.146	0.122
Black-white segregation						
Regression coefficient	0.001	0.000	0.003	−0.000	0.002	0.002
t-statistic	(1.48)	(0.50)	(0.95)	(−0.19)	(1.74)	(1.42)
Beta coefficient	0.078	0.023	0.068	−0.010	0.116	0.103
Percentage living in central city						
Regression coefficient	−0.016	−0.038	0.743	0.375	−0.473	−0.463
t-statistic	(−0.48)	(−1.43)	(4.08)	(3.23)	(−6.07)	(−5.81)
Beta coefficient	−0.025	−0.058	0.283	0.143	−0.406	−0.400
Tightness of city versus suburban labor market						
Regression coefficient	0.011	0.002	0.085	0.029	−0.053	−0.045
t-statistic	(0.72)	(0.13)	(0.98)	(0.53)	(−1.53)	(−1.27)
Beta coefficient	0.037	0.005	0.067	0.023	−0.095	−0.080
Adjusted R^2	0.57	0.76	0.22	0.71	0.37	0.41

Source: Based on author's calculations using the Five Percent Public Use Micro Sample of the 1980 and 1990 U.S. Censuses.
Note: The basic model includes the following additional variables: percentage change in female-headed households, in households headed by a person over age sixty-five, in mean household size, in median education, in educational inequality (Gini for years of attainment), and in the 1980 population and the 1980 level of the dependent variable. The full model, in addition to the variables listed in the basic model, includes percentage change in no-earner households, multiple-earner households, wage and salary inequality (Gini), employment-to-population ratio, percentage of MSA population who migrated into the MSA in the past five years, mean per capita income, MSA population, and a dummy variable indicating an MSA boundary change.

dized ordinary least squares regression coefficients, their *t*-statistics, along with standardized or beta coefficients. The beta coefficient represents the association between a one standard error change in the independent variable and the standard error of the dependent variable. It standardizes for differences in measurement units across variables to enable direct comparisons about the relative importance of effects.

The results of two different specifications are presented in table 11.2. The first specification, the basic model, includes changes in demographic structure (age, race, gender, household size), skill composition (median education and the Gini coefficient for years of education among persons twenty-five to sixty-four years of age), and structural characteristics (whether located in the South Central region, the 1979 household income Gini coefficient for the MSA, and changes in the proportions of residents living in the central city, the proportions of metropolitan jobs to residents in the central city, and the levels of residential segregation). The second specification, the full model, controls for local labor market conditions and growth by adding in changes in the Gini coefficients for wages across all wage and salary earners in each MSA and changes in the ratio of total metropolitan employment to population ages twenty-five to sixty-four. It also controls for demographic characteristics (changes in the growth in the proportion of in-migrants and in the proportions of no-earner, multiple-earner households) and several structural characteristics (growth in population, growth in mean income, and changes in the boundary of the MSA between 1980 and 1990) that are highly correlated with one another and with economic growth.

Changes in the wage and salary Gini coefficients fully measure the association between household income inequality and any changes in the distributions of wage and salary alternatives in the metropolitan area, whereas changes in the employment-to-population ratio reflects changes in the overall tightness of the labor market. Although other studies (for example, Danziger 1976) have used measures of industrial composition to reflect wage distribution and have estimated two-stage equations in order to infer the effect of the labor market on household or family income distribution, the data used here allow direct measurement of the wage and salary distribution available to individual workers.

By comparing coefficients between these specifications, one can infer the robustness of the results and the sensitivity of the correlation between changes in an independent variable and inequality, poverty, or the concentration of poverty to the other characteristics included in the estimation. The additional variables permit assessment of the pathways through which changes in metropolitan characteristics affect inequality. Differences in coefficients between the first and second specification show the extent to which racial composition or segmentation is associated with inequality beyond the association with the local labor market and economic growth.

The first two columns of table 11.2 show how household income inequality within MSAs changes with racial composition, residential segregation, and economic structure. The next two columns examine how changes in these same MSA characteristics are correlated with changes in their poverty rate, and the last two columns examine the tendency of poverty to concentrate in the central city of the MSA. There are important similarities and differences between these measures of inequality.

While changes in the poverty rate in a metropolitan area may reflect changes in the equality of household income distribution within the area, poverty rates and income inequality are not the same phenomena. The Gini coefficient measures changes in household income across the entire distribution of household income. The poverty rate measures the proportion of households that receive an income below a level defined as necessary to maintain a minimal standard of living, which is defined for the entire nation and does not reflect differences between metropolitan areas in prices or in climate. Movements toward inequality can arise from changes in all parts of the income distribution, whereas the poverty rate measures changes for the poorest segment of the population.

Although the household income Gini and the poverty rate measure different aspects of the distribution, the correlations between racial composition, residential segregation, and segmentation are remarkably similar. MSAs with greater changes in racial composition have no statistically significant change in their household income inequality or their poverty rate compared with MSAs that experience less change in racial composition, once measures of change in the local labor market and economic growth are included. If these economic characteristics are not considered, an increase in the representation of African Americans does tend to decrease inequality and poverty, although not significantly so for household income inequality. In short, there is no statistical evidence that MSAs with more African Americans have greater inequality, a result that is inconsistent with unobserved productivity differentials that account for racial differences in income.

Changes in the extent of racial segregation in housing (the second row of table 11.2) likewise have no relationship with changes in the MSA household income, Gini, or poverty rate. Similarly, changes in the ratio of the central city's share of MSA employment to the central city share of MSA residents (the fourth row) have insignificant effects on changes in MSA income inequality or poverty rates. These results provide no evidence that residential segregation by race or spatial distribution of jobs and residents contributes to increases in MSA income inequality. This finding is consistent with the view that persons who have less success in the labor market reside in ghettos and are more isolated from jobs; it is not consistent with the hypothesis that segregation and job isolation *cause* inferior job outcomes.

MSAs that have less of a decrease in the proportion of residents living in the central city experience no significant difference in income inequality, but they have significantly greater rates of growth in their poverty levels. About half of the poverty effect appears to arise because MSAs with a relative increase in population in the central city have slower growth (evidenced by the lower coefficients for the percentage living in the central city when local labor market and economic growth characteristics are added). After considering the effects of economic growth and local labor market conditions (column 2), a change in the proportion of MSA residents in the central city that is one standard error above average increases the growth in the MSA poverty rate by 0.143 standard error.

The direction of this correlation is surprising. Metropolitan fragmentation—that is, increasing numbers of municipalities or local governments in a metropolitan area—is expected to worsen poverty by making it easier for the wealthier to separate themselves from the poor. Metropolitan fragmentation increases as the proportion of the population living in the central city decreases. The separation of richer from poorer is expected to lead to greater spatial concentration of the poor that, in turn, leads to spatial mismatch or urban underclass effects. Furthermore, such segmentation undermines the fiscal ability of the local government to provide compensatory goods and services to the poor.

The unexpected direction of this result may indicate that change in the percentage living in the central city is correlated with another unmeasured characteristic. While the second specifications in table 11.2 take into account the effects of the local labor market and of economic growth, they may not do so completely. Other studies (Madden 2000) conducted with these data show that MSAs with relatively greater increases in the proportion of the MSA population resident in the central city are more likely to be smaller, are more likely to have experienced increases in female-headed households, and are less likely to have experienced increases in in-migrants, per capita income, average education, or population. The results for this MSA characteristic thus are likely to reflect the effect of stagnant economies rather than a direct causal relationship with local government fragmentation on inequality.

Another clue to the puzzling effect of this variable appears in the analysis of the spatial concentration of poverty, shown in the last two columns of table 11.2. These columns use a different measure of inequality, the rate of change in the ratio of the central city to the MSA poverty rate, thus assessing the *spatial inequality* of income within MSAs. Because MSAs vary in the size of the central city relative to the overall MSA, I measure the percentage change in that ratio during the 1980s, while adding to the regression analysis a control for changes in the boundaries of the MSA and of the central city.

As with the growth in MSA poverty, growth in the spatial concentration of poverty is strongly influenced by the proportion of MSA residents in the central city. Increases in the proportion of MSA residents in the central city strongly decrease the rate of concentration of poverty in the central city. An increase that is one standard error above the mean decreases the rate of concentration of poverty by 0.40 to 0.41 standard error. Because this characteristic has an opposite effect on MSA poverty, however, this represents a rearrangement of poverty from the city to the suburbs in a way that actually is *correlated* with increases in overall MSA poverty. Local governmental fragmentation does not increase MSA poverty, although it does concentrate MSA poverty in the central city. Local governmental segmentation thus affects who is poor (central city or suburban residents) and where the poor live (not in suburbs), but it does not disadvantage the MSA as a whole. This result is consistent with the view that segmentation affects where the poor live but does not itself produce more poverty.

MSAs that experience increases in the representation of African Americans (first row of table 11.2) have significantly greater growth in the concentration of poverty. As a comparison of the basic and full models indicates, part of that association arises because those MSAs have slower growth. Thus the growing representation of African Americans does not increase MSA poverty or change the equality of the income distribution per se, but it does have some effect on where the poor live: MSAs with more African Americans appear to have more spatially concentrated poverty. MSAs that become more racially segregated also experience a statistically significant increase in the concentration of poverty in the central city (second row), although the effect becomes only marginally significant once economic growth and local labor markets are considered. MSAs that have an increase in job accessibility for central city residents (as evidenced by an increase in the ratio of jobs to residents in the central city) have no significant change in the concentration of poverty in the central city.

In sum, the sorting of employment between cities and suburbs does not appear to be relevant to metropolitan-wide poverty or inequality. My analysis of MSA variation in rates of change in household income inequality, the poverty rate, and spatial inequality finds no support for the hypothesis that job access and spatial mismatch contribute to inequality or to poverty. The effect of the ratio of jobs to residents also is not evident even to the spatial concentration of poverty in the central city (the sign is right, but the coefficient is not significant). Racial composition, meanwhile, affects where the poor are located in an MSA, but not the overall level of MSA poverty.

EFFECTS BY INCOME QUINTILE

Income inequality (as measured by the Gini coefficient) may change because of shifts occurring within the upper segments of the distribution as well as changes that move income from the upper segments to the bottom segments. The top panel of table 11.3 shows the average share of household income in the metropolitan area that went to each quintile of the income distribution in 1979 and 1989. In 1979, for example, the bottom quintile received 0.9 percent of the metropolitan household income and the top quintile received 47.6 percent. The bottom row of the panel shows the average change (measured as the absolute change in percentage points, not as a percentage change) in shares for each quintile. The share of all quintiles, other than the richest, declined between 1979 and 1989.

To investigate the segments of the income distribution that account for the tendencies of the distribution to converge or diverge, changes in metropolitan racial and segmentation characteristics are regressed on the change in income share within each quintile in the distribution. The results are reported in the lower panel of 11.3. The dependent variable in this analysis is the 1989 share minus the 1979 share accruing to the quintile; it reflects the absolute change in percentage share, not the percentage change in share. As before, I control for the 1979 share for each quintile, which is comparable to the approach used in table 11.2, although differences in specification of the dependent variable can affect the results.

There is much agreement between the regression results of tables 11.2 and 11.3. Similar to the findings for overall household income inequality and for the poverty rate, racial composition has little effect on the distribution by quintile. Although race is strongly significant in explaining *which* households receive lower incomes within an MSA, it is not related to the overall equality of distributions within MSAs. Although racial segregation has no significant effect on overall inequality or the poverty rate in table 11.2, table 11.3 shows that MSAs with rising segregation levels experience a decrease in the share of income accruing to the top quintile and an increase in the share of quintiles two and three.

TABLE 11.3 Mean Income Shares by Quintile and Metropolitan Characteristics Associated with Changes in Share Accruing to Quintile in 182 Metropolitan Areas, 1979 to 1989

Variable	Quintile of Household Income Distribution				
	Lowest 1	2	3	4	Highest 5
Changes in income share					
1979	0.009	0.081	0.169	0.265	0.476
Standard deviation	(0.007)	(0.018)	(0.011)	(0.006)	(0.031)
1989	0.008	0.075	0.160	0.256	0.501
Standard deviation	(0.007)	(0.018)	(0.011)	(0.007)	(0.033)
Change, 1979 to 1989	−0.001	−0.006	−0.009	−0.009	0.025
Standard deviation	(0.004)	(0.013)	(0.007)	(0.005)	(0.021)
Regression coefficients for associated changes in independent variables					
Percentage African American					
Regression coefficient	−0.000	−0.001	−0.002	0.000	0.003
t-statistic	(−0.00)	(−0.20)	(−1.94)	(0.22)	(0.75)
Beta coefficient	−0.000	−0.016	−0.119	0.020	0.051
Black-white segregation					
Regression coefficient	0.0001	0.0003	0.0002	−0.0001	−0.0006
t-statistic	(1.16)	(1.96)	(2.57)	(−0.72)	(−2.25)
Beta coefficient	0.087	0.145	0.151	−0.061	−0.148
Percentage living in central city					
Regression coefficient	0.011	0.035	0.012	−0.008	−0.049
t-statistic	(2.99)	(3.26)	(2.35)	(−1.60)	(−3.04)
Beta coefficient	0.189	0.208	0.119	−0.118	−0.156
Tightness of city versus suburban labor market					
Regression coefficient	−0.002	−0.000	−0.000	−0.001	0.004
t-statistic	(−0.98)	(−0.00)	(−0.05)	(−0.62)	(0.50)
Beta coefficient	−0.061	−0.000	−0.002	−0.044	0.028
Adjusted R^2	0.35	0.41	0.63	0.30	0.53

Source: Based on author's calculations using the Five Percent Public Use Micro Sample of he 1980 and 1990 U.S. Censuses.

This effect is consistent with the argument that segregation has high social costs, decreasing efficiency and overall income in the MSA by decreasing the quality of the match between workers and jobs. Segregation may reduce competition from households in quintile one for jobs typically taken by members of households in quintiles two and three, increasing the incomes of quintiles two and three, while decreasing the incomes of quintile one. Segregation thus appears to reduce the productivity and profitability of MSA businesses, contributing to a reduction in the income share of quintile five.

Consistent with the results reported in table 11.2 for the household income Gini coefficient and for poverty, an increase in the relative proportion of jobs in the central city (a measure of the spatial match between jobs and central city residents) has a positive, but statistically insignificant, effect on growth in the share of the top quintile and a negative effect on the share of the bottom four quintiles. Increases in the ratio of the share of jobs in the central city to the share of residents in the central city should favor the lower quintiles if poorer households are more likely to reside in the central city and if proximity to jobs increases income. There is no evidence here of such an effect.

There are also some important differences, however, between the regression results reported in tables 11.2 and 11.3. MSAs experiencing relative increases in the proportion of residents residing in the central city display no differential change in overall household income inequality but do have a greater growth in poverty (table 11.2). Table 11.3, in contrast, shows that the MSAs with relative growth in central city residents have growth in the income share of their bottom three quintiles and decreases in that of their top two quintiles, with the greatest changes occurring for the first, second, and fifth quintiles. The quintile results can be reconciled with the poverty rate results in two ways:

(1) The positive effect on the income share of the bottom quintile may be attributed to the second decile, with the first decile, where most poor households are counted, experiencing the opposite relationship. The fact that the bottom quintile shows less of a positive effect than the second quintile in table 11.3 suggests that the positive effect of larger central cities on income shares decreases at the lower levels of income.

(2) Differences between the households included in the bottom quintile and the households included in the group with incomes below the poverty level, which are defined with respect to age and household size but ignoring MSA price levels, account for the differences. The MSAs that have less of a decrease (or an increase) in the proportion of residents living in the central city are different with respect to other attributes that are associated with poverty rates, but not with household income shares. MSAs in California and Florida generally dominate the outlying increasers and decreasers in central city population. Because the two coasts generally experience greater economic growth, their changes in poverty rates (which depend more on income level than on distribution, like the Gini) may lead to different results.

The quintile analysis thus generally confirms the conclusions drawn from other measures of inequality discussed in the prior section. One exception is that the quintile analyses provide some evidence that segregation and segmentation directly affect income distribution. Income shares of the top quintile decrease as racial residential segregation increases, whereas income shares of the second and third quintiles increase. Racial segregation, in other words, appears to benefit the middle of the income distribution at the expense of the high end of the distribution, as measured by changes in quintile shares. Likewise, the shares of the three lower quintiles increase and that of the highest quintile decreases as the central city increases in population. A reduction in the degree of local governmental segmentation thus raises the share of the lower 60 percent of the income distribution but decreases the share of the top quintile.

EFFECTS ON THE DISTRIBUTION
OF WAGES AND SALARIES

The distribution of wages and salaries among individual workers within a labor market is the result of interactions between the demand for labor and the supply of labor. The local demand for labor is derived from the demand for the outputs of local industry.

Consumer tastes and the attractiveness of the MSA as a production site affect local demand for labor. The demographic and skill characteristics of local residents affect local labor supply as well as demand. The MSA outcome is shaped, then, by MSA demographic and skill characteristics of the labor force, by the structure of the MSA and its industrial composition, and by the extent of current discrimination in the labor market.

Table 11.4 shows the effects of racial composition, residential segregation, and segmentation on wage and salary inequality for all workers and for selected subgroups of workers. The first column reports the relationship between changes in racial composition and segmentation, on the one hand, and changes in the Gini coefficient for wage and salary income for all workers, on the other. The second column repeats the regression for those wage and salary workers who worked full-time for the entire year. The last five columns repeat the analysis for subgroups defined by occupation (managers and professionals, men in precision and operative occupations, women in clerical occupations, sales workers) and by industry (producer service workers).

MSAs experiencing relatively greater increases in the representation of African Americans experience less of an increase in wage and salary inequality (column 1), and when the analysis is restricted to full-time, year-round workers, the effect increases, indicating that it is greater equality in the rate of pay rather than in hours of work that accounts for the increase in equality as the proportion of African Americans increases. The last five columns show varying signs and no statistical significance for the effects of increases in African American representation on equality within industries and occupations. The statistical insignificance for these subgroups may occur simply because the Gini coefficients are measured with less precision for the smaller occupational and industry groups. Alternatively, the significant correlation of this characteristic with overall wage inequality may arise from differences in the industrial and occupational distribution of MSAs with greater increases in African American representation.

MSA changes in residential segregation by race have no relationship to wage and salary inequality overall or within industries or occupations (second panel of table 11.4). The results show no difference for jobs more concentrated in the central city (manage-

TABLE 11.4 Metropolitan Characteristics Associated with Changes in Gini Coefficients for Earnings Distributions in 182 MSAs, 1979 to 1989

Variable	All Wage and Salary Earners	Year-Round, Full-Time Earners	Managerial and Professional Workers	Male Precision Operative Workers	Female Clerical Workers	Producer Service Workers	Sales Workers
Percentage African American							
Regression coefficient	−0.012	−0.019	−0.013	−0.006	0.007	0.003	−0.005
t-statistic	(−1.924)	(−2.112)	(−1.410)	(−0.566)	(0.730)	(0.329)	(−0.574)
Beta coefficient	−0.133	−0.160	−0.106	−0.032	0.053	0.025	−0.041
Black-white segregation							
Regression coefficient	0.000	−0.000	−0.000	−0.000	−0.000	0.000	0.001
t-statistic	(0.072)	(−0.130)	(−0.263)	(−0.014)	(−0.248)	(0.291)	(1.177)
Beta coefficient	0.005	−0.011	−0.023	−0.001	−0.020	0.024	0.095
Percentage living in center							
Regression coefficient	0.026	0.012	0.051	0.120	0.122	0.111	0.043
t-statistic	(0.879)	(0.271)	(1.120)	(2.469)	(2.709)	(2.931)	(1.095)
Beta coefficient	0.059	0.020	0.081	0.137	0.193	0.217	0.076
Tightness of city versus suburban market							
Regression coefficient	0.017	0.028	0.036	0.016	−0.021	−0.004	−0.004
t-statistic	(1.239)	(1.378)	(1.719)	(0.688)	(−0.979)	(−0.205)	(−0.196)
Beta coefficient	0.080	0.097	0.121	0.037	−0.068	−0.015	−0.013
Adjusted R^2	0.34	0.22	0.22	0.55	0.24	0.18	0.29

Source: Based on author's calculations using the Five Percent Public Use Micro Sample of the 1980 and 1990 U.S. Censuses.

ment and professionals, producer service workers) or for those suburbanizing most rapidly (men in precision and operative occupations). Measures of MSA structural segmentation, however, show greater effects. The proportion of the population residing in the central city is associated significantly with increasing inequality of wages for those jobs that are most spatially concentrated in the MSA (third panel). Men employed in semiskilled and skilled manufacturing jobs (precision and operatives), women in clerical positions, and producer service workers all show greater wage inequality as the proportion residing in the center increases (and governmental segmentation decreases). Manufacturing jobs are largely in the suburbs, whereas clerical and producer service jobs are more centralized. The effect is insignificantly positive for management and professionals, an occupation that also is relatively centralized. The direction of this effect is surprising if the percentage living in the central city is interpreted only as a measure of local governmental fragmentation; it is less surprising if it reflects lagging economic growth rates. These results may simply indicate that more stagnant economies have more wage inequality.

The relative accessibility of jobs for central city residents (fourth panel) has no significant effect on wage inequality. The evidence on the effects of MSA racial composition and segmentation on wage and salary inequality among individual workers is consistent with the evidence for the various measures of income inequality among households. MSAs with more African Americans do not have more wage and salary inequality; neither residential segregation by race nor income and governmental segmentation has an effect on wage and salary inequality.

CONCLUSIONS

There is no positive relationship between MSA income inequality (measured in a variety of ways for households and individuals) and the relative representation of African Americans within MSAs. This result is consistent with the view that current discrimination accounts for racial differentials in income, poverty, and earnings within MSAs. There is no evidence that MSAs with proportionately more African Americans have higher poverty rates, household income inequality, or individual wage inequality. Rather, MSAs with more African Americans are more likely to have poverty concentrated in their central cities. Race thus affects *which* residents are poor in the MSA but has no effect on the proportion or number of persons who are poor.

There also is no correlation between MSA income inequality, no matter how it is measured, and either residential segregation by race, local government fragmentation, or relative job suburbanization. Because these characteristics of the economy do not appear to influence aggregate economic outcomes for the MSA, there is no evidence that they affect overall productivity in the region. There is evidence, however, that poverty becomes more concentrated in the central city as racial segregation and, possibly, local government fragmentation increase. The greater spatial concentrations mean that racial segregation (and the governmental segmentation that often accompanies it) isolates the poor but does not contribute directly to their poverty.

REFERENCES

Danziger, Sheldon. 1976. "Determinants of the Level and Distribution of Family Income in Metropolitan Areas, 1969." *Land Economics* 52(4): 467–78.

Farbman, Michael. 1975. "The Size Distribution of Family Income in W.S. SMSAs, 1959." *Review of Income and Wealth* 21(2): 217–37.

Garofalo, Gasper, and Michael S. Fogarty. 1979. "Urban Inequality and City Size: An Examination of Alternative Hypotheses for Large and Small Cities." *Review of Economics and Statistics* 61(3): 381–88.

Holzer, Harry J. 1991. "The Spatial Mismatch Hypothesis: What Has the Evidence Shown?" *Urban Studies* 28(1): 105–22.

Ihlanfeldt, Keith R. 1992. *Job Accessibility and the Employment and School Enrollment of Teenagers.* Kalamazoo, Mich.: W.E. Upjohn Institute for Employment Research.

Jencks, Christopher, and Susan E. Mayer. 1990. "Residential Segregation, Job Proximity, and Black Job Opportunities." In *Inner-City Poverty in the United States,* edited by Lawrence E. Lynn Jr. and Michael G. H. McGeary. Washington, D.C.: National Academy Press.

Kain, John F. 1968. "Housing Segregation, Negro Employment, and Metropolitan Decentralization." *Quarterly Journal of Economics* 82(May): 175–97.

———. 1992. "The Spatial Mismatch Hypothesis: Three Decades Later." *Housing Policy Debate* 3(2): 371–460.

Madden, Janice Fanning. 2000. *Changes in Income Inequality within U.S. Metropolitan Areas.* Kalamazoo, Mich.: W.E. Upjohn Institute for Employment Research.

Manski, Charles F. 1993. "Identification of Endogenous Social Effects: The Reflection Problem." *Review of Economic Studies* 60(3): 531–42.

Massey, Douglas S., and Nancy A. Denton. 1993. *American Apartheid: Segregation and the Making of the Underclass.* Cambridge, Mass.: Harvard University Press.

Nord, Stephen. 1980a. "An Empirical Analysis of Income Inequality and City Size." *Southern Economic Journal* 40(6): 863–72.

———. 1980b. "Income Inequality and City Size: An Examination of Alternative Hypotheses for Large and Small Cities." *Southern Economic Journal* 40(6): 863–72.

Wilson, William J. 1987. *The Truly Disadvantaged: The Inner City, the Underclass, and Public Policy.* Chicago: University of Chicago Press.

—— Chapter 12 ——

Segregation and Violent Crime in Urban America

Douglas S. Massey

Americans believe they are living through an unprecedented boom in violent crime. They are wrong. Serious crimes reported to the police actually dropped 3 percent during 1994 and 1995, and the murder rate fell 9 percent from 1980 to 1992. These declines do not stem from the underreporting of crimes to the police, since similar shifts are evident in nationwide surveys carried out by the National Institute of Justice. According to their data, criminal victimization rates are at their lowest levels in two decades: the reported incidence of aggravated assault and robbery dropped 11 percent between 1973 and 1992, the victimization rate for rape fell 28 percent, the burglary rate fell 30 percent. Over roughly the same period, the percentage of households experiencing a crime fell substantially, from 32 to 25 percent of the population (Zucchino 1994).

One would never guess that crime rates were on the wane by watching television, however. News coverage of violent crime by the three major networks doubled from 1992 to 1993, while coverage of murders tripled (Zucchino 1994). In addition, a spate of new reality-based cop shows, rescue programs, and tabloid offerings has given crime extensive airplay *after* the nightly news. Despite constant or declining crime rates in the United States, therefore, Americans are *exposed*, albeit vicariously, to more crime and violence than ever before; consequently they feel more vulnerable and threatened.

317

These feelings are exacerbated by two very real shifts in the nature of crime in the United States. Although rates of crime are declining, those crimes that are committed are more likely to involve guns and are more likely to be committed by children (Zucchino 1994). As a result, crime has become more lethal, and the age of both criminals and victims has fallen. Crime now seems more "senseless" because deadly acts are carried out by people too young to realize the implications of their decisions. Altercations that twenty years ago would have ended in a fistfight and a bloody nose now terminate in a corpse riddled with twenty-millimeter bullets fired from an automatic machine pistol.

In addition to the rise in coverage of violent crime, the increasing use of lethal weapons, and the growing involvement of children in criminal activity, there is one more fact about contemporary crime that increases its visibility and resonates strongly in the American psyche: race. Although rates of crime may be going down for the United States generally, they are spiraling upward for one specific group of Americans: those of African origin.

According to a 1992 National Institute of Justice survey, African Americans are now more likely to become victims of violence than at any point in the past two decades (Zucchino 1994). Black teenagers are eleven times more likely to be shot to death and nine times more likely to be murdered than their white counterparts. Among black males, in particular, homicide rates have skyrocketed. Whereas black men were killed at the rate of 45 per 100,000 in 1960, by 1990 the rate was 140 per 100,000, compared with a figure of around 20 per 100,000 for white males (still the highest rate in the industrial world; see Zucchino 1994). This alarming trend has prompted some observers to dub young black men "an endangered species" (Prothrow-Stith and Weissman 1991, 64).

Thus when television viewers (who are mostly white) see rising criminal violence on television, the people they see committing increasingly lethal crimes are predominantly young, male, and black, a fact that carries profound and disturbing consequences for American race relations. Although virtually all the victims of black criminals are also black (94 percent of those killed by black murderers, for example, are African American), the people whom viewers learn to fear are young black men. As a result, calls for harsher sentences, more police, and tougher treatment inevitably carry strong racial overtones, since such measures will be directed predominantly at African American males.

A variety of theories have been put forth to explain the new wave of violent crime in black America. Some observers have attributed black violence to the unique set of stresses experienced by urban black communities (see Rose and McClain 1990). Others have linked it to persistent racial inequality, which has produced frustration that is expressed as violence (Blau and Blau 1982; Blau and Golden 1986; Messner and Golden 1985; Sampson 1986). Others argue that black crime is a natural consequence of prolonged poverty, joblessness, and income deprivation (Bailey 1984; Williams 1984; Loftin and Parker 1985; Sampson 1985, 1987; Williams and Flewelling 1988). Still others hold that it stems from a distinctive subculture that accepts and condones high levels of violence (Curtis 1975). Herrnstein and Murray (1994) have gone so far as to imply that black criminality stems from the lower intelligence of African Americans.

Missing from all of these explanations is any serious attempt to come to terms with the most salient and far-reaching fact about black America: its high degree of residential segregation. Simply put, African Americans are unique: they are more segregated than any other racial or ethnic group in the United States, now or at any point in the country's history (Massey and Denton 1993). Blacks are segregated so highly, and on so many geographic dimensions simultaneously, that Massey and Denton (1989) have coined the term hypersegregation to describe their situation. According to the 1990 census, blacks in twenty metropolitan areas, containing nearly 40 percent of the African American population, live under conditions of hypersegregation (Denton 1994).

This unusual degree of segregation is largely involuntary and stems from the operation of three interrelated and mutually reinforcing forces in American society: high levels of institutionalized discrimination in the real estate and banking industries, high levels of prejudice among whites against blacks as potential neighbors, and discriminatory public policies implemented by whites at all levels of government (see Massey and Denton 1993; Farley et al. 1994; Yinger 1995). Racial segregation is not simply a historical legacy of past prejudice and discrimination. On the con-

trary, it is actively perpetuated by institutional actions, private behaviors, and public policies that continue to the present day (see
Galster 1990a, 1990b, 1990c).

A growing body of research has examined the deleterious
consequences of segregation for the black community, linking it
to high rates of joblessness, unwed parenthood, welfare dependency, infant mortality, and poverty (see the arguments and evidence presented in Massey and Denton 1993; Galster and Killen
1994; Yinger 1995). With two exceptions, however, neither theorists nor researchers have sought to link racial segregation to the
cycle of violent crime now overtaking inner cities, but when the
link has been examined, it has proven to be quite strong.

Logan and Messner (1987) study the connection between segregation and crime using a sample of suburbs surrounding fifty-
four metropolitan areas. They measure the degree of segregation
between blacks and whites across municipalities within suburban
rings and relate it to the rate of suburban crime, while statistically
controlling for other factors such as poverty, population mobility,
the minority percentage, age composition, and population size.
They find that racial segregation was very strongly associated with
rates of violent crime in both 1970 and 1980. According to their
results, the more racially segregated a suburban ring is, the higher
is its rate of violent crime.

Although Logan and Messner (1987) find a clear, positive relationship between segregation and criminal violence, the level of
black-white segregation is not the strongest predictor in their statistical model; other factors, such as poverty and income inequality appear to carry more explanatory weight. The investigators,
however, do not examine the effect of racial segregation on *black*
crime rates; they only examine the relationship between racial
segregation and *overall* rates of crime in suburban rings. Since
blacks constitute a small fraction of most suburban populations,
the crimes they commit would not be expected to have a large
effect on overall rates, even if segregation were strongly related to
the incidence of black crime.

In order to circumvent this problem, Peterson and Krivo
(1993) study the relationship between black segregation and black
homicide in 125 central cities. They find that black-white segregation is by far the most important variable in explaining intercity
variation in the black murder rate, dwarfing the effect of control

factors such as income inequality, poverty, education, occupation, age composition, population size, and region. Standardized coefficients show that the effect of segregation is 2.5 times that of the next closest factor in their statistical model.

When Peterson and Krivo (1993) break homicide rates down into murders committed by different types of persons—family members, acquaintances, and strangers—they find that segregation is not related to homicide within families; it only predicts murder between acquaintances and strangers. In other words, whatever segregation is doing to influence rates of homicide in urban black communities, the causal processes operate largely outside the home and within the public sphere. The Peterson-Krivo study provides strong prima facia evidence of a direct link between high levels of segregation and high rates of violent crime within black America. Nonetheless, social scientists have paid scant attention to segregation as a possible explanatory factor in accounting for the recent wave of criminal violence in inner cities.

The purpose of this chapter is to explain in theoretical terms the link between segregation and violent crime and to show logically how high levels of racial segregation in U.S. metropolitan areas help to bring about a distinctive pattern of violence within urban black communities. In particular, I show that two conditions known to exist within urban America—high levels of black segregation and high rates of black poverty—interact to create a unique ecological niche for black Americans, within which violent behavior becomes a logical, rational adaptation. I then review recent ethnographic research on racially isolated, crime-ridden areas to show how residents adapt behaviorally to this structurally produced environment. I then attempt to explain why it has been so difficult to implement policies that promote desegregation, pointing out the economic and political benefits that whites derive from residential segregation. I conclude with alternative scenarios for the future of urban America.

CREATING THE NICHE OF VIOLENCE

High rates of crime are structurally built into the experience of urban blacks by virtue of their residential segregation because, during periods of economic dislocation, segregation concentrates poverty and anything associated with it. Since crime and violence are strongly correlated with income deprivation, any social process that concentrates poverty also concentrates crime and violence to create an ecological niche characterized by a high risk of physical injury, violent death, and criminal victimization.

In a racially segregated city, any increase in black poverty is necessarily confined to a small number of geographically isolated and racially homogeneous neighborhoods. During times of recession, therefore, viable and economically stable black neighborhoods are transformed into areas of intense socioeconomic deprivation, where joblessness, welfare dependency, and single parenthood become the norm and where crime and social disorder are inextricably woven into the fabric of daily life. The coincidence of rising poverty and high levels of segregation *guarantees* that blacks will be exposed to a social and economic environment that is much harsher than anything experienced by whites.

Scientists customarily demonstrate the effect of one variable on another by carrying out an experiment. In an experiment, all factors except the one under investigation are held constant, and the investigator then manipulates it to observe the effect on some outcome of interest. Social scientists cannot, of course, conduct experiments in the social world. They cannot randomly assign blacks to live in segregated and integrated urban cities, raise the rate of black poverty, and observe what happens to the geographic concentration of poverty.

They can, however, carry out the equivalent of a laboratory experiment by defining hypothetical cities, giving them constant characteristics that correspond to those in the real world, and then varying the level of racial segregation and black poverty to observe what happens to the geographic concentration of poverty. In prior work (Massey 1990), I have carried out just such an exercise, the results of which are summarized in table 12.1.

To carry out the experiment, I begin with an ideal city of 96,000 whites, 32,000 blacks, and sixteen neighborhoods of 8,000 residents each, yielding a total city population with 128,000 inhabitants and a black percentage of 25 percent. Blacks are initially assumed to have a poverty rate of 20 percent, compared to 10 percent for whites. I then raise the black poverty rate to 30 percent, while keeping the white rate constant to replicate trends that

TABLE 12.1 **Effect of Rising Black-White Segregation and Rising Rates of Black Poverty on the Geographic Concentration of Poverty and Crime in Black Neighborhoods (Percentage)**

Segregation and Black Poverty Rate	For Typical Poor Black Person	
	Neighborhood Poverty Rate	Neighborhood Crime Rate
Without class segregation		
Racially integrated city		
Black poverty rate 20 percent	12.5	47.9
Black poverty rate 30 percent	15.0	49.9
Racially segregated city		
Black poverty rate 20 percent	20.0	52.4
Black poverty rate 30 percent	30.0	60.3
With class segregation		
Racially integrated city		
Black poverty rate 20 percent	25.0	57.8
Black poverty rate 30 percent	30.0	60.3
Racially segregated city		
Black poverty rate 20 percent	40.0	69.7
Black poverty rate 30 percent	60.0	84.0

Source: Massey 1990.

actually occurred in large American cities during the 1970s and 1980s, particularly those in the Northeast and Midwest (see Massey and Eggers 1990; Abramson and Tobin 1994).

The experiment consists of examining what happens to the geographic concentration of poverty when this shift in black poverty occurs under different conditions of class and racial segregation. Concentrated poverty occurs when poor people live in very poor places. In the original experiment, I perform the simulation using two levels of class segregation (no segregation by income and high segregation by income) and four levels of racial segregation (complete integration, low segregation, high segregation, and complete segregation). For simplicity, table 12.1 reports the extreme cases of low and high class segregation and of no and complete racial segregation. The full range of assumptions may be viewed in Massey (1990).

The figures in the first column show how poverty is concentrated geographically whenever the overall rate of poverty increases in a racially segregated group. The top panel illustrates what happens under the assumption of no class segregation among blacks (that is, poor and nonpoor blacks display no propensity to live in different neighborhoods). This is the simplest case and displays in the most straightforward fashion the mechanism by which segregation concentrates poverty, so I consider it first.

Under conditions of racial integration, the neighborhood poverty rate experienced by the average black citizen increases from 12.5 to 15.0 percent as a result of the shift in black poverty rates from 20 to 30 percent. That is, after the increase in black poverty the average poor African American lives in a neighborhood where 15 percent of the people are poor. Although the black poverty rate itself increases from 20 to 30 percent, in an integrated city only 25 percent of the inhabitants of each neighborhood are black, while the remaining 75 percent are white, so the effect of rising black poverty is buffered by the presence of a large number of whites who are not poor. The increase in black poverty is spread widely among many integrated neighborhoods, and in each place the overall increase in poverty is muted because most residents are whites whose poverty rate does not rise. After the period of economic dislocation, therefore, the rate of neighborhood poverty experienced by blacks in a racially integrated city is just slightly higher than it was before.

Under conditions of racial segregation, in contrast, the increase in black poverty is not spread evenly around the city, and there are no whites within neighborhoods where blacks live to buffer the effect of rising black poverty. All of the increase in black poverty is absorbed by a small number of all-black neighborhoods that are clustered together and spatially isolated from the rest of the city. As a result, when the overall rate of black poverty increases from 20 to 30 percent, the rate of poverty experienced by poor blacks in their neighborhoods *must* likewise increase from 20 to 30 percent. When all blacks are confined to 100 percent black neighborhoods, any increase in black poverty *necessarily* yields a sharp increase in the geographic concentration of poverty: no other outcome is possible.

These results illustrate clearly the underlying mechanism by which rising segregation and increasing poverty interact to produce an increase in the geographic concentration of poverty. Moving from racial integration and a black poverty rate of 20 percent to racial segregation and a black poverty rate of 30 percent yields a sharp increase (from 12.5 to 30 percent) in the level of poverty that poor blacks are exposed to in the neighborhoods where they live.

Although these results are clear, the simulation is unrealistic in the sense that no class segregation is assumed. In reality, of course, poor and nonpoor blacks tend to live apart from one another. Although incorporating class segregation into the simulation makes the mathematics somewhat more complicated, the basic principle is the same: racial segregation still concentrates poor blacks within a small number of neighborhoods and raises the rate of poverty to which they are exposed, only now *poor* black neighborhoods bear the brunt of the increase in black poverty.

The addition of class segregation to the simulation exacerbates the degree of poverty concentration that racial segregation imposes on poor blacks because of racial segregation. Given class segregation and a black poverty rate of 20 percent, the typical poor black resident lives in a neighborhood that is 25 percent poor if the city is not segregated by race; but the neighborhood poverty rate becomes 40 percent poor if racial segregation is also imposed. When the overall rate of black poverty is increased to 30 percent, the neighborhood poverty rate experienced by poor blacks jumps to 60 percent under conditions of racial segregation. In a city segregated by race as well as class, therefore, an increase in black poverty will constrain poor blacks to live in a social world where most of their friends and neighbors are also poor.

In short, rising black poverty and racial segregation interact to produce a sharp increase in the geographic concentration of poverty. Under general conditions of class segregation, moving from a city with no racial segregation and a black poverty rate of 20 percent to complete racial segregation and a black poverty rate of 30 percent means the difference between a residential environment where the vast majority of people are not poor (a neighborhood poverty rate of 25 percent) to one where a large majority of people live below the poverty line (a neighborhood poverty rate of 60 percent). All other conditions are held constant, so the difference is entirely due to the increase in black poverty and racial segregation.

As poverty is concentrated, of course, all things associated with it are concentrated, including crime. In earlier work, I use data from Philadelphia to estimate the empirical relationship between neighborhood poverty rates and major crime rates, controlling for racial composition (Massey 1990). Major crimes include murder, rape, aggravated assault, robbery, burglary, larceny, and auto theft. Using least squares regression, I estimate the relationship between crime and poverty to be major crime rate = 36.55 + 0.02 (percentage white) + 0.79 (poverty rate), where the units are census tracts and crime rates are expressed per one thousand inhabitants.

This formula is applied to predict the crime rate associated with each neighborhood poverty level generated by our simulation. The predicted crime rates are shown in the right-hand column of table 12.1. Although I show predictions for scenarios with and without class segregation, I focus on the realistic case of a class-segregated city and consider what happens to neighborhood crime rates when black poverty rises under varying conditions of racial segregation.

In the absence of racial segregation, the level of crime to which poor blacks are exposed in a class-segregated city increases modestly from 57.8 to 60.3 percent as a result of the increase in overall black poverty, a small rise that few inhabitants of the neighborhood probably would notice. When the same increase in black poverty occurs under conditions of racial segregation, however, the neighborhood crime rate increases rather dramatically from 69.7 to 84.0 percent. The difference between these extremes—a neighborhood crime rate of 57.8 percent and a neighborhood crime rate of 84.0 percent—is the difference between a city with no racial segregation and a black poverty rate of 20 percent and a city with complete racial segregation and a poverty rate of 30 percent. Everything else, including class segregation, has been held constant.

This dramatic 45 percent difference in the concentration of crime stems entirely from the interaction of segregation with rising poverty, yielding two social environments that are diametrically opposed to one another. With a crime rate of 57.8 percent, the likelihood that a person will be victimized over a ten-year period is about 0.45; with a crime rate of 84.0 percent the probability is

0.59. In one case, therefore, a typical person has better than even odds of not being victimized, whereas in the other case, the same person more likely than not will become the victim of a major crime.

Thus segregation interacts with rising black poverty to concentrate poverty geographically and, in concentrating poverty, to concentrate crime, thus creating an ecological niche characterized by a high level of violence and a high risk of victimization. The concentration of crime is brought about by just two conditions that we know to have characterized U.S. metropolitan areas during the 1970s and 1980s: high levels of racial segregation and rising rates of black poverty. Given the correlation between poverty and crime, the concentration of crime follows axiomatically from these structural conditions: no other outcome is possible.

The ecological niche created by racial segregation and high black poverty defines the social environment to which poor blacks must adapt. Given the barriers to black residential mobility, escape is difficult, if not impossible. How does a person adapt to a harsh environment where violence is endemic, the odds of criminal victimization are high, and the risk of death or injury substantial? The most logical individual adaptation is to become violent oneself. By adopting a threatening demeanor, cultivating a reputation for the use of force, and selectively backing up that reputation with actual violence, one can deter potential criminals and increase the odds of survival.

In a social world characterized by endemic, exogenously induced violence, therefore, violent behavior and an obsessive concern with respect become rational strategies for survival. Given a geographic concentration of violence, some people within the community are sure to adopt violent attitudes and behavior as survival strategies. As more people adopt more violent strategies for self-preservation, the average level of violence within the niche rises, leading others to adopt more violent behavior. As the average level of violence rises over time, more people adopt increasingly violent strategies to protect themselves from the growing threat of victimization, ultimately producing a self-perpetuating upward spiral of crime and violence.

Although a cycle of black violence may follow axiomatically from racial segregation and black poverty, what has made the spiral so frightening and appalling in recent years is the concomitant availability of lethal weapons of spectacular firepower. Precisely at the moment when forces in U.S. society were interacting to maximize the conditions for violence in one segment of the population, guns became cheaper, more deadly, and less controlled than ever. The existence of a racially distinctive ecological niche of violence within a society that has chosen to permit unparalleled access to automatic weapons can only produce one outcome: the spectacle of black men killing each other in increasingly violent ways.

Thus racial segregation is deeply implicated in the tide of violence that is sweeping black America. The transformation of the urban economy from manufacturing to services, the suburbanization of employment, the decline in the real value of welfare, and the stagnation of wages combined over the past two decades to raise the rate of black poverty, but high levels of segregation confined this increased poverty to a small number of racially isolated neighborhoods clustered around the urban core. As a result, the concentration of poverty was dramatically increased within segregated black communities to create an ecological niche in which crime was prevalent and violence a logical adaptation to the harsh conditions of daily life.

ADAPTING TO THE NICHE OF VIOLENCE

This theoretical explanation for the rising tide of black violence is generally consistent with the observed facts. It explains the strong association between racial segregation and crime rates observed by Logan and Messner (1987); it explains the findings of Peterson and Krivo (1993) that segregation is associated with killings between strangers and acquaintances, but not relatives; it explains why crime rates continue to rise in the black community even though they are falling for other groups (Zucchino 1994); and it explains why repressive police measures have done little to stem the tide of black violence, since they do not address the fundamental causes of black crime.

Even though the theory of segregation explicitly links high rates of black crime to structural arrangements in society, ultimately it is a theory of micro-behavior: it makes specific predictions about how people adapt to conditions of life that have been imposed on them by virtue of their confinement to an ecological niche characterized by extreme levels of violence that cannot be avoided. Building a prima facie case for a connection between segregation and crime, therefore, requires information about how people negotiate the difficult conditions of life in poor, inner-city neighborhoods.

Anderson (1994, 1999) has carried out precisely this sort of analysis. His ethnographic research draws on years of participant observation within one poor black neighborhood of Philadelphia, a city that manifestly exhibits the structural predeterminants of concentrated poverty and violence. Not only is Philadelphia characterized by a very high rate of black poverty (according to the 1990 census it stood at 39 percent, compared with just 8 percent for whites), it also is one of the metropolitan areas that Massey and Denton (1989) describe as hypersegregated, owing to the extreme segregation of blacks on multiple geographic dimensions, a condition that Denton (1994) has reconfirmed as of 1990.

As a result of these two features of Philadelphia's social structure—high segregation and high black poverty—Massey and Eggers (1990) find a remarkably high concentration of black poverty. According to their calculations, the average poor black family lived in a neighborhood that was 30 percent poor in 1980, whereas the average poor white family lived in a neighborhood that was only 10 percent poor. An average value of 30 percent means that many poor black families experience substantially higher rates of neighborhood poverty, in some cases living in neighborhoods where more than 50 percent of the families are below the poverty line. Poor whites almost never live in such neighborhoods (Massey, Gross, and Eggers 1992).

The specific neighborhood studied by Anderson (1994, 82) typifies the ecological niche of violence that follows from Philadelphia's structural conditions: it is a place of "muggings, burglaries, car jackings, and drug-related shootings, all of which may leave their victims or innocent bystanders dead." According to Anderson, this social environment reflects the disproportionate concentration of "street families" within it. People from such families

show a lack of consideration for other people and have a rather superficial sense of family and community . . . [Their lives are] marked by disorganization. In the most desperate circumstances [they] frequently have a limited understanding of priorities and consequences, and so frustrations mount over bills, food, and, at times, drink, cigarettes, and drugs. Some tend toward self-destructive behavior. [Anderson 1994, 83.]

Anderson links this destructive behavior to persistent poverty:

The seeming intractability of their situation, caused in large part by the lack of well-paying jobs and the persistence of racial discrimination, has engendered deep-seated bitterness and anger in many of the most desperate and poorest blacks. . . . [T]he frustrations of persistent poverty shorten the fuse in such people—contributing to a lack of patience with anyone, child or adult, who irritates them. [Anderson 1994, 83]

In other words, long-term poverty produces the proclivity toward violence. By concentrating the persistently poor in certain neighborhoods, segregation concentrates a "street orientation" to create a social world characterized by high levels of interpersonal hostility and aggression.

Low-income black neighborhoods also contain what Anderson (1994, 82–83) calls "decent families," who

tend to accept mainstream values more fully and attempt to instill them in their children. . . . They value hard work and self-reliance and are willing to sacrifice for their children. . . . Extremely aware of the problematic and often dangerous environment in which they reside, decent parents tend to be strict in their child-rearing practices, encouraging children to respect authority and walk a straight moral line.

Even if children come from decent families, however, they must adapt to a social world that is disproportionately influenced by the culture, values, and behavior of the street. According to Anderson (1994, 81–82), "Simply living in such an environment places young people at special risk of falling victim to aggressive behavior. . . . Above all, this environment means that even youngsters whose home lives reflect mainstream values . . . must be able to handle themselves in a street-oriented environment."

Thus the fundamental need to adapt to conditions of endemic violence that are structurally imposed and inescapable has led to the evolution within poor, inner-city black neighborhoods of a "code of the streets" that encourages and promotes the use of force, even among "decent" families. According to Anderson (1994, 82), this code

> amounts to a set of informal rules governing interpersonal public behavior, including violence. The rules prescribe both a proper comportment and a proper way to respond if challenged. They regulate the use of violence and so allow those who are inclined to aggression to precipitate violent encounters in an approved way. The rules have been established and enforced mainly by the street-oriented, but *on the streets the distinction between street and decent is often irrelevant*; everybody knows that if the rules are violated, there are penalties. Knowledge of the code is thus largely defensive; it is literally necessary for operating in public. Therefore, even though families with a decency orientation are usually opposed to the values of the code, they often reluctantly encourage their children's familiarity with it to enable them to negotiate the inner-city environment. [Emphasis added.]

This passage provides, in essence, a succinct description of the self-perpetuation of violence through rational, micro-level decisions taken by families and individuals who are forced to confront a hostile social environment. Asking residents of poor, racially isolated neighborhoods to "choose" a less violent path or to say "no" to the temptation of the streets is absurd, given the threatening character of the niche in which they live. To survive on the streets of segregated, inner-city America, one must learn, and to a significant extent internalize, the code of violence. In this way, violent behavior is passed from person to person and parents to children in a self-feeding, escalating fashion, precisely in the manner predicted by the theory of residential segregation.

A primary concern of those invested in the code of the streets is the maintenance of respect, which is "loosely defined as being treated 'right,' or granted the deference one deserves" (Anderson 1994, 82). Within a hostile and violent social world, the maintenance of respect is much more than a vain concern with appearances; it a critical social resource that promotes physical security and survival, since "with the right amount of respect [a person] can avoid 'being bothered' in public" (Anderson 1994, 82).

In essence, the code of the streets provides a framework for negotiating respect. In a niche of violence, respect can only be built and maintained through the strategic use of force. Beginning in childhood and continuing into adulthood, young people are socialized to fight in order to earn respect. In doing so, they lower their odds of victimization and forestall an even larger number of fights in the future. "The violent resolution of disputes, the hitting and cursing, gains social reinforcement. The child in effect is initiated into a system that is really a way of campaigning for respect. . . . Many parents actually impose sanctions if a child is not sufficiently aggressive" (Anderson 1994, 87).

Within an ecological niche characterized by high rates of crime and violence, therefore, respect is a scarce, but important, social resource that individuals attempt to cultivate in order to lower the risk of criminal victimization. The cultivation of respect through the strategic use of violence represents a logical, instrumental strategy pursued by rational individuals as a means of adapting to the harsh conditions of daily life created by structural arrangements in American society that are beyond the individual's control.

The inhabitants of poor, inner-city neighborhoods not only pursue individual strategies to reduce their risk of victimization; they also act collectively. Perhaps the most common collective response to the niche of violence is the formation of gangs, whose role and function in low-income neighborhoods have been studied in detail by Sánchez Jankowski (1991). In essence, gangs collectivize the code of the streets, which he calls "defiant individualism," through an explicit organizational structure that controls and regulates the use of force.

According to Sánchez Jankowski (1991, 45), individuals join gangs for a variety of reasons, but one central motivation is self-protection: "Individuals also join gangs because they believe the gang can provide them with personal protection from the predatory elements active in low-income neighborhoods." People, quite rationally, "are either tired of being on the alert or want to reduce the probability of danger to a level that allows them to devote more time to their effort to secure more money."

Joining a gang thus provides a way of substantially increasing one's respect, while minimizing personal effort and risk. Membership in a gang provides a deterrent against attacks and victimization, since an attack on one gang member constitutes an attack on the group and can trigger a violent response not simply from the victim, but from all members of the gang. Whereas respect is a form of human capital that individuals must laboriously cultivate through their actions and behavior, gang membership is a form of social capital that may be accessed simply by joining up.

Gangs also provide benefits to the neighborhood as a whole. Although gangs do not eliminate violence, they at least control and regulate it and generally deflect it away from territories and groups they cover. Residents of the neighborhoods studied by Sánchez Jankowski (1991, 184) "emphasized that gangs are more able to deter crime in their community than the police because gang members are distributed throughout the community and are able to identify strangers. . . . [T]hey are not restrained from taking immediate action against anyone considered a community threat. . . . [And] unlike the police, the gang can administer physical injury without regard to laws designed to restrain such action."

Gangs also provide special protection for the weakest members of the community: children and the elderly. According to Sánchez Jankowski (1991, 185–86),

> In 84 percent (thirty-one) of the cases that I studied, gangs provided at least escort service for anyone in the community who asked for it. . . . In addition to trying to assume responsibility for protecting residents from being accosted and/or robbed, all but three of the gangs that I studied also tried to protect them from other social predators, like loan sharks, unethical landlords, and/or store owners who overcharged for their products.

Despite these benefits to individuals and communities, gangs carry costs since they inevitably become engines of violence themselves. In order to ensure their own survival as organizations, gangs must acquire capital, which moves them into illegal activities, notably the marketing and distribution of narcotics and other illegal drugs. The resulting proliferation of addicts promotes crime indirectly, since unemployed junkies must acquire cash to support their habit, thereby inflating rates of robbery and burglary. In addition, to survive, gangs often must use force against rival gangs who seek to enter their market areas or zones of social influence. They also must apply force whenever the well-being or reputation of a member is threatened. Rather than a spiral of individual-level violence, therefore, gangs more often produce a spiral of collective violence between competing organizations.

Thus two detailed ethnographic studies of poor, inner-city

areas yield descriptions of individual and collective behavior that are consistent with the line of theoretical reasoning developed here. The ecological niche of violence promotes and perpetuates high levels of violence among blacks in two ways: by encouraging the formation of criminal gangs at the collective level and by fostering an obsessive concern for respect at the individual level. The wave of crime in urban black America is not simply a product of individual moral failings; it is an inevitable outgrowth of social conditions created by the coincidence of racial segregation and high rates of black poverty.

VIOLENCE AND THE POLITICS OF SEGREGATION

If segregation is a fundamental factor behind the crime wave now sweeping American inner cities, a logical question is why so little has been done to desegregate U.S. urban areas. In the years since passage of the 1968 Fair Housing Act, levels of black-white segregation have hardly changed, particularly in metropolitan areas with large black populations (see Farley and Frey 1994). In thirty metropolitan areas with the largest black populations, for example, the level of black isolation stood at sixty-nine in 1970 and sixty-seven in 1990 on a scale of zero to one hundred (Massey 1994).

A major reason for the lack of change is that most Americans, particularly whites, perceive themselves to benefit from the social arrangements that produce racial segregation. If poverty rates are higher for blacks, and if crime is associated with poverty, then by isolating blacks in segregated neighborhoods the rest of society insulates itself from the crime and other social problems that stem from the higher rate of black poverty.

The benefits accruing to the rest of society from racial exclusion are illustrated in table 12.2, which examines what happens to the neighborhood environment experienced by the average poor white person as a result of racial segregation. As before, I begin with an initial black poverty rate of 20 percent, compared with 10 percent for whites, and then raise the black rate to 30 percent, while keeping the white rate constant. This is intended to show what happens to the neighborhood of poor whites when a shift in

TABLE 12.2 **Effect of Rising Black-White Segregation and Rising Rates of Black Poverty on the Geographic Concentration of Poverty and Crime in White Neighborhoods (Percentage)**

	For Typical Poor White Person	
Segregation and Black Poverty Rate	Neighborhood Poverty Rate	Neighborhood Crime Rate
Without class segregation		
Racially integrated city		
Black poverty rate 20 percent	12.5	47.9
Black poverty rate 30 percent	15.0	49.9
Racially segregated city		
Black poverty rate 20 percent	10.0	46.5
Black poverty rate 30 percent	10.0	46.5
With class segregation		
Racially integrated city		
Black poverty rate 20 percent	25.0	57.8
Black poverty rate 30 percent	30.0	60.3
Racially segregated city		
Black poverty rate 20 percent	20.0	54.4
Black poverty rate 30 percent	20.0	54.4

Source: Massey 1990.

black poverty rates occurs under conditions of no and high class segregation and of no and complete racial segregation.

Assume that class segregation gives the most realistic assessment of what will happen to whites as a result of increasing black poverty and the imposition of racial segregation. In a city that is segregated by class, but not race, the average poor white person will inhabit a neighborhood where 25 percent of the residents are poor. Increasing the black poverty rate to 30 percent but keeping other conditions the same produces a relatively high neighborhood poverty rate of 30 percent.

Imposing racial segregation, however, yields substantially lower levels of neighborhood poverty for poor whites. Isolating blacks within their own neighborhoods means that only blacks experience the problems stemming from their elevated income deprivation: whites end up with lower rates of neighborhood poverty. In the simulation, the rate of poverty in the neighborhood of the average poor white person drops to 20 percent when racial segregation is imposed, a situation that does not change even if the black poverty rate is increased to 30 percent, since under conditions of racial segregation all of the increased poverty is, by definition, confined to black neighborhoods.

As a result of the lower rate of neighborhood poverty, therefore, poor whites experience significantly lower crime rates by imposing racial segregation, since crime follows poverty. Rather than a neighborhood crime rate of 60.3 percent (in a city with a black poverty rate of 30 percent and racial integration), whites experience a neighborhood crime rate that is roughly 11 percent lower at 54.4 percent (in a racially segregated city with the same poverty rate). By segregating blacks and their social problems, in other words, poor whites derive a benefit in the form of lower rates of neighborhood crime. Even though society as a whole may be damaged by this arrangement, and long-term costs may be greater, whites generally perceive themselves to be better off as a result of segregation.

In fact, this simulation understates the degree to which whites perceive themselves to be better off. In reality, whites do not compare their current crime rate with the one that would occur if there were no racial segregation, since they do not have an opportunity to observe the counterfactual situation of racial integration. Rather, they compare their neighborhood crime rate with the one they currently observe in segregated black communities. Instead of a crime rate of 60.3 percent in the counterfactual case of a racially integrated city, whites actually see a crime rate of 84.0 percent in segregated black communities, a differential of almost 50 percent. In contemplating desegregation, therefore, whites imagine themselves to be exposed to the high crime rates they observe in the ghetto, which are themselves a product of segregation.

Thus by creating a niche of violence and establishing the social conditions for a self-perpetuating cycle of crime, segregation paradoxically raises the perceived costs of desegregation for whites, while imposing ever higher penalties on blacks. In short, segregation simultaneously victimizes blacks, while giving whites greater incentive to maintain the residential status quo, leading to a vicious cycle whereby segregation promotes poverty among blacks, leading to behavior that hardens white prejudice and discrimination, which in turn promotes further socioeconomic damage to the black community, which leads to continued segregation (see Galster and Keeny 1988).

In addition to lower crime rates, racial segregation provides benefits to whites in the form of lower taxes. If blacks have a higher poverty rate than other groups in American society, then their inclusion within the same taxing district necessarily generates higher costs for the rest of society in the form of greater expenses for health, education, welfare, and criminal justice. To the extent that segregation isolates poor blacks within separate jurisdictions, it also lowers the tax burden for whites.

This outcome, however, requires that residential segregation occur not only at the neighborhood level but also at the administrative level. Although neighborhood-level segregation may confine blacks and their social problems to certain residential areas, if whites and blacks still live in the same municipality, whites still have to shoulder the costs of black poverty. If, however, blacks are segregated across *municipal* as well as neighborhood boundaries, not only can whites minimize their exposure to crime and other social problems but also, to a large extent, they can avoid paying the costs as well.

Historically, of course, blacks were isolated from whites across state and county boundaries. Prior to 1900 blacks resided largely in rural counties of the South, and most whites were neither exposed to problems arising from black poverty nor affected by the costs. Within the South, whites were protected from the deleterious consequences of black poverty by the Jim Crow system. With massive out-migration from the rural South to cities of both the North and South, however, this regional segregation ended, and whites and blacks came to occupy common municipalities around the United States.

As blacks moved into cities, successively higher levels of residential segregation were imposed to minimize racial mixing within neighborhoods (Lieberson 1980), but until 1950 this segregation occurred primarily at the level of blocks or census tracts. Up through World War II, urban blacks and whites lived under common municipal governments, forcing whites to share the costs of black social problems. After 1950, however, segregation increasingly occurred not only at the neighborhood level but also at the municipal level.

According to Massey and Hajnal (1995), the degree of segregation between blacks and whites across city boundaries steadily rose after 1950. Using an index of segregation that varies from zero to one hundred (the index of dissimilarity), they found that the level of black-white segregation increased from thirty-five to forty-nine from 1950 to 1990, an upward shift of 40 percent—or 10 percent a decade. The degree of black isolation within municipalities increased correspondingly.

During the postwar period, significant municipal-level segregation emerged throughout the urban hierarchy—in small and large cities located at the urban core, in suburbs, as well as in nonmetropolitan areas. Among cities with one hundred thousand or more inhabitants, for example, none was predominantly black in 1950; but by 1990, fourteen cities were at least half black (including Atlanta, Baltimore, Detroit, Gary, Newark, New Orleans, and Washington, D.C., among others). Among cities of twenty-five thousand or more inhabitants, only two municipalities were half black in 1950 (both in the South); by 1990 the number had increased to forty. Many observers have noted the recent emergence of black suburbs (Long and DeAre 1981; Logan and Schneider 1984; Stearns and Logan 1986; O'Hare and Frey 1992; Schneider and Phelan 1993); and at least one observer has documented the growth of black cities in nonmetropolitan areas of the South (Aiken 1990).

The segregation of blacks within all-black municipalities adds a new layer of isolation to that already achieved by segregation at the neighborhood level: fiscal isolation. Given segregation at the municipal level, whites not only benefit by limiting their exposure to crime and the other social problems arising from black poverty but also by escaping the financial burdens as well.

In summary, racial segregation persists in the United States because whites benefit from it. In undermining the socioeconomic status and well-being of African Americans and deepening their social problems, segregation simultaneously increases the incentives for whites to maintain the residential status quo. As social conditions in the nation's ghettos deteriorate, policies to promote desegregation become less popular politically, thereby making a resolution of the nation's crime problem that much more remote.

CONCLUSIONS: SEGREGATION AND CRIME

I have developed a line of theoretical reasoning that connects the rising tide of crime in inner-city black neighborhoods to basic structural features of American society, as opposed to the individual failings of African Americans. I have shown how two features of metropolitan social structure—high rates of black poverty and high levels of black segregation—interact to produce an ecological niche within which poverty is concentrated and crime is prevalent.

African Americans who are forced to inhabit this structurally produced niche must adapt to a violent social world where the chance of criminal victimization is great. According to ethnographic data from high-crime areas, adaptive responses to this environment have occurred at both the individual and collective level. At the individual level, rational actors attempt to build and cultivate respect through the strategic and frequent use of violence. A willingness to use violence provides a deterrent against predators inhabiting the niche and thereby lowers the odds of victimization. As such, it constitutes a valuable form of human capital in the ghetto. As more people adopt more violent strategies of survival, however, the average level of violence rises, causing even more people to adopt even high levels of violence, leading to a self-perpetuating cycle of violence.

At the collective level, people turn to gangs to protect themselves from the ongoing threat of violence. Membership in a gang gives an actor access to the deterrence of violence without having to build and cultivate an individual reputation for violence. A person simply taps into the respect accorded the gang though its reputation for the use of violence and mutual defense. Gang membership provides a valuable form of social capital that can significantly lower the odds of victimization within the niche of violence. Once again, however, gangs create new opportunities and motivations for the expression of violence and in the long run produce better-organized violence on a larger scale, even as they protect the interests of certain individuals.

Thus the present cycle of urban violence does not stem from

individual failings, but rather from basic structural features of urban society that create a niche of violence to which black Americans must adapt. Sadly, in promoting high levels of violence among blacks, segregation simultaneously gives whites a strong incentive to maintain the status quo and to perpetuate the ghetto as a basic feature of American life. As a result, segregation has grown more intense in recent years as it has moved beyond the neighborhood level to occur increasingly at the municipal level. At present, blacks and whites are not just socially isolated; they are fiscally isolated as well. Through municipal-level segregation, blacks are forced to bear a larger share of the costs of their own victimization, while whites escape the high costs of black poverty, at least in the short term.

Elsewhere I and others have outlined the federal policy initiatives that would need to be undertaken to end the legacy of American apartheid (see Massey and Denton 1993; Yinger 1995). Despite the fact that most of these policies were implemented by the Secretary of Housing and Urban Development, Henry Cisneros, during the first two years of the Clinton administration, it is hard to be optimistic about the future welfare of either cities or black America, given the understanding of the origins and nature of black crime developed here.

In the current political climate, which emphasizes a reduced role for government, limited discretionary spending at the federal level, and a profound reluctance to embrace race-specific remedies, the chances of a major new desegregation initiative seem remote indeed. Yet unless forceful action is undertaken soon to desegregate urban America, the cycle of black, urban violence can be expected to continue. As the cycle of violence continues, political support for a policy of desegregation will wither and become even more remote, perpetuating the multiple problems created by the coincidence of segregation and black poverty.

At present, the United States appears to be locked into a set of institutional arrangements that will only exacerbate racial inequalities, perpetuate urban violence, deepen the socioeconomic problems of African Americans, and erode the status and well-being of American cities. As central cities in general, and urban black communities in particular, continue to deteriorate fiscally, socially, and economically, the socioeconomic health of the nation will also erode. Despite the efforts of white Americans to escape through segregation, inevitably they will end up paying the costs—directly in the form of higher expenses for insurance, health care, criminal justice, security, and education and indirectly in the form of reduced competitiveness on world markets, a diminished quality of life, and a retreat from American democratic ideals.

"Segregation and Violent Crime in Urban America," by Douglas S. Massey, is a revised version of a paper also presented at the University of Pennsylvania Law School and published as "Getting Away with Murder: Segregation and Violent Crime" in the *University of Pennsylvania Law Review* 143(5, 1995): 1203–32.

REFERENCES

Abramson, Alan J., and Mitchell S. Tobin. 1994. "The Changing Geography of Metropolitan Opportunity: The Segregation of the Poor in U.S. Metropolitan Areas, 1970–1990." Paper presented at the 1994 Fannie Mae annual housing conference.

Aiken, Charles S. 1990. "A New Type of Black Ghetto in the Plantation South." *Annals of the Association of American Geographers* 80(2): 223–46.

Anderson, Elijah. 1994. "The Code of the Streets." *Atlantic Monthly* 273: 80–94.

———. 1999. *Code of the Street: Decency, Violence, and the Moral Life of the Inner City.* New York: Norton.

Bailey, William C. 1984. "Poverty, Inequality, and City Homicide Rates: Some Not So Unexpected Findings." *Criminology* 22(3): 531–50.

Blau, Judith R., and Peter M. Blau. 1982. "The Cost of Inequality: Metropolitan Structure and Violent Crime." *American Sociological Review* 47(1): 114–29.

Blau, Peter M., and Reid M. Golden. 1986. "Metropolitan Structure and Criminal Violence." *Sociological Quarterly* 27(1): 15–26.

Curtis, Lynn A. 1975. *Violence, Race, and Culture.* Lexington, Mass.: Lexington Books.

Denton, Nancy A. 1994. "Are African Americans Still Hypersegregated?" In *Residential Apartheid: The American Legacy,* edited by Robert D. Bullard, J. Eugene Grigsby III, and Charles Lee. CAAS Publications. Los Angeles: University of California, Los Angeles.

Farley, Reynolds, and William H. Frey. 1994. "Changes in the Segregation of Whites from Blacks during the 1980s: Small Steps toward a More Integrated Society." *American Sociological Review* 59(1): 23–45.

Farley, Reynolds, Charlotte Steeh, Maria Krysan, Tara Jackson, and Keith Reeves. 1994. "Stereotypes and Segregation: Neighborhoods in the Detroit Area." *American Journal of Sociology* 100(3): 750–80.

Galster, George C. 1990a. "Racial Discrimination in Housing Markets during the 1980s: A Review of the Audit Evidence." *Journal of Planning Education and Research* 9(2): 165–75.

———. 1990b. "Racial Steering by Real Estate Agents: Mechanisms and Motives." *Review of Black Political Economy* 19(1): 39–63.

———. 1990c. "Racial Steering in Urban Housing Markets: A Review of the Audit Evidence." *Review of Black Political Economy* 18(1): 105–29.

Galster, George C., and Mark Keeney. 1988. "Race, Residence, Discrimination, and Economic Opportunity: Modeling the Nexus of Urban Racial Phenomena." *Urban Affairs Quarterly* 24(1): 87–117.

Galster, George C., and Sean P. Killen. 1994. "The Geography of Metropolitan Opportunity: A Reconnaissance and Conceptual Framework." Paper presented at the 1994 Fannie Mae annual housing conference.

Herrnstein, Richard J., and Charles Murray. 1994. *Intelligence and Class Structure in American Life.* New York: Free Press.

Lieberson, Stanley. 1980. *A Piece of the Pie: Blacks and White Immigrants since 1880.* Berkeley: University of California Press.

Loftin, Colin, and Robert Nash Parker. 1985. "An Errors-in-Variable Model of the Effect of Poverty on Urban Homicide Rates." *Criminology* 23(3): 269–85.

Logan, John R., and Steven F. Messner. 1987. "Racial Residential Segregation and Suburban Violent Crime." *Social Science Quarterly* 68(3): 528–38.

Logan, John R., and Mark Schneider. 1984. "Racial Segregation and Racial Change in American Suburbs: 1970–1980." *American Journal of Sociology* 89(4): 874–88.

Long, Larry, and Diana DeAre. 1981. "The Suburbanization of Blacks." *American Demographics* 3(4): 17–44.

Massey, Douglas S. 1990. "American Apartheid: Segregation and the Making of the Underclass." *American Journal of Sociology* 96(2): 329–58.

———. 1994. "The Residential Segregation of Blacks, Hispanics, and Asians: 1970–1990." In *Immigration and the Changing Status of Race Relations,* edited by Gerald D. Jaynes. Charlotte: University of Virginia Press.

Massey, Douglas S., and Nancy A. Denton. 1989. "Hypersegregation in U.S. Metropolitan Areas: Black and Hispanic Segregation along Five Dimensions." *Demography* 26(3): 373–93.

————. 1993. *American Apartheid: Segregation and the Making of the Underclass.* Cambridge, Mass.: Harvard University Press.

Massey, Douglas S., and Mitchell L. Eggers. 1990. "The Ecology of Inequality: Minorities and the Concentration of Poverty, 1970–1980." *American Journal of Sociology* 95(5): 1153–89.

Massey, Douglas S., Andrew B. Gross, and Mitchell L. Eggers. 1992. "Segregation, the Concentration of Poverty, and the Life Chances of Individuals." *Social Science Research* 20(3): 397–420.

Massey, Douglas S., and Zoltan L. Hajnal. 1995. "The Changing Geographic Structure of Black-White Segregation in the United States." *Social Science Quarterly* 76(3): 527–42

Messner, Steven F., and Reid M. Golden. 1985. "Economic Sources of Homicide: Reconsidering the Effects of Poverty and Inequality." Paper presented at the annual meetings of the American Sociological Association.

O'Hare, William P., and William H. Frey. 1992. "Booming, Suburban, and Black." *American Demographics* 14(a): 30–38.

Peterson, Ruth D., and Lauren J. Krivo. 1993. "Racial Segregation and Black Urban Homicide." *Social Forces* 71(4): 1001–26.

Prothrow-Stith, Deborah, and Michaele Weissman. 1991. *Deadly Consequences.* New York: HarperCollins.

Rose, Harold M., and Paula D. McClain. 1990. *Race, Place, and Risk: Black Homicide in Urban America.* Albany: State University of New York Press.

Sampson, Robert J. 1985. "Race and Criminal Violence: A Demographically Disaggregated Analysis of Urban Homicide." *Crime and Delinquency* 31(1): 47–82.

————. 1986. "Effects of Inequality, Heterogeneity, and Urbanization on Intergroup Victimization." *Social Science Quarterly* 67(4): 751–66.

————. 1987. "Urban Black Violence: The Effect of Male Joblessness and Family Disruption." *American Journal of Sociology* 93(2): 348–82.

Sánchez Jankowski, Martín. 1991. *Islands in the Street: Gangs and American Urban Society.* Berkeley: University of California Press.

Schneider, Mark, and Thomas Phelan. 1993. "Black Suburbanization in the 1980s." *Demography* 30(2): 269–81.

Stearns, Linda B., and John R. Logan. 1986. "The Racial Structuring of the Housing Market and Segregation in Suburban Areas." *Social Forces* 65(1): 28–42.

Williams, Kirk R. 1984. "Economic Sources of Homicide: Reestimating the Effects of Poverty and Inequality." *American Sociological Review* 49(2): 283–89.

Williams, Kirk R., and Robert L. Flewelling. 1988. "The Social Production of Criminal Homicide: A Comparative Study of Disaggregated Rates in American Cities." *American Sociological Review* 53(3): 421–31.

Yinger, John. 1995. *Closed Doors, Lost Opportunities: The Causes, Consequences, and Cures for Racial and Ethnic Discrimination in Housing.* New York: Russell Sage Foundation.

Zucchino, David. 1994. "Call of the Streets Can Be Hard to Resist." *Philadelphia Inquirer,* November 13, 1994, p. 1.

— Part IV —

Race at Work and School

— Chapter 13 —

Gender, Race, Local Labor Markets, and Occupational Devaluation

Jerry A. Jacobs and Mary Blair-Loy

EMALE-DOMINATED OCCUPATIONS pay less than male-dominated fields with similar educational requirements. Many studies find that the higher the representation of women in an occupation, the lower the pay (England 1992; Kilbourne et al. 1994). Other studies focus on the pay of particular jobs, rather than on the broad aggregation of jobs that fall into the same occupational classification. These studies find an even more striking relationship between female concentration and low pay (Jacobs and Steinberg 1990, 1995; Tomaskovic-Devey 1993; Petersen and Morgan 1995). This devaluation of feminine work makes a significant contribution to the gender gap in wages.

The same issue has been explored with respect to race, yet national studies have not consistently found an effect of minority representation on wages (England 1992). Sorensen (1989) finds minority composition effects for white men, but not for other groups and only in some industries. Comparable worth studies conducted within organizations generally fail to find significant effects of racial composition on the earnings of jobs (Jacobs and Steinberg 1990; Orazem and Mattila 1989; see Baron and Newman 1990 for a counterexample). Tomaskovic-Devey (1993), for example, gathers survey data on jobs in North Carolina and finds dramatic evidence of gender effects on wages, but few statistically

significant race effects. Moreover, most studies find that controlling for education accounts for much of the apparent effect of
racial composition, while education accounts for little, if any, of
the gender composition effect.

Race and gender are often conceptualized similarly because
both are classic ascriptive variables. Individuals are born with
their race and sex fixed—neither can be altered without undertak-
ing extreme measures—and neither race nor gender is reducible
to class distinctions. Although cultural stereotypes differ for race
and gender, most researchers in this area expect to find similar
effects of race and gender composition on wages.

The assumption that race and gender should affect stratification processes in similar ways is held by sociologists of many theoretical persuasions. Studies as diverse as Siegel's (1971) research
on occupational prestige, England's (1992) national analysis of
comparable worth, Tomaskovic-Devey's (1995) analysis of North
Carolina employers, and Baron's analysis of the California civil
service (Baron and Newman 1990) all explore whether race and
gender have parallel effects on earnings processes. The inability
of researchers to detect consistent racial composition effects on
job rewards thus represents a puzzle for the sociological perspective on labor markets.

Race and gender can affect social stratification in many ways.
One way is through barriers to access; another way is through the
devaluation of jobs in which women and minorities concentrate.
The current findings show that African American men are allocated to positions that are established as low status for reasons
unconnected with race, while women are segregated into positions that are devalued in part because of women's presence.
These different processes, in turn, reflect different levels of educational attainment. Access to high-status occupations is constrained
for African Americans in part by their limited educational attainment. Given women's high educational attainment relative to
men, however, male privilege cannot be ensured with credential
screening alone. Instead, a high level of workplace segregation
between men and women, accompanied by a systematic devaluation of women's fields, must occur in order to preserve men's advantage in the workplace.

Still, it is curious that race does not appear to affect the valuation of jobs, while gender does. The goal of this chapter is to account for the presence of gender devaluation and the absence of consistent evidence of racial devaluation. We attempt to explain this puzzle by noting differences in the demographic distribution of women and African Americans in local and national labor markets. We focus on variation across metropolitan areas in order to highlight the distinctive position of these two groups and use 1990 census data to assess the effects of race and gender composition in local labor markets.

We begin by contrasting the composition of occupations by race and gender and then move on to develop hypotheses about the role of local labor markets in accounting for the devaluation of work. We then consider the relationship between minority concentration in cities and the race gap in earnings before introducing the data employed in our analysis. Our results consist of a descriptive analysis of the distribution of women and African Americans across occupations and metropolitan areas, followed by a regression analysis to test "local labor market" explanations for race and gender composition effects on wages.

COMPOSITION OF OCCUPATIONS
BY RACE AND GENDER

A primary reason that gender has a stronger effect on occupational earnings than does race is that there is more gender segregation in the labor market. In other words, there is more potential for gender to have an effect because women are more occupationally segregated from men than are African Americans from whites. Reskin and Cassirer (1996) calculate indexes of dissimilarity from the 1990 census for a variety of race-gender groups. They find that 55.3 percent of white women would have to change occupations in order to be distributed in the same manner as white men. For African American men, the degree of segregation from white men is only 30.0 percent; but among African Americans in general, the level of gender segregation is nearly as high as it is among whites ($D = 51.7$). Among women, the level of racial segregation is slightly lower than among men ($D = 26.6$).

Thus sex segregation is much higher than racial segregation no matter what comparison of race with sex is employed.

A second way in which gender differs from race is that many female-dominated occupations are *overwhelmingly* female. In contrast, no occupations exist in which African Americans comprise the majority of incumbents throughout the country. While many occupations are *disproportionately* African American (in that African Americans constitute a larger share of the occupation than the labor force as a whole), none of these occupations is ever *predominantly* African American in the way that many occupations are predominantly female.

Third, African Americans are not distributed evenly across locales; instead they are concentrated in certain metropolitan areas. This means that in some cities, occupations with the highest representation of African Americans are still overwhelmingly white. Women's labor force participation varies across metropolitan areas, but to a much more limited degree. Consequently, most female-dominated occupations are predominantly female in all areas.

The demographic differences by race and gender are important because many social processes are predicated on the presence of a clear majority of one group. The creation of occupational stereotypes, for example, requires a *typical* incumbent, not simply disproportionate representation of one group. Occupations thus develop clear gender associations in our culture: even young children can distinguish jobs typically performed by women from those typically performed by men (Stockard and McGee 1990; McGee and Stockard 1991; Nemerowicz 1979). These associations are only possible because stereotypically female work is performed overwhelmingly by women in all locales.

In contrast, fewer cultural stereotypes are associated with African American representation in occupations. Indeed, we are not aware of any study that has asked individuals to judge the racial composition of occupations. It thus is difficult to label a particular occupation as "African American" in the same way that a position can be labeled "female," because the proportion of African Americans in occupations varies significantly across cities. This fact does not deny the importance of racial stereotypes, of course; it simply suggests why racial stereotypes are associated with individual characteristics rather than occupational roles.

Social and geographic distributions by race and gender also have important implications for recruitment practices. Employers can expect to fill vacancies in female-dominated occupations with women regardless of the city in which they are located. The exclusive recruitment of one gender is possible only because women are available in all locales. In contrast, recruiting exclusively among African Americans would not be a successful strategy for employers in any occupation, and in many cities it would be an extremely foolhardy approach given the scarcity of African American workers who are available locally. Consequently, the recruitment of women into female-dominated occupations can become institutionalized throughout the country in a way that is simply not possible for African Americans. Employment stereotypes and nationally institutionalized recruitment processes require significant numbers of workers in targeted groups evenly distributed throughout the country. The demographics of women's employment fit these requirements, but the case of African Americans does not.

Studies that focus on variation in women's employment across metropolitan areas (Abrahamson and Sigelman 1987; Jones and Rosenfeld 1989) emphasize the importance of demand-level factors in women's employment patterns, although there is evidence for supply effects as well. The small variation across metropolitan areas that does exist partly reflects differences in the extent of labor demand within fields designated as female. In other words, women are available as needed for recruitment in female-dominated positions. Thus women's availability is even more uniform than the observed level of women's employment in different cities.

This discussion leads to a view of the devaluation of women's work as an institutional or cultural feature of our social structure. Occupations acquire gender stereotypes that reflect the profile of the typical incumbent (Milkman 1987), and particular features of these occupations are highlighted to emphasize their association with masculine or feminine roles. The gender of an occupation becomes one of its defining features and is institutionalized in national culture and recruitment practices. As a result, the same occupations are performed more or less uniformly by women throughout the country. Once established, the sex label of an occupation becomes a self-sustaining social arrangement.

In contrast, the demographics of race make it difficult, if not impossible, to associate a particular occupation with the racial characteristics of its incumbents. If our understanding of the process of gender devaluation is correct, it would account for the presence of gender composition effects and the absence of racial composition effects within U.S. labor markets. The systematic devaluation of women's work is an enduring cultural attribute that has been embedded in a wide variety of institutional arrangements.

Of course, wages are set locally in the United States and not by a national board (as in Australia) or by national collective bargaining (as in Germany). Yet we are suggesting that local decisionmakers draw on stereotypes deeply rooted in national culture to make decisions on who to hire and what jobs are worth. The availability of these occupation-specific stereotypes leads to a different form of wage setting for women as opposed to minorities. National media may promote a variety of negative stereotypes about African Americans as a group, but this does not translate into wage setting for individual occupations. In contrast, the close cultural association between occupations and gender roles leads to the devaluation of all labor that is assumed to be "women's work."

NATIONAL INSTITUTIONS AND LOCAL LABOR MARKETS

One prominent piece of evidence may appear inconsistent with the institutional view just outlined. Many researchers have noted that an occupation captures only a portion of workplace segregation by sex. Job-level segregation is much higher than occupational segregation, and job-level segregation explains much more of the gender gap in wages than does occupational segregation. Tomaskovic-Devey (1995, 24) views gender segregation as a *local* phenomenon of the labor market rather than as a national phenomenon:

> Is there some national occupational sex-typing process that sets wage rates? Few social scientists would argue that this is a dominant process in the United States. Wage rates, with few exceptions, are set in local labor markets and are attached to jobs within firms. More compelling are explanations that the observed effects of occupational sex composition on earnings reflect processes that operate at the job level.

He thus contends that job-level processes operating in local labor markets are principal forces behind the devaluation of women's work. Indeed, Tomaskovic-Devey follows Baron and Newman (1990) as well as Bridges and Nelson (1989) in insisting on the firm-specific nature of decisionmaking with respect to hiring and wage setting. Unfortunately, we do not have data that allow us to distinguish firm-specific from other local wage-setting practices. To the extent that firms respond to their local labor markets (Bridges and Nelson 1989), however, the present analysis captures the degree to which wages reflect the local sex and racial composition of specific occupations, recognizing that the wage policies of individual firms vary around the local mean.

So far we have outlined two opposing views of the devaluation of women's work: national cultural and institutional devaluation, on the one hand, and local labor market processes, on the other. We have suggested that the effects of racial composition on wages are rarely observed because they cannot be embedded in cultural beliefs and national institutions. Race can only affect job valuation through a local labor market process affecting individuals. Yet some analysts claim that the devaluation of women's work is also a local labor market process and, in this way, operates in the same way as does race.

We propose to draw on interurban variation in racial and gender composition to obtain leverage on these questions. If race and gender affect the valuation of work through local labor market processes, then we would expect the variation across cities in the sex and racial composition of particular occupations to be associated with their relative valuation or devaluation. In other words, within a given occupation, earnings should be lower in those cities with a higher representation of women among incumbents of that occupation. Such a finding would support the local-labor-markets interpretation of the gender devaluation process. A failure to find such effects would be consistent with the institutional or cultural interpretation of gender devaluation. Similarly, within a given occupation, earnings should be lower in those cities with a higher representation of African Americans among incumbents.

We test the national devaluation hypothesis indirectly, based on the lack of evidence for the alternative, local explanation. The less variation between locales, the more the evidence is consistent with a national explanation. The more variation between metropolitan areas, the more importance theories must place on local factors. As noted, Tomaskovic-Devey infers the impact of local labor markets from data on the sex composition of jobs, as opposed to the more common focus on occupations. We propose to assess the effects of local labor markets by examining particular occupations across a range of cities. This strategy enables us to bring census data to bear on the operation of wage-setting practices in particular locales.

RACE AND THE CITY

Another line of research focuses on the relationship between race and cities. A number of researchers have examined the effects of minority concentration in metropolitan areas on socioeconomic inequality (Blalock 1956; Reich 1971; Frisbie and Neidert 1977; Tienda and Lii 1987; Parcel and Mueller 1983; Grant and Parcel 1990). These studies treat the metropolitan area as a local labor market and conclude that income disparities between majority and minority members grow as the concentration of minorities in the labor market increases and that white income rises at the expense of minorities. Tienda and Lii (1987) disaggregate minority concentration into separate components for blacks, Hispanics, and Asians in each metropolitan area. They find that a higher concentration of African Americans in a local labor market is associated with lower earnings for African Americans, Asians, and Hispanics. In contrast, white incomes benefit from an overrepresentation of African Americans but are not affected by an overrepresentation of Hispanics.

There are two principal interpretations of these associations. Blalock (1956) suggests a positive relationship between minority presence and discrimination. He maintains that white resistance to minorities grows as the minority presence in a city increases. Blalock's approach interprets the association between minority concentration and the race gap in earnings as evidence of increased discrimination against minorities due to the greater threat they pose to whites. Lieberson (1980), however, suggests a demographic alternative that does not depend on increased hostility. He offers a queuing model that predicts increased minority concentration in the lowest-status occupations as minority presence increases. Lieberson's approach suggests that the majority's advantage grows as a result of the demography of occupational distribution, not necessarily because of greater resistance to minority groups (Lieberson 1980, 298).

A possibility not considered thus far is that minorities are penalized in local labor markets because their occupations are devalued. The demographics of race make it difficult for any occupation to be devalued nationally because of an association with minority incumbents. It is possible, however, that a particular occupation that is disproportionately nonwhite within a given locale may be devalued locally by labor market processes. England (1992, 162) suggests that this process may be operating in the case of African Americans: "It is possible that this sort of race bias in wage setting may exist at a local or organizational level but not be revealed by a national analysis such as this."

If this effect is evident, it is consistent with Blalock's premise that resistance to minorities increases as their presence grows. Such an effect would be inconsistent with Lieberson's notion that the distribution of minorities across occupations by itself accounts for the association between minority concentration and the race gap in earnings. Although we cannot test Blalock's and Lieberson's hypothesis directly because we do not examine the level of earnings across an entire metropolitan area, we do try to bring their reasoning to bear on the issue of interest here—namely, the valuation of particular occupations within local labor markets based on race and gender composition. In doing so, we follow the example of other studies (Pfeffer and Davis-Blake 1987; Jacobs 1992) that have brought the work of Blalock, Lieberson, Kanter, and others to bear on understanding the process of wage setting within occupations.

We delve more deeply than previous research into the effects of minority concentration, however, by examining the effects of African American representation within specific occupations in particular locales. If race affects the valuation of particular occupations through local labor market processes, then we expect variation across cities in the racial composition of particular occupations to be associated with the devaluation of jobs. In other words, within a given occupation, earnings should be lower in those cities with a higher representation of African Americans among incumbents. In this sense, we specify and test one specific mechanism that might influence the relationship between race and earnings in a local context.

DATA AND METHODS

Our analysis draws on the one in one hundred sample of the 1990 census of population. We select men and women who were employed during 1989 and restrict our sample to African Americans and non-Hispanic whites. We explore variation in the representation of African Americans and women across metropolitan areas by analyzing the fifty occupations with the largest numbers of incumbents, where each one represents at least 0.5 percent of the labor force. We focus on large occupations in order to obtain as many occupations with a reliable racial composition for as many metropolitan areas as possible. Our cross-classification of race by detailed occupation by metropolitan area requires a large sample size to produce results in which we have much confidence. Even in those occupations with large numbers of African American men, cases become sparse in smaller metropolitan areas.

In order to maintain an adequate sample size, we limit the analysis to the one hundred largest metropolitan areas. The one-hundredth metropolitan area includes 2,272 respondents (0.2 percent of the sample), which means that occupations comprising 1 percent of the labor force have only twenty-three incumbents in the smallest of our locales. Sampling variability would begin to overwhelm useful information if the samples became much smaller. These one hundred metropolitan areas included 55 percent of employed Americans in 1990.

The final sample includes 132,347 white women, 117,033 white men, 30,406 African American women, and 24,333 African American men. The fact that women constitute the majority of the sample reflects the fact that we select the largest occupations in the census for analysis, which tend to be predominantly female. Sample sizes for individual occupations are more modest. For white women, the largest occupation includes 24,993 cases, while the smallest includes only 11 cases. The median of the fifty occupations includes 1,601 white women for inclusion in the regression analysis. For white men, the largest occupation includes 10,135 working men, while the smallest includes 122 men. The median is 1,785 cases. For African American women, the smallest occupation includes 1 case; the largest includes 3,088 cases; the median sample size for an occupation is 287. For African American men, the largest occupation includes 2,178 cases, the smallest includes 4 cases, and the median is 321.

In order to assess the impact of locale-specific race and gender composition of occupations on individuals' earnings, we calculate the proportion of women in each of the fifty largest occupations in each metropolitan area. We then assign this sex composition score to all incumbents in these occupations. We then calculate the proportion of African American women in each occupation in each metropolitan area and assign this black female composition score to all incumbents. Next we calculate a black male composition score and assign it to all incumbents. Finally, we estimate individual-level earnings analyses with the metropolitan area–specific female, black female, and black male composition scores as predictor variables.

For incumbents in each of the fifty occupations, we estimate an earnings function of the following form:

$$\log(\text{earnings}) = a + b_1 (\text{ed}) + b_2 (\text{age}) + b_3 (\text{hours}) + b_4 (\text{weeks}) + b_5 (\text{female}) + b_6 (\text{black female}) \quad (13.1) + b_7 (\text{black male}) + b_{8\text{-}17} (\text{industry}),$$

where "earnings" are annual earnings in 1989 of all men employed one or more hours and one or more weeks in 1989; "ed" is the number of years of schooling completed; "age" is respondents' age in years; "hours" is the number of hours usually worked in 1989; "weeks" is the number of weeks worked in 1989; and "industry" is a vector of nine industry dummy variables.

We employ a modified list of the major industry groups as control variables: (1) agriculture, forestry, fishing, and mining; (2) construction; (3) manufacturing; (4) transportation, communications, and utilities; (5) wholesale trade; (6) retail trade; (7) finance, insurance, and real estate; (8) business and repair services; (9) personal services; (10) professional services; and (11) government employment. Manufacturing serves as the reference category.

The variables "female," "black female," and "black male" represent the proportion of each of these demographic groups in each occupation in each metropolitan area. The "black female" variable tests whether the proportion of African American women in an occupation has the effect of devaluing an occupation above and beyond the effect of female representation. In all earnings analyses, we adjust the earnings data to take into account variation in the cost of living across metropolitan areas. We deflate earnings using the metropolitan statistical area deflator figures for 1989 developed by Bartik (1993). We estimate these equations separately for each race and sex group. We thus estimate two hundred earnings equations, one for each of the four race and sex groups in each of the fifty occupations examined. In our analyses we treat the local sex and racial composition of the respondent's occupation as an individual variable, in the same manner that industry and occupation are often treated.

THE ECONOMIC GEOGRAPHY OF RACE AND GENDER

Whereas African Americans are distributed unevenly across metropolitan areas in the United States, working women are distributed much more evenly across locales. We order the one hundred largest metropolitan areas in terms of the representation of working African American men. Table 13.1 lists the percentage of male workers who are African American for every tenth case. In Memphis, African American men comprise more than 30 percent of metropolitan area employment. At the other extreme, in Bakersfield, California, African American men comprise less than 5

TABLE 13.1 **African Americans as a Percentage of Employed Individuals by Metropolitan Area and Sex**

Metropolitan Area	Blacks as a Percentage of	
	Employed Males	Employed Females
Washington, D.C.	23.9	29.0
Norfolk, Virginia Beach	23.7	28.3
Baltimore	22.4	26.7
Atlanta	21.8	27.1
New York	21.7	27.2
Newark	19.1	24.3
Miami	16.7	20.5
Charlotte	16.5	20.9
Chicago	15.4	19.7
Detroit	15.1	18.9
Philadelphia	14.8	18.7
Cleveland	14.8	19.2
Houston	14.6	19.7
Ft. Lauderdale	12.9	14.7
St. Louis	12.6	16.2
Dallas	12.2	15.8
Oakland	11.2	14.7
Orlando	10.6	11.2
Kansas City	9.6	12.0
Columbus	9.5	11.4
Cincinnati	9.4	11.5
Los Angeles	9.2	12.3
Ft. Worth	8.3	10.9
Tampa, St. Petersburg	7.8	8.9
Bergen, Passaic, N.J.	7.6	9.2
San Diego	7.1	5.2
Rochester	6.8	8.7
San Francisco	6.5	6.0
Riverside	6.3	6.8
Boston	6.2	7.1
Middlesex, Somerset, N.J.	6.2	6.8
Nassau, Suffolk, N.Y.	6.2	7.8
Pittsburgh	6.1	6.6
Sacramento	5.4	5.8
Denver	5.0	5.3
San Jose	4.0	3.9
Seattle	3.8	3.6
Phoenix	3.2	3.4
Minneapolis, St. Paul	3.1	2.8
Anaheim, Santa Ana	1.9	1.8

Source: Authors' tabulations of U.S. 1990 Census Public Use Micro Sample.

percent of the employed men in the metropolitan area. In Salt Lake City, they represent less than 1 percent of the employed male workforce. These results show that there are many locales with few African Americans in the employed population.

Table 13.1 also presents data on the representation of African American women across metropolitan areas. The share of women's employment that is composed of African American women is generally slightly greater than that for men. Nonetheless, the variation of African American women across metropolitan areas closely mirrors that of their male counterparts. Indeed, the correlation between the share of employed black men and black women in a metropolitan area is 0.94, calculated across the one hundred metropolitan statistical areas examined in this study.

The contrast with the case of gender representation becomes evident in table 13.2. Women's representation does vary across metropolitan areas, but within a much more restricted range. Among the one hundred metropolitan areas examined, the fraction of female among employed persons ranges only from 42.8 to 48.8 percent. We also analyze women's representation among full-time, full-year employees. This fraction is lower but has a similar range, from 36.3 to 43.0 percent. Working women are thus well represented in all major metropolitan areas, and their representation varies within a more restricted range than is the case for African Americans. Moreover, much of this variation reflects the local demand for employment in female-dominated occupations.

The effect of the distribution of African Americans and women on the composition of individual occupations can be seen in the next three tables. In table 13.3, we report the range of African American men's representation within occupations across the one hundred metropolitan areas. The table shows the twenty occupations with the largest fraction of African American males from our list of the fifty largest occupations. In some metropolitan areas even those occupations with the highest proportions of African American men are overwhelmingly white. Truck drivers, for example, range from 2 to 56 percent African American among the one hundred largest metropolitan areas.

The data in table 13.3 also include the interquartile range (Q3 to Q1) because we are concerned that the minimum and maximum cases might include excessive measurement error due to small sample sizes that inflate the range. Results based on the in-

TABLE 13.2 **Women as a Percentage of Employed Persons, by Metropolitan Area, 1990**

Metropolitan Area	Women as a Percentage of	
	Employed Persons	Full-Time Workers
Tampa, St. Petersburg	48.8	43.0
Boston	48.8	41.5
Cincinnati	48.6	39.7
Rochester	48.5	39.6
Atlanta	48.4	42.1
Washington, D.C.	48.2	43.0
Charlotte	48.2	41.0
New York	48.0	43.6
Kansas City	47.9	42.1
Baltimore	47.8	41.3
Minneapolis, St. Paul	47.5	39.5
Denver	47.5	42.0
Philadelphia	47.5	40.3
St. Louis	47.5	40.1
Miami	47.4	42.3
Newark	47.4	40.4
Cleveland	47.3	38.6
Sacramento	47.2	40.5
Ft. Lauderdale	47.1	40.6
Middlesex, Somerset, N.J.	47.0	39.2
San Francisco	47.0	42.1
Columbus	47.0	40.7
Dallas	46.9	42.0
Pittsburgh	46.7	39.2
Bergen, Passaic, N.J.	46.6	38.9
Oakland	46.6	39.8
Detroit	46.5	38.4
Nassau, Suffolk, N.Y.	46.5	37.1
Ft. Worth	46.4	40.7
Chicago	46.3	40.4
Phoenix	46.1	39.8
Orlando	46.0	39.8
Seattle	45.5	38.5
Houston	45.2	39.2
San Jose	44.7	38.8
Anaheim, Santa Ana	44.3	38.0
Riverside	44.2	35.8
Los Angeles	44.0	39.3
Norfolk, Virginia Beach	43.7	34.5
San Diego	42.8	36.3

Source: Authors' tabulations of U.S. 1990 Census Public Use Micro Sample.

TABLE 13.3 Racial Composition of Twenty Occupations with the Largest Representation of African American Men Nationally Across One Hundred of the Largest Metropolitan Areas, 1990

Occupation and Census Code	Percentage Black	Number	Median	Minimum	Maximum	Q1	Q3	Q3 to Q1	Number
Nursing aides, orderlies, and attendants (447)	25.5	542	33.3	6.3	65.4	22.0	44.6	22.6	227
Guards and police except public service (426)	20.3	1,148	17.2	3.5	58.0	12.3	32.1	19.9	768
Noncommissioned officers and other enlisted (904)	19.8	544	25.0	7.7	100.0	20.3	41.7	21.4	154
Janitors and cleaners (453)	19.7	2,959	23.0	6.5	73.0	14.4	38.8	24.4	1,334
Cooks (436)	19.0	1,874	26.7	4.7	53.2	9.6	33.6	24.0	861
Industrial truck and tractor operators (856)	18.1	736	27.3	4.3	66.7	15.0	38.9	23.9	250
Traffic, shipping, and receiving clerks (364)	15.8	603	18.9	2.3	55.0	10.7	28.6	17.9	326
Stock and inventory clerks (365)	15.4	691	17.4	2.4	43.9	11.1	29.0	17.9	327

Laborers, except construction (889)	15.3	1,444	23.8	3.5	69.2	9.6	33.6	24.0	597
Assemblers (785)	14.3	1,100	18.2	1.9	83.3	9.0	28.8	19.8	424
Construction laborers (869)	13.5	1,416	13.1	2.1	77.5	8.3	24.5	16.2	554
Truck drivers (804)	12.9	3,060	12.9	1.5	56.0	9.5	24.4	14.8	1,395
Groundskeepers and gardeners, except farm (486)	12.2	732	16.7	3.7	52.9	6.7	25.8	19.1	261
Stock handlers and baggers (877)	12.1	839	11.8	1.5	46.3	8.1	21.2	13.0	386
Cashiers (276)	11.9	649	13.7	1.4	50.0	6.5	22.7	16.3	350
Farm workers (479)	8.4	612	18.5	5.3	100.0	11.1	30.0	18.9	37
Auto mechanics (505)	8.1	571	7.5	2.1	42.1	5.2	14.9	9.8	264
Supervisors, production occupations (628)	7.5	725	7.1	1.3	28.8	3.8	13.0	9.2	329
Carpenters (567)	5.6	549	5.0	0.8	28.0	2.7	10.2	7.5	224
Supervisors and proprietors, sales (243)	4.1	674	3.7	0.7	19.8	2.1	6.9	4.9	410

Source: Authors' tabulations of U.S. 1990 Census Public Use Micro Sample.
Note: Weighted results are presented with unweighted numbers.

terquartile range are obviously less dramatic than those based on the entire range. Nonetheless, in ten of the twenty cases the interquartile range is 10 percentage points or more. These results slightly modify our earlier conclusion about the absence of African American majorities in particular occupations. Although there are certain *locales* in which African Americans comprise a majority of certain occupations, in other metropolitan areas whites represent the overwhelming majority of incumbents in the same occupations.

Table 13.4 describes the range of African American women's representation across metropolitan areas in the twenty occupations. The pattern of results reinforces the conclusions reached for African American men. In eighteen of twenty cases, the interquartile range is 10 percentage points or more. For the majority of occupations considered, in other words, African American women's representation is far higher in some locales than in others.

Table 13.5 presents parallel results for the twenty occupations that are mostly female-dominated (selected from the fifty largest occupations). In all of these cases, women represent the majority of incumbents. For many of the cases, the occupations are overwhelmingly female; and in most cases, the range in women's representation is relatively small. For example, secretaries range from a low of 96.4 percent female to a high of 100 percent female. In only seven cases is the interquartile range 10 percentage points or more, in contrast to half or more of the cases for African American occupations. The greatest variation is observed among occupations that are less than two-thirds female. In the most female-dominated occupations, in other words, there is very limited variability between the highest and lowest metropolitan areas. In five cases, the interquartile range is less than 5 percentage points. Thus there is enough variation to conduct interesting regression analyses, but not as much as in the case of African Americans.

These distributions underscore points made in the introductory section of this chapter, which highlighted differences in the demographic distribution of women and African Americans. Whereas women nationally represent the majority of incumbents in many occupations, this never occurs for African American men or women in the national occupational structure. Women are also

TABLE 13.4 Racial Composition of Twenty Occupations with the Largest Representation of African American Women Nationally Across One Hundred of the Largest Metropolitan Areas, 1990

Occupation and Census Code	Percentage Black Women	Number	Median	Minimum	Maximum	Q1	Q3	Q3 to Q1	Number
Private household cleaners (407)	32.7	1,132	44.2	6.7	90.3	24.3	64.5	40.2	387
Nursing aides, orderlies, and attendants (447)	28.2	4,209	35.1	6.7	85.7	23.6	55.1	31.4	2,051
Maids and housemen (449)	27.6	1,473	40.0	4.3	94.6	20.0	63.9	43.9	570
Janitors and cleaners (453)	23.3	1,695	30.0	5.3	46.7	15.6	46.7	31.0	645
Social workers (174)	21.4	810	19.4	2.4	62.5	10.3	37.8	27.5	495
Cooks (436)	18.9	1,949	21.0	1.4	58.6	9.4	37.2	27.8	543
Data-entry keyers (385)	17.9	831	20.0	2.1	52.1	13.0	30.8	17.8	528
Typists (315)	17.6	934	18.2	5.6	58.5	10.6	30.2	19.6	623
Textile sewing machine operators (744)	17.5	1,364	28.6	3.7	93.3	16.7	38.5	21.8	168
Production inspectors, checkers, examiners (796)	17.4	610	25.0	2.9	72.7	16.0	37.1	21.1	168
Licensed practical nurses (207)	16.7	596	28.6	5.6	72.7	13.0	43.3	30.3	303
Assemblers (785)	16.1	1,046	23.1	2.3	81.3	11.8	35.1	23.4	359
Cashiers (276)	14.7	3,368	13.8	2.5	65.1	7.1	27.6	20.5	1,492
General office clerks (379)	13.9	1,513	8.2	3.4	44.4	8.2	23.0	14.7	969
Teachers, elementary school (156)	10.2	2,294	11.1	1.8	33.3	4.3	17.9	13.6	1,105
Registered nurses (95)	8.6	1,277	7.7	1.1	39.8	3.2	15.9	12.7	790
Receptionists (319)	8.5	612	9.9	1.4	33.3	5.3	16.4	11.1	405
Secretaries	7.2	2,466	6.3	1.1	30.3	3.7	12.4	8.7	1,604
Supervisors and proprietors, sales (243)	6.4	599	6.8	0.9	24.1	3.7	15.7	11.9	328
Bookkeepers, accounting, and auditing clerks (337)	5.6	763	6.1	0.7	20.1	3.8	9.9	6.1	515

Source: Authors' tabulations of U.S. 1990 Census Public Use Micro Sample.

Note: Weighted results are presented with unweighted numbers.

TABLE 13.5 **Gender Composition of Fifty Occupations with Largest Representation of Women Nationally Across One Hundred of the Largest Metropolitan Areas, 1990**

Occupation and Census Code	Percentage Women	Number	Median	Minimum	Maximum	Q1	Q3	Q3 to Q1	Number
Secretaries (313)	98.5	41,911	98.4	96.4	100.0	98.0	99.1	1.1	17,458
Receptionists (319)	95.7	8,318	96.4	90.3	100.0	94.3	97.7	3.4	3,800
Registered nurses (95)	94.3	17,885	95.0	88.6	100.0	93.3	95.6	2.3	7,209
Typists (315)	93.1	6,252	95.2	82.4	100.0	92.9	96.3	3.4	2,942
Hairdressers and cosmetologists (458)	90.3	4,949	87.4	73.2	98.4	85.1	91.6	6.4	1,917
Textile sewing machine operator (744)	89.0	7,971	89.3	66.7	100.0	82.0	92.2	10.2	1,904
Bookkeepers, accounting, and auditing clerks (337)	89.0	17,600	88.3	74.4	95.0	86.5	91.2	4.7	6,951
Nursing aides, orderlies, and attendants (447)	86.9	17,601	87.0	75.8	92.4	83.9	89.9	5.9	5,404
Data-entry keyers (385)	85.6	5,488	85.4	72.7	97.7	81.4	89.3	7.9	2,650
Waiters and waitresses (435)	81.1	14,096	77.3	45.9	91.6	71.0	82.3	11.3	4,377
Maids and housemen (449)	81.1	6,072	78.3	60.6	91.2	76.7	81.8	5.1	1,875
General office clerks (379)	80.8	13,085	81.3	71.4	91.0	78.4	84.4	5.9	5,654
Cashiers (276)	79.8	26,384	77.6	59.5	89.8	73.3	81.4	8.1	8,796
Teachers, elementary school (156)	78.9	26,218	79.2	64.2	89.4	76.1	83.1	7.0	9,173
Social workers (174)	68.9	4,481	69.3	52.9	88.2	63.4	76.0	12.7	1,830
Computer operators (308)	62.0	4,189	57.3	45.5	80.0	53.6	64.3	10.7	1,690
Teachers, secondary school (157)	57.1	3,967	56.5	41.5	74.2	49.6	62.4	12.8	1,254
Designers (185)	54.6	2,861	56.1	34.3	67.4	47.2	58.9	11.8	1,349
Accountants and auditors (23)	54.4	7,951	51.8	35.9	68.8	47.9	56.6	8.7	4,035
Production inspectors, checkers, and examiners (796)	54.0	3,920	49.7	25.8	77.4	40.2	58.0	17.8	1,013

Source: Authors' tabulations of U.S. Census Public Use Micro Sample.
Note: Weighted results are presented with unweighted numbers.

distributed more uniformly across locales than are African Americans, and female-dominated occupations are consequently quite uniform in their sex composition from place to place, as are male-dominated occupations. In contrast, occupations vary markedly from place to place in the extent to which African Americans are represented.

EFFECTS OF GENDER AND RACIAL COMPOSITION

We have seen that African American representation varies substantially across locales, while women's representation varies as well, but in a more restricted range. Are earnings lower in metropolitan areas where African American representation in particular occupations is higher? Is the same pattern observed for women? We now turn to an analysis of the effect of local variation on earnings in order to answer these questions.

Summary results for the regression analyses of the fifty largest occupations are reported in table 13.6. We have estimated equations on each of fifty occupations for four groups: white men, white women, African American men, and African American women. In these two hundred equations, there are three coefficients of theoretical interest: female, black female, and black male. Our results consequently include six hundred coefficients of interest (full regression results will be provided on request).

Assuming a 5 percent chance of a false positive (following conventional significance levels), we expect thirty significant coefficients across all of these equations even if no relationship exists. Thus we should be careful not to overinterpret every statistically significant coefficient. Nevertheless, if the results were truly a matter of chance, we would see significant coefficients distributed equally between positive and negative coefficients, and we would see an equal number of significant coefficients for each of the three variables. Instead, we see forty-one negative coefficients for female composition and only one positive one. We consequently believe that the pattern of results is meaningful, even if not every individual coefficient requires interpretation.

Our results provide limited evidence of local gender composition effects. In thirteen of the fifty occupations examined, white

TABLE 13.6 **Summary of the Effects of Local Occupational Composition on Earnings: Female Composition**

Group	Coefficient Number of Occupations
Employed white men	
Negative significant	17
Not significant	30
Positive significant	3
Employed white women	
Negative significant	16
Not significant	31
Positive significant	3
Employed African American men	
Negative significant	13
Not significant	33
Positive significant	4
Employed African American women	
Negative significant	15
Not significant	31
Positive significant	4

Source: Authors' tabulations of U.S. 1990 Census Public Use Microsample.

male incumbents in metropolitan areas with larger proportions of women are paid less than their counterparts in areas with lower concentrations of women in their occupations; the reverse holds in only one case. In the remaining thirty-six cases, the effect is not statistically significant. The same pattern holds for white women. The presence of more women depresses the wages of female incumbents in nineteen of fifty cases, with no cases having the opposite effect. Among African American males, female composition has virtually no effect on earnings. Among African American females, in contrast, the presence of women depresses earnings in eight of fifty occupations; in no occupation does a higher concentration of women raise earnings. When we restrict the analysis to full-time, full-year workers, the results are largely the same.

Turning to the effects of racial composition, local black male composition generally has no statistically significant *negative* effect on the wages earned in any of the four populations. Of the fifty equations estimated for white men, the local black male composition variable has the predicted statistically significant negative effect in only one case and has the opposite effect in ten cases. A similar pattern is found among the population of white women. In none of the fifty cases does the presence of African American men in an occupation reduce white women's wages, while it has the opposite effect in six cases. Among African American men, the presence of other African American men reduces earnings in only two occupations and raises earnings in one occupation. Finally, in the African American female population, the presence of African American males reduces earnings in only one occupation, while raising earnings in six occupations. In sum, for white men, white women, black men, and black women, working in a city with a larger share of African American men in their occupation does not reduce their wages.

A surprising finding is that in some occupations the presence of higher percentages of African American males *increases* the earnings of incumbents. This effect may be due to an intervening variable, such as unionization, that increases both African American representation and earnings, but we were unable to test this speculation with these data.

Moreover, the positive coefficients for black male composition appear most frequently in the white male population but are virtually absent in the African American male population. A similar pattern is evident for African American women. We speculate that white males may earn more in occupations with larger shares of African American males because whites are more likely to hold the jobs that yield higher earnings within an occupation. This effect is similar to that found by Tienda and Lii (1987) in their analysis of local labor markets, although their study does not focus on the racial gap in earnings within occupations.

One interpretation of this result, then, is that this is evidence of a race-based queuing of jobs within occupations (Lieberson 1980; Reskin and Roos 1990). However, in only four cases is the effect statistically smaller for African American men than for white men. In the remaining cases, the large standard error in the equations for African American men (due to more limited sample size) accounts for the lack of a statistically significant effect. Thus the basis for speculation regarding queuing effects is somewhat limited. Moreover, a queuing explanation must address the disparate results of female and minority concentration. If queuing advantages white men as black men's presence increases, it is necessary to explain why there is no similar effect when white women's presence increases.

We also consider whether the concentration of African American women reduces the earnings of incumbents in occupations. We do not expect the presence of African American women to depress the wages of occupations above and beyond the effect of other women's representation, and indeed the evidence is consistent with this expectation (see table 13.6). In other words, an African American woman's wages are depressed by the fact that she works in a female-dominated occupation and by the fact that she is African American, but not because the presence of African American women has an additional effect on the earnings of her occupation.

CONCLUSIONS

We posited that racial composition can affect wages only in local labor markets, since the representation of African Americans in occupations is too limited in extent and too uneven in geographical distribution to allow for national occupational devaluation based on race. Gender composition, in contrast, can affect wages either through local labor markets or via national cultural and institutional processes. We assessed whether the local labor market explanation fit the data for women and for African Americans by examining variation in wages across one hundred metropolitan areas.

We found no evidence that racial composition reduces wages through a local labor market process. Our analysis revealed that the presence of larger fractions of African Americans in individual occupations in particular metropolitan areas does not result in lower wages of incumbents. In contrast, we found that there is modest evidence that gender composition operates through local labor markets. In other words, for both men and women, working in a metropolitan area in which there is a relatively high proportion of women in one's occupation reduces a worker's earnings. The prevalence of this devaluation varies across groups, from about 10 percent of the cases for white men to nearly 40 percent of the cases for white women. We suggested that gender composition effects operate through national cultural institutions but that occupational racial composition cannot affect compensation because of the demographics of race. We then showed that gender operates locally as well as nationally, while race does not operate on the wages of occupations at either level.

Why should gender, but not race, be a factor in wage setting in labor markets? Our explanation is that local effects simply amplify national cultural and institutional processes. Employers see gender as a legitimate basis for structuring jobs. Race surely is significant in labor markets, but it seems to play a larger role in the hiring process than in the wage-setting process. Our results suggest that the common finding of an inverse relationship between the concentration of African Americans in a metropolitan area and African American earnings (for example, Tienda and Lii 1987) cannot be explained by the devaluation of the particular occupations in which minorities are located. Race continues to influence the earnings of individuals, but not the wage rates of occupations in which individuals are employed.

We suspect that race remains significant because it is used to channel individuals into jobs, not because it is used to set the wage rates of the jobs themselves. African Americans are more likely to work in lower-paying occupations than whites, on average. This may indicate a race-based queuing of workers into occupations, as Lieberson (1980) has argued. African Americans are channeled into lower-paying occupations in part because their educational attainment is lower, on average, than that of whites. However, education alone cannot explain the overrepresentation of African Americans in lower-paying jobs. African American men earn less than white men with the same amount of schooling (Jencks 1992; Bound and Freeman 1992). This race-based queuing perspective suggests that even highly educated African Americans end up in lower-paying jobs than do their white counterparts.

Another possible interpretation of our results is that our analysis of employed persons ignores a potentially significant locus of racial discrimination—the hiring process. Jencks (1992, 49–57) argues that affirmative action increased the pressure on employers to pay blacks as much as whites in the same job. However, laws prohibiting hiring discrimination are harder to enforce than laws barring pay discrimination among current employees, and Jencks thus concludes that the locus of racial discrimination moved from pay to hiring. This means that the lowest place in the labor market queue is unemployment, a place in the queue where African Americans are overrepresented.

We found limited evidence that an increased presence of women in a local labor market lowers the wages earned. However, local labor market effects for women are of greater theoretical than practical significance. Because women's representation in an occupation varies little across metropolitan areas and because the coefficients for women's representation are of modest size, the local labor market effects we detected are not of fundamental importance in understanding the devaluation of women's work. In other words, secretaries in Tulsa earn only slightly less than secretaries in Raleigh-Durham because this occupation is only slightly more dominated by women in the former locale (99 and 96 percent female, respectively) and because every additional percentage female has only a small effect on earnings. Our results are consistent with the premise that national cultural and institutional arrangements are critical elements in the devaluation of women's work.

"Gender, Race, Local Labor Markets, and Occupational Devaluation," by Jerry Jacobs and Mary Blair-Loy, is a revised version of a paper that originally appeared in a special issue of *Sociological Focus* 29 (3): 209–29 entitled "Gender in the Workplace," edited by Barbara F. Reskin.

Another draft of this chapter was presented at the meetings of the Society for the Advancement of Socio-Economics, Washington, D.C., April 1995. We thank Brian Powell, Donald Tomaskovic-Devey, Paula England, Janet Gornick, Barbara Reskin, Toby Parcel, and Brian Powell for comments on earlier drafts of this work.

REFERENCES

Abrahamson, Mark, and Lee Sigelman. 1987. "Occupational Sex Segregation in Metropolitan Areas." *American Sociological Review* 52(5): 588–97.

Baron, James N., and Andrew E. Newman. 1990. "For What It's Worth: Organizations, Occupations, and the Value of Work Done by Women and Nonwhites." *American Sociological Review* 55(2): 155–75.

Bartik, Timothy J. 1993. *Economic Development and Black Economic Success.* Report 93–001 for the W. E. Upjohn Institution for Employment Research, Kalamazoo, Mich.

Blalock, Herbert. 1956. "Economic Discrimination and Negro Increase." *American Sociological Review* 21: 584–88.

Bound, John, and Richard Freeman. 1992. "What Went Wrong? The Erosion of the Relative Earnings and Employment of Young Black Men in the 1980s." *Quarterly Journal of Economics* 107(1): 201–32.

Bridges, William P., and Robert L. Nelson. 1989. "Markets in Hierarchies: Organizational and Market Influences on Gender Inequality in a State Pay System." *American Journal of Sociology* 95(3): 616–58.

England, Paula. 1992. *Comparable Worth: Theories and Evidence.* New York: Aldine de Gruyter.

Frisbie, W. Parker, and Lisa Neidert. 1977. "Inequality and the Relative Size of Minority Populations: A Comparative Analysis." *American Journal of Sociology* 82: 1007–30.

Grant, Don Sherman II, and Toby L. Parcel. 1990. "Revisiting Metropolitan Racial Inequality: The Case for a Resource Approach." *Social Forces* 68(4): 1121–42.

Jacobs, Jerry A. 1992. "Women's Entry into Management: Trends in Earnings, Authority, and Values among Salaried Managers." *Administrative Science Quarterly* 37(2): 282–301.

Jacobs, Jerry A., and Ronnie J. Steinberg. 1990. "Compensating Differentials and the Male-Female Wage Gap: Evidence from the New York State Pay Equity Study." *Social Forces* 69(2): 439–68.

———. 1995. "Further Evidence on Compensating Differentials and the Gender Gap in Wages." In *Gender Inequality at Work,* edited by Jerry A. Jacobs. Thousand Oaks, Calif.: Sage Press.

Jencks, Christopher. 1992. *Rethinking Social Policy.* Cambridge, Mass.: Harvard University Press.

Jones, Jo Ann, and Rachel A. Rosenfeld. 1989. "Women's Occupations and Local Labor Markets: 1950 to 1980." *Social Forces* 68(3): 666–92.

Kilbourne, Barbara S., Paula England, George Farkas, Kurt Beron, and Dorothea Weir. 1994. "Returns to Skill, Compensating Differentials, and Gender Bias: Effects of Occupational Characteristics on the Wages of White Women and Men." *American Journal of Sociology* 100(3): 689–719.

Lieberson, Stanley. 1980. *A Piece of the Pie: Blacks and White Immigrants since 1980.* Berkeley: University of California Press.

McGee, Jeanne, and Jean Stockard. 1991. "From a Child's View: Children's Occupational Knowledge and Perceptions of Occupational Characteristics." *Sociological Studies of Child Development* 4: 113–35. Greenwich, Conn.: JAI Press.

Milkman, Ruth. 1987. *Gender at Work*. Urbana: University of Illinois Press.

Nemerowicz, Gloria M. 1979. *Children's Perceptions of Gender and Work Roles*. New York: Praeger.

Orazem, Peter F., and J. Peter Mattila. 1989. "Comparable Worth and the Structure of Earnings: The Iowa Case." In *Pay Equity: Empirical Inquiries*, edited by Robert T. Michael, Heidi I. Hartmann, and Brigid O'Farrell. Washington, D.C.: National Academy Press.

Parcel, Toby L., and Charles W. Mueller. 1983. *Ascription and Local Labor Markets: Race and Sex Differences in Earnings*. New York: Academic Press.

Petersen, Trond, and Lauri Morgan. 1995. "Occupation-Establishment Sex Segregation and the Gender Wage Gap." *American Journal of Sociology* 101(2): 302–28.

Pfeffer, Jeffrey, and Allison Davis-Blake. 1987. "The Effects of the Proportion of Women on Salaries: The Case of College Administrators." *Administrative Science Quarterly* 32(1): 1–24.

Reich, Michael. 1971. "The Economics of Racism." In *Problems in Political Economy: An Urban Perspective*, edited by David M. Gordon. Lexington, Mass.: D.C. Heath and Company.

Reskin, Barbara, and Naomi Cassirer. 1996. "Segregating Workers: Occupational Segregation by Sex, Race, and Ethnicity." *Sociological Focus* 29(3): 231–44.

Reskin, Barbara, and Patricia Roos. 1990. *Job Queues, Gender Queues*. Philadelphia: Temple University Press.

Siegel, Paul. 1971. "Prestige in the American Occupational Structure." Ph.D. diss., University of Chicago, Department of Sociology.

Sorensen, Elaine. 1989. "Measuring the Effect of Occupational Sex and Race Composition on Earnings." In *Pay Equity: Empirical Inquiries*, edited by Robert T. Michael, Heidi I. Hartmann, and Brigid O'Farrell. Washington, D.C.: National Academy Press.

Stockard, Jean, and Jeanne McGee. 1990. "Children's Occupational Preferences: The Influence of Sex and Perceptions of Occupational Characteristics." *Journal of Vocational Behavior* 36(3): 287–303.

Tienda, Marta, and Ding-Tzann Lii. 1987. "Minority Concentration and Earnings Inequality: Blacks, Hispanics, and Asians Compared." *American Journal of Sociology* 93(1): 141–65.

Tomaskovic-Devey, Donald. 1993. *Gender and Racial Inequality at Work: The Sources and Consequences of Job Segregation*. Ithaca, N.Y.: ILR Press.

———. 1995. "Sex Composition and Gendered Earnings Inequality: A Comparison of Job and Occupational Models." In *Gender Inequality at Work*, edited by Jerry A. Jacobs. Thousand Oaks, Calif.: Sage.

—— Chapter 14 ——

Working Steady: Race, Low-Wage Work, and Family Involvement Among Noncustodial Fathers in Philadelphia

Kathryn Edin and Timothy J. Nelson

SEVERAL YEARS AGO William Julius Wilson (1996) argued that chronic joblessness among men is at the heart of the problem in many impoverished inner-city neighborhoods. Chronic jobless-ness, argued Wilson, makes community life difficult to sustain. Without jobs, men cannot marry the mothers of their children or provide adequate role models for those children. Without work, communities become disorganized and chaotic. Without employ-ment, social institutions (businesses, churches, local newspapers) falter and disappear.

> The disappearance of work has adversely affected not only individuals, families, and neighborhoods, but the social life of the city at large. A neigh-borhood in which people are poor but employed is different from a neigh-borhood in which people are poor and jobless. Many of today's problems in the inner-city ghetto neighborhoods—crime, family dissolution, welfare, low levels of social organization, and so on—are fundamentally a conse-quence of the disappearance of work. (Wilson 1996, xii)

The employment prospects of unskilled and semiskilled Ameri-can men *in the formal sector* have declined dramatically since the

375

1970s. The percentage of men who work year-round, full-time in the formal sector and have low annual earnings (those who earn less than the poverty line for a family of four) increased from 7 percent in 1974 to 14 percent in 1990. For white males, the rate increased from 7 to 13 percent; for African American males, it increased from 14 to 22 percent; and for men of Spanish-speaking origin, it increased from 12 to 28 percent (U.S. House of Representatives 1993, 597, table 46).

As the earnings of full-time, full-year male workers dropped, the percentage of men working full-time, full-year in the formal sector also declined. This is particularly true for poorly educated males. For white males ages twenty to twenty-four without a high school diploma, only 42 percent worked full-time in 1989, as compared to 55 percent in 1967. For similarly educated young black men, the drop was from 47 to 21 percent. For somewhat older unskilled men (ages twenty-five to thirty-four), the drop was from 74 to 55 percent for whites and from 65 to 33 percent for African Americans (U.S. House of Representatives 1993, tables 51, 52).

These trends in formal sector wages and employment for unskilled men reflect the fact that income inequality grew dramatically during the 1980s and early 1990s (see Danziger and Gottschalk 1993). The earnings of the college educated held steady or increased slightly, whereas the wages of those with less education plummeted, along with their ability to command full-time, year-round work. Although the number of low-skill jobs grew, the supply of workers for these jobs increased even more, yielding an excess of supply over demand for low-skill workers (Blank 1995). This was particularly true in some of America's inner cities, where unemployment rates were substantially higher than in the metropolitan region as a whole.

Although Wilson's book offers a multidimensional view of the effect that chronic joblessness may have, other scholars have focused primarily on the implications for family life. Many have argued that, given the rapidly deteriorating job prospects for unskilled men (especially minority men), mothers and fathers who want to marry are forced apart by economic circumstances (see Edin 2000). Those researching this question have often focused on African Americans, since it is among blacks that marriage rates have declined most dramatically. Some have addressed the question of whether the decline in marriage among African Americans is due to an insufficient and declining supply of marriageable black men as a result of unemployment (Wilson 1996, 1987), earnings losses (Oppenheimer 1988), or unbalanced sex ratios (South and Lloyd 1992; Tucker and Mitchell-Kernan 1996). There is ample evidence to support the "male marriageable pool" or "marriage squeeze" hypothesis (Fossett and Kiecolt 1993; Lichter, LeClere, and McLaughlin 1991; Rank 1987; Schoen and Kluegel 1988; South and Lloyd 1992; Tucker and Mitchell-Kernan 1996). Nevertheless, the growth in the number of mothers raising children apart from fathers is much greater than this approach would predict.

Even if fathers do not marry their children's mothers, they may still make significant contributions that enhance their children's lives. Thus, the effect that deteriorating employment prospects have on the ability or willingness of noncustodial fathers to involve themselves in their children's lives—both economically and emotionally—has also been the subject of scholarly work. For example, research has shown that noncustodial fathers who do not pay child support earn about half as much on an annual basis as those who do, suggesting that economic involvement is significantly related to men's earnings (Garfinkel, McLanahan, and Hanson 1998). Low paternal earnings are perhaps part of the reason why only a minority of those fifteen million children with a child support award received any substantial help from their fathers in 1990 (Bloom, Conrad, and Miller 1998, 1). It also is reasonable to assume that poor job prospects among fathers might contribute to the fact that about 60 percent of mother-only households have a child support award in place (Freeman and Waldfogel 1998, 4–5).

If fathers' declining employment prospects are even partly to blame for their failure to marry, or for low levels of economic and emotional involvement with their noncustodial children, then the relationship between the experience of low-wage employment and family involvement merits additional study. Although quantitative analyses have established a relationship between low-wage employment and father involvement, there are several problems with such analyses. First, low-income noncustodial fathers are seriously underrepresented in national surveys (Garfinkel, McLanahan, and Hanson 1998). Second, even if our target group of fathers was adequately represented in surveys, many of the fathers are evading child support orders and might be hesitant to tell a stranger (that is, a survey researcher) that they have noncustodial children whom they do not support. Third, many of these fathers work in the informal or underground economy, which also might make them hesitant to talk to survey researchers about their income-generating activities. Finally, even the best quantitative data cannot provide a full picture of what fathers think about their own experience with low-wage employment and its relationship to their ability or willingness to participate in family life.

Drawing on in-depth qualitative data in moderate- and high-poverty neighborhoods throughout the Philadelphia metropolitan area (Philadelphia City, Pennsylvania, and Camden, New Jersey), we attempt to show that work has not disappeared; rather, it has gone underground. Most of the noncustodial fathers we interviewed are indeed working—they just are not working in the formal economy. We also show that, contrary to popular belief, most fathers do not sell drugs when formal sector work is unavailable. Although many participate in the drug trade at some point in their work careers, most believe that such work is not a legitimate form of employment, particularly for fathers of young children. Thus most fathers work in jobs that fall in between the formal sector and the drug trade—in what scholars have variously termed the informal, irregular, or unregulated economy.

We argue that the lack of opportunity in the formal sector (a lack that is exacerbated by criminal records and drug and alcohol abuse), on the one hand, and strong norms about appropriate jobs for fathers, on the other hand, conspire to push men into legal but unregulated jobs. We also argue that racial and ethnic inequalities in wages and employment, so evident in the formal sector, are equally present in the unregulated sector and that these differences are primarily due to differences in network ties, on which the employers in the unregulated sector depend so heavily (Castells and Portes 1989).

METHOD

Our data are drawn from qualitative, in-depth interviews with low-income noncustodial fathers living in moderate- to high-poverty census tracts in Philadelphia, Pennsylvania, and Camden, New Jersey (which border each other and form part of the same metropolitan statistical area). This area includes several very poor neighborhoods containing large numbers of low-skilled male workers of African American, Latino, and European American descent. These neighborhoods are located throughout the South, North-Central, West Kensington, and Kensington areas of Philadelphia and throughout Camden, a very poor industrial suburb separated from downtown Philadelphia by the Delaware River.

The 1990 census reveals that these neighborhoods contain a large number of poor single mothers of black, white, and Latin descent (U.S. Bureau of the Census 1990). We thus assumed that we would find large numbers of noncustodial fathers in these neighborhoods as well. These neighborhoods essentially form a ring around downtown Philadelphia and have been home to the metropolitan area's low-income population for decades. The selection of these neighborhoods means that the white, African American, and Latino fathers in the study share a similar ecological context, a rare feature in sociological studies of poverty (the white poor are far more likely to live in mixed-income neighborhoods than the minority poor).

Many of the economic outcomes for unskilled and semi-skilled male workers are influenced by the health of the overall labor market. Within the Philadelphia MSA, the rate of unemployment in 1997 averaged nearly 6 percent, but Philadelphia city's rate was 7 percent and Camden's was above 15 percent. Philadelphia is a fast-shrinking northern rustbelt city where blue-collar manufacturing jobs have been in decline for over four decades, causing occupational dislocations among the sons of a stable working class of white and black men. In the past decade alone, the city lost more than fifty thousand jobs. Although Philadelphia has seen very modest job growth in recent years, losses have outweighed or kept even with the gains. Most job loss has occurred within the city limits, whereas eleven of every twelve new jobs created have been in Philadelphia's suburban ring (an hour or more away by bus or train from most of our target neighborhoods).

In addition to employment, policies regarding child support

payments from noncustodial fathers affect our study population as well. Both New Jersey and Pennsylvania are among the top five states in terms of child support collections. Both states now have investigators who pursue nonpaying fathers at home, on their jobs, and anywhere else they can find them. Fathers who do not pay face thirty days in jail. The efforts to collect child support in both of these states are quite aggressive.

In our interviews with fathers, we had five main goals. Our first goal was to obtain a detailed picture of the economic realities of low-wage employment among low-income noncustodial fathers. To do this, we had to get a sense of their budgets. Second, we wanted to collect extensive data on fathers' employment experiences in the formal and unregulated sectors of the economy, as well as information on how they move between job opportunities in these sectors. Third, we were interested in how low-income noncustodial fathers view employment opportunities in these different economic sectors. Fourth, we wanted to learn what income from these various low-wage sources of employment "buys" men in terms of family involvement. We were interested in both the *amount* of money earned and its *source*. Finally, we wanted to document the entire range of other factors that fathers say impede or enhance their ability to participate economically and emotionally in family life.

To explore the themes outlined, we conducted a study of roughly one hundred fathers, using multiple, in-depth interviews. The resulting sample includes thirty-two men of European American heritage, fifty-four of African American heritage, and sixteen of Latin American descent (mostly first- or second-generation migrants from Puerto Rico). All respondents are noncustodial fathers who earn less in the formal sector than the poverty line for a family of four. This means that our sample is limited to fathers earning $16,000 a year or less ($1,333 a month on average) *in the formal sector*. For full-time employees, this is the equivalent of about $8 per hour. In terms of educational level, our sample is limited to fathers without college degrees and captures the full range of heterogeneity in schooling in the noncollege category for each subgroup.

Many scholars have pointed to the large underrepresentation

of such fathers in nationally representative surveys—as many as half of all nonresident fathers could be missing from some surveys—and no survey is free from large underrepresentation problems. This situation is more acute among low-income fathers than among fathers on average, so our task was doubly difficult. For an excellent review of the literature regarding this issue, see Garfinkel, McLanahan, and Hanson (1998).

Because of these difficulties in survey samples, we identified our sample using the maximum heterogeneity approach that Edin and Lein used to recruit low-income single mothers in four U.S. cities (Edin and Lein 1997). We describe this approach in detail here. This approach does not fully satisfy concerns about *validity*, but the difficulties and cost associated with generating a random sample are extremely daunting, as we will show. In addition, in our interviews with fathers, we wanted to gather *reliable* data about highly sensitive issues such as income from illegal and informal employment. We also wanted fathers to talk freely about their involvement or lack of involvement in the lives of their children, and these conversations can be painful or embarrassing. Thus we chose the maximum heterogeneity method over a random sampling approach.

In each target neighborhood, we garnered referrals from a wide variety of third parties (local employers, single mothers, social service agencies, block captains, and grassroots community organizations) and from informal contacts we made while walking the streets of the neighborhood. We selectively pursued these referrals based on our sampling criteria. For each ethnic group, we pursued roughly half of our referrals from these sources. Then we asked successfully interviewed subjects to refer us to one or two other individuals. We instructed respondents to refer us to someone we probably would not have been able to recruit by relying on our other sources of referral.

We worked through a wide range of trusted third parties to get referrals to our fathers. These individuals were able to convince fathers that we were trustworthy, that we were not child support officials or undercover police officers (a very real worry for many of them), and that the information they shared was truly confidential. Though an exact response rate is nearly impossible to calculate given our recruitment practices, our economic and family involvement data from fathers were very detailed, and fathers were very forthcoming.

THE PREVALENCE OF WORK

Our interviews revealed that fathers are engaged in a lot of work that is not captured by official employment statistics. In fact, no father we interviewed who was not disabled (that is, receiving Supplemental Security Income) was completely without work during the previous year (even though General Assistance was available to men in both Pennsylvania and New Jersey), and most worked at least part-time for most of the year.

In table 14.1 we describe all of the jobs that the fathers in our sample had held during the twelve months preceding the interviews. Only about a third of the jobs were in the regulated sector of the economy, whereas two-thirds were in the unregulated sector.

The fathers we interviewed often distinguish between various types of regulated and unregulated work, distinctions that are important for understanding both ethnic and racial differences in types of employment and men's hierarchy of job preferences. What are the dimensions of these various types of regulated and unregulated jobs? Castells and Portes (1989) and others have developed various ways of categorizing regulated and unregulated work. We have developed a classification scheme inductively, based on the actual types of work that men reported doing and on their views of what kinds of distinctions were important in choosing between available jobs.

In table 14.1 we distinguish between jobs in three ways. First, some are formal sector jobs, and some are not. We define formal sector jobs as any job that is regulated by the Internal Revenue Service—in other words, any job for which the employer or the employee reports the work to government authorities, making it subject to taxation and other government regulation. Second, some jobs are legal in and of themselves (in other words, the work activities themselves are legal), and some are not. This dis-

TABLE 14.1 Classification of All Jobs Held in the Prior Twelve Months: Low-Income Fathers in Camden and Philadelphia

Legality and Independence	Regulated Sector	Unregulated Sector
Legal activities		
Employee	Day labor	Roofing
	Construction	Painting
	Social service agency	Commercial salvage
	Teacher's aide	Truck driver
	Sales	Rehabilitation-construction
	Store clerk	Distributing fliers
	Shipping clerk	Landscaping
	Factory work	Lawn maintenance
	Stock boy	Janitorial
	Line cook	Building superintendent
	Prep cook	Sandwich maker
	Security guard	
	Horse and carriage driver	
Entrepreneur		Auto repair
		Car stereo installation
		Car window tinting
		Catalog resale
		Junking
		Roofing
		Construction
		Exterminator
		Plumbing
		Painting
		Appliance repair-resale
		Car washing
		Handyman
		Speakeasy
		Artisan (makes bookmarks)
		Recycling (cans)
Illegal activities		
Entrepreneur		*Recycling (copper)*
		Liquor from New Jersey
		Prostitution
		Stealing or selling to fences
		Drug sales

Source: Authors' compilation.
Note: Jobs involving illegal activities are printed in italics.

tinction interacts with the first in interesting ways. A job may involve activity that is legal (roofing, for example), but the employee is hired informally (paid "under the table"). Other jobs involve activity that is both illegal and informal (like selling drugs).

This second distinction does not work perfectly in that ambiguities over the legality of specific work activities prevent any tidy solution. To offer a few examples, it is, of course, legal to install car radios in the cars of friends and neighbors for a fee. However, the method of acquiring the radio (which may be stolen and purchased through a fence) may be illegal. Tinting car windows may be illegal or legal, depending on which window is tinted. Similar difficulties arise in classifying the work of one of our respondents, who orders items from a popular auto and home stereo catalogue and resells them for a large markup to neighbors and friends. We categorize these activities as legal even though some aspect of the work is illegal, because the men themselves do not generally view them as criminal.

Furthermore, some activities, though clearly illegal, involve only misdemeanors rather than felonies like drug dealing, robbery, and so on. Two examples are buying liquor in New Jersey and taking it illegally across the state line for resale to Philadelphia restaurant owners and stealing copper wire and other valuable metal from vacant and boarded up buildings throughout the city and selling it to recyclers. To resolve this problem, we draw an additional distinction between jobs that involve misdemeanor crimes and those that involve a felony.

Third, we distinguish between jobs that involve working for an employer (a store owner or a contractor, for example) and jobs that are entrepreneurial (operating one's own car-washing business or repairing and reselling lawn mowers, televisions, washers and dryers, and other household implements). Sometimes the same activity can be employer based or entrepreneurial, depending on the working arrangements. Roofers, for example, sometimes work for contractors informally, while others are entrepreneurs and operate their own informal roofing businesses.

These distinctions leave us with a classification scheme that has eight possible cells. We have observations in some of these

FIGURE 14.1 **Principal Job Categories Reported by Low-Income Fathers Interviewed in Poor Neighborhoods of Camden and Philadelphia**

Regular jobs ———————————→	Regulated, legal, employee
Off-the-books jobs — ———————→	Unregulated, legal, employee
Informal businesses ——————→	Unregulated, legal, entrepreneur
Hustles ———————————→	Unregulated, illegal, entrepreneur, no drug involvement
Drug dealing ———————→	Unregulated, illegal, entrepreneur, drug involvement

Source: Authors' compilation.

cells, but not in others. Some are theoretically implausible (for example, regulated work that is illegal), and some are plausible but have not yet been observed in our sample (we did not interview any men working at regulated and legal entrepreneurial jobs, like hot dog cart operators or street vendors). It also is possible that if the drug trade were more organized in Philadelphia, we might classify street-level dealing as an illegal employer-based job.

Since we have only four cells with observations, our job of describing the range of work is simpler. We use the term "regular job" to refer to regulated employer-based jobs (see figure 14.1). We call work that is unregulated and employer-based "off-the-books jobs." Jobs that are unregulated and entrepreneurial are called "informal businesses," since that is what some of our respondents call them. Jobs that are unregulated, entrepreneurial, and illegal are called "hustles" if they are outside the drug economy and "drug sales" if they are within the drug economy. All of these labels are what some of our fathers actually call these jobs (what anthropologists call "member terms"). Let us take each of these types of jobs in turn.

Regular Jobs

Jobs in this sector include service, construction-related, and low-level manufacturing jobs. Men in these jobs earn between the legal minimum and $8 an hour. This category includes both jobs that are full-time and stable as well as jobs that are highly erratic (like day labor). Almost none includes any kind of health benefits. Regular jobs are preferred over many types of work, including some of the lower-level off-the-books jobs, many of the lower-end informal businesses, and especially any strictly illegal form of employment. This valuation occurs for several reasons.

First, fathers recognize the secondary advantages associated with work in the formal economy. Several spoke of how formal sector work is preferable to other types of employment because of the Social Security survivors insurance benefits their legal children can claim in the event of their early deaths (we use the term "legal children" because not all have established legal paternity for all of their children). Moreover, work in formal sector jobs might provide access to other government benefits, such as worker compensation and unemployment insurance. Men dream of landing formal sector jobs with employer-provided benefits like health care and life insurance. No father mentioned the availability of government-provided Social Security retirement benefits or employer-provided pensions as an advantage of formal sector employment, possibly because many doubt they will live to retirement age. It also is possible that retirement worries seem far off when their current economic situations are so unstable.

Second, fathers almost universally feel that landing a steady, full-time job would make them more desirable fathers in the eyes of both their children and the mothers, and that making steady contributions would give them more access to their children. Full-time employment is seldom available in the unregulated sector. In addition, fathers said that mothers often are very concerned about the source of their earnings, a theme we return to later.

Third, fathers thought that formal work might bring them *some* level of respectability among their family members, friends, and neighbors. In addition, many fathers said they want to feel that they are full participants in society and want to become taxpaying citizens. It is fascinating that these marginally employed men equate citizenship with paying taxes. More than one man told us, "I want to be able to say 'I pay taxes' like everyone else."

Fourth, fathers almost universally see the formal sector as the only road to substantial social mobility. Most feel that if they could find civil service or union work, they would advance to the respectable working class. This working-class respectability would bring them more than physical comforts; it might also mean that they could reunite with their children and their mothers or enter into a long-term relationship with a woman who has not yet borne them a child. Later in this chapter, we explain why fathers feel that drug proceeds cannot buy them this respectability.

Not all men view formal sector work in these positive terms, and not all types of formal sector work are viewed positively. Fathers nearly always distinguish between different types of formal sector employment. Of course, hourly wages are crucial, but the steadiness of the work, and the ability to claim full-time hours are as important to men as the amount they earn hourly. When added to considerations of whether the jobs bring government or employer benefits, most men have a complex set of criteria on which they rate formal sector work. In reality, however, many of the jobs in this imaginary hierarchy are not available to these fathers.

Although most fathers have held at least one fairly good (well-paying and stable) formal sector job in the past, they also reported considerable difficulty moving laterally from one good job to another when they are laid off or fired or when they quit. Thus most fathers also have had several very unstable and poorly paid formal sector jobs. Day labor is chief among these. The major distinctions men make between types of formal-sector labor are between steady jobs, part-time and seasonal work they find on their own, and temporary jobs they find through a day labor agency. Steady jobs are full-time, are relatively permanent, and pay more than the minimum wage. Part-time and seasonal work includes jobs at a fast food restaurant, jobs working retail during the Christmas rush, and so on.

Day labor is on the bottom of the formal sector hierarchy. Like cities everywhere, Philadelphia's economy offers scores of opportunities for employers to make minimal commitments to less-skilled employees. Day labor operators in Philadelphia contract with businesses who need strong arms, legs, and backs, but little skill, to fill out their factory shop floors, move equipment before and after trade shows, clean up construction sites, and so on. Although traditional day labor operators pay workers at or slightly above the minimum wage, they charge employers considerably more. Employers like the arrangement because they do not have to recruit, screen, and hire laborers. They also are freed from regulations regarding employee benefits. To preserve their "take" from their operation, day labor operators often have rules prohibiting these employers from hiring any of their day labor employees directly for a substantial period of time after the contract ends (generally four months). Thus short stints as a day laborer rarely lead to long-term employment.

There are nine day labor operators in the City of Camden, where we conducted about a third of our interviews. Camden unemployment rates have been four times the national average over the last decade, so there is heavy competition for day labor positions. Several of the fathers we interviewed are "loyal" to one day labor operation or another and said that their loyalty and reputation for working hard are rewarded during the winter months, when cold weather means that outdoor construction work dries up and day labor jobs are very scarce.

Other men work in teams, with each team member assigned to a particular agency. When a given team member learns that there is work to be had at his agency, he beeps the others, who then make their way over if prospects for work at their own agency look less promising. Since most of Camden's agencies are within walking distance of one another, even men with no transportation can get from one agency to another in no more than ten to fifteen minutes. Being part of a team enhances their prospects of finding work on any given day. However, in the long term, men who move from agency to agency to get work are perceived as less loyal by any given operator and thus move down the queue for work in the winter months when work is scarce.

The day labor operators in our Philadelphia neighborhoods are less concentrated, and men cannot go from one to another quickly. Thus day labor is less viable as a source of employment in most of our Philadelphia neighborhoods than in Camden. Agencies provide work that is very labor intensive and seldom lasts for more than a few weeks or even several days. In addition, most jobs are seasonal, like construction or landscaping, so although summer work is plentiful, these opportunities become scarce when the temperature begins to fall. Only in rare cases does day labor lead to more permanent employment.

Off-the-Books Jobs

Off-the-books jobs paid an hourly wage ranging from $5 to $15 an hour, but these jobs did not offer full-time, year-round employment. The most common off-the-books jobs we observed were roofing and other low-skilled, construction-related work, which offer little employment in winter months. The most steady among them typically pay the most poorly (for example, the part-time jobs as sandwich maker at a Korean convenience store and delicatessen, apartment building superintendent, and janitor). Most of the higher-paying jobs are not only seasonal (roofing, painting, landscaping) but also subject to weather-related interruptions. The exception is local truck driving, which pays a relatively high wage and provides part-time work throughout the year.

In Philadelphia, many of these jobs would be unionized if they were in the formal sector. Presumably, this is part of the reason why employers like to hire their least-skilled employees this way. Because unions have lost much of their ability to ensure high wages, and because they impose high dues on members, most of the men who work at these relatively high-wage jobs said they would rather work off-the-books.

Informal Businesses

The main feature that distinguishes informal businesses from off-the-books employment is that the men who work them are entrepreneurs rather than employees. This type of unregulated entrepreneurship can be highly profitable, but several factors limit the ability of fathers to become successful in their efforts or even to participate in this type of work activity at all. First, many informal businesses involve the construction trades (roofing, painting, and plumbing). The fathers who practice these trades informally either own their own tools or are able to borrow them from friends or employers. They need to have ready capital in order to purchase materials needed for specific jobs, and not the least important, they need to have reliable transportation for themselves and their equipment (which generally means a truck and a valid driver's license).

One of our fathers works full-time for a beer distributor (a regulated job). He purchased his own exterminating equipment with the wages from his regular job and started an unregulated weekend exterminating business by posting fliers throughout his neighborhood. Junking is an activity that involves driving a truck around Philadelphia's wealthier neighborhoods and suburbs and picking up any salvageable items for resale in scrap yards and thrift stores. This activity can be quite lucrative, but on many evenings fathers make nothing at all. Junking requires a truck and a driver's license, and some fathers told us they are saving money in order to capitalize a junking business.

Not all informal businesses are this lucrative, however. This category also includes some very low-level jobs that men engage in only when they cannot get any other type of work. These jobs generally are held only by individuals who are drug addicted or have other serious problems. For example, some fathers wipe down cars at car washes for tips, often making as little as $1 an hour. Others collect aluminum cans and sell them to a recycling plant, again making only $1 or $2 an hour. Selling newspapers on the street is a similar activity, although we did not interview anyone in this category. What is fascinating is that men work these jobs rather than participate in the drug economy, which is far more lucrative. Oftentimes, these very low-level jobs only provide men with enough cash to get high on a couple of "forties" of malt liquor or a six-pack of beer.

Hustles

Hustles include activities that are against the law, but are not related to the drug trade. Most men work at these jobs only a few hours a day or week, generally to supplement other types of work. One father is paid $10 each time he allows a customer to perform oral sex on him. This takes about half an hour, so he earns $20 an hour in this activity. However, he only engages in this activity a few times a week. Our sole thief steals ladders, rakes, and other tools from yards and garages and resells them door to door or at informal flea markets. Another father makes extra cash by purchasing liquor in New Jersey, illegally bringing it over the state line, and reselling it to thrifty restaurateurs in Pennsylvania. Finally, some men scavenge copper pipes, wire, and other metals from boarded up and vacant buildings. They sell these items to a local recycling plant, which pays them quite well for the material.

The Drug Economy

Although hustles are illegal, most fathers do not view them as serious crimes. However, drug dealing is another matter, and most fathers place it into a category of its own. Although half of the fathers in the sample said they had sold drugs at some point in their lives, most felt that dealing is a morally reprehensible activity for fathers, especially as they grow older. Perhaps because of the low esteem in which this occupation is held, the vast majority of fathers who deal drugs only do so as a side activity combined with other, more acceptable forms of employment. One father, for example, was laid off of a regular job and could only find part-time formal sector work to replace it. In order to make up the difference between his part-time earnings and his bills, he bought an "eight-ball" of crack and sold it to old high school friends in the neighborhood.

Another father began dealing when his day labor agency could not provide him with sufficient hours:

> When I seen that they really wasn't keeping me busy, that's when I started doing the drug thing. That kept me busy, [it] gave me more money and everything than just the temp service. So it was just whenever [the temp service] called me or whenever I felt as though the cops was trying to lock people up that I worked with the temp services.

For some of our fathers, participation in the underground economy began as a form of youthful employment. Others generally began selling drugs in their late teens and early twenties, after losing a formal sector job, getting laid off in the winter, or not getting enough hours of work. As fathers matured into early adulthood, many continued to use underground work as a way of smoothing income flows when other more "legitimate" types of work were unavailable. By the time they reached the age of twenty-five, however, most fathers reported that they had aged out of the drug trade.

When young inner-city boys enter their teenage years, their taste for expensive clothing, tennis shoes, and so on grows. Generally, their mothers are either on welfare or working at a low-wage job. If their fathers are involved, their employment is generally low paying and unstable. In many cases, however, no father is involved. Thus parents cannot provide the kinds of things teen-agers feel they need to have to earn respect among their peers. It is not surprising that these teenagers become obsessed with making money. Since their communities offer few legitimate avenues for earning money, the drug trade becomes a major form of youth employment.

In addition, the school-to-work transition often presents un-skilled young men with few full-time or steady work opportunities, so low-level drug dealing often helps young adult men smooth income flows. When boys and young men are still living at home and have few financial or relational responsibilities, working in the drug trade provides enough cash to buy an expensive sweat suit, a pair of tennis shoes, a fast food meal after school, and gifts for a girlfriend. But as men age, the trade begins to take a toll. Dealers work late into the night in all kinds of weather. Although these older boys and young men might have a week or two with fantastically high earnings, such weeks are rare. Far more common are weeks when they net only $7, $8, or $9 an hour for their efforts, or even less.

Meanwhile, these older boys and young men are in constant fear of police detection, arrest, and incarceration. Dealers perceive the risk of arrest as extremely high, and even if arrest does not lead to incarceration, such men become "known" to the police, lessening their ability to ply their trade openly on the street. Arrest and incarceration mean less to a juvenile than to an adult, and as boys move beyond their eighteenth birthday their altercations with the police become part of their permanent record. From then on, the stakes increase dramatically with each arrest and conviction, and the prospect of spending years in jail becomes frighteningly real. The mounting penalties serve as a strong disincentive to working in the drug economy, and as men approach their middle twenties, most no longer think it is worth the risk.

Along with the risk of incarceration, drug dealing carries with it two other potential risks. First, men fear the street violence that often accompanies work in the drug trade. Most young men know of someone in their community who was killed as a result of drug-related activity. As their involvement grows, so does their belief that they themselves constitute potential victims of street violence. Second, the drug itself poses a substantial risk. Men who sell seldom use at first (although some begin using first and then try to sell in order support their habit), but many succumb eventually. As they begin using, they are more likely to smoke or shoot up all of their profits, meaning that they get nothing but high for their labors. They also are more likely to get in trouble on the street or with the police. If men become addicts, their criminal employers often deem them unreliable, and their addiction eventually locks them out of the trade.

Finally, men who work in the underground economy often find that the money they earn cannot get them ahead in the long term. Respondents who sell drugs described how they spend the money they earn selling drugs on their own habit, on alcohol, on fast food, on clothing, and on extravagant gifts for their girlfriends. No father has saved any of the money he earns; no father has bought a house (row houses can sometimes be had for $20,000 or less in these neighborhoods) or paid for a college education; and only one father has bought a car for cash (which he abandoned while fleeing from the police). More important, fathers seldom use any of the money they earn from drugs to support their children or other kin.

Indeed, men told us that such contributions are likely to be refused if offered. Working in the drug trade is viewed in such strongly negative terms by the community at large that fathers who work in it often find themselves completely cut off from family and friends. This exile is both self-imposed (fathers are ashamed of their activities) and imposed from the outside (their children's mothers and their own mothers and other kin generally revile them for their activities). Thus proceeds from the underground economy cannot buy fathers what most desperately want—to have ongoing contact with their children, to have a stable common-law or marital relationship, and to live a moderately respectable life in the eyes of their kin, friends, and neighbors.

For all these reasons, in the end, most men take one of three paths out of the trade by their middle twenties: incarceration, addiction, or a move to other types of employment. In the first two cases, the father frequently cannot find or keep work in the formal sector. Men with criminal records told us of repeated failures in trying to find legitimate employment (except through day labor and specialized niches like food preparation, where employers know that prisons train convicts for the job). Men with drug addictions are seldom steady enough to keep their formal sector jobs even if they manage to get them. Only traditional day labor agencies are able or willing to employ these men, and those whose work habits are erratic quickly become known around the day labor circuit and are locked out of the formal sector entirely. These fathers are relegated to the unregulated sectors.

ETHNIC AND RACIAL INEQUALITY
IN THE INFORMAL SECTOR

Wage inequalities by race and ethnicity among similarly skilled men are well-established in the formal sector, but we are aware of no research that looks at wage inequalities in unregulated sectors of the economy. For each racial and ethnic group, a distinctive labor market queue spans both the regulated and unregulated sectors of the economy. Table 14.2 shows employment over the past twelve months for fathers in each of our racial and ethnic groups. It reveals that these fathers live and work in a highly racialized low-wage labor market that confers advantages to whites at all levels and disadvantages African Americans and Latinos (in our case, mainly Puerto Ricans).

Our interviews suggest that informal sector jobs (both informal and underground) are as highly racialized as formal sector jobs. Indeed, the only informal sector occupation that is common among all groups is selling drugs! We find that the primary reason that whites are paid more than African Americans is *not* the disproportionate involvement of blacks with the criminal justice system or differences in substance abuse patterns, although these play a role; nor is employer discrimination at the root of the problem (although black men felt that this plays a role in the *formal* sector). Rather, fathers in different groups get their jobs in radically different ways, reflecting important differences in the composition of their social networks. Since the literature shows that the informal sector is more highly dependent on network ties than the formal sector, our discovery of the importance of social networks should not be surprising.

TABLE 14.2 **Classification by Race and Ethnicity of Jobs Held by Low-Income Fathers in Camden and Philadelphia**

Legality, Race, and Independence	Regulated Sector	Unregulated Sector
Whites (n = 30)		
Legal		
Employee	Stock boy ($6)	Roofing ($12 to $15)[a]
	Warehouse clerk ($6.50)	Truck driving ($12)[a]
		Rehabilitation-construction ($8 to $10)
		Painting ($8 to $10)
		Commercial salvage ($7.50)
		Residential salvage ($10)
Illegal		
Entrepreneur		Auto repair ($10)
		Drug sales ($7 to ?)
African Americans (n = 40)		
Legal		
Employee	Construction ($5.60)	Landscaping ($6.25)
	Social service agency ($8)	Lawn maintenance ($7.50)
	Teacher's aide ($7.50)	Cleaning ($6)
	Cashier ($6.50)	Painting ($8)
	Shipping clerk ($8)	Building superintendent ($7.50)
	Machine operator ($6)	Sandwich maker ($6)
	Day laborer ($5.15 to $5.50)	
	Fast food ($5.15)	
	Line cook ($8)	
	Prep cook ($7)	
	Security guard ($5.15)	
	Stock boy ($6)	
Entrepreneur		"Recycling" ($0 to $5)
		Car washing ($1 to $5)
		Appliance repair ($1 to $5)
Illegal		
Entrepreneur		"Recycling" ($5 to $10)
		Drug sales ($7 to ?)
		Theft-resale ($1 to ?)

TABLE 14.2 *Continued*

Legality, Race, and Independence	Regulated Sector	Unregulated Sector
Latinos (n = 16)		
Legal		
Employee	Social service agency ($8)	
Entrepreneur		"Yunquear" ($1 to $20)
		Roofing ($12 to $15)
		Install stereos ($10)
		Tint car windows ($10)
		Crutchfield resale ($8)
		Speakeasy ($8)
Illegal		
Entrepreneur		Liquor from New Jersey ($10)
		Prostitution ($20)
		Drug sales ($7 to ?)

Source: Authors' compilation.
Note: Hourly wages are in parentheses.
a Though these jobs paid more than $8 per hour, the men that held them only worked part time or part year. Thus, their incomes were below $16,000 per year.

Race and ethnicity operate through a multitude of channels to affect jobs in the informal sector. One-third of our African American fathers have criminal records, about the same proportion as our white fathers. For both races, the jobs held by fathers with criminal records are more likely to be in the informal sector than the jobs held by fathers in their group generally. However, one group of ex-criminals does *not* tend to be more disadvantaged than the other (in terms of holding a formal sector job). Current drug use is somewhat more common among our African American fathers (about one in five is addicted) than among whites (only about one in ten said that drug or alcohol abuse prohibits him from holding a more stable job), and those fathers all work in very low-level informal businesses or underground jobs. Far more important than these other factors are ethnic-racial differences in the composition of men's networks.

Whites generally find work through their social networks. Most whites have both kin and friends from the "old neighbor-hood" who are contractors or owners and operators of other for-mal sector businesses. These employers hire many of their unskilled or semiskilled laborers informally. It is fascinating to read through the interview transcripts and find white fathers who, despite chronic alcohol problems or drug addition, lengthy criminal histories, and erratic work behavior, find relatively good unregulated jobs again and again through network contacts (even though they have considerable difficulty gaining work in the *formal* sector). The only white men who are really badly off in terms of employment are those whose behavior is so reprehensible (or whose drug addiction is so severe) that they have burned their bridges with friends and kin. These men sometimes work through employment services where, for a hefty fee, the agency sets them up with a formal sector job. Most of these jobs are not as well paying as those they can get through network members in the informal sector.

Moreover, the white men working in high-paying off-the-books jobs do not, in general, aspire to anything more that the kinds of jobs they already hold. They just want the work to be more regular. They have little or no desire to hold a formal sector union job, because at their skill level the union dues make such work less profitable than informal sector work. Their work histories show that they have never been very attached to the formal sector.

In general, the white men we interviewed prefer employment opportunities in the informal or legal sector to jobs in the formal economy or underground jobs. Their work is seldom entrepreneurial. Thus whites cluster in what we call off-the-books jobs. Although the white men in our sample are very marginal to the communities in which they live and are on the very bottom end of the labor market for white males, they generally are able to capitalize on childhood ties with others from their home neighborhoods who have been more successful.

White men's employers are generally building, siding, or painting contractors or owners of small businesses such as bakeries. These employers hire their most-skilled laborers through formal channels and hire their less-skilled workers informally (probably to evade union pay rates). Building contractors hire men with whom they have such ties to help with roofing and site cleanup informally. Bakery owners hire these same men informally to drive their bakery trucks. Because these jobs are generally unionized in the formal sector, they pay far better than mini-mum wage in the informal sector. Our white roofers, for example, generally are paid a flat rate of between $95 and $125 a day, re-gardless of how many hours they work. Our bakery truck drivers earn upward of $10 an hour ($12 on average). However, both types of jobs are episodic or seasonal.

For these white fathers, moving to the formal sector in these same occupations would mean three things: work would be harder to get (they would have difficulty getting into the union), they would have to pay taxes, and they would be forced to absorb hefty union dues. The only other formal sector occupations open to them involve low-paying factory and service sector jobs, which pay far less an hour. Nearly all have worked in the formal sector at least once in the past, but well-paying formal sector jobs are scarce, and when they lose or quit these jobs, they often cannot find another formal sector job with the same rate of pay.

Latino and African American men almost never mentioned communal and family ties as a source for jobs. African Americans generally find regulated work through day labor agencies, news-paper advertisements, and help wanted signs. Off-the-books jobs of the kinds that whites hold are generally unavailable to blacks because they do not have the network ties to employers. Only infrequently do they find either formal or informal sector jobs through family members and friends. Roughly one-third of our African American fathers use their entrepreneurial skills to create informal sector jobs for themselves. These jobs, however, tend to pay substantially less than minimum wage, and men only tend to make these jobs for themselves when their drug addiction has be-come so bad that they can no longer get even a day labor job.

The interview transcripts reveal another difference between white and African American fathers. African American fathers nearly universally prefer stable, formal sector jobs over any other type of employment. Their desired wages are not exorbitant—$7.00 to $7.50 an hour—but they want the job to be full-time and year-round. The African American fathers talked a lot about how motivated they are to find these kinds of jobs. The exceptions are the drug addicts, who know that such jobs are out of their reach for now. Even those with criminal records work to find such jobs.

One interesting niche is food preparation. It is relatively

steady and pays moderately well, and employers seldom care if the employees have criminal histories, since many men train for food preparation in prison. Other formal sector niches for black men, like private security and dietary aid work, are generally less available to African American men with criminal records. For African American fathers, the unregulated sector is merely a stopgap measure, while they seek formal sector work.

Typically, African American fathers prefer formal sector work to either informal or underground jobs. Many of these fathers have held such jobs in the past—some of them quite well paying. But as they lose or quit these jobs, few find equivalent jobs with other employers. Others believe that they will never be able to get these jobs, even if they desire them, because they have a criminal record. Still others believe they will not be able to keep formal sector jobs because of their substance abuse (too often they need to skip a day of work). For all of these reasons, older African American fathers generally find work in formal sector day labor or in informal jobs. However, the types of informal sector jobs they reported are not nearly as lucrative as those of their white counterparts. No one in this group works at roofing or in the construction trade, for example. Some work informally for employers and some as entrepreneurs, but the more entrepreneurial the activity, the more poorly it pays (with the exception of drug sales).

Latinos generally gravitate toward entrepreneurial, unregulated employment and tend to do far better economically than African Americans. This may be because most of our Latino respondents are recent migrants who have a greater familiarity with entrepreneurship in the informal sector (which is often more prevalent in Puerto Rico than on the mainland). In other words, their greater socialization into the informal sector may confer advantages. Again, we did not interview very many men in this group, so it is important to resist making too much of these findings.

Jobs and Fathering

Children play a powerful role in the lives of the fathers in our study. Some are heavily involved with the economic and emotional support of their children, and some have never seen them. Nevertheless, men told us that being a father is one of the most important things in their lives. When we asked fathers what their lives would be like without their children, we expected that fathers would tell us that they would have more money for themselves, would have less hassle from authorities in regard to child support, would be able to finish high school and enroll in a training program, and so on. Instead, nearly every father told us, "I'd be dead or in jail."

One father said, "If I didn't have none, then I guess I would be out trying to get some." Another said, "I just want to know that when I die, there will be something out there to show that I was on the planet, something that looks like me. That way, people will remember that I existed." Still another said, "Having a son is very important to me, because I know that even if I don't make nothin' out of my life, he might go beyond me and make something of his life. Something I can be proud of. He might go beyond me, you know." Several described their lives before fatherhood as "falling apart" or "spinning out of control." These men told us that children help them "settle down" or "leave the fast life" and give them "something to live for, something to strive for" or "a reason to get myself together and make something of my life, so's he can be proud of me" (men talked far more about their sons than their daughters). These views illustrate the powerful symbolic importance that children have for the men who fathered them, even if those men do not actually parent or support the child in any way.

Fathers view some jobs as compatible with being a father and some as incompatible (see table 14.3). In general, fathers agree that activities that are both informal and illegal and that involve a felony offense (underground jobs) are not compatible with fathering. Off-the-books work and informal businesses do not always have such a stigma, particularly if they pay well or are stable. Jobs that pay quite well and are only illegal in some respects also carry little stigma (hustles). The most incompatible jobs are the most dangerous for the fathers and, according to them, would be dangerous for the children should they follow their fathers' example and take them up as adults. They involve a significant risk of incarceration or even death and could bring danger into the household of anyone involved with them.

There are also formal sector jobs that are generally viewed as

TABLE 14.3 **Compatibility of Jobs with Fathering, as Seen by Low-Income Fathers from Poor Neighborhoods in Philadelphia and Camden**

Legality and Independence	Regulated Sector	Unregulated Sector
Legal		

Employee	Generally acceptable
	Depending on pay and
	  regularity
	  No fast food
	  No other minimum wage
	  Service job that is not full
	    time
	  No day laboring
	  Especially for older fathers
		Generally acceptable
		Depending on pay and
		  regularity

Entrepreneur		Depending on pay and
		  regularity
		More acceptable for Latinos
		  than for blacks

Illegal		
Entrepreneur		Generally not acceptable Depending on pay and regularity
Drugs		Not acceptable

Source: Authors' compilation.

incompatible with fathering. These are minimum-wage jobs in the service sector, such as working at McDonald's, and day labor jobs in the formal sector. Low-level service sector jobs are seldom full-time, offer no benefits, and generally pay poorly. Fathers said that these jobs are "good enough for me, but won't do anything for my kids." The same can be said for day labor work in the formal sector, which also pays badly and is extremely unstable. Fathers use such jobs for their own subsistence when necessary, but they are constantly looking for something that offers better pay or stability. Age might also be a factor in explaining whether jobs are viewed as legitimate. Drug sales, for example, are more acceptable for teenage and young adult fathers than for grown men who should "know better."

CONCLUSIONS

In this chapter, we have made three main points. First, low-income fathers are engaged in a lot of work that is not likely to be captured by official employment statistics. Work for unskilled inner-city fathers has not disappeared; it has simply gone underground. Second, we found persistent racial differences between blacks and whites in the informal as well as the formal economy, although the situation was more complicated for Latinos. Whereas direct discrimination may play an important role in the formal economy, racial differentials within the informal economy reflect intergroup differences in the mechanisms of job acquisition and recruitment. In contrast to low-income whites, Latino and African American men almost never mention communal and family ties as a source for jobs. Third, some jobs are considered more or less compatible with their roles as fathers. Jobs in the drug economy are the clearest example of this perception, and as men seek to activate their fathering roles they move away from drug sales into other occupations that are less morally reprehensible in the eyes of the community and less dangerous for them and their families.

The data reported in this chapter are part of a larger study that is still in progress. In the summer of 2001, we (with Laura Lein) completed interviews with 480 low-income, noncustodial fathers of black, white, and Latino descent in the Charleston, South Carolina, Philadelphia, and Austin, Texas, metropolitan areas. With this larger data set, we will be able to refine and extend the analysis presented here. Because Austin's and Charleston's labor markets are significantly tighter than Philadelphia's, we expect to observe how the greater availability of formal sector employment affects the racial dynamics and patterns of family involvement discussed in this chapter.

The authors would like to thank Antwi Akom, Susan Clampet-Lundquist, Mirella Landriscina, David Mitchell, Magaly Sánchez, and Eric K. Shaw for their invaluable assistance with interviews and analysis. This research was funded by the Department of Health and Human Services and by the Russell Sage Foundation.

REFERENCES

Blank, Rebecca. 1995. "Outlook for the U.S. Labor Market and Prospects for Low-Wage Entry Jobs." In *The Work Alternative*, edited by Demetra Smith Nightingale and Robert Haveman. Washington, D.C.: Urban Institute Press.

Bloom, David, Cecilia Conrad, and Cynthia Miller. 1998. "Child Support and Fathers' Remarriage and Fertility." In *Fathers Under Fire: The Revolution in Child Support Enforcement*, edited by Irwin Garfinkel, Sara S. McLanahan, Daniel R. Meyer, and Judith A. Seltzer. New York: Russell Sage Foundation.

Castells, Manuel, and Alejandro Portes. 1989. "World Underneath: The Origins, Dynamics, and Effects of the Informal Economy." In *The Informal Economy: Studies in Advanced and Less Developed Countries*, edited by Alejandro Portes, Manuel Castells, and Lauren A. Benton. Baltimore, Md.: Johns Hopkins University Press.

Danziger, Sheldon, and Peter Gottschalk, eds. 1993. *Uneven Tides: Rising Inequality in America*. New York: Russell Sage Foundation.

Edin, Kathryn. 2000. "What Do Low-Income Single Mothers Say about Marriage?" *Social Problems* 47(1): 112–33.

Edin, Kathryn, and Laura Lein. 1997. *Making Ends Meet: How Single Mothers Survive Welfare and Low-Wage Work*. New York: Russell Sage Foundation.

Fossett, Mark A., and K. Jill Kiecolt. 1993. "Mate Availability and Family Structure among African Americans in U.S. Metropolitan Areas." *Journal of Marriage and the Family* 55(2): 302–31.

Freeman, Richard B., and Jane Waldfogel. 1998. "Does Child Support Enforcement Affect Male Labor Supply?" In *Fathers under Fire: The Revolution in Child Support Enforcement*, edited by Irwin Garfinkel, Sara S. McLanahan, Daniel R. Meyer, and Judith A. Seltzer. New York: Russell Sage Foundation.

Garfinkel, Irwin, Sara S. McLanahan, and Thomas L. Hanson. 1998. "A Patchwork Portrait of Nonresident Fathers." In *Fathers under Fire: The Revolution in Child Support Enforcement*, edited by Irwin Garfinkel, Sara S. McLanahan, Daniel R. Meyer, and Judith A. Seltzer. New York: Russell Sage Foundation.

Lichter, Daniel T., Felicia B. LeClere, and Diane K. McLaughlin. 1991. "Local Marriage Market Conditions and the Marital Behavior of Black and White Women." *American Journal of Sociology* 96(4): 843–67.

Oppenheimer, Valerie K. 1988. "A Theory of Marriage Timing." *American Journal of Sociology* 94(3): 563–91.

Rank, Mark R. 1987. "The Formation and Dissolution of Marriages in the Welfare Population." *Journal of Marriage and the Family* 49(1): 15–20.

Schoen, Robert, and James R. Kluegel. 1988. "The Widening Gap in Black and White Marriage Rates: The Impact of Population Composition and Differential Marriage Propensities." *American Sociological Review* 53(6): 895–907.

South, Scott J., and Kim M. Lloyd. 1992. "Marriage Opportunities and Family Formation: Further Implications of Imbalanced Sex Ratios." *Journal of Marriage and the Family* 54(2): 440–51.

Tucker, Belinda B., and Claudia Mitchell-Kernan, eds. 1996. *The Decline in Marriage among African Americans: Causes, Consequences, and Policy Implications.* New York: Russell Sage Foundation.

U.S. Bureau of the Census. 1990. *Census of Population and Housing.* Washington: U.S. Government Printing Office.

U.S. House of Representatives Committee on Ways and Means. 1993. *Overview of Entitlement Programs (Green Book).* Washington: U.S. Government Printing Office.

Wilson, William Julius. 1987. *The Truly Disadvantaged: The Inner City, the Underclass, and Public Policy.* Chicago: University of Chicago Press.

———. 1996. *When Work Disappears: The World of the New Urban Poor.* New York: Alfred A. Knopf.

Chapter 15

The Social Situation
of the Black Executive:
Black and White Identities
in the Corporate World

Elijah Anderson

African Americans in executive-level positions in the United States today must deal with extremely complex social dynamics. As blacks they are identified first and foremost as members of a historically stigmatized group; as corporate executives they are identified as members of an elite and powerful class. This ethnographic case study examining their problems and efforts to deal with them will yield insights into the situation not only of black executives but also of marginalized minorities more generally.

In preparing to enter the field, I requested complete access to the workers in a major financial service corporation in central city Philadelphia. Such access would have afforded me the opportunity to follow and observe the subjects of the study in their daily activities and to question them at will. I would have liked to have engaged in intensive participant observation, an ideal situation for generating slice-of-life portrayals of the work setting and for gleaning important insights into the corporate culture generally and the social situation of minority employees of the company more particularly. The company rejected this plan. Instead, I was permitted to roam the premises and interview persons referred to me by the vice president for employee relations, who is himself black.

The representation here is therefore based both on observation of the social setting and on intensive ethnographic interviews with a small sample of executive-level minority employees including blacks, Jews, and women. The resulting observations are meant to be not representative but rather suggestive of the quality of experience within the company. Over the course of six months, I conducted interviews on the work premises or at area restaurants during the workday, and they frequently extended to ninety minutes. (In order to build on this primary research, I have been informally interviewing a variety of black and white, male and female executives of organizations throughout the Philadelphia area over the past ten years.) The company provided office space as well as time for employees to be interviewed, and the interviewees were most helpful and candid in their discussion of the questions put to them. The interviews were open-ended and informal in an attempt to elicit information and insights into the personal lives of employees and their situation within the organization.

HISTORICAL BASIS OF AFFIRMATIVE ACTION

An adequate assessment of the present-day situation of executives in this company, and in the American corporate world in general, requires some historical perspective on black mobility. Such a viewpoint is important since social change within this corporate environment is related to important changes in other major institutions of American society. Over the past half century, American society changed profoundly in the area of race relations (see Myrdal 1944; Drake and Cayton 1962 [1945]; Cox 1948; Hacker 1995; Wilson 1980, 1987, 1996). Largely as a consequence of affirmative action programs, black Americans, long segregated in ghettos and treated as second-class citizens, began to participate in the wider society in ways previously restricted to privileged members of the white majority. This process of racial incorporation signaled the beginning of the still very slow decline of the American caste-like system of race relations, and it may be traced to certain general sociohistorical developments. The most dramatic changes were spurred by the civil rights movement, the subsequent major civil disorders, and the social and political responses to these new and provocative developments (see Kerner et al. 1968).

Major policy responses included the civil rights legislation of 1964, 1965, and 1968. Perhaps most important for the subject of this chapter was the executive order issued and signed by President John F. Kennedy in 1961 and later revised by President Lyndon Johnson in 1964 prescribing "affirmative action" as an important remedy for racial discrimination, social injustice, and the resulting inequality. At the time, public support for these remedial measures was widespread and overwhelming, but by no means unanimous. Some critics have argued that because of the overarching concern of government, business, and academia for social peace, these policies were simply desperate measures to "cool out the long hot summers," in particular, and to mollify alienated black Americans and their white allies, more generally.

Although there was desire on the part of policymakers to prevent further outbursts of violence and disorder in American cities, there also appeared to be a genuine national consensus on the need to make the socioeconomic system more equitable, particularly for members of the nation's black community. Also important was the provocative international specter of black Americans being whipped and beaten daily in their efforts to obtain the basic right to vote in the world's leading democracy. This image was simply too much of a contradiction for many Americans, including policymakers, to bear, particularly with the emergence of so many newly independent "colored" nations of Africa and other parts of the Third World, which were in the process of trying to decide, in the midst of the cold war, whether to follow in the orbit of the Soviet Union or the West.

Whatever the reasoning or intentions of policymakers, American social life has moved toward equality for blacks since that time. Moreover, to a significant degree, the events that have provided more mobility for blacks also have done so for other minority groups. Blacks, women, and members of other minority groups, including newly arrived immigrants, have become the beneficiaries of significant civil rights legislation, including affirmative action, which has been strictly enforced by successive federal administrations, with the exception of those of presidents Reagan and Bush. As a result, members of these groups, most notably white women, are now participating in the American occupational structure at levels inconceivable a few decades ago.

Consistent with these trends, the black middle class has expanded in both size and outlook and appears to be in the process of transforming from a class of small business operators and professionals serving the black community almost exclusively to one that is increasingly economically independent of that community (see Frazier 1957; Wilson 1980; Landry 1987; Collins 1997). With such developments, more and more middle-class blacks are involved in the corporate and business sectors of society at large. Even to the casual observer, black Americans appear to be included more fully in American life than ever before. Largely shut out from becoming bankers, stockbrokers, corporate executives, and responsible government agents before the social upheaval brought on by the civil rights movement (see Stryker 1953), blacks have become increasingly visible in such occupations, although very few move beyond the middle levels to areas of major influence.

Beginning in the 1960s, as part of the general movement toward greater black incorporation, an impressive number of African Americans began attending predominantly white colleges and universities from which they were previously excluded, at times by law; the number of black professors, particularly those teaching at predominantly white institutions, also increased. This general process of incorporation did not bypass the corporations, some of which gladly recruited blacks; others, though, needed to be pressured into establishing affirmative action programs to remedy past underrepresentation and discrimination.

However, as African Americans became ostensible beneficiaries of affirmative action, leading to a growing presence of middle-class blacks in major social positions, especially in corporate life, growing numbers of white Americans began to feel highly threatened. In an era of de-industrialization, corporate downsizing, and the resulting insecurities of the American workforce, policies that were once indulged and viewed as noble efforts against racial discrimination became increasingly viewed as so many "race preferences" for blacks. In these circumstances, efforts to include blacks worked to create a growing backlash and resentment among a number of those whites with whom individual black beneficiaries would share work settings. Indeed, many whites, and some blacks, have gone so far as to mount legal and ideological challenges to affirmative action programs, arguing "reverse discrimination" (see Glazer 1987 [1975], 1997; *Regents of the State of California v. Bakke,* 438 U.S. 265, 1978; Skrentny 1996; Bearak 1997). All this has culminated in a growing nationwide movement to legally dismantle affirmative action programs through state initiatives. Proposition 209 outlawed affirmative action in California, foreshadowing what could happen throughout the United States.

Ironically, along with the apparent growth of black representation and participation in various areas of American life, but particularly in the workplace, fewer citizens see a need for affirmative action. With such visible black participation, as well as the growing presence of other minorities, including white women, in the workplace, it becomes increasingly difficult to make the argument that racism is the sole factor denying opportunities to blacks and that the system itself is racially exclusionary. In these circumstances, race is prematurely degraded as a powerful explanation for inequality. In essence, the power of the concept has been weakened by the proliferation of symbolic elements that contribute to the appearance of inclusiveness in the corporate workplace; by their presence and high visibility, successful blacks imply that the occupational structure is now open and egalitarian, if not entirely meritocratic.

Nevertheless, black executives often express their doubts. Although it is clear that social conditions have improved considerably for many middle-class blacks and that the resulting progress toward attaining social parity with middle-class whites has given many hope, racial inequality is endemic to American society, and tremendous numbers of blacks as well as other people of color are segregated in ghettos, are poor, and continue to be treated as second-class citizens (see Massey and Denton 1993; Feagin and Sikes 1994; Cose 1993). In fact, as improvements in the condition of the black middle class become more pronounced, a social and economic split between members of the black middle class and the black lower class becomes more discernible.

The affirmative action initiatives and policies had their most direct and immediate effect on blacks who were well prepared and poised to take advantage of any opportunity that arose in the occupational system. In this scenario, the lower class was largely ignored at a time when the jobs on which this class depended were disappearing due to automation, de-industrialization, and the rise of the global economy (see Wilson 1980, 1987, 1996; Anderson 1990; Rifkin 1995). This historical context is important for understanding aspects of the social life of the company on which this chapter is based.

After President Johnson issued his executive order prescribing affirmative action, the company I studied instituted programs to recruit and train blacks. Without such pressure and the initiatives that followed, the number of blacks working and being promoted within the company would have been significantly smaller. To be sure, affirmative action has produced conflicting results in this corporate setting. A few blacks have indeed been highly successful, occasionally reaching upper-level management positions. Many others are frustrated, feeling strongly that they are being detained and kept from rising by an invisible job ceiling. They believe that there are certain jobs that blacks will never obtain and others into which blacks are being channeled. They do not feel or act as if they are accepted as full participants in the organization (see Cose 1993).

Since skin color, particularly its social and political significance, appears to be a problematic issue for the personnel of the organization, it would be conceptually useful, following Goffman (1963), to consider its relationship to the concept of stigma, or spoiled identity. Goffman distinguishes three categories: the own, the wise, and the normal. The own represents the stigmatized group in society. This group consists of individuals with a similar negative difference. Within the group, there is a discrepancy between each person's virtual and actual social identities, which can be seen as the difference between his or her good, virtuous, and positive qualities and his or her negative attributes. Stigma thus is a matter of degree and perhaps best viewed as a product of social interaction; in effect, it is a transaction between those who are stigmatized and those who assign stigma (see Becker 1973 [1963]). For Goffman, those who assign stigma include the normals (those members of the organization who feel that corporate life is fair to them and to others and who have few complaints), the wise (normals who have the capacity for empathy toward outsiders and who tend to extend themselves to the own, assisting them and making them feel welcome within the organization), and members of the own themselves.

However, much has happened in the politics of difference since Goffman advanced his position. Today, Goffman's view of stigma appears rather absolutist insofar as he has a generally clear conception of what does and does not constitute stigma. In his view, the one person in our society without stigma is the young, married, white, urban, northern, heterosexual, Protestant father, who is college educated, fully employed, and of good complexion, weight, and height and who has a recent record in sports (Goffman 1963, 128). All others, we are to presume, are in some way compromised and would rather be "normal"; they would be more than ready to trade in their status and identity as stigmatized if that were possible.

With respect to the tribal stigma of race, such an analysis is weakened by the fact that, since the beginning of the civil rights and black (cultural) nationalist movements that have culminated in today's Afro-centrism, many black people, but not all, appear increasingly black and proud and would cringe at the thought of giving up their blackness for promises of racial inclusion or assimilation. Such positions have their parallels among feminists, gays, and various ethnic groups. In present-day America there seems to be an emerging concern with valuing one's differences, playing up one's particularity, be it ethnic, racial, or sexual, and attempting to compete effectively for place and position among so many others who make up our pluralistic society (see Rose 1990 [1973]; Schlesinger 1992; Feagin and Sikes 1994; Glazer 1997). Nevertheless, Goffman's typology, taken as conventional commentary on race and difference, provides us with a conceptually useful, if ideologically conservative, benchmark from which to approach the social situation of the black executive.

THE OWN

Within the organization I studied, the own may be characterized as a loosely knit collection of black employees. Such people may at first glance appear, especially to outsiders, to be a monolithic, tightly knit, self-interested group. The actual situation, however, is more complicated than that. Membership in the own is usually involuntary and persistent, because it is determined by skin color, although in reality its members at times may fade in and out of the association. To a certain degree, this is a matter of perception, and putative members become more or less closely affiliated with the own depending on the issue at hand and the attendant social circumstances. Moreover, individuals with observable phenotypical features identifiable by all Americans, but especially by blacks, as "black" or black African in origin are automatically eligible for membership. During social interaction and instances of sociability, fellow blacks in effect claim them, and whites readily associate them with the own.

Among some blacks in the organization, the sense of affiliation with the own can be situational, while for others it can be a full-time preoccupation. At the same time, however, their awareness of the job ceiling and other indications of negative differential treatment, mixed with hurt but often hidden feelings, may set them apart from others in the company, including other minorities. Many feel strongly that their experiences in the workplace are unique and that other minorities—women, Asians, Jews, and Hispanics—do not confront the same personal and social problems. They see their skin color and the social significance it has acquired over the centuries as their chief and lingering problem, not just in the workplace but in society in general (see Cose 1993). Hence, for a large number of blacks in the organization, skin color *is* the persistent issue, a conspicuous and observable characteristic that often makes them subject a priori to negative consideration and treatment. They tend to keep such views to themselves or to share them mainly with fellow blacks who they think are trustworthy or, rarely, with whites who have earned their confidence.

At the same time, many of those blacks who are doing well in the organization have found it necessary to distance themselves from the own and to present themselves as individuals who have struggled despite great odds and have made it. Indeed, for them, it is generally considered bad form to define oneself as publicly preoccupied with race, as a "race man" or "race woman," or as one who promotes "the race" over others (see Drake and Cayton 1962; Goffman 1963; Anderson 1997). In this context, at times with deep ambivalence, some feel it prudent to tone down their enthusiasm for company policies that appear to favor "the race" (see Steele 1990; Carter 1991; Kennedy 1997). For instance, such people may feel that they must publicly distance themselves from the concept of affirmative action, even though without this policy and the accompanying governmental pressure many probably would not hold the positions they do.

Accordingly, it is not uncommon to hear some of these blacks voice complaints about the wisdom of affirmative action programs and quotas. These complaints often stem from a complex psychological need to identify publicly with a corporate culture that at times denies them full participation. In working to resolve this dilemma, many have internalized conceptions of the organization as a virtual meritocracy, while others are left embittered by what they see as a sham of equal opportunity.

Generally in their daily behavior at work, most find themselves enacting their versions of the corporate orientation, a clear commitment to organizational rules and values that their white counterparts and superiors readily sanction. To enact such a role effectively implies that the individual him or herself is a standing member of that system. But in terms of feeling fully included, most are left with reservations. At least some of this acceptance of the corporate orientation may have to do with the felt need to present oneself as a team player or the desire to benefit—or at least to cover oneself—by "going along to get along," while offering up the classic caveat about not selling out and "remembering where you came from."

It is conceptually useful to divide black executives into two groups: the core own and the peripheral own. The core own are those blacks who have recently emerged from traditional, segregated black communities or who maintain a strongly expressed or a racially particularistic sense of identity. The peripheral own are often the products of less racially isolated backgrounds and tend to be more universalistic in outlook (see Anderson 1990, 40–42). Generally speaking, the core own tends to be organized around the belief that American society is irredeemably racist and that relationships with whites are to be entered into with a certain amount of suspicion, if at all, and that such relationships are best understood as being primarily instrumental. Those taking this position tend to interact with whites only on a formal level, and their friendships are mainly with other blacks who are "black enough," meaning those who place race first and emphasize solidarity with the African American community.

The peripheral own tend toward a more cosmopolitan orientation, while regarding the problem of American race relations as difficult but hopeful. In deference to norms of racial caste, they tend to engage other blacks for close friendships but are open to friendships with whites and others. Imbued with values of social tolerance, such blacks tend to be comfortable in relationships with various kinds of people and tend to see them as individuals first and people of a certain race second. As a result of these differential identifications, the core and the peripheral own tend to have different corporate experiences.

Complicating the picture, however, is the fact that certain coworkers, black and white alike, lump all blacks together into a single group. For such people, the member's skin color and physical attributes help define the person's special relationship with the company. Members of the own, who are generally expected to acknowledge, befriend, and support one another on the basis of skin color, thus assume a common social and cultural history with respect to racial prejudice and discrimination toward blacks (see Hughes 1945; Blumer 1958; Wellman 1977; Pettigrew 1980; Feagin and Sikes 1994; Hacker 1995). These assumptions serve as an important organizing principle for the own.

When brought to the organization, the core own's identity and its related values are sharpened by the distinctions they draw between themselves, the peripheral own, and other coworkers, who tend to be white and of middle-class background. Therefore, a member of the core own whose sense of identity is threatened by the everyday vicissitudes of life within the organization, particularly by the extent to which he or she is required to interact closely with whites, often gravitates to others who are black and have similar social attitudes and values. These individuals then find racial solidarity as a valuable defense because of what they view as a generalized pattern of bad treatment at the hands of whites and, by extension, of white oppression of black communities.

In these circumstances, many of the black employees are reminded of the strong adversity their people traditionally have experienced in their everyday dealings with whites. When the experience is not personally remembered, it may be socially reconstructed. Collectively, the own, particularly those in the core, tend to define the present situation as a hostile one, making it ever more difficult for them to trust white coworkers and easier to trust fellow blacks. This oversimplified view further encourages association on the basis of color and as a result reifies a racial division of labor, while undermining comity and goodwill among blacks and whites in the workplace.

Among themselves, functionally backstage, members of the own commune and commiserate with one another. Here they may "talk black," both articulating the frustrations they experience in working among insensitive whites and identifying the work-related issues they believe are racially based. They may greet one another as "sister" and "brother," invoking feelings of familial solidarity. On these occasions, members of the own appear relatively relaxed, but they may not be so: many feel that they must be alert and aware of those who might turn on them, selling them out to those in authority.

Highly motivated to succeed, they feel competitive not only with their white coworkers but at times with their black colleagues as well. As the issue becomes survival, they learn to watch and protect their backs. Yet as they meet and talk, and to a degree collude, they learn to trust and find themselves socializing, often on the basis of racial unity. Not only do they make small talk, perhaps discussing what was on television last night, but they also discuss public issues of the day, particularly issues that affect the lives of blacks in corporate life. They pass around relevant news clippings and, through sociability, gain perspective on the corporate world. Equally important, they compare notes on experiences with their white colleagues, at times collectively distinguishing between enemies and friends, or the "wise," in the general organization and discussing issues pertinent to their jobs. Here also, some might complain about problematic supervisors or about an errant white secretary who shows too little respect for blacks, or they might even single out members of the peripheral own who have shown themselves to be outside the fold or to have blatantly violated the rules of the own.

As a group, the peripheral own tend to have a more cosmopolitan orientation and in general are better educated than the
core own. They tend to occupy a higher status in the organization.
Such blacks have a strong need to believe that they are present in
the organization not solely because of the color of their skin, but
because of their own success in the business world. Furthermore,
in cases where racial particularism among blacks might be invoked to favor a black or other minority individual, these individuals might hesitate to offer an endorsement. Rather, they sometimes bend over backward to judge an individual not on the basis
of color, but with regard to the issue at hand and on their own
perceptions of that person's merit.

A major reason for this hesitancy and the attempt to neutralize
racial particularism in public has much to do with the standing
power relationships within the organization, as well as with feelings of insecurity experienced by members of this group. One
way of dealing with such feelings is by embracing the corporate
culture, including the meritocratic norms of the organization, and
by demonstrating their team loyalty and worthiness at every opportunity. Such norms may be strongly affirmed through close attention to presentational rituals in the areas of dress, speech, and
manners. If such behavior promises the approval of corporate
higher-ups, such rituals also may put off members of the core
own, sharpening the division between the two groups.

Compared with others in the company—both whites and
blacks—members of the peripheral own appear utterly polished.
The men usually dress in stylish fashions, wearing expensive corporate outfits tending toward dark pinstriped suits; their appearance seems carefully chosen to conform to some handbook on
dressing for success. The women often are glamorous, not limiting
themselves to the dark and subdued colors worn by the white
women of their corporate status. In general, the peripheral own
tend to be impressive looking to their white coworkers, particularly for persons of their color-caste. Moreover, their use of language suggests that they have been well educated; over the phone
they are at times mistaken for educated whites.

Not only do they seem to feel at ease in the company of
whites, but their demeanor seems almost casual and certainly confident. During such interactions, they leave no doubt that they are

the social and intellectual equals of their white coworkers. More-over, they give the impression of having had personally satisfying interactions and positive experiences with whites, and they are mostly willing to blame whatever bad experiences they may have had on errant individuals, not on whites generally.

In managing the various and sundry issues of the corporate world, members of the periphery like to appear to be color-blind, indicating that race plays a limited role in their understanding of the social world. However, they display some ambivalence in this regard, particularly as the conservative political establishment ef-fectively assaults the very basis of their existence by actively ques-tioning affirmative action and other policies they feel have pro-vided blacks with opportunities in the corporate world. Such actions and news reports give them pause, causing them to re-serve judgment and to hold on to a racial analysis of the social and corporate world. Such reservations, and the dynamic tensions they create, allow race to continue to play an important role in their work and personal lives. Such ambivalence may encourage some of these individuals to defer to the powers that be, at times playing along with what they think their white colleagues would like them to think.

In such circumstances these individuals experience most acutely the racial "twoness" of which Du Bois spoke almost a cen-tury ago (Du Bois 1995 [1905]). Some others, to be sure, less am-bivalent but well schooled by the dominant system and its ideol-ogy of egalitarianism, individualism, and merit, embrace the corporate culture more fully. It is with these ambivalences and reservations that, on a social basis, the peripheral own tend to fraternize with both blacks and whites, often believing they are making little distinction on the basis of skin color, yet doing so all the while.

Within this context, this benchmark, they project a cosmopoli-tan ideal. Yet when it comes to most issues affecting them person-ally, they do make distinctions based on color. Moreover, because of their class position, and the sense of privilege flowing there-from, the peripheral own are likely to pursue activities that the core own most often associate with whites: golf and tennis as well as occasional evenings at the symphony, the opera, or the theater, at times in the company of white coworkers and friends. During backstage sessions, the core own sometimes jokingly accuse them of selling out or of being co-opted by the system. These barbs sometimes hit home. According to one male black senior vice president with whom I discussed my analysis:

> In terms of their lifestyles, some do the opera thing and the art museum thing. But all black executives will also do the jazz. They also do the house party. They wouldn't do it with the core group, but it would be a high-class house party. You'd have some where you'd do some socializing and you'd bring a few whites into it. But the ones that were really serious parties were kind of isolated. You'd have two different sets of agendas: one where you'd want to create some cohesion with some of the whites so they could see how nice you could socialize, but where you'd really want to let yourself go and get down and talk about issues, then it would be blacks only. The core would never do that [invite whites to a party]. And they play golf, play tennis. About ten, twelve years ago, my wife bought me some golf clubs for Christmas. I never thought about playing golf before that. She said, "You need these to be a part of the team." So I took up golf. I bought her golf clubs the following Christmas. And I play several times a year. Before that, whenever we would go on a company retreat, there was always some free time, and there would be some golf and some tennis and some volleyball. And I would be in the volleyball game because I didn't have the skills to play tennis—I wasn't too good at that—and I never touched a golf club. And those folks are into a different group. I think that whole thing's gonna change twenty years from now because of Tiger Woods. We'll still have exclusive clubs because of the money, but it will be less so. So it won't be as prestigious because everybody's out there doing it.

To members of the peripheral own, such experiences support their values of openness to new social experiences and to social relationships more general than those bounded by color and race. Bent on upward mobility, they usually have some plan for realizing success, and to a degree most have already experienced it within the firm. However, because of their ambivalent relationship with the own, they run a distinct risk of becoming the subject of ambiguity for some whites. This question of their place in the structure becomes especially acute when whites see that they are congregating or fraternizing closely with other blacks. Outsiders might interpret such close associations as a violation of organizational etiquette regarding the relationships between superiors and subordinates. Such members harbor a certain ambivalence with respect to the own because they are haunted by the concern that associating closely with the own may seriously impair their own chances of advancing in the organization. Yet they feel some obligation to engage in such association.

When blacks rise in the company, they tend to move away from the core own to the more loosely knit peripheral own. A person whose status changes may easily be accused of disavowing membership in the own, for his or her behavior, including styles of interacting with white associates, can suggest a certain distancing from more ordinary black employees. As this occurs, depending on his or her status and behavior, the individual may be subject to sanctions by the loosely knit group of the own; to deal with such an individual, members of the own may come together. Their sanctions may amount to expressions of hostility—including angry looks and gossip—and the threat of ostracism. However, because of the professional nature of business occupations, these sanctions are usually mild and somewhat indefinite. Their real impact is negated by the possibility that the person being sanctioned at one moment may be needed for support at a later point in time.

Instead of forcing issues, some people simply "stew" and gossip when they observe one of the own violating group norms. When this happens, it usually occurs behind a person's back, not to his or her face. Thus the complaints often remain subtle and only marginally effective. In general, the own becomes and remains something of a shadow group, emerging when it or one of its members is being or is feeling threatened; seldom, if ever, does it strike out as a major force.

The basis for the club of the own has to do primarily with the insecurities of its members about their standing in the wider group. This standing is thought to be strongly affected by their blackness and its meaning within a predominantly white firm. The members of the own believe that skin color has a direct impact on the way they are regarded within the firm. Many have the recurring feeling of being persecuted or "on" when in the presence of whites, a sense that someone is always watching and "just waiting to get something on me." There is also a general belief that although individuals may be unsure of themselves, the members of the own may be able collectively to do something about their situation. There is a sense that they are strangers in hostile territory and that the formation of an informal club is partly a matter of self-defense. Hence, "unity" becomes an important social value, if not a major principle of social organization.

Some of the own, particularly those on the periphery, are not sure how much legitimacy the group deserves. Accordingly, those seriously attempting to negotiate the organizational ladder tend to be careful about the racial and political implications of their public associations, particularly when on the job. They are cognizant of the fact that they have to avoid compromising themselves in the eyes of the powerful members of the organization. This set of issues operates to confuse and frustrate certain members of the own, contributing to their worries about appearing "too black" in one set of circumstances and "too white" in another. Whites are inclined to see these ambivalent blacks in one way, and fellow blacks are inclined to see them in another. Many of the whites may become disturbed by what appears to be insincerity on the part of a trusted black friend and colleague. Often this "insincerity" is an outgrowth of the black person's attempts to manage the various and sometimes conflicting demands placed on him or her by color and by its social meanings within the organization. The own and the larger group of whites are deeply implicated in the black executive's mode of operation.

The members of the own appear to understand and to be somewhat tolerant of the black executive's excesses, appreciating this member's need to deal with his or her white colleagues. In the words of one executive, it is acceptable to be "white," but only to a degree. To venture beyond the acceptable degree of association—and thus of perceived identification—is to risk the sanctions of the own. It is important to understand that such limits on behavior are in reality a matter of social negotiation and, depending on the executive's social resources in the situation, he or she may be able to get away with more or fewer transgressions in the face of the own. The executive's behavior may be interpreted simply as competence on the job and not as a conscious attempt (without good reason) to approximate "white" ways.

However, when the person negotiates effectively with the own group, he or she runs the distinct risk of alienating white coworkers and superiors. Given the political realities of this situation, the black executive often resolves the conflict by risking his or her relationships with other members of the own, assuming that those other members lack real power and influence in comparison with supervisors and other higher-ups, who tend to be white. From this perspective, fellow blacks are politically expendable, whereas upper-level whites are not. Understanding this reality creates tolerance in members of the own for the "deviance" of their members. In the words of the senior vice president referred to earlier:

The [peripheral] own was like a support group. At the same time, I went to great lengths to keep a good relationship with the core own. I couldn't do everything that they would do because some things I didn't think were correct or politically savvy in terms of progressing. One of the issues is [as a member of the peripheral own] you can go along with the core and do everything they do, but the end result is you have no influence with the company. So by doing that you hurt the core. So even though the more astute ones will say, "What he's doing is OK," some of the core folks say that if you don't act the way I act, you've sold out. But some of them give the peripherals slack, because they understand you have to do that to stay in the good graces and have some kind of minimal power, marginalized power, whatever it is. So they don't call it acting white necessarily; it varies by the individual.

Some folks who were black executives whom I saw in that vein, whom I saw identifying a lot less than I did with blacks -at the bottom line, I also found out that they were doing things, low-key things, that would improve the plight of the black employees, but they just weren't raising the banner about it. They were keeping a low profile. I think it's a rare black executive who has no conscience about reaching back and doing something for his people. Some will go out of their way to relate, mentor, and coach, etc. Others will keep a distance. But even with that distance they will do things as the opportunity arises. And the thing is that the further you stay away from the core, the more power you have to make things happen. You might meet with the core privately, but some of these folks didn't meet with the core at all, didn't want to be seen with them.

I could see those things being played out. For the most part, I got very positive feedback [from the core], but I'm sure there were some folks saying, "He sold out. He's not one of the brothers." So even with myself I think it was a negative reaction [at times], but those folks who got an even more negative reaction were the very same folks who had the ability to make change. Those people would never socialize with the core, [although] they would say hi. They would take the company position on issues. They would not assume that everything was racist. They [the peripheral own] would ask questions as if they were objective arbitrators versus somebody who's going to defend their race to the end. So they would do things that would come across as being conservative or not understanding. And I think they were going through the process of trying to appear to be super-objective even to the point of being overly so and making you prove your case. I think in their heart, in small settings among the club, you'd hear what was really happening. But they would behave as if the structure was correct. And that would give them coin [leverage] with the power structure.

I had a lot of positive feedback, but just reading it as a possibility that there were folks who thought I sold out was painful. [But] in your heart you know you're doing good things and you're trying to do the right thing and you're doing what you need to do to not assimilate but at least have people not be concerned about you in terms of wanting to cut you out of any kind of power, decisionmaking process. In terms of who's going to be downsized, you need to act in a certain civil manner, so they'll say, "This guy, he's part of the group." You're never really part of the group, but you're close enough that you can sit in the room. And the thing is that once you get on that management track, either you change right away and you start wearing different suits and different clothing, or you never rise any higher. They're never going to envision you as being a white male, but if you can dress the same and look a certain way and drive a conservative car and whatever else, they'll say, "This guy has a similar attitude, similar values. He's a team player." If you don't dress with the uniform, obviously you're on the wrong team. I've talked to young guys who are becoming managers about the dress, the style, and why it's important. The way I would always put it to them would be, "It's a choice. You don't have to do what they do, but let me tell you what you're giving up. You dress like this [in a flamboyant, stereotypically black way], you're not part of the team. It shouldn't be important, but these are the rules." And so they can make conscious choices.

At the same time, for the larger organization, the members of the peripheral own often serve (although sometimes their role is not acknowledged) as cultural brokers, working to bridge the social gap between members of the minority community and management (see Collins 1997); in fact, such peripheral blacks often informally see themselves as communication links between people of their own racial background and the predominantly white firm. In informal conversations, they sometimes attempt to edify and sensitize their white colleagues about black life. They are sometimes successful in this regard and are often highly valued by those of the enlightened management group who increasingly must come to terms with minority issues. Because of this communication function and because blacks are so poorly represented at the higher reaches of the organization, the black executive runs the further, often debilitating, risk of becoming all-consumed by this role.

Sensitive to the risks involved, many black executives strongly resist this feature of their positions, at least formally. They would much rather see and identify themselves as persons with more general roles (or with roles they view as more central to the mission of the organization) than that of managing the minority community. When they feel themselves being used simply as communication links and representatives of blacks, many feel themselves seriously compromised and complain that they are unable to do the work for which they have been trained. They worry that they will be seen as tokens, and they often begin to question the roles they play in the organization. For some, this perception leads to demoralization, cynicism, or deeper questions concerning their real value to the organization. This role can also create difficulties for them within the own. Although whites may view their role as mainly helping to expand the horizons and influence of blacks within the company and as being leaders and role models, members may enact it somewhat grudgingly.

In general, however, the members of the peripheral own tend to display a positive attitude about life in the company and may become spokespersons for the company. This outlook is enhanced by their perception of the individual as master of his or her own destiny. If they have complaints, they take them to those in authority, as individuals, not as members of the own, thereby creating fewer tensions with white leadership. Also, with their presentation of self, including their dress and demeanor and general social outlook, they are the ones who seem most able to seek and gain effective relationships with white mentors or with white political allies in the company.

For members of the general organization, however, the distinctions between the core own and the peripheral own are often invisible. Rather, "the blacks" signify a reference group, although whites and blacks see the significance and meaning of the group quite differently (see Shibutani 1961; Merton 1957). When whites think of blacks, they may find it conceptually convenient to consider the individual as part of the black group. Although some whites may pride themselves on seeing and treating blacks as individuals, blacks often remain unconvinced of their ability to do so.

THE WISE

This brings us to the wise. The wise are people in the organization who are privileged in some respect (usually upper-middle class) but who, because of their upbringing, education, or general life experiences, have developed a deeply sympathetic or empathetic orientation toward people they define as unfortunate victims of social injustice. The members of the wise have an appreciation of the special background of the own and so bring a unique brand of social awareness to the corporate setting. This awareness, mixed with their own intelligence and their understanding of the corporate world, generates in them a rare ability to appreciate the contributions of minorities to the corporation and to society in general. Combining this sense of appreciation with a real sensitivity to life within their own caste and its relation to the minority caste, such persons have developed a certain wisdom mixed with a sense of tolerance in the area of human relations. Compared with others in the organization, executives in the wise are particularly strong in the field of human affairs.

The wise are often made up of Jews, women, successful blacks (members of the peripheral own), and other minority members who occupy high-status positions within the firm. Significantly, liberal Jews tend to be overrepresented in this category. Because of the Jews' long history as victims of prejudice and discrimination at the hands of the majority group, they are often in a position to observe and to appreciate the plight of blacks in American society in general and in the corporation in particular. Because of their own group and personal experience with prejudice and discrimination or simply because they have taken a liking to the member of the own with whom they work, the wise are often able to empathize with the dilemmas of the black executive, particularly if he or she is young and located low on the corporate ladder.

Occupying positions of authority and influence, as well as having a certain independence, these executives have a chance to do something to alleviate the problems they see. They often go on record to demonstrate their empathy for the plight of blacks and other minorities in the organization. Among the own, such persons may be identified and spoken of as allies. With an understanding of the ways of both whites and blacks, the wise are able to express their special identity in ways that other whites might not notice but that are unambiguous to many blacks. They may demonstrate this quality by assisting a black employee during a difficult period or by associating closely with blacks at certain corporate functions, by showing a real and sincere interest in issues important to minorities, by displaying a tolerant manner toward minorities, or by appreciating contributions of the own and other minorities in the company. Of all the whites of the organization, in the minds of members of the own, the wise are viewed as the most likable and trustworthy. Because of these abilities, the wise more readily appreciate contributions of the own and other minorities to the company.

Although members of the wise are usually privileged and white, they may be located almost any place within the organization. In addition, blacks on the corporate ladder sometimes report how they have been befriended by a black janitor or doorman. In their encounters with such individuals, they discover how much more they have to discuss with them than with white peers or superiors who are not members of the wise. At times, a lower-level white person may serve a similar purpose. The main quality that all such persons have in common with the member of the own is their perception of him or her as alone, as needing social support, or simply as approachable. Key features of the wise are their ability to understand the situation and their general receptivity to members of the own.

Because of their openness, the well-connected members of the wise often provide valuable connections for the upwardly mobile members of the own, particularly people who tend to make up the peripheral own. By developing this connection into a social relationship, the member of the own can gain even more mobility as well as a rare and useful perspective on the hierarchy of the organization and on how it may or may not be negotiated. A protégé-mentor relationship often grows out of such connections. One male black executive had such an experience:

My first mentor in the corporate world was a Jewish man, and he helped me quite a bit. This man helped me, and after he left our company, he still stayed in contact. When my brother lost his job, I reached out to him, and he hired my brother. My brother was desperate. But he had the power to bring people in. If he said it would happen, it would happen. So he said to my brother, "Based on my knowledge of your brother, I know you must have some of the same qualities. So you're hired."

Normally you don't have that kind of leverage, that kind of ability to reach out and say, "Hey, would you mind so-and-so, and have somebody help?" He could really shut the door, but I had nurtured this relationship with him for several years at one company. Then when he left, he was there to help. And again, this was a Jewish man. I wouldn't call him racially sensitive, where he was on top of all the issues, but he was a fair-minded man.

The relationship [between us] started when I was having a problem. I was, I guess, pretty much full of myself, and I knew I was good at what I did. If I was at a meeting and somebody wanted to do something that was bureaucratic or would slow me down or whatever, I would say that. And this person would not raise an issue at the meeting, but they would go behind my back and undermine what I was doing behind the scenes. So this Jewish guy came to me and told me what was happening: "You need to learn how to not wear your emotions on your sleeve." It was the first time I thought about that, but he was right. He played cards quite a bit. He was talking about, "It's like playing poker and you're gonna gain, and everybody else is holding their cards, and you can't see what they are, but your cards are lying face up on the table." And I was used to being straight out and honest—this is how I feel. A lot of people wouldn't come out with it, but if they had some agenda, they would go about taking care of it. And I learned that. He explained it to me, how you need to mellow out and not be face to face in terms of how you address issues and how you deal with people. I guess the expression he used was that you have enough enemies in the corporate world without creating new ones. And it may not even be obvious that they're going after you, they're gunning for you. But he said, "If you put somebody down, say something ugly at a meeting, and the person has the opportunity to hurt you, they will." My attitude at the time was, because I'm good at what I do and I know what I'm doing, I could just say what I felt like saying. But that was not really the case at all.

So we would socialize. I played golf with him. We played racquetball together several times. He had my wife and me over to his house. I had risen to middle-management just acting a certain way. So since that carried me that far, why change? He explained to me why change, because it would hinder you as you went forward. And I used that same logic in terms of choosing your battles with my children, family, friends, other employees, whatever. I explained to them I had the wisdom that I picked up and used and now I was passing it on to them.

At the same time, the member of the own has a chance to mentor the wise and even sometimes the normals. Michelle is a case in point. A black manager who considers herself a member of the peripheral own, she in fact transcends all three categories, while maintaining links to all of them. She has used her considerable understanding to get on in the corporation and, in the process, has herself become wise in its ways. She has become a strategic actor (see Goffman 1961) who can, in turn, edify and assist members of the various categories with their problems in the organization. As such, she reverses the model by mentoring normals in the ways of the own and in their sensitivities to race issues. In return, she can wield a certain amount of power by helping people perform better for the organization. Unlike the male executive quoted earlier, Michelle is not ambivalent about her intermediate position between the core own and the normals; she is not concerned about being seen by the core as selling out because she is convinced that her style of behavior benefits all blacks:

First of all, when I joined the department, I was basically the only black professional. There was one other black person who was, as far as they were concerned, the typical ghetto Negro, because she came from there. She lived in North Philadelphia, made no bones about it, she looked as the stereotype, she behaved as the stereotype. And I wanted to create my own positive image, not just as a black person, but as a person who is committed to professionalism but who happens to be black. So that my blackness would not be the only thing that they're concerned about.

I would always deal with people in a way that respected who they were so that I would get the respect that I was demanding by my behavior. I also reported to someone who was a bright, young, Catholic male, who went to a Jesuit school and recognized that we have something in common in that he was Catholic and I was Catholic. He was young. He came to the position, of course, because of his father. And he certainly recognized that, so he took pains to always tell me how hard he worked and how he worked from the mail room up to where he is, which was not true—he spent maybe two minutes in the mail room of his entire career. And he was made in charge of the department very young, probably at the age of thirty something. And he was not in a sense filled with all the old traditional tapes of people who would think about black people in a certain way. To him it was something that you looked at sort of funny or joking or whatever, but he was not punitive. If he did it, it would not be what I consider malicious. He would have done it based on what I think most white people have a problem with, and that is not by commission but by omission, by not realizing what it means. If confronted with it, which I constantly did, he was always, "Oh, I didn't realize. Oh, I'm sorry."

There was another manager who was there who was also Italian, that he tried to be buddy-buddy with, but this Italian person had been with me for a long time so he knew me. So he would also share with me what they shared in the bathroom that he didn't tell me. He told me, "Michelle, a lot of decisions are made in the bathroom." So he would tell me. So I had this other relationship with this other person that sort of helped me deal with the boss.

My boss let me hire one other professional person [a black man], and he also put me in charge of the word-processing pool, and I made sure that I hired people of color. So I changed the complexion of the pool.

Even today, I'll tell you something else: when our jobs [her job and that of the Italian manager] were downsized, I went and interviewed for a job at Merrill Lynch, and it was clear to me they didn't want a woman because how could a woman know anything about financial stuff? So he had a job he didn't like. So I called him and said, "Why don't you go and apply for the job?" He got the job and eventually became a vice president. Now he's still at Merrill Lynch, and I call him frequently, and he still calls me for advice. And every once in a while I have lunch with him, and I make him pay for it, and I say, "You still owe me."

Ironically, members of the core own group, because of different styles of communication and the social distance that normally exists between the core own and whites, have relatively little opportunity to make positive impressions on members of the wise. Members of the core group, more sensitive to race than the color-blind peripheral own, are likely to perceive such a wise person as white first, making him or her ineligible for trust. In an important sense, the members of the core own are handicapped by their inability to make distinctions among whites, to trust whites, or to conceive of a white person being able to go out of his or her way for a black person. For the core own, all relationships with whites tend to be instrumental, whereas the peripheral own are able to establish and sustain expressive friendships and associations with white people.

THE NORMALS

The last group, the normals, are people who make up and identify with the majority in the corporate culture. Handicapped by their close identification with the majority, they are generally oblivious to the special situation and plight of blacks and other minorities in the company. Even when they understand the special problems that minorities encounter, many tend to be unsympathetic to them; they often feel that the workplace has done enough for minorities. They may feel this way in part because they have been conditioned to perceive the minority person as a threat to their own interests. Many such people emerge from a situation without advantages, and they are inclined to look on a black person or another minority group member as a competitor within the organization, even when there is no basis for such thinking. Furthermore, many are of the opinion that the company has already done enough or too much. These people often believe that blacks and other minorities, assisted as they are by government programs to remedy past prejudice and discrimination, do not deserve to be employed by the company, particularly when there are so many well-qualified normals around.

This outlook is at times shared, perhaps to an increasing degree, by some of the minority employees of the corporation themselves, including a number of the blacks. Such beliefs reflect an ethos that emphasizes homogeneity in a culture where white skin color and male gender predominate. There exists a need for all members of the corporation to present themselves as and to pass as normals. Blacks, women, Jews, and other minorities with conspicuous and observable differences find passing difficult. Those who more readily approximate the dominant standards and values, including language, dress, and style of self-presentation, may find it easier to pass. This group includes white minorities, particularly when their members are almost indistinguishable from the white majority.

In such an environment, certain minorities in pursuit of status within the organization may assume the posture of the majority, including a degree of indifference to the special needs of minorities within the company. Some minority individuals may consciously sever all connections with their group. And given what has become an increasingly competitive context, striving minorities may find some reward—psychological or otherwise—in ignoring or de-emphasizing the importance of the special concerns of blacks and others.

Because of a certain dissonance that results from being caught between the poles of fully accepting this position and identity as members of the own, blacks are more sensitive to the shortcomings of this outlook. Thus most blacks find themselves working to reshape the corporate ideology and culture to allow their own incorporation. Such actions ultimately place them outside of the normal group. Those minority group members who are white may not suffer the same dissonance, and, because of their own group's divergent interests within the corporation, they may find it difficult to display a tolerance of blacks and others who may be viewed as outsiders within the corporation.

In their efforts to embrace the identity of the normal, such people may show their annoyance with the black presence by actively discrediting blacks whenever possible. They seldom facilitate the hiring of blacks in their immediate surroundings and recount sad tales of the last one who failed to work out, stories that the wise and the own must often suffer through. In their conversations on the subject, they like to emphasize "standards." Members of the own, being aware of such implicit charges against their competence and integrity, are then encouraged, if not required, to be more formal, distant, and guarded with whites in general. Such experiences, and the responses to them, help to solidify the own's generally negative working conception of life in the company. The prevalence of such experiences encourages an ambivalent stance by members of the peripheral own as they try to negotiate the organizational ladder of the company.

CONCLUSIONS

A major result of this country's civil rights movement of the 1960s was the incorporation of large numbers of blacks into the American occupational structure. Since then, through antidiscrimination legislation, including affirmative action, the black middle class has grown. It presently amounts to roughly a third of the black population. In addition, with the arrival of fair housing legislation, it has gravitated away from the inner-city black communities. Over the years, in effect, middle-class black people have begun to participate in the broader society in ways that would have astounded their predecessors.

However, a primary instrument of this process of incorporation—affirmative action—is now being seriously challenged and becoming increasingly untenable ideologically and politically. The process, at least in part, is being undermined by its seeming success: the apparent proliferation of blacks, and other minorities of color, in the professions, academia, business, and government, at a time when the workplace is becoming increasingly competitive. In effect, the advent of diversity seems to have been the political price required by affirmative action to survive. In addition, the appearance of such diversity serves as impressive evidence that the system is open, fair, and egalitarian, while restrictions of race become obscured. With such ostensible success, the former participants and their allies (the wise) in the civil rights movement recede, feeling that they have little left to fight for, especially when preferences are severely criticized as racially based in the current social and political context. Moreover, de-industrialization, corporate downsizing, and increased immigration have led to a highly competitive workplace, in which established but insecure workers tend to be much less generous in their support of social programs of almost any kind, but particularly those viewed as favoring one race over another. In these circumstances, many former liberals question their earlier support for remedial measures like affirmative action as a tool for achieving equal opportunity.

In this context, they simultaneously degrade racism as an explanation for a black person's inability to succeed, a position strongly held by powerful and well-organized conservatives. Moreover, conservative activists have been successful in challenging and outlawing affirmative action policies in California and are presently waging similar campaigns in other states. Their goal is to redefine affirmative action ideologically as a beatable menace that is inimical to the interests of whites and others who view their rights as threatened, if not abrogated, by such policies. If success-

ful, such campaigns will have important implications and consequences not just for colleges and universities throughout the land,
but for the American workplace as well. As the black presence in
such settings seriously declines, the struggle for black equality is
set back, further alienating many black people.

In the organization I studied, before affirmative action policies
were initiated, almost no black people were present. In the average firm of thirty years ago, when present at all, blacks were
found most often in the lowliest positions, including those of janitor, night watchman, doorman, elevator operator, secretary (at
times required to work out of sight), or an occasional assistant
director of personnel. With the arrival of affirmative action policies, the situation began to change, as the workplace became
more inclusive. Accordingly, top executives and supervisors began to recruit blacks, providing them with a new kind of racial
coin. This development enabled blacks to negotiate not only with
their talents, including education and people skills, but also with
their skin color. One of the important effects, if not a goal, of
affirmative action was to place a premium on black skin color,
negating its historical demerit.

Traditionally, the racial system provided preferences to those
with white skin color, but now the tables are somewhat turned.
For many corporate, political, and civic leaders, the social good of
racial incorporation, at least for a time, outweighed the ambiguous, if sometimes arbitrary, invocations of meritocratic standards.
During the tensions of the civil rights movement, and later the
civil disorders occurring in many cities, business and government
leaders encouraged racial peace and social progress, creating incentives that strongly motivated their organizations to absorb and
use black workers. Many who were now being recruited as corporate employees had once been involved or sympathized with the
college student and black power movements of their day. Now
they were upwardly mobile, residing outside the ghetto, driving
nice cars, sporting expensive dress, lunching in upscale restaurants with white colleagues, and at times discussing business strategy with high corporate officials.

In time, these direct beneficiaries of affirmative action, particularly members of the peripheral own described in this chapter,
gravitated from group concerns long associated with liberating

subjugated blacks to more individualistic concerns associated with personal economic well-being. In general, theirs was often a socially tense passage through a kind of nether world, fraught with risks, including taunts and criticisms of being an "oreo," a "sellout," or an "Uncle Tom." Most dealt with their dilemmas with ambivalence, either by forging a strong relationship with the own or by actively distancing themselves from it. Regardless, such tensions and choices took their toll on black unity.

As suggested throughout this chapter, many executives occupied an ambiguous position, which was at times resolved superficially by code switching. Depending on the issue and the audience at hand, they might behave in a racially particularistic manner in private, while embracing more mainstream behavior in public. Most had the strong desire to be included as full participants in the organization and to meet the standards that everyone else was expected to meet. Yet, on their jobs, many experienced all manner of reaction to their presence in the organization—from effective mentoring and acceptance with open arms to cold stares and hostile receptions and persistent racial discrimination.

With the increasingly effective assaults on affirmative action policies, many black executives have become disillusioned and insecure. Over time, alienation takes a toll, and people become more isolated in the workplace, gravitating to what I call the core own. Here, in response to perceptions of an unreceptive work environment, they may keep to themselves, looking inward, while becoming racially energized to collaborate in the outright racial polarization that infuses so many work settings today (see Cose 1993).

Such behavior often exacts a social cost that compounds the initial problems at work. In the corporate setting, blacks who become so isolated often remain a group apart, inhabiting a social ghetto on the lower rungs of the corporate ladder. From this perspective, when the occasional black person achieves success, the promotion may be met with cynicism rather than unqualified praise; ambiguity often rules. Among those strongly associated with the own, depending on how they wear success, epithets like token or sellout may be whispered behind their backs. Although government pressures and policies have enabled many blacks to land executive positions in major corporations—and most perform their duties with real competence—many have been unable to attain the corresponding informal social power, along with relative feelings of security, that are taken for granted and enjoyed by many of their white counterparts in the workplace.

Moreover, in the changing economy and the increasingly competitive workplace, uncertainty often prevails, negating feelings of generosity and empathy with those who are most often marginalized and excluded. Accomplishing the unfinished business of equal opportunity, and the full incorporation of blacks, promises to be extremely difficult. The task at hand cannot be fully achieved without the support and active engagement of the wise—enlightened normals with the strong capacity for empathy with outsiders—who willingly go about the sometimes daunting social task of reaching out to blacks in the firm, recruiting, welcoming, befriending, and carefully mentoring them. In actively supporting the prevailing levels of black presence in the workplace, such socially liberal people were at times actively engaged as though they were on some kind of mission, and many were: their collective, if unstated, goal was to move our society forward by creating black access to meaningful positions in the workplace, furthering the process of incorporation and racial equality. Ironically, in the present socially and politically competitive context, enacting such roles may seem inappropriate, even quaint, a throwback to the do-gooder era of not so long ago. Such people who once reached out to blacks are much less visible in today's workplace.

For the laudable goal of equal opportunity, the real challenge is that of somehow edifying, encouraging, cultivating—in essence, growing—the wise, including blacks who have risen in the firm. All this, at a time when many feel the economic pie to be shrinking, when often ambiguous notions and tests of merit are invoked, and when blacks are at times portrayed as unworthy and undeserving of close mentoring or a hand up. Without the full engagement of such allies in the struggle for racial justice, blacks and other minorities will remain marginalized, creating ever more tension in the workplace. Thus a major task is that of growing the wise and bringing them together with the own in spite of unrelenting social forces that are hard at work to create fewer of their collective number.

"The Social Situation of the Black Executive," by Elijah Anderson, is a revised version of a paper of the same title published in *The Cultural Territories of Race: Black and White Boundaries*, edited by Michelle Lamont (Chicago, University of Chicago Press; New York, Russell Sage Foundation, 1999).

REFERENCES

Anderson, Elijah. 1990. *Streetwise: Race, Class, and Change in an Urban Community*. Chicago: University of Chicago Press.

———. 1997. "The Precarious Balance: Race Man or Sellout?" In *The Darden Dilemma: 12 Black Writers on Justice, Race, and Conflicting Loyalties*, edited by Elis Cose. New York: HarperCollins.

Bearak, Barry. 1997. "Between Black and White." *New York Times*, July 27, sec. 1, p. 1.

Becker, Howard S. 1973 [1963]. *Outsiders: Studies in the Sociology of Deviance*. Glencoe, Ill.: Free Press.

Blumer, Herbert. 1958. "Race Prejudice as a Sense of Group Position." *Pacific Sociological Review* 1(1): 3–7.

Carter, Stephen L. 1991. *Rejections of an Affirmative Action Baby*. New York: Basic Books.

Collins, Sharon M. 1997. *Black Corporate Executives*. Philadelphia: Temple University Press.

Cose, Ellis. 1993. *The Rage of a Privileged Class*. New York: HarperCollins.

Cox, Oliver. 1948. *Caste, Class, and Race*. New York: Doubleday.

Drake, St. Clair, and Horace Cayton. 1962 [1945]. *Black Metropolis: A Study of Negro Life in a Northern City*. New York: Harper and Row.

Du Bois, W. E. B. 1995 [1905]. *The Souls of Black Folk*. New York: Dutton.

Feagin, Joe R., and Melvin P. Sikes. 1994. *Living with Racism: The Black Middle Class Experience*. Boston: Beacon.

Frazier, E. Franklin. 1957. *The Black Bourgeoisie*. New York: Free Press.

Glazer, Nathan. 1987 [1975]. *Affirmative Discrimination*. Cambridge, Mass.: Harvard University Press.

———. 1997. *We Are All Multiculturalists Now*. Cambridge, Mass.: Harvard University Press.

Goffman, Erving. 1961. *Strategic Interaction*. Indianapolis: Bobbs-Merrill.

———. 1963. *Stigma: Notes on the Management of Spoiled Identity*. Englewood Cliffs, N.J.: Prentice-Hall.

Hacker, Andrew. 1995. *Two Nations: Separate, Hostile, Unequal*. New York: Ballantine.

Hughes, Everett C. 1945. "Dilemmas and Contradictions of Status." *American Journal of Sociology* 50(5): 353–59.

Kennedy, Randall. 1997. "My Race Problem, and Ours." *Atlantic* 279(5): 55–66.

Kerner, Otto, et al. 1968. *Report of the National Advisory Commission on Civil Disorders*. Washington, D.C.: Bantam.

Landry, Bart. 1987. *The New Black Middle Class*. Berkeley: University of California Press.

Massey, Douglas S., and Nancy A. Denton. 1993. *American Apartheid: Segregation and the Making of the Underclass*. Cambridge, Mass.: Harvard University Press.

Merton, Robert K. 1957. *Social Theory and Social Structure*. New York: Free Press.

Myrdal, Gunnar. 1944. *An American Dilemma: The Negro Problem and Modern Democracy*. New York: Harper and Row.

Pettigrew, Thomas. 1980. *The Sociology of Race Relations*. New York: Free Press.

Rifkin, Jeremy. 1995. *The End of Work: The Decline of the Global Labor Force and the Dawn of the Post-Market Era*. New York: Putnam.

Rose, Peter I. 1990 [1973]. *They and We*. New York: Random House.

Schlesinger, Arthur M., Jr. 1992. *The Disuniting of America*. New York: Norton.

Shibutani, Tamotsu. 1961. "Social Status in Reference Groups." In *Society and Personality: An Interactionist Approach to Social Psychology*. Englewood Cliffs, N.J.: Prentice-Hall.

Skrentny, John David. 1996. *The Ironies of Affirmative Action*. Chicago: University of Chicago Press.

Steele, Shelby. 1990. *The Content of Our Character: A New Vision of Race in America*. New York: St. Martin's.

Stryker, Perrin. 1953. "How Executives Get Jobs." *Fortune* 48(2): 117ff.

Wellman, David T. 1977. *Portraits of White Racism*. New York: Cambridge University Press.

Wilson, William Julius. 1980. *The Declining Significance of Race: Blacks and Changing American Institutions*. Chicago: University of Chicago Press.

———. 1987. *The Truly Disadvantaged: The Inner City, the Underclass, and Public Policy*. Chicago: University of Chicago Press.

———. 1996. *When Work Disappears: The New World of the Urban Poor*. New York: Knopf.

── Chapter 16 ──

Race and Ethnic Differences in Peer Influences on Educational Achievement

Grace Kao

M ORE THAN AT any other time during the life course, adolescence is marked by the increasing influence of friends relative to parents in the everyday lives of youths. While most researchers agree that peers play a role in shaping students' school orientations (or their valuation of school), there is considerable debate over the relative importance of peers in determining academic outcomes, compared to that of the family. Part of the difficulty in determining the extent of peer influence lies in the simple fact that adolescents tend to choose friends who are like themselves (in terms of socioeconomic status, sex, race, and attitudes). It is thus unclear whether indicators of peer influence actually reflect the influence of friends or simply proxy for characteristics and attitudes that were present before the friendships were formed.

In this chapter I examine racial and ethnic differences in the attitudes of friends toward school, social life, and work and consider their influence on academic aspirations and achievement. I argue that systematic intergroup differences in attitudes and behavior contribute significantly to intergroup variation in performance outcomes. Characteristics of peers differ, in part, because peer groups tend to be racially and ethnically segregated, so that group differences in academic performance often yield distinct peer cultures structured along racial and ethnic lines. Using the National Education Longitudinal Study (NELS) of 1988, I document these differences with respect to value orientation and educational plans among friends, as well as the degree to which the extent of peer influence differs from group to group. If families in some groups are more tightly knit, for example, then we might expect their group members to be more resilient to peer influences than members of other groups (Keefe, Padilla, and Carlos 1979; Valenzuela and Dornbusch 1994; Schneider and Lee 1990).

PEER INFLUENCES ON EDUCATIONAL ATTAINMENT

Educational researchers have expended considerable energy investigating the relative influence of peer groups and the mechanisms through which they operate to affect educational outcomes. For the purposes of this analysis, I review three elements of prior research on peer influence: the relative degree of influence enjoyed by friends versus parents; the relative effect of selection versus socialization in friends' apparent influence (selection refers to that part of the estimated peer effect that stems from friends' similarity to respondents); and the specific mechanisms of peer influence. I then review previous work on the role played by race and ethnicity in determining peer culture.

Researchers have long been concerned with the relative importance of peers versus parents in determining educational outcomes. Adolescence is marked by increased social interaction with friends at the expense of time spent with parents; consequently one expects youth to be influenced increasingly by friends more than families. A particular concern is whether peer culture actually promotes antiachievement (or antiadult) norms, as portrayed in popular media and by early research on adolescent society (Petersen 1988). Coleman's (1961) landmark study on adolescent society, for example, suggests that peer culture draws teenagers to rebel against adult norms.

Subsequent work has generally found that teenagers choose friends with comparable long-term goals and educational outlooks. Even in real or hypothetical situations where parents and peers offer conflicting advice, students do not automatically choose to act on their peers' suggestions. In fact, Brown (1990) finds that teenagers are more likely to follow their parents' advice in decisions regarding future educational and occupational plans. Peer pressure is most effective in regulating social behavior (such as styles of clothing and music), and when peer groups influence educational achievement, they tend to support positive educational goals (such as staying in high school).

Since youth are likely to choose peers who have similar outlooks, it may be that the peer effect found empirically in many studies actually results from early family and school socialization than from socialization by peers. The debate over selection versus socialization arises because of the relative difficulty of distinguishing the effects of selection from the effects of peer socialization (Epstein 1983; Hallinan 1983; Brown 1990; Savin-Williams and Berndt 1990; Hallinan and Williams 1990). It often is unclear whether peer effects actually reflect background characteristics known to influence educational outcomes or the real influence of an adolescent's friends. Confusion also arises because peer groups tend to be homogeneous not only in background characteristics but also in outlook and behavior. One review argues that peer effects stem primarily from selection of similar peers as friends rather than from processes of peer influence (Brown 1990).

Other work, however, suggests that even when controlling for selection bias, peer influence remains a significant determinant of educational performance (Savin-Williams and Berndt 1990). Epstein (1983), for example, finds that having high-scoring friends improves the test scores of previously low-scoring and high-scoring students, while having low-scoring friends depresses the test scores of previous high-scorers. Kandel's (1978) study of friends also finds that assortative pairing (similarity in selection) and peer socialization (friends' influence) are about equally responsible in determining marijuana use, political orientation, and educational aspirations. Although there may be disagreement over the relative importance of selection versus actual influence in accounting for peer effects, there is little doubt that both contribute to the "total peer effect." Even the most "pro-selection" researchers will admit that some peer socialization must occur.

According to Brown (1990), theorizing about the diverse mechanisms of peer influence has been limited. One exception is the work of Deutsch and Gerard (1955), who distinguish between normative influence (pressure to conform to others' expectations) and information influence (pressure to accept information from friends). They find that normative influence is a more powerful mechanism of peer pressure. Another exception is Kandel (1978), who specifies two distinct transmission mechanisms: modeling (where teenagers imitate peer behavior) and reinforcement (where adolescents adopt values of their peer group). She finds that modeling is a stronger influence on eventual drug use.

In contrast to educational researchers' concern with the structure of peer influence, ethnicity researchers have been concerned primarily with how the content of peer norms is affected by a student's minority status. Ogbu (1978, 1991) argues that black peer groups often espouse antischool norms, mandating members to "act black," a term that is defined partly by values antithetical to high academic performance. Ogbu links these attitudes to blacks' minority experience in the United States, which produces ambivalent beliefs about the value of education for their socioeconomic mobility. Similarly, Mickelson (1990) finds that black youths are more likely to agree with abstract statements about the importance of education but are less likely to believe in the value of education for themselves, compared to white youths. Although black peer groups may abstractly promote positive educational values, at the same time they may negatively influence others through their behavior. Drawing on previous research, my analysis considers both positive and negative peer influences on academic performance and aspirations.

Specifically, the longitudinal design of the NELS data allows me to consider the effect of current friends on academic outcomes after taking into account previous grade performance or aspirations. Since prior research suggests that networks of adolescent friends are sorted at least in part by ethnicity, I expect to observe clear intergroup differences in friends' orientation toward school, social life, and work. In particular, I expect that friends of Asian students will be more oriented toward school than friends of whites. Similarly, although black youths may report having friends that value school, they also may value social activities more than white youths. Finally, I expect that Hispanic youths will be more likely than black youths to value work, as Hispanic adults are better able to convert their educational attainments into labor market success than are African Americans (Bean and Tienda 1987).

The actual behavior of friends also should differ by race and ethnicity. Specifically, given the high dropout rate among Hispanics, I expect them to be better acquainted with others who have dropped out than either whites or blacks; given the remarkably low dropout rate among Asians, I expect them to be least likely to report having friends who have dropped out. Employing these data on attitudes and behavior among friends, differentiated by race and ethnicity, I can distinguish whether friends' antischool attitudes or behaviors are most detrimental to respondents' academic outcomes.

Finally, if cultural arguments about the influence of ethnicity on family relationships are right, we should find discernable racial-ethnic differences in how much friends influence academic outcomes. Specifically, if Hispanics are more family-oriented, and if Asians are more parent-oriented, we might infer Hispanics and Asians to be less susceptible than whites or blacks to their friends' attitudes or behavior (Valenzuela and Dornbusch 1994; Schneider and Lee 1990).

DATA AND METHODS

To explore these research questions, I use data from the National Education Longitudinal Study. The NELS is based on a two-stage probability sample that first selected a nationally representative sample of 1,052 schools and then surveyed 24,599 respondents from these schools who were eighth graders in 1988. The survey followed them at two-year intervals through 1994, when most of the sample members were about twenty years old. This data set is unique not only because it begins before the transition to high school but also because it oversampled Hispanics and Asians and surveyed administrators, parents, and teachers as well as students (National Center for Educational Statistics 1990).

For descriptive tabulations, I use data from the second and third waves of the NELS, administered when the cohort was in tenth and twelfth grades, respectively. I use these waves for two reasons. First, there were relatively few items about peer influence in eighth grade, the base year of survey. Second, and most important, by focusing on later grades, I can include the eighth-grade grade point average (GPA) or aspirations as a control for previous academic achievement and thus consider the relative importance of selection versus peer influence to evaluate how much of the apparent peer effect can be attributed to prior differences.

Sample attrition is relatively unproblematic in the second wave, as very few students drop out between the eighth and tenth grades. By twelfth grade serious attrition has occurred, however, especially among Hispanic and black students. This attrition is quite selective, with the lowest-achieving students being most likely to have dropped out of school, removing themselves from the sample. Although NELS does follow these dropouts, by definition they do not have current grade point averages and are not eligible for analysis. Therefore my analysis of educational outcomes focuses on tenth-grade GPA and aspirations.

In order to examine whether racial and ethnic groups differ systematically with respect to the attitudes and behaviors of friends in tenth grade, I present t-tests comparing the orientation of each group's friends toward school, social life, and work to those of whites (see table 16.1). The first set of items relates to school orientation, drawing on a series of questions that ask respondents, "Among your friends, how important is it to attend classes regularly, study, get good grades, finish high school, and continue education after high school?" For each item the response categories are (1) not important, (2) somewhat important, and (3) very important. At the bottom of the top panel, these items are combined into a single social scale constructed using factor analysis.

In general, blacks and Asians report higher pro-school values than whites, and, overall, Asians have the highest school factor score. Hispanics are more likely than whites to report that their friends value studying and getting good grades, although their friends are less likely to value high school completion. Overall, the average factor score of Hispanics is statistically indistinguishable from that of whites.

The next set of items refers to social orientation, asking re-

TABLE 16.1 **Orientation of Respondents' Friends Toward School and Social Life in Tenth Grade by Race and Ethnicity**

Orientation	Asian	Hispanic	Black	White
School orientation: how important is it				
To attend classes regularly	2.598***	2.507	2.591***	2.529
	(0.555)	(0.582)	(0.565)	(0.573)
To study	2.442***	2.294*	2.382***	2.262
	(0.580)	(0.619)	(0.617)	(0.610)
To get good grades	2.583***	2.483***	2.582***	2.400
	(0.571)	(0.605)	(0.568)	(0.600)
To finish high school	2.816*	2.749**	2.803	2.785
	(0.421)	(0.496)	(0.459)	(0.459)
To continue education	2.605***	2.455	2.520***	2.446
	(0.575)	(0.645)	(0.632)	(0.642)
School factor score	0.227***	−0.012	0.159***	−0.037
	(0.932)	(1.037)	(0.981)	(0.996)
Social orientation: how important is it				
To be popular	2.227*	2.194***	2.181***	2.273
	(0.641)	(0.669)	(0.667)	(0.644)
To have a boyfriend or girlfriend	1.908***	2.033*	2.078***	1.997
	(0.649)	(0.679)	(0.691)	(0.651)
To be willing to party	1.850***	2.000*	1.855***	2.039
	(0.721)	(0.739)	(0.756)	(0.735)
Social factor score	−0.175***	−0.017*	−0.083***	0.031
	(1.007)	(1.031)	(1.059)	(0.982)
Competing orientation: how important is it				
To have a job	2.161**	2.304***	2.419***	2.092
	(0.720)	(0.685)	(0.687)	(0.726)
Actions and desires of friends: percentage who				
Dropped out of school	0.170***	0.404***	0.361***	0.233
	(0.417)	(0.567)	(0.576)	(0.467)
Wanted to go to college	0.478***	0.365**	0.378	0.396
	(0.500)	(0.481)	(0.485)	(0.489)
Number of cases	1,097	1,984	1,673	12,139

Source: Author's compilation.
Note: Numbers in parentheses are standard deviations.
*Significantly different from whites at $p < 0.05$ level.
**Significantly different from whites at $p < 0.01$ level.
***Significantly different from whites at $p < 0.001$ level.

spondents, "Among your friends, how important is it to be popular, to have a boyfriend or girlfriend, or to be willing to party?" These items are again combined into a single factor score at the bottom of the panel. With respect to friends' attitudes about the importance of social life, whites have the highest overall scores, while Asians have the lowest. In other words, friends of whites are most likely to value social activities, while friends of Asians are least likely to do so. These differences are generally reflected in the tabulations of individual items with the exception of having a boyfriend or girlfriend. Here, blacks and Hispanics are most likely to have friends who value romantic relationships.

Strong orientations toward work and earning money may also diminish academic performance and aspirations (Rosenberg 1989). For this reason, I also examine the importance of having a job among respondents' friends. Overall, it is least important to whites to have a job and most important to blacks. This measure may signal a competing priority since the peer valuation of work may lower students' own school orientation.

Finally, I examine friends' actual behavior and perceived desires for respondents. On average, a smaller proportion of Asians' friends have dropped out of high school, while a larger proportion of Hispanics' friends have done so compared to whites. Blacks also are more likely than whites to befriend high school dropouts. Similarly, Asians are more likely than whites to believe that their friends want them to go to college after high school, while Hispanics are least likely to receive such support. Blacks are just as likely as whites to have such support from their friends.

From these descriptive accounts of friends' values, we see that Asian students have friends who are most academically oriented and least likely to have dropped out of school. Black students have friends with pro-school values, yet they also have greater exposure to friends who have dropped out of school. Similarly, while friends of Hispanics have school values comparable to those of whites, their friends are far more likely to have already dropped out. Hence, while blacks and Hispanics may have friends who espouse pro-school attitudes, the behavior of their friends is more likely to discourage educational goals than it is for Asians and whites. The friends of whites tend to value social activities more than the friends of Asians, Hispanics, or African Americans.

Table 16.2 presents comparable peer influence items and factors among NELS seniors using the richer battery of items available in the twelfth-grade survey. With respect to school, race and ethnic variation in friends' orientation and behavior is comparable to the patterns described in tenth grade. Overall, Asians have the most academically oriented friends, while the friends of whites and Hispanics are the least likely to be academically oriented. These racial differences are somewhat muted since a greater proportion of Hispanic (compared to white or Asian) students have already dropped out of high school, and those who have dropped out presumably are the least enthusiastic about school (Stevenson et al. 1993).

The twelfth-grade survey offers a more detailed picture of friends' attitudes toward social life. Here I can distinguish between attitudes toward merely socializing with friends and more troublesome behavior. To construct these two dimensions of behavior, I separate those items that demarcate more "delinquent" behavior known to lower academic performance (importance of partying, having sex, using drugs, and drinking) from those that have more to do with socializing with friends (Jessor, Donovan, and Costa 1991). Then I construct factors using each of these groups of items separately. (When I load all of the items together, the factor analysis also results in two factors: the "nondelinquent" social factor and the factor for delinquent behavior.)

Overall, patterns of social behavior in twelfth grade are comparable to those in tenth grade. On average, friends of Asians are least oriented toward social activities, while those of whites consider social life to be more important. Friends of blacks are much less likely to consider both nondelinquent and delinquent social activities to be important compared to whites; in fact, their average ranking of nondelinquent activities is similar to that of Asians. However, blacks are more likely than Asians to have friends who value delinquent social activities. Hispanics are also less likely than whites to have friends who value nondelinquent social activities, but their friends value delinquent activities as much as do those of whites.

Asians also benefit from friends who are less oriented toward having a job or making money than other groups, in contrast to blacks and Hispanics, whose friends are significantly more geared

TABLE 16.2 Orientations of Friends Toward School and Social Life in Twelfth Grade, by Race and Ethnicity (Standard Deviations in Parentheses)

Orientation	Asian	Hispanic	Black	White
School orientation: how important is it				
To attend classes regularly	2.496**	2.439	2.507***	2.434
	(0.608)	(0.636)	(0.617)	(0.624)
To study	2.397***	2.266**	2.359***	2.227
	(0.616)	(0.640)	(0.636)	(0.643)
To get good grades	2.509***	2.433***	2.519***	2.378
	(0.610)	(0.617)	(0.607)	(0.629)
To finish high school	2.815	2.770***	2.793	2.812
	(0.448)	(0.506)	(0.474)	(0.458)
To continue education	2.617***	2.477*	2.513	2.510
	(0.611)	(0.655)	(0.645)	(0.645)
School factor score	0.166***	−0.018	0.110***	−0.026
	(0.953)	(1.033)	(0.992)	(0.996)
Nondelinquent orientation: how important is it				
To be popular	2.025***	2.031***	2.043**	2.103
	(0.678)	(0.709)	(0.734)	(0.692)
To have a steady boyfriend or girlfriend	1.753***	1.867	1.906***	1.843
	(0.656)	(0.676)	(0.713)	(0.646)
To get together with friends	2.509***	2.489***	2.352***	2.608
	(0.571)	(0.575)	(0.624)	(0.538)
Nondelinquent factor score	−0.149***	−0.076***	−0.142	0.046
	(0.997)	(1.039)	(1.100)	(0.973)
Delinquent orientation: how important is it				
To go party	2.006***	2.191	2.093***	2.193
	(0.734)	(0.719)	(0.734)	(0.725)
To have sexual relations	1.574***	1.797	1.871*	1.821
	(0.699)	(0.749)	(0.785)	(0.747)
To use drugs	1.134**	1.202	1.137***	1.184
	(0.410)	(0.500)	(0.418)	(0.465)
To drink alcohol	1.369***	1.524***	1.343***	1.602
	(0.606)	(0.669)	(0.590)	(0.686)
Delinquent social factor score	−0.304***	0.002	−0.142***	0.045
	(0.939)	(0.997)	(0.923)	(1.007)
Competing priorities: how important is it				
To have a job	1.983*	2.178***	2.216***	2.032
	(0.723)	(0.678)	(0.719)	(0.697)

TABLE 16.2 *Continued*

Orientation	Asian	Hispanic	Black	White
To make money	2.344**	2.494***	2.559***	2.406
	(0.705)	(0.652)	(0.634)	(0.674)
Work factor score	−0.143**	0.155***	0.243***	−0.047
	(1.040)	(0.952)	(0.964)	(1.001)
Plans of friends: percentage who				
Dropped out of high school	1.397	1.832***	1.694***	1.437
	(0.629)	(0.869)	(0.812)	(0.673)
Have no plans for college	1.906***	2.373***	2.348***	2.091
	(1.095)	(1.117)	(1.137)	(1.115)
Plan to work after high school	2.106***	2.857***	2.795***	2.464
	(1.140)	(1.162)	(1.210)	(1.225)
Plan to attend two-year college	2.332	2.687***	2.581***	2.373
	(1.100)	(1.054)	(1.063)	(1.015)
Plan to attend four-year college	3.772***	3.096***	3.329***	3.495
	(1.043)	(1.168)	(1.139)	(1.103)
Friends' plans factor score	0.340***	−0.451***	−0.284***	0.084
	(0.972)	(0.932)	(0.938)	(0.989)
Number of cases	1,119	1,851	1,459	11,269

Source: Author's compilation.
Note: Numbers in parentheses are standard deviations.
*Significantly different from whites at $p < 0.05$ level.
**Significantly different from whites at $p < 0.01$ level.
***Significantly different from whites at $p < 0.001$ level.

toward working and making money than those of whites. Employment goals may stem from economic necessity and compete with immediate educational goals. Asians are also more likely to have friends who plan to go to a four-year college, while their friends are least likely to have dropped out of high school, to have no plans for college, or to plan to work full-time after high school compared to any other group. Much smaller proportions of both Hispanic and black students' friends plan to attend a four-year college, while a greater portion have dropped out of high school, have no plans for college, or plan to work full-time after high school compared to whites. Blacks are slightly more likely to have friends who plan to attend some kind of college after high school than their Hispanic counterparts.

Overall, despite the generally pro-education stance of Asians' and blacks' friends (as evidenced by their school factor score), the actual plans of blacks' friends center less on postsecondary schooling than those of whites or Asians. Friends of Hispanics are more likely than friends of whites to consider it important to study and get good grades, but they are less concerned about actually finishing high school and continuing their education beyond high school. In fact, they are more likely to have dropped out of high school or to plan to begin working full-time after high school.

Racial and ethnic differences in the behavior of peers closely match the patterns of educational achievement documented elsewhere. Asian Americans tend to earn higher grades, followed by whites, Hispanics, and then blacks. These differences in grade performance persist even after controlling for differences in parental characteristics, with the exception of Hispanic students, who are statistically indistinguishable from their white counterparts (Farkas et al. 1990; Miller 1995; Kao, Tienda, and Schneider 1996).

FRIENDS' INFLUENCE ON EDUCATIONAL ACHIEVEMENT

The descriptive tabulations clearly show that friends' orientations toward school, social life, and other activities differ along race and ethnic lines among high school students. However, from descriptive tabulations I cannot say whether these differences result from variation in socioeconomic background that partly coincide with ethnicity or students' own orientations. It may be that students who are more oriented toward school simply select peers with similar viewpoints. In order to control for students' academic orientations prior to their association with current friends, measures of previous levels of achievement must be included.

To separate the initial preferences of respondents from the influences of friends, table 16.3 presents ordinary least squares estimates of the effects of friends' orientations on tenth-grade GPA controlling and not controlling for eighth-grade GPA. I examine grades rather than achievement test scores because grades are more sensitive to peer influence (since it is a performance measure that is more dependent on current academic orientation and behavior than achievement test scores; see Fehrman, Keith, and Reimer 1987).

TABLE 16.3 **Ordinary Least Squares Estimates of Effects of Friends' Orientations on Tenth-Grade GPA**

Explanatory Variables	Without Control for Prior Achievement		With Control for Prior Achievement	
	B	SE	B	SE
Background characteristics				
Asian	0.147***	0.041	0.105**	0.037
Hispanic	−0.049	0.029	−0.041	0.023
Black	−0.098***	0.026	−0.051*	0.023
Mother's education	0.034***	0.008	0.011	0.007
Father's education	0.042***	0.007	0.015*	0.006
Family income (in $10,000s)	0.009**	0.003	0.003	0.003
Friends' school orientation				
Important to attend school regularly	0.064**	0.021	0.047*	0.019
Important to study	0.006	0.020	0.005	0.018
Important to get good grades	0.082***	0.021	0.068***	0.019
Important to finish high school	0.053*	0.024	0.026	0.021
Important to continue education	0.088***	0.018	0.055***	0.016
Friends' social life orientation				
Important to be popular	0.064***	0.015	0.031*	0.013
Important to have a boyfriend or girlfriend	−0.058***	0.016	−0.026	0.014
Important to party	−0.106***	0.014	−0.081***	0.012
Friends' job orientation				
Important to have a job	−0.111***	0.013	−0.067***	0.012
Friends' actions and desires				
Number of friends who are dropouts	−0.169***	0.019	−0.115***	0.016
Friends who want to go to college	0.127***	0.019	0.084***	0.017
Control for prior achievement				
Middle school GPA			0.453***	0.011
Constant	2.232***	0.071	1.198***	0.068
Adjusted R^2	0.176		0.359	
Number of cases	26,900		26,900	

Source: Author's compilation.
*Significant at $p < 0.05$ level.
**Significant at $p < 0.01$ level.
***Significant at $p < 0.001$ level.

The first model only includes indicators of race, parental education, and family income, whereas the second model adds the eighth-grade GPA as a control measure. By controlling for prior academic achievement, I seek to determine the portion of current academic achievement that is attributable to peer influence rather than preexisting orientation of youth. Once the control for prior achievement has been added, what remains of the peer influence is more clearly the result of peer socialization (having "geeky" friends improves one's academic achievement) rather than peer selection ("geeky" kids are more likely to hang out with other "geeky" kids; see Eckert 1989). The difference between the "total" peer influence, as measured in model one and the "socialization" component of peer influence, as measured in model two (after adding previous levels of achievement) provides an estimate of the portion of peer influence we can attribute to selection processes.

As Kandel (1978) finds in her study of drug use, both components play a significant role in determining academic performance. Even after I control for prior achievement, almost all of the peer effect is maintained. In addition, friends' actual behavior (as measured by the number of friends who are high school dropouts) has a persistent and substantial effect on student achievement. Holding constant race, family background, friends' orientations, and prior achievement, each percentage point increase in the share of friends who have dropped out lowers grades by one-tenth of a grade point. As a result, those students whose friends have *all* dropped out of high school earn about four-tenths of a grade point lower than students whose friends are all still in high school, other things remaining equal.

Table 16.4 examines the effects of friends' orientation (using factor scales to conserve degrees of freedom) on tenth-grade GPA and evaluates whether peer influences differ by ethnicity. The first model serves as the baseline, only including background characteristics and friends' orientations. The second adds prior achievement in order to control for the effects of peer selection, and, finally, the third adds interactions with group membership to assess the extent to which peer influences differ by race and ethnicity.

Clearly, positive peer orientations toward school are associated with higher grades, and this effect remains significant after controlling for prior achievement, suggesting that most of the apparent peer effect is attributable to friends' influence. Although a one-point increase in friends' academic orientation (about one standard deviation) yields an increase of about 0.158 grade point in the first model, it only accounts for an increase of 0.110 grade point in the second. Hence the actual peer influence on grades is 0.110 grade point, or about two-thirds (0.110/0.158) of its baseline estimate, meaning that peer socialization indeed plays a role in influencing grades distinct from selection mechanisms that group academically oriented children with each other.

At the same time, peer orientation toward social life significantly lowers academic achievement, and, as before, this influence persists throughout various specifications of the model, suggesting that both selection and socialization are at work. Social life orientation maintains about three-fourths ($-0.042/-0.055$) of its effect on grades when I add controls for previous achievement levels.

Thus peer socialization seems to account for a large portion of the total peer influence effect of both school and social life orientations. It is clear that the negative impact on achievement of having friends who are socially oriented has more to do with current socialization than with preexisting value orientations. Overall, peer effects on achievement are persistent and cannot be attributed simply to students' prior valuation of academic achievement. Indeed, peer influences through socialization appear to have a greater impact than peer influences through selection.

Peer influences differ by group, but only for African Americans. Friends' orientation toward the importance of having a job lowers the GPA of blacks more than that of whites. Thus orientation toward work competes with educational orientations more among blacks than among whites. However, the negative influence of social orientation on GPA does not hold for blacks—having friends who value their social life has no effect on the GPA of black youths. Finally, after controlling for background characteristics and friends' valuation of school and social life, the number of friends who are high school dropouts is not associated with lower grades among blacks. No other race interactions are significant. This suggests that the effect of friends' orientations is quite similar for Hispanics, Asians, and whites, but that blacks differ from whites in their sensitivity to their friends' influence.

Overall, then, it appears that blacks are less susceptible to peer influence (due to socialization) than whites. The only exception to this general pattern is that friends' orientation toward work

TABLE 16.4 Ordinary Least Squares Estimates of Effects of Friends' Orientation Factors on Tenth-Grade GPA with and Without Race Interactions

Explanatory Variables	Model One[a]		Model Two[b]		Model Three[c]	
	B	SE	B	SE	B	SE
Background characteristics						
Asian	0.153***	0.042	0.109**	0.037	0.156	0.093
Hispanic	−0.052	0.029	−0.042	0.025	0.043	0.051
Black	−0.096***	0.026	−0.046*	0.023	0.121*	0.048
Mother's education	0.036***	0.008	0.011	0.007	0.012	0.007
Father's education	0.042***	0.007	0.014*	0.006	0.014*	0.006
Family income (in $10,000s)	0.009**	0.003	0.002	0.003	0.002	0.003
Friends' orientation factors						
School factor score	0.158***	0.010	0.110***	0.009	0.113***	0.010
Asian × school score					−0.024	0.043
Hispanic × school score					−0.011	0.029
Black × school score					0.002	0.028
Social factor score	−0.055***	0.009	−0.042***	0.008	−0.063***	0.009
Asian × social					0.042	0.038
Hispanic × social					0.057*	0.027
Black × social					0.088***	0.024

	Model [a]		Model [b]		Model [c]	
Friends' job orientations						
Important to have a job	−0.117***	0.013	−0.068***	0.012	−0.048***	0.012
Asian × job					−0.016	0.040
Hispanic × job					−0.043	0.024
Black × job					−0.098***	0.022
Number of dropout friends	−0.183***	0.019	−0.122***	0.016	−0.141***	0.019
Asian × dropout					0.006	0.087
Hispanic × dropout					0.005	0.051
Black × dropout					0.155***	0.046
Friends who want to go to college	0.137***	0.019	0.089***	0.017	0.098***	0.019
Asian × college					−0.031	0.077
Hispanic × college					−0.019	0.056
Black × college					−0.057	0.050
Control for prior achievement						
Middle school GPA	0.457***	0.011	0.460***	0.011		
Constant	2.791***	0.041	1.542***	0.047	1.493***	0.048
Adjusted R^2	0.167		0.356		0.360	
Number of cases	26,900		26,900		26,900	

Source: Author's compilation.

[a]Baseline model including only background characteristics and friends' orientations.

[b]Model one plus prior achievement.

[c]Model two plus interactions with group members.

*Significant at $p < 0.05$ level.

**Significant at $p < 0.01$ level.

***Significant at $p < 0.001$ level.

is more detrimental to the academic achievement of African Americans than of whites. Perhaps the meaning attached to having a job is different for black tenth graders than for their counterparts in other groups, or, as Ogbu (1991) suggests, blacks may be less likely to link employment options to their educational success. The fact that blacks are more likely to have friends who value employment may result from their greater difficulty in finding jobs.

Additional evidence for this rationale is found in the patterns of work by race or ethnicity among NELS tenth graders. Auxiliary analysis reveals that blacks and Hispanics are less likely to be currently employed or to have ever worked than whites. However, among those who do work, blacks and Hispanics work longer hours than their white or Asian counterparts. This pattern, along with well-documented evidence of high unemployment among black adolescents, suggests that African American teenagers are more oriented to work because they have more difficulty finding employment.

In summary, then, my examination of the relative influence of friends' school, work, and social life orientations yields four basic findings:

1. Friends' orientations toward social life are negatively associated with achievement and affect respondents' outcomes primarily through friends' socialization rather than by their selection of peers on the basis of academic, social, or job orientation.
2. Overall, race and ethnic differences are apparent in the extent to which friends are oriented toward school, work, and social life. Part of the reason Asians have better schooling outcomes than whites is that they are more likely to have academically oriented friends, on average, than their white counterparts.
3. There are a few racial and ethnic differences in the relative influence of friends. In other words, a Hispanic student and a white student in the same circle of friends should respond similarly to the socialization effects of peers. The only exception is for blacks, who are particularly sensitive to their friends' beliefs and behavior, although their friends' orientations toward work in tenth grade are more detrimental to their academic perfor-

mance than those of other groups. This probably reflects exceptionally high unemployment among black youth, which may drive a sense of hopelessness and decrease academic achievement (Farley and Allen 1987; Ogbu 1978, 1991).

PEER EFFECTS ON EDUCATIONAL ASPIRATIONS

Because part of the paradox of minority educational outcomes is their low achievement coupled with high aspirations, it makes sense to discuss how friends influence the educational aspirations as well as achievement of minority youth (Kao and Tienda 1998). Table 16.5 shows how friends' orientations toward educational attainment, their plans and actions, and their desires for their friend influence student aspirations to attend a four-year college as tenth graders. As before, the first model includes no controls for prior aspirations, while the second controls for aspirations to finish college as expressed in eighth grade. The table excludes race interactions because auxiliary analyses find no significant interaction effects.

The main finding here is that peer influences matter a great deal in maintaining high educational aspirations and that the primary mechanism is socialization rather than selection.

Specifically, all components of friends' valuation of additional education past high school are important for maintaining high educational aspirations through tenth grade. Friends' abstract valuation of continuing one's education beyond high school as well as friends' specific desire for the respondent to go to college significantly increases the odds of aspiring to graduate from college. Those students whose friends think they ought to go to college are two and a half times ($e^{0.914} = 2.49$) more likely to aspire to graduate from college than their counterparts; even when controlling for eighth-grade aspirations, these students are still twice as likely to have such high aspirations.

The effects of friends' abstract valuation is quite powerful as well. Those whose friends consider it "very important" to continue one's education beyond high school are almost three and a half

TABLE 16.5 **Logistic Regression Estimates of Effects of Friends'
Orientation and Behavior on Educational
Aspirations in the Tenth Grade**

Explanatory Variables	Without Control for Prior Aspirations		With Control for Prior Aspirations	
	B	SE	B	SE
Background characteristics				
Asian	0.282	0.204	0.405	0.220
Hispanic	0.131	0.135	0.077	0.144
Black	0.502***	0.132	0.418**	0.141
Mother's education	0.240***	0.032	0.179***	0.034
Father's education	0.253***	0.029	0.184***	0.031
Family income (in $10,000s)	0.121***	0.017	0.097***	0.017
Friends' orientation and behavior				
Important to continue education	0.617***	0.049	0.548***	0.050
Number of dropout friends	−0.536***	0.040	−0.459***	0.042
Friends who want to go to college	0.914***	0.079	0.717***	0.084
Control for prior aspirations				
Aspired to finish college in eighth grade			1.793***	0.085
Constant	−3.226***	0.152	−3.741***	0.165
Pseudo R^2		0.207		0.291
Number of cases		13,859		13,859

Source: Author's compilation.
*Significant at $p < 0.05$ level.
**Significant at $p < 0.01$ level.
***Significant at $p < 0.001$ level.

times ($e^{2 \times 0.617} = 3.43$) as likely to aspire to graduate from college than those with friends who think it is "not important." When I control for eighth-grade aspirations, the odds are reduced only slightly, and these friends are still three times as likely to have these aspirations. Could it be that friends are simply reacting to respondents' own achievement levels? Perhaps they are simply using respondents' achievement in evaluating their likelihood of success in college. To consider this competing hypothesis, I have added measures of eighth-grade GPA in auxiliary analyses. Overall, the effects of peer orientation and behavior persist and remain statistically significant.

CONCLUSIONS

The search for one's self-identity is a major aspect of adolescent development. For minority youth, a major component of self-identity is ethnic identity. More than at any time during the life course, characteristics of one's social circle determine how one is viewed by others. In addition, group images that emphasize the link between race or ethnicity and ability encourage group specialization in academic and extracurricular activities. Pressures of loyalty to one's own group, the desire to find others similar to oneself, and the prevalence of racially segregated activities and classes work together to reinforce race or ethnicity as a primary filter in selecting friends.

The pressures of ethnic loyalty and the prevalence of racially segregated peer groups are especially strong for blacks. After all "acting white" and "acting black" are defined in direct opposition to one another (Ogbu 1978, 1991). Hence, I expected black teenagers to be most likely to have other black friends, which may result in greater heterogeneity on other characteristics, such as age. In fact, I found greater racial and ethnic differences in peer behavior than in peer orientation. Specifically, friends of Asian teenagers are more oriented to school and less oriented toward social activities than the friends of white teenagers. Their friends are also less likely to have dropped out of high school and more likely to plan to go to college than the friends of white youth.

In contrast to Ogbu's expectation that minority youth have antischool values, however, I found minority students to have extremely positive school orientations. Specifically, the friends of blacks are more oriented toward school and less oriented toward social activities than the friends of whites, but they are more concerned with working, more likely to have dropped out of school, and less likely to aspire to a four-year university. Finally, friends of Hispanics are just as oriented toward school life as those of whites, but they are more oriented toward working. Their valuation of social activities is lower than that of white peers, but higher than that of black and Asian peers.

My analysis of NELS data showed that black youth are most likely to have older friends and that, along with the higher rate of high school dropout of blacks, this fact may explain their greater likelihood of having friends who have dropped out of high school and who have more modest plans for education following high school. For Hispanics, the desire to find similar others, which is additionally driven by language homogeneity, limits their association with non-Hispanic youth. Qualitative studies I have done suggest the severity of racial segregation in peer groups. Coupled with the quantitative finding that the friends of blacks and Hispanics are older and less educationally successful, this finding suggests that, independent of their own achievement, black and Hispanic adolescents have more exposure to similar others who have already experienced school failure. These results support Kandel's argument that modeling is far more important than normative influences on student academic performance.

REFERENCES

Bean, Frank D., and Marta Tienda. 1987. *The Hispanic Population of the United States*. New York: Russell Sage Foundation.

Brown, B. Bradford. 1990. "Peer Groups and Peer Cultures." In *At the Threshold: The Developing Adolescent,* edited by S. Shirley Feldman and Glen R. Elliott. Cambridge, Mass.: Harvard University Press.

Coleman, James S. 1961. *The Adolescent Society: The Social Life of the Teenager and Its Impact on Education*. Glencoe, Ill.: Free Press.

Deutsch, Morton, and Harold B. Gerard. 1955. "A Study of Normative and Informational Social Influence upon Individual Judgement." *Journal of Abnormal and Social Psychology* 51: 629–36.

Eckert, Penelope. 1989. *Jocks and Burnouts: Social Categories and Identity in the High School*. New York: Columbia University Press.

Epstein, Joyce. 1983. "The Influence of Friends on Achievement and Affective Outcomes." In *Friends in School: Patterns of Selection and Influence in Secondary Schools,* edited by Joyce Epstein and Nancy Karweit. New York: Academic Press.

Farkas, George, Daniel Sheehan, Robert P. Grobe, and Yuan Shuan. 1990. "Cultural Resources and School Success: Gender, Ethnicity, and Poverty Groups within an Urban School District." *American Sociological Review* 55(February): 127–42.

Farley, Reynolds, and Walter R. Allen. 1987. *The Color Line and the Quality of Life in America*. New York: Russell Sage Foundation.

Fehrman, P. G., T. Z. Keith, and T. M. Reimer. 1987. "Home Influence on School Learning: Direct and Indirect Effects of Parental Involvement on High School Grades." *Journal of Educational Research* 80(6): 330–37.

Hallinan, Maureen T. 1983. "Commentary: New Directions for Research on Peer Influence." In *Friends in School: Patterns of Selection and Influence in Secondary Schools,* edited by Joyce Epstein and Nancy Karweit. New York: Academic Press.

Hallinan, Maureen T., and Richard A. Williams. 1990. "Students' Characteristics and the Peer-Influence Process." *Sociology of Education* 63(April): 122–32.

Jessor, Richard, John E. Donovan, and Frances M. Costa. 1991. *Beyond Adolescence: Problem Behavior and Young Adult Development.* Cambridge, Mass.: Cambridge University Press.

Kandel, Denise. 1978. "Homophily, Selection, and Socialization in Adolescent Friendships." *American Journal of Sociology* 84(2): 427–36.

Kao, Grace, and Marta Tienda. 1998. "Educational Aspirations among Minority Youth." *American Journal of Education* 106(May): 349–84.

Kao, Grace, Marta Tienda, and Barbara Schneider. 1996. "Racial and Ethnic Variations in Academic Performance." *Research in Sociology of Education and Socialization* 11: 263–98.

Keefe, Susan E., Amado M. Padilla, and Manuel L. Carlos. 1979. "The Mexican-American Extended Family as an Emotional Support System." *Human Organization* 38(2): 144–52.

Mickelson, Roslyn Arlin. 1990. "The Attitude-Achievement Paradox among Black Adolescents." *Sociology of Education* 63(January): 44–61.

Miller, L. Scott. 1995. *An American Imperative: Accelerating Minority Educational Advancement.* New Haven, Conn.: Yale University Press.

National Center for Educational Statistics. 1990. *National Education Longitudinal Study of 1988: Base Year Student Component Data File User's Manual.* Washington: Department of Education, Office of Educational Research and Improvement.

Ogbu, John U. 1978. *Minority Education and Caste: The American System in Cross-Cultural Perspective.* New York: Academic Press.

———. 1991. "Immigrant and Involuntary Minorities in Comparative Perspective." In *Minority Status and Schooling: A Comparative Study of Immigrant and Involuntary Minorities,* edited by Margaret A. Gibson and John U. Ogbu. New York: Garland.

Petersen, Anne C. 1988. "Adolescent Development." *Annual Review of Psychology* 39: 583–607.

Rosenberg, Morris. 1989. *Society and the Adolescent Self-Image,* rev. ed. Middletown, Conn.: Wesleyan University Press.

Savin-Williams, Ritch C., and Thomas J. Berndt. 1990. "Friendship and Peer Relations." In *At the Threshold: The Developing Adolescent,* edited by S. Shirley Feldman and Glen R. Elliott. Cambridge, Mass.: Harvard University Press.

Schneider, Barbara, and Yongsook Lee. 1990. "A Model for Academic Success: The School and Home Environment of East Asian Students." *Anthropology and Education Quarterly* 21(4): 358–77.

Stevenson, David, Jeffrey Link, Barbara Schneider, and Kathryn Schiller. 1993. "Early School Leavers." Paper presented at the 1993 annual meetings of the American Sociological Association. Miami Beach, Fla.

Valenzuela, Angela, and Sanford Dornbusch. 1994. "Familism and Social Capital in the Academic Achievement of Mexican Origin and Anglo Adolescents." *Social Science Quarterly* 75(1): 18–36.

Index